Angel Eyez

By Rashma Mehta

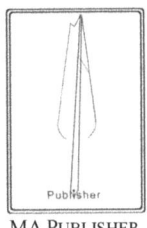

MA PUBLISHER

Rashma Mehta

Copyright © Rashma Mehta 2020

Published by MA Publishing
Published in London, UK
1st Edition printed on 15.02.2020
ISBN-13: 978-1-910499-53-5

All rights reserved. No part of this publication may be reproduced, stored in a retrieval system, or transmitted, in any form or by any means, electronic, mechanical, photocopying, recording, public performances or otherwise, without prior written permission of the copyright holder, except for brief quotations embodied in critical articles or reviews.

Disclaimer
All expressions and opinions of the work belong to the artists and MAP does not share or endorse any opinions in this book, other than to provide the open platform to publish their work. For further information on WC policies please email: mapublisher@yahoo.com for further information and submission guidelines.

Cover designed by Mayar Akash
Cover photo: Shutterstock
Typeset in Times New Roman

Paper printed on is FSC certified, lead-free, acid-free, buffered paper made from wood-based pulp. Our paper meets the ISO 9706 standard for permanent paper. As such, paper will last several hundred years when stored.

Dedication

Dedicated to Vishal

You break through, Loyalty, Hold you, You are my hero, Inspiration, You make me feel, Human being, Personality, You are a star, Host, Best friend, You, Storm, Held my hand, What If, There for me, Thank you, Role model, Had my back, Helped me, Eliminate, Under your wing, Approach, Living proof, Heal me, Unlock, Rise above it, Against me, Light me up, Tear me apart, Reach out to me, Lean on me, Count on me, Vent to me, Have your back, Be your rock, Won't let you fall, Rely on me, Always have me, Won't turn you away, Look my way, Hear you call, Turn to me, Never leave your side, Trust in me, Never let you down, Glue you back together, I will make sure no one hurts you, in a blink of an eye, Always be in your corner, I will know when you need me, drag you down, won't walk away, free you, knock you down, look for me, in the blink of a light, in the flesh, in a flash, believe in you, care for you, look out for you, loyal to you for life, take you aside and make you smile, I give you, brave face, fake smile, put on an act, shed a teardrop, inseparable for life, be yourself around me, close by, stick by my word, lead you astray. When I'm around you, never question, you shield me, underground, bring you down, dreams. Backstab you, take advantage of you, betray you, hit a brick wall, doubt yourself, you mean the absolute world to me, never change you, Bring out the warrior in you, bring you out of your shell, look up to you, look up to me, admire you, walk all over you, screw you over, bring out the worst in you, bring out the best in you, perfect to me, walk on fire for you, never run a mile, go that extra mile for you, best intentions, best interest at heart.

Revenge, Positive impression, looking in the mirror, Blinded, Regrets. Never be ashamed, push in the right direction, echoes, its ok to admit, imprint, words, Different side of me. Confidence, came into my life, Overlooked, Reasons, found my way, you reassure me, because of you, I'll find the truth, Block out, Don't hold it in, Twist the truth, The weight on ur shoulders, Build a wall, The poem starting with come and find me, Good enough, Important to me, As I go under, Take a risk on you, Pick up the pieces, Take a bullet for you, Sidekick, Jump to ur defense, didn't know, close chapter, at a standstill, rejected, only you can, hard to admit, back from the edge, not a word, give in, give up, u turn, quit, safe place, won't be far, lifeline, every step of the way, out in the cold. I don't wanna be awake, make me feel good enough, abandon you, watch over you, make time for you, this mess, daylight or not, insecure, struggle, VBBS, bite, release, invisible to me, confide in you. Burn out, End of the earth for you, Black cloud, keep me in the dark, open up to me. open up to you, keep you on the straight and narrow, keep me on the straight and narrow. Free me, my rock, ur faith in me, cry on the inside. My emotional stain, reality, my side, purpose, my true calling, proud of me, proud of you, be my lookout. Abandon me, won't let me struggle, know me inside out. stick by you, stick by me, give me hope, give me strength, somebody, valued, take me as me, belong, true friends like you are hard to find, my hour of need, make a difference, make my day, give me stability, won't let me down. Take you under my wing, Hold back my tears, Hold back my pain, Hold back my hurt, Don't have to be ashamed of my disability, I put on a brave face, Don't have to be ashamed of my scars & burns, Hear me, See the best in me, Start to question myself, stuck by me, appreciate you.

Bulletproof, Ease, Wreck, Judge me, Lifetime journey, Look ur way, Leave me out in the cold, Reach out to you, Rely on you, Count on you, Lean on you, Warrior in me, Untangle me, Wild side of me, Reckless side of me, Bring me out of my shell, Vent to you, Adventurous side of me, Rebel in me, Bring me out of my comfort zone, Bring out the real me, never alone, dark place, breaking point, at my lowest, numb. World of possibilities, When I am a mess, Face it with me, Not alone, Mask, Stick by ur word, Stumble, Matter to me, Matter to you, Comfort me, nothing stops me achieving my goals, Force to be reckoned with, Slip under the cracks, Loyal to me for life, Helping hand, believe in myself. Surface, jump to my defense, patch me up, never let anything go wrong, watch over me, Always make sure I'm ok, Confide in me, Knock me down, Put me down, Stronger than ever before, Shatter into a million pieces, Drag me down, Walk all over me, Shed a tear on you, Escape my reality, find a way to make me smile, Whatever life throws my way, Whatever life throws ur way, Won't let go without a fight, Precious to me, Precious to you, Won't let anything keep you down, Ripped apart, Get me down, Keep me afloat, A lost soul, I have nothing to fear, You have nothing to fear, Trapped, Treasure you, Treasure me, Take everything on, The weight of everything, Get you down, Up & downs, Isolate me, Lead me astray, Fragile. Doubt myself, backstab me, come out stronger, braver & the best you can be, disguise you, changed my life, I turned my life around, fly alone, fly beside you, Have a voice, Karma, Window of opportunity, Escape route, Massive influence on me, Catch every tear, Drop my guard, Cast a doubt, Troublesome road of defeat, Its ok to show the world who I truly am, Trick me, confessions. Destructive ways. Upper hand. Approval uncertainty, hold you together, value you. My door will always be open for you. Searching for something within me with you right beside me, burning bridges. Witness, crisis, won't let anything come between us. Come & find me

Contents

Dedication	3
Introduction	15
Angel Eyez	16
Protector	16
Connection	17
Illusion	17
Individuality	18
You Break Through	18
Imperfections	19
Loyalty	19
You Have	20
Let My Voice	20
Let Me Drown	20
Spiral	21
Family Loyalty	21
Stand Tall	22
Keep Close	22
I Pick Myself Back Up	22
Crumble	22
Own Worst Enemy	23
When I	23
Every Inch	24
Crossroads	24
I'm So Caught Up	24
Power	25
Vision	25
Intoxicated	26
My Only Wish	26
Errors	27
Reservations	27
You Are A Star	28
Host	28
Best Friend	29
Fall Out	30
Hold You	31
You Are My Hero	31
Never Cling	32
Inspiration	33
You Make Me Feel	34
Human Being	35
Personality	36

What If	37
Storm	37
Held My Hand	38
There For Me	39
Thank You	40
Blame Game	42
You Are My Role Model	43
Had My Back	44
You Helped Me	46
Eliminate	46
Take Me Under Your Wing	47
Approach	48
Living Proof	49
I Unlock	51
Against Me	52
Rise Above It	52
Heal Me	53
Light Me Up	53
Tear Me Apart	55
Reach Out To Me	56
Lean On Me	57
Vent To Me	58
Count On Me	59
Have Your Back	60
Be Your Rock	61
Rely On Me	62
Won't Let You Fall	63
Won't Turn You Away	64
Always Have Me	65
Hear You Call	66
Look My Way	67
Trust In Me	68
Turn To Me	69
Never Leave Your Side	70
Never Let You Down	71
Glue You Back Together	72
Hurt You	73
Blink Of An Eye	74
In Your Corner	75
When You Need Me	76
In The Flesh	77
Blink Of A Light	78

Won't Walk Away	80
Free You	81
Knock You Down	82
Look For Me	83
Cave In	84
Care For You	85
Look Out For You	86
Loyal To You For Life	87
In A Flash	88
Believe In You	90
Never Let You Face Anything Alone	91
Take You Aside And Make You Smile	92
Drag You Down	94
I Give You	95
Brave Face	95
Fake Smile	97
Put On An Act	99
You Can Be Yourself	100
Shed A Teardrop On Me	102
Inseparable For Life	103
Close By	104
Stick By My Word	105
Untangle You	106
Lead You Astray	107
Look Up To You	109
Look Up To Me	110
Bring You Out Of Your Shell	111
Admire You	113
Bring Out The Warrior In You	114
Screw You Over	115
Bring Out The Best In You	116
Perfect To Me	118
Reality	119
Walk All Over You	119
Bring Out The Worst In You	120
Walk On Fire For You	122
Never Run A Mile	123
Go That Extra Mile For You	124
Best Intentions	125
Best Interest	127
When I'm Around You	128
Defeat You	129

You Shield Me	130
Dreams	131
Bring You Down	131
Never Question	133
Take You Underground	133
Vision Impairment	134
Backstab You	135
Take Advantage Of You	136
Betray You In Any Way	138
Hit A Brick Wall	139
Doubt Yourself	141
You Mean The Absolute World To Me	142
Never Change You	143
Revenge	144
Positive Impression On Me	145
Looking In The Mirror	146
Blinded	146
Regrets	147
Never Be Ashamed	147
Push In The Right Direction	148
Echoes	149
Its Ok To Admit	150
Imprint	150
Words	151
Different Side Of Me	152
Confidence	152
Until You Came Into My Life	153
I Don't Wanna Be Overlooked	154
Reasons	155
Found My Way	156
Someone Understands Me	156
I Can	157
Release	157
At A Standstill	158
I Don't Wanna Be Awake	159
You Reassure Me	160
Close Chapter	160
Dictate	161
I'll Find The Truth	162
Didn't Know	162
Because Of You	163
Bite	164

To The Back Of My Mind	164
Confide In You	166
Block Out	166
Don't Hold It In	167
Twist The Truth	168
The Weight On Ur Shoulders	169
Build A Wall Around You	171
Come & Find Me	172
You Are Good Enough	173
Important To Me	174
As I Go Under	175
I'd Take A Risk On You	176
Pick Up The Pieces	177
I'd Take A Bullet For You	178
Be Ur Sidekick	179
I'd Jump To Ur Defence	180
Won't Let You Feel Rejected	181
Only You Can	182
It's Hard To Admit	183
Bring Me Back From The Edge	184
Don't Have To Say A Word I'll Know	185
You Are Not Invisible To Me	186
Give In	187
Won't Leave You Out In The Cold	188
I'll Be Ur Safe Place	189
I'll Be Ur Lifeline	190
Give Up	191
I'll Be Ur U Turn	192
Won't Be Far	193
I'll Be With You Every Step Of The Way	194
Won't Let You Quit	195
Vbbs	196
I Know	197
Good In Me Only You Can See	198
Open With You	199
Open With Me	200
Keep You On The Straight & Narrow	201
Keep Me On The Straight & Narrow	202
Free Me	204
You Are My Rock	205
Ur Faith In Me	206
Don't Have To Cry On The Inside	208

My Emotional Strain	209
Won't Leave My Side	211
Help Me Find Purpose	212
Help Me Find My True Calling	213
Proud Of Me No Matter What	214
Always Be My Lookout	215
Proud Of You No Matter What	216
Know Me Inside Out	218
Won't Let Me Struggle	220
Won't Abandon Me	221
Stick By Me Through Thick & Thin	222
Give Me Hope	223
Give Me Strength	224
Stand By You Through Thick & Thin	225
Make Me Feel Like Somebody	227
Make Me Feel Valued	228
Always Take Me As Me	229
My World In Tatters	230
Make Me Feel Like I Belong	231
True Friends Like You Are Hard To Find	232
My Hour Of Need	233
Make A Massive Difference To Me & My Life.	234
Make My Day	236
Give Me Stability	237
Won't Let Me Down	237
Take You Under My Wing	238
Hold Back My Tears	239
Hold Back My Pain	241
Hear Me	242
Hold Back My Hurt	244
Don't Have To Be Ashamed Of My Scars & Burns	245
Don't Have To Be Ashamed Of My Disability	247
Hold Back My Honesty	249
Give Me Courage	250
Best In Me	251
I Don't Have To Put On A Brave Face	252
When I Question Myself	254
Stuck By Me	255
Appreciate You	256
When I Am A Wreck	257
Never Judge Me	258
Take Me On A Lifetime Journey	258

Look Ur Way	259
You Ease	260
Bulletproof	261
Won't Leave Me Out In The Cold	261
Reach Out To You	262
Rely On You	263
Count On You	264
Lean On You	265
Warrior In Me	266
Untangle Me	267
Bring Out The Wild Side Of Me	267
Bring Out The Reckless Side Of Me	268
Bring Me Out Of My Shell	269
Vent To You	270
Bring Out The Adventurous Side Of Me	271
Bring Out The Rebel In Me	272
Bring Me Out Of My Comfort Zone	273
Bring Out The Real Me	274
When I Felt Numb	275
When I Am At My Lowest	276
When I Am At Breaking Point	277
Dark Place	278
Mask	279
I Am Never Alone	280
Kerry	281
Drain You	281
In A Heartbeat	282
Ups & Downs	283
Get You Down	285
The Weight Of Everything You Carry On Ur Shoulders	286
Take On Everything You Hold Within	287
Disguise You	289
Fly Alone	289
You Won't Fly Alone	290
I Find My Voice	292
Karma	293
Window Of Opportunity	294
Escape Route	296
Massive Influence On Me & My Life.	298
Catch Every Tear	299
Drop My Guard	301
Cast A Doubt	302

Troublesome Road Of Defeat	303
It's Ok To Show The World Who I Truly Am	306
Trick Me	309
Confessions	311
Destructive Way	312
Upper Hand	312
Approval	313
Uncertainty	315
Hold You Together	316
Value You	317
My Door Will Always Be Open For You.	318
Searching For Something Within Me	320
Burning Bridges	320
Witness	321
Crisis	322
I'll Be Right Here Waiting	323
Won't Let You Struggle	324
Won't Let You Feel Insecure	325
Daylight Or Not	326
Never Let You Face A Mess Alone	327
Never Abandon You	328
Always Make Time For You	329
Always Watch Over You	330
Make Me Feel Good Enough	331
Burn Out	332
Go To The End Of The Earth For You	333
Won't Let You Carry A Black Cloud Around With You	335
Don't Have To Keep Me In The Dark	336
When I Am A Mess	338
Stick By Ur Word	339
Face It With Me	340
Ur World Of Possibilities	341
Know When I Start To Stumble	342
Always Matter To Me	343
Always Matter To You	344
Comfort Me	345
Nothing Will Stop Me Achieving My Goals.	346
A Force To Be Reckoned With	347
Won't Let Me Slip Under The Cracks.	348
Loyal To Me For Life	349
You Give Me A Helping Hand	350
Believe In Myself	351

Surface From Below	352
Jump To My Defence	353
Patch Me Up	354
Never Let Anything Go Wrong When I'm Around You.	355
Always Watch Over Me	357
Always Make Sure I'm Ok	358
Confide In Me	359
Knock Me Down	359
Put Me Down	361
Make Me Stronger Than Ever Before	362
Won't Shatter Into A Million Tiny Pieces	363
Drag Me Down	364
Walk All Over Me	365
Shed A Tear On You When I Cry	366
Escape My Reality	367
Find A Way To Make Me Smile	368
Keep You Down	369
Precious To Me	370
Precious To You.	371
Won't Let You Go Without A Fight	372
Whatever Life Throws My Way	373
Whatever Life Throws Ur Way	375
Won't Let Us Get Ripped Apart	377
Treasure Me	378
Treasure You.	379
Trapped No Longer	380
Nothing To Fear When Ur In My Life & Around Me.	381
Have Nothing To Fear When I'm In Ur Life & Around You	382
Won't Let Anything Come Between Us	384
When I Am A Lost Soul	385
Keep Me Afloat	386
Get Me Down	387
Come Out Stronger, Braver And Best You Can Be.	388
Backstab Me	389
Doubt Myself	390
Know How Fragile I Can Be	391
Lead Me Astray	392
Won't Let Me Feel Isolated	393
Not Invisible To You.	394
Find Closure	395
You Changed My Life	396
I Turned My Life Around	397

Index 399
Mapublisher Catalogue 408

Introduction

Following on from my second book the experiences and journey to this point has made me a writer who tries to explores every angle of my world and life journey of those I have close to me, around me to help and assist me to overcome, conquer the obstacles that one may face in life, especially a person like me as my life journey is a lifelong struggle and hopefully I am seeing a light at the end of the tunnel.

I hope my book will leave readers itching to read even more leaving them wanting to know how I go about my life experiences through my writings that have changed even more as I aim to take my writing in a different direction, to a higher level that would test my skill and determination. This book is filled with even more exciting original material, hopefully it shows the readers my way of life and how I have conquered the numerous obstacles right from birth.

As my writing journey continues with the support and encouragement of my loved ones I try and conquer the struggles, the obstacles & challenges I come across. I still find a way to overcome this and I thrive & become even stronger and determined than I was before.

I want to allow readers to see what I am all about experience my world & find that I got to this point with the help of those close to me and around me they have been massively involved showing me that there is more to me than I originally thought.

As I write, I find I am developing my skill as a writer, being inspired in the way I am by those who inspire me is just so wonderful. It allows me to chase this very long-awaited dream and further my writing to the next chapter as I continue to write and show the world as well as those around me and close to me just how much I can do, am capable of when I have such a passion in this journalistic world.

I would like to thank Vishal Bhatnagar, Bhupendra Gandhi, Sonal Makim for continuing to be a part of this ongoing journey, being right by my side during this wonderful experience. I would also like to thank Vishal Bhatnagar for continuing to be my ongoing inspiration and inspiring me the way you have stood by me no matter what. I would also like to thank Elizabeth & Vishal Bhatnagar for always proofreading my work when I needed it.

Angel Eyez

Angel eyez shine on you when you least expect it.
Angel eyez look down on your reality and help you rally around.
When no one around you understands you angel eyez accepts you for you.
When no one believes your problems angel eyez will help you solve them.

When you feel you Can't face reality angel eyez will keep you on the straight and narrow.
When you feel low angel eyez will guide you through the unnecessary burden on your shoulders.
Angel eyez will always find a way in to your horrific past.
Angel eyez will always hold you close and help you take steps forward.
Angel eyez will always be beside you.
Angel eyez will never judge the choices and decisions you make.

Protector

Protector of the extension of your heartfelt traumatic past.
Protector of your innocent minds.
Protector of the hurtful reminders that follow you around.
Protector of the devil that tries to corrupt you.

Protector of the pain your soul holds within.
Protector of the unnoticed defence you try and bring out.
Protector of the determination you hold within.
Protector of your inner world.

Protector of your close inner circle.
Protector of your breaking point.
Protector of your heart.
Protector of your weakness.
Protector of the real you.

Connection

Connection is possible.
Connection is a turning point.
Connection is being true to those around you.
Connection allows you to face reality with the support of those around you.

Connection allows you to find yourself.
Connection allows you to see what is around the corner.
Connection allows you to believe in yourself and those around you.
Connection allows you to do what is best for you with the encouragement of those around you.

Connection allows you to forget the hurt you feel and turn to those around you.
When you feeling low connection allows you to be able to turn to those around you.
Connection allows you to see the people who will stick by you.
Connection allows you to see the people who love you for you.

Illusion

Fear is an illusion.
Reality is a false sense of how to be.
False hope is an illusion.
False predictions is an illusion.

False sense of choice is an illusion.
False sense of doubt is an illusion.
False sense of determination is an illusion.
False sense of insecurity is an illusion.

Individuality

I am a determined individual.
I am a free individual that knows my mind.
I am an inspirational individual.
I am a strong individual.

I am true to the point individual.
I am an individual that says what's on my on my mind.
I am an individual who use to struggle.
I am an individual who is supportive.

I am an individual who will do anything to be heard.
I am an individual with a wild heart.
I am an individual who will never let anything get in the way of my dreams.
I am an individual with a tough outlook on life.

I am an individual not to be messed with.
I am an individual who is unique.
I am an individual if crossed will let out rage.
I am an individual that can let out a real temper.

I am an individual who won't be held back.
I am an individual that will take potential to the next level.
I am an unstoppable individual.

You Break Through

You break though my fragile past.
You break though my never-ending pain
You break though my over turning reality
You break though my heart to find the unknown answers

You break though my weakness to see me at my lowest and help me beat it
You know when to break me away from suffering silently
You know when to understand me
You know when I am in denial

You know when I need to escape from my reality
You know when I need to be held together as you are there

You know when I will crack and break
You know when I cry you wipe away my tears that fall

You know when I fall you pick me back up in a way only you know how
You know when I am in a dark place or sad you always know how to make my day.
You give me hope
You give me strength

You know when I start to question myself
You love me for me and never want me to change for anyone
You are always there for me when no one is

Imperfections

Imperfections are not easy to find.
Imperfections are what make you.
Imperfections are not far from the truth.
Imperfections are not what define you.

Imperfections will not defeat you.
Imperfections are what you make them.
Imperfections are not a weakness.
Those around you will accept your imperfections and take them as they see them.
Imperfections do not rule what those around you think about you.

Loyalty

Loyalty to those who accept your past.
Loyalty to those who stick by you through thick and thin.
Loyalty to those who have made an impact on you and your life.
Loyalty to those who stand by you for the person you are.

Loyalty to those who support you for the right reasons.
Loyalty to those who accept you for you.
Loyalty to those who accept you as you are.
Loyalty is not a weakness.
Loyalty is a way to tell who your true friends are.
Loyalty is never facing anything alone.

You have

You have always believed in me.
You have always supported me in everything I've done.
You have always seen the best in me no matter what.
You have always been there for me through the hectic stuff.

You have been my rock.
You have raised my spirits.
You have picked me up when I've fallen to the ground.
You have always stood by me.

I can be me when I'm around you.
I never have to hide who I am from you.
When I feel lost, you always find me and bring me back to reality.
You take me as I am.

We are inseparable.
You are loyal to me.
You understand me like no one else does.
You are true to me in no uncertain way.
You show me the best way to be.

Let My Voice

Let my voice be a way of telling you how much you mean to me.
Let my voice be a little reminder of how I wanna be.
Let my voice be true to those around me.
Let my voice be my reaction to things I've had to keep to myself.
Let my voice be the answer to your uncertainty.
Let my voice be the one to give you reassurance about what you feel within.

Let Me Drown

Let me drown the past out.
Let me drown the troubles that follow me.
Let me drown out the hurtful remarks that come my way.
Let me drown out the hurtful words that make me feel like a nobody.
Let me drown out the way I was.
Let me drown out the endless games some people play with my emotions.

Let me drown out the endless resentment I feel.
Let me drown out the pain that comes my way.
Let me drown out the endless mind games some people won't let me forget.

Spiral

Things that spiral out of control you know you can get it sorted with the right encouragement.
Things that conspire without your knowledge is easily turned with the right mindset.
When things get difficult you come across a way to deal with it when you turn to the people beside you or in your life.
When things turn ugly you can escape reality for a while by turning your attention to the people beside you.
When things turn against you, you don't let it defeat you, you turn to the people who will stick by you.
Don't let those things that don't want you to succeed define you in any way.

Family Loyalty

Family loyalty is never simple.
Family loyalty is draining.
Family loyalty is the way to destroy someone they love if they can't believe in them.
Family loyalty can hurt.

Family loyalty can leave you feeling alone.
Family loyalty can leave you feeling betrayed.
Family loyalty can leave you feeling uneasy.
Family loyalty can leave you further from when you were once close.

Family loyalty can leave you feeling unwanted.
Family loyalty can leave you feeling rejected.
Family loyalty can leave you feeling broken more than ever.
Family loyalty can leave you feeling distant form them.

Stand Tall

Don't let your past define you stand tall.
Don't let your fears determine you stand tall.
Don't let trouble chase you stand tall.
Don't let confidence knock you sideways stand tall.
Don't doubt your expectations stand tall.
Don't matter how hard you try keep going and stand tall.
Don't let gravity drop you to the ground stand tall

Keep Close

Keep the past close so you can learn from it.
Keep the fears close to learn the way you tackle them.
Keep your insecurities close to learn the truth about what led you to them.
Keep troubles close to learn how to overcome situations that occur.
Keep being you and the best you can be.
Keep fighting to be heard.
Stand your ground and overachieve the things that you want.

I Pick Myself Back Up

I pick myself back up from my horrific past.
I pick myself back up from my traumatic journey of life.
I pick myself back up from my fragile heartache.
I pick myself back up from all the pain I had.
I pick myself back up from the hurt I go through.
I pick myself back up from failure that comes my way and I keep going to make those around me proud.
I pick myself back up from when something tries to break me.
I pick myself back up from the emotional baggage I had.

Crumble

Don't let your past crumble to tiny pieces.
Don't let your fears dictate the way it crumbles.
Don't let your pain be the reason it crumbles.
Don't let your own strength force your own hand to crumble.
Don't let your voice be shattered when it crumbles.

Don't let emptiness crumble to the floor.
Don't let emotional strain crumble.
Don't let your determination crumble.

Don't let your demons tackle you to crumble.
Don't let your true self crumble
Don't let the real you crumble.
Don't let the pressure of things around you crumble.
Don't let hope crumble.
Don't let your darkest way crumble.
Don't let your lowest point crumble.
Don't let the tiger in you crumble.

Own Worst Enemy

Don't let your past be your own worst enemy.
Don't let your fear torture you when it becomes your own worse enemy.
Don't let denial become your own worst enemy.
Don't let your darkness path become your own worst enemy.
Don't let your emotional strain become your own worst enemy.
Don't let my silence be your own worst enemy.
Don't let negativity become your own worst enemy.
Don't let strength overpower you and become your own worst enemy.

When I

When I Came off the rails, I tried to get back on track but something was holding me down.
When I came across a solution, I always get knocked however I always get back and leap forward.
When my heart turns dark you shine a light that shows me a way out
When I become reckless you see another side of me.

When I have doubts you always keep me on the straight and narrow.
When I feel alone, I know I'm not as I have people around me that care about me and will walk alongside me when I least expect it.
When I break no matter how hard or bad I know I have a flood of people around me.
When battles I face is worth it as it shows that things are worth standing my ground over.

Every Inch

Every inch of your past face it with all ur energy you have.
Every inch of your fear show you can beat the beast.
Every inch of the darkest hour you try and stop from appearing in front of you.
Every inch of struggling ways that show the deep down corner of you.

Every inch of doubt is just a very close call to over think that you will not be in doubtful thoughts.
Every inch is a true battle with experience that you are someone that don't run from battles and you face them head on.
Every inch of the true you that show who you really wanna be as a person.
Every inch of the real world that shows it can be cruel in a way no one sees coming.
Every inch of the real you is not allowing you to be you.
Be who you are and not a fake show that you are original.

Crossroads

Crossroads appear to block your past.
Crossroads appear to turn that terrorising look on ur face into hope.
Crossroads appear to help chase ur troubles away before they take over ur life.
Crossroads appear to help you with ur echoing voices.

Crossroads appear to be a revolution.
Crossroads appear to help you stay afloat.
Crossroads appear to help you survive the cruel way of the world outside.
Crossroads appear to show you that you are unique.
Crossroads appear to help you realise the battles you face can be vanished from ur life.

I'm So Caught Up

I'm so caught up in the past I've created.
I'm so caught up in fearless fears of my world that I try and conquer.
I'm so caught up in the hardship of this cruel world.
I'm so caught up in my own uniqueness.
I'm so caught up in making my own memories in any way I possibly can.
I'm so caught up in making people around me proud.
I'm so caught up in my own struggling ways to make them disappear.

I'm so caught up in my own doubts.
I'm so caught up in making an impact o the people around me.
I'm so caught up in making a difference.
I'm so caught up in making memorable moments with the people around me.

Power

You got the power to determine if ur past will be a constant loss.
You got the power to come face to face with things that antagonise you and solve it.
You got the power to not give the wrong people ammunition over you.
You got the power to not let things escalate in any situation.
You got the power to escape the pain you feel.
You got the power to deal with difficulties in life that try and overtake us.
You got the power to figure out who you wanna be.
You got the power to let people that love you into ur life and know they will stay with you step by step.
You got the power to deflate the doubts in ur head.
You got the power to turn the atmosphere of the environment ur in around.

Vision

Vision of ur past.
Vision of ur terrorising fears.
Vision of ur territory that you hold close.
Vision of ur own strength.
Vision of ur own enemy.
Vision of ur chemistry.
Vision of ur nightmare.
Vision of ur negativity.
Vision of ur outlook on life.
Vision of ur struggling ways.
Vision of ur doubts.
Vision of ur positivity.
Vision of ur fearless ways.
Vision of ur possible reality.
Vision of ur success.
Vision of ur future which is in ur own very hands.
Vision of ur destiny.
Vision of ur own strong mind.

Vision of ur own path.
Vision of ur own decisions.
Don't let anything stand in ur way be who you wanna be.

Intoxicated

When ur past become intoxicated.
When ur fears become intoxicated.
When ur troubles become intoxicated.
When ur inner cries become intoxicated.

When ur inner voice become intoxicated.
When ur terrified demons become intoxicated.
When ur enemy become intoxicated.
When ur pain become intoxicated.

When ur darkest moments become intoxicated.
When ur emotional strain become intoxicated.
When ur emotional baggage become intoxicated.
When ur nightmares become intoxicated.

When ur bad memories become intoxicated.
When ur unbearable secrets become intoxicated.
When the non-existent from ur life become intoxicated.
When the words some people say to you become intoxicated.

Let what people who are not important to you or ur life and what they think go over ur head and keep the close people you care about and have in ur life close and let them in.

My Only Wish

My only wish of my past becoming a distant memory in the back of my mind.
My only wish is to make my friends proud of me.
My only wish is to have the perfect year.
My only wish is to make my dreams a reality.

My only wish Is to have those who accept me for me around me.
My only wish is not to mess up.

My only wish is to spend time with the people in my life that don't see me as a failure.
My only wish is not to feel the pain.

My only wish is to feel free.
My only wish is to choose who I spend my time with.
My only wish is not to get hurt in any way.
My only wish is not to feel betrayed by anyone.

Errors

Errors of my past don't define me.
Errors of my fearless fears won't stop me confronting them.
Errors of my underlying issues don't have a hold on me.
Errors of my unexpected consequences will not redirect me.

Errors of hatred won't boil over me.
Errors of my ways won't let me hit the ground.
Errors of my darkest moments will not let me go underground.

Reservations

Reservations of my past won't stop me.
Reservations of my fears won't stop me confronting them.
Reservations are not a way to trap me.
Reservations of my opportunities won't stand in my way.

Reservations won't leave me considering my options.
Reservations won't drag me down.
Reservations of my failed attempts won't drop me to the ground.
Reservations of the missing pieces won't determine my outlook on life.

Reservations of this cold winter won't stop me achieving what I want.
Reservations of my reality won't try and avoid me.
Reservations of putting on a brave face in front of the closest people I care about won't stop me doing just that.
Reservations of how strong I can be is undeniable.
Reservations won't stop the people that are close to me and by my side from being there when I need them and this will show who I have and who I don't.

You Are A Star

You are a star in my mind.
You are a star in my reality.
You are a star in the way you thrive.
You are a star to me.

You are star quality.
You are a superstar in no uncertain ways.
You got the stardom in you.
You are the star that you wanna be.

You are a true star.
You are an amazing talented star.
You are an incredible star.
You are a fabulous star.

You are a tremendous star.
You are a spectacular star.
You are an awesome star.
You are an excellent star.

You are an extraordinary star.
You are a magnificent star.
You are a mega star.
You are a marvellous star.

You are the rarest star.
You are the most loyalist star.
You are the most genuine star.
You are a firestorm star.
You are a firely star.
You are a Rock-star to me.

Host

You are the best host.
You are an amazing host.
You are an awesome host.
You are a very very talented host.

You are a fabulous host.
You are a tremendous host.
You are a great host.
You are a perfect host.

You are an incredible host.
You are a fair host.
You are an excellent host.
You are an extraordinary host.

You are the host with the most.
You are a blast of a host.
You are a mega host.
You are a magnificent host.

You are a fantastic host.
You are a magical host
You are the host we love.
You are a natural host

You are a superior host.
You are a brilliant host.
You are an epic host.
You are a spectacular host.
You are a trouper of a host.
You are a super genius host.
You were born to be a host.
You are a passionate host.
You are a carefree host.
You are a loyal host.
You are an inspirational host.

Best Friend

Ur my amazing best friend.
Ur my incredible best friend.
Ur my great best friend.
Ur my fantastic best friend.

Ur my fabulous best friend.
Ur my excellent best friend.

Ur my extraordinary best friend.
Ur my magnificent best friend.

Ur my golden best friend.
Ur my genuine best friend.
Ur my best friend forever.
Ur my one in a million best friend.

Ur my tremendous best friend.
Ur my true best friend.
Ur my best friend that never lets me go through rough times alone.
Ur my best friend that will not let me walk alone and will always walk with me.

Ur my best friend that sees me at my lowest point.
Ur my best friend that will help me in my hour of need.
Ur my best friend who helps me beat my battles.
Ur my best friend who never judges me for who I am.

Ur my best friend who takes me as I am.
Ur my best friend who lets me wipe my tears on you.
Ur my truthful best friend.
Ur my best friend who won't let me fall to the ground.
Ur my best friend who wants to see the best in me.
Ur my best friend who don't wanna see me fail.
Ur my best friend for life.

Fall Out

Fall out of my mind.
Fall out of my heart.
Fall out of my pain.
Fall out of my heartbreak.

Fall out of my heartache.
Fall out of my emotional strength.
Fall out of my emotional strain.
Fall out from the forbidden pathway.
Fall out from my weakness.
Fall out from my limitless limits.

Hold You

I'm going to hold you as you face ur fragile past.
I'm going to hold you as you face ur energetic demons.
I'm going to hold you as you face the tough things that are thrown ur way.
I'm going to hold you as you face the nightmares that occur.

I'm going to hold you if you fall apart.
I'm going to hold you if something tries to break you.
I'm going to hold you as you take one step at a time towards ur dreams.
I'm going to be there to hold you as you face ur reality.

I'm going to hold you as you chase the uncertainty.
I'm going to hold you as you face backlashes of ur wrong doing.
I'm going to hold you as ur inner cries take control.
I'm going to hold you if and when you become sad.

I'm going to hold you during ur darkest moments.
I'm going to hold you at ur lowest point.
I'm going to hold you at ur weakest point.
I'm going to hold you at ur bravest point.
I'm going to keep hold of you when ur scared.
I'm going to hold you at ur strongest.
I'm going to hold you as you take on challenging days.
I'm going to hold you as you face ur toughest choices.

You Are My Hero

You are my hero helping me to process my fragile past.
You are my hero helping me to oversee my fearless fears head on.
You are my hero helping me to overcome my overturn of troubles that follow me.
You are my hero helping me to rise above my difficulties.

You are my hero in no uncertain ways.
You are my hero helping me to overshadow my doubts in my mind.
You are my hero helping me turn the various things that make a barrier.
You are my hero helping me stay on the straight and narrow.

You are my hero helping me to redirect my energy in a way that is used in a good way.

You are my hero helping me to realise my purpose.
You are my hero helping me turn my negativity in to a positive.
You are my hero helping me to realise my dreams.

You are my hero helping me to get the real me to shine.
You are my hero helping me to get the true me to light up.
You are my hero lighting up my smile any way you can.
You are my hero helping me through my darkest moments.

You are my hero helping me find answers to unknown questions I have.
You are my hero helping me by having such a massive heart of gold.
You are my hero helping me by having an massive impact on me and my life.
You are my hero helping me by having such a massive influence on me and my life.

You are my amazing hero. You are my inspirational hero.
You are my tremendous hero. You are my outstanding hero.

You are my extraordinary hero. You are my fabulous hero.
You are my fantastic hero. You are my hero in my reality.

You are my hero helping me to see that not everyone is as genuine as you.
You are my hero in keeping me calm in situations.
You are my loyal hero. You are my hero just by being by my side.

You are my hero not letting me face anything alone.
You are my hero just by being you.
You are my hero because you brighten up my days.

Never Cling

Never cling on to ur fragile past.
Never cling on to ur energetic demons.
Never cling on to ur troubles that cast a doubt.
Never cling on to difficult times they will only drag you down.

Never cling on to the people that want you to drown and fail.
Never cling on to the people that don't see the best in you.
Never cling on to the people that try and break you.
Never cling on to the people who show hatred at how well you do in life.

Never cling on to anger it will destroy you.

Never cling on to bitterness it will always find a way to keep you from moving on.
Never cling on to people you ghost from ur life.
Never cling on to the people who don't wanna see you thrive.

Never cling on to the people who don't see you for you.
Never cling on to the people that judge you.
Never cling on to ur emotional strain it will only make you miserable.

Always cling on to the people that are close to you and stand with you no matter what.

Inspiration

You are my incredible inspiration.
You are my amazing inspiration.
You are my fabulous inspiration.
You are my never ending inspiration.

You are my epic inspiration.
You are my one in a million inspiration.
You are my awesome inspiration.
You are my extraordinary inspiration.

You are my true inspiration.
You are my tremendous inspiration.
You are my only inspiration.
You are my outstanding inspiration.

You are my lucky inspiration.
You are my unstoppable inspiration.
You are my forever inspiration.
You are my loyal inspiration.

You are my best inspiration.
You are my wonderful inspiration.
You are my superhero inspiration.
You are my supportive inspiration.

You are my kind hearted inspiration.
You are my golden inspiration.

You are my true natured inspiration.
You are my superstar inspiration. You are my inseparable inspiration.
You are my inspiration through my reality.
You are my inspiration as you watch me thrive.
You are my inspiration in my mind.

You Make Me Feel

You make me feel alive.
You make sure I am never feeling frighten.
You make me feel I am a somebody.
You make me feel good enough.

You make me want to just go that extra mile for you.
You make me feel like I am worth it.
You never let me walk alone.
You make the true me come out.

You make me smile like no other can.
You make me believe in myself.
You make sure nobody else can hurt me.
You make sure nobody can harm me.

You make sure nobody betrays me.
You make sure I don't face my worst.
You have seen me thrive.
You have seen me sad.

You make sure I don't give up.
You make sure I don't give in.
You make me feel like I can be me.
You make me feel like I don't have to hide the real me from you.

You make me feel like I can do anything.
You bring out the best in me.
You make sure I am never alone.
You always stand by me no matter what.
You make me feel less scared.
You and me have a special bond.
We are inseparable.

Human Being

You are an amazing human being.
You are an incredible human being.
You are an excellent human being.
You are an extraordinary human being.

You are a carefree human being.
You are a rare human being.
You are an tremendous human being.
You are a kind hearted human being.

You are a huge inspirational human being.
You are the best human being.
You are a go getter human being.
You are a wonderful human being.

You are a believer in making things a reality.
You are a genuine human being.
You are a soul searcher.
You are a truthful human being.

You are a diamond human being.
You are a protective human being.
You are a mega human being.
You are a one in a million human being.

You are a loyal human being.
You have a golden heart.
You are a trustworthy human being.
You are an unusual human being.

You are a unique human being.
You are a passionate human being.
You are a brilliant human being.
You are an awesome human being.
You are a spectacular human being.
You are a bright spark of a human being.

Personality

You have an amazing personality.
You have an incredible personality.
You have an excellent personality.
You have a tremendous personality.

You have a rare personality.
You have a brilliant personality.
You have an extraordinary personality.
You have a unique personality.

You have a perfect personality.
You have an awesome personality.
You have a wonderful personality.
You have a personality that shows deep within you.
You make people around you proud in so many ways.
You always make an impact on people close to and around you
You have a massive influence on people
You make such a massive difference to people and their lives.
You have a genuine personality.
You have a one in a million personality.
You have a passionate personality.
You have an outstanding personality.

You have a courageous personality.
You have a firestorm personality.
You have a mega personality.
You have a magnificent personality.

You have a carefree personality.
You have a fighting sprit personality.
You have a superb personality.
You have a kind hearted personality.
You have a golden personality.
You have a superior personality.

What If

What if my past comes flooding back.
What if my troubles come flooding around the corner.
What if my fears come looking for revenge.
What if my circumstances are at a standstill.

What if my denial is crumbling out.
What if my walls around me crack wide open.
What if my world comes crashing down around me.
What if I feel abandoned.

What if I feel unnoticed.
What if I feel reality is not what it seems.
What if a memory resurfaces.
What if I feel I am going to make a success of myself.

What if I lean on people close to and beside me.
What if I sense the worst.
What if I fall hard as stone.
What if my heart burns with passion.

Storm

Ur an amazing storm.
Ur an incredible storm.
Ur an inspirational storm.
Ur a fabulous storm.

Ur an excellent storm.
Ur an extraordinary storm.
Ur a tremendous storm.
Ur a fighting spirit storm.

Ur a force of nature storm.
Ur an outstand storm.
Ur a carefree storm.
Ur a free spirit storm.

Ur a loyal storm.
Ur a great storm.

Ur a passionate storm.
Ur a mega storm.

Ur a magical storm.
Ur a determined storm.
Ur a magnificent storm.
Ur a star storm.

Ur a true storm.
Ur a worthy storm.
Ur a firestorm.
Ur a genuine storm.
Ur a rare storm.
Ur a strong storm.

Held My Hand

You held my hand when I looked back at my fragile past.
You held my hand at the trouble I try and block out.
You held my hand through my toughest times.
You held my hand through the difficult pain.

You held my hand through the dark moments.
You held my hand through the battles I faced.
You held my hand through my challenging times.
You held my hand through my failures.

You held my hand as I fall hard.
You held my hand when I try and make a life for myself.
You held my hand as my world comes crashing down around me.
You held my hand when I am sad.

You held my hand when I thrive.
You held my hand when I wipe my tears on you.
You held my hand when I needed you the most.
You held my hand when I am at my worst.

You held my hand when I am at my lowest.
You held my hand at my weakest.
You held my hand as you never let me face anything alone.
You held my hand when you walk beside me.

You held my hand when I got knocked down.
You held my hand through my achievements.
You held my hand when I didn't have hope.
You held my hand when I didn't have strength.

You held my hand when I tried to give in.
You held my hand when I felt broken.
You held my hand when I tried to give up.
You held my hand and never let go.

There For Me

You were there for me when I looked back at my fragile past.
You were there for me when I continued to confront my energetic demons.
You were there for me when I overcame lifelong fears.
You were there for me when I needed to vent.

You were there for me when I needed the support.
You were there for me when I needed to escape my reality.
You were there for me when I needed you the most.
You were there for me when I needed a shoulder to cry on

You were there for me when I needed the encouragement.
You were there for me when I struggled.
You were there for me when I was at my lowest.
You were there for me when I was at my weakest.

You were there for me when I needed you in my hour of need.
You were there for me when I wanted to let out a scream.
You were there for me when I wanted to explode.
You were there for me when I was sad.

You were there for me when I needed to let out rage.
You were there for me when I felt broken.
You were there for me when I needed to fight my inner cries.
You were there for me when I felt abandoned.

You were there for me when I felt alone.
You were there for me when I felt insecure.

You were there for me when I needed you to make a massive difference in me and my life.
You were there for me when I needed you to make a massive influence on me and my life.

You were there for me when I needed comfort.
You were there for me when I fall apart.
You were there for me when I faced my underlying issues.
You were there for me when I needed a hug.
You were there for me when I needed to find a way of being me.
You were there for me when I needed cheering up.
You were there for me when I felt unnoticed.
You were there for me when I felt let down by others.
You were there for me when I needed a laugh.
You were there for me when I needed to face a challenging day.
You are there for me when I am in crisis.
You are there for me when I am going through my hard times.
You are there for me when I face my worst.
You are there for me when I cry.
You are there for me when I needed you to make me smile.

Thank you

Thanks to you I can face my fragile past.
Thanks to you I can face my lifelong fears.
Thanks to you I can put my endless battles to the back of my mind.
Thanks to you I feel good enough.

Thanks to you I feel wanted.
Thanks to you I feel free.
Thanks to you I know I have people who care about me.
Thanks to you I feel endlessly happy.

Thanks to you I am following my dreams and making them a reality.
Thanks to you I feel valued by those who want me in their lives.
Thanks to you I don't feel low.
Thanks to you I make myself a success.

Thanks to you I realise I have a purpose.
Thanks to you I make a life for myself.
Thanks to you I realised I have a voice.

Thanks to you I feel I can be the person I wanna be.

Thanks to you I believe in myself.
Thanks to you I don't let people who I ghosted from my life walk all over me.
Thanks to you I have hope.
Thanks to you I have strength.

Thanks to you I am the best I can be as you bring out the best in me.
Thanks to you I am never alone.
Thanks to you I never feel lost.
Thanks to you I am so passionate about the things I can do.

Thanks to you I know I can do anything.
Thanks to you I have the best people around me.
Thanks to you I feel so much stronger.
Thanks to you I feel a lot more braver.
Thanks to you I am me.
Thanks to you I have a burning sensation.
Thanks to you I can achieve the things I want from life.
Thank you for being you

Thank you for being in my life.
Thank you for bringing out the real me.
Thank you for bringing out the true me.
Thank you for being so loyal to me.

Thank you for helping me find myself.
Thank you for encouraging me.
Thank you for always being there for me when I needed you the most.
Thank you for always being beside me.

Thank you for always making me smile.
Thank you for being my role model.
Thank you for being my rock.
Thank you form the bottom of my heart.

Blame Game

I took the blame for this toxic environment.
I took the blame for the way I was raised in a toxic environment.
I took the blame for the vengeance I hold within.
I took the blame for the way I was treated.

I took the blame for feeling like a nobody.
I took the blame for the way I turned out.
I took the blame for the protection of those that are close to and beside me.
I took the blame for the rebel I became.

I took the blame for the screw up I was.
I took the blame for feeling like an outsider.
I took the blame for feeling unwanted.
I took the blame for anything and everything that got thrown my way.

I took the blame for the rejection I felt.
I took the blame for the people around me to keep them safe.
I took the blame for the rage I held within.
I took the blame for feeling invisible.
I took the blame for believing things that weren't true.

You Are My Role Model

You are an amazing role model to me.
You are an incredible role model to me.
You are an extraordinary role model to me.
You are an excellent role model to me.

You are a superior role model to me.
You are a fabulous role model to me.
You are a fantastic role model to me.
You are the best role model to me.

You are a tremendous role model to me.
You are a brilliant role model to me.
You are a mega role model to me.
You are a one in a million role model to me.

You are an outstanding role model to me.
You are a loyal role model to me.
You make such a massive impact on me and
my life just by being a role model to me.
You make such a massive difference in me and
my life just by being a role model to me.

You are a magnificent role to me.
You are a rare role model to me.
I admire you.
I look up to you.

I wanna be more and more like you.
You are a trouper of a role model to me.
You are an awesome role model to me.
You are an epic role model to me.
You are a wonderful role model to me.
You are an inspirational role model to me.
You are a spectacular role model to me.

Had My Back

You have always had my back from the very beginning.
You have had my back since we first met.
You have had my back for over many years.
You have had my back during my time at school.

You have had my back when I felt I couldn't face my fragile past.
You have had my back when I couldn't face my bullies.
You have had my back when I had low self-esteem.
You have had my back when I couldn't face my insecurities.

You have had my back when I needed you the most.
You have had my back when I felt alone.
You have had my back when I couldn't face my days at college.
You have had my back from day one.

You have had my back when I needed to escape.
You have never let me down not once.
You have guided me through things I didn't think I could get through.
You have made me a better person.

You have had my back through the pain I endured.
You have had my back when I was so fragile.
You have had my back when I wasn't myself.
You have had my back through the difficulties I faced throughout.

You have had my back since I needed a shoulder to cry on.
You have always had my back when I faced any challenges throughout the years.
You have had my back on so many occasions.
You have had my back when I needed a push in the right direction.

You have had my back when I was feeling low.
You have had my back when I lost my way.
You have had my back when I struggled.
You have had my back when I felt I couldn't go on.

You have had my back when I fall apart.
You have had my back when no one else but you understand me.
You have had my back even when I've been a nightmare.
You have had my back when I couldn't see what was best for me at the time.

You have had my back and never left my side.
You have had my back even when I wanted out.
You have had my back even given me a chance to express myself.
You have had my back just by making a massive impact on me and my life.

You have had my back just by showing me I have a voice and I will be heard.
You have had my back when I just wanted to hide away.
You have had my back just by making a massive difference in me and my life.
You have had my back just by being there for me no matter what.

You have had my back through difficult situations I faced.
You have had my back when I face my worst.
You have had my back when I didn't feel good enough.
You gave me the courage I needed.

You have had my back when I felt broken.
You have had my back when was feeling down.
You have had my back when I felt betrayed.
You have had my back when I felt I couldn't cope.

You have had my back when I didn't feel brave enough.
You have had my back when I didn't feel strong enough.
You had my back when I finally realised you are one of a kind.
You have had my back when I needed a hug.

You have had my back through everything.
You have had my back just by being so loyal to me.
You have had my back just by being in my life.
You have had my back just by being you.

You have had my back just by showing me I can stand my ground.
You have had my back just by showing me I can achieve my goals.
You have had my back just by showing me I can be me.
You have had my back just by showing me that I have confidence to be who I wanna be.

You have had my back just by showing me I can make a success of myself.
You have had my back just by letting me show you the true me.
You have had my back just by letting me show you the real me.
Nothing will ever break us apart.
I wouldn't be me if it wasn't for you.

You Helped Me

You helped me figure out how to get past my traumatic past.
You helped me vanish my lifelong fears that terrorise me to no end.
You helped me find a purpose in life.
You helped me realise my potential.

You helped me turn my life around.
You helped me put my doubts to the back of my mind.
You helped me find myself.
You helped me realise I am worthy of being.

You helped me realise I am as unique as everyone else.
You helped me shape the person I am today.
You helped me by putting a smile on my face
You helped me defy the odds.

You helped me defy my expectations.
You helped me defy my pain.
You helped me defy my ongoing traumas.
You helped the true me to surface.

You helped the real me to show.
You helped me realise I am my own person.
You helped me realise I am who I wanna be.
You helped me raise my spirits.
You helped me by being apart of my life.

Eliminate

You eliminate my past.
You eliminate my pain.
You eliminate my lifelong fears.
You eliminate my underlying issues.

You eliminate my energetic demons.
You eliminate my loneliness.
You eliminate my sadness.
You eliminate my rage.

You eliminate the blame I hold within.

You eliminate my nightmares.
You eliminate my obstacles that are in my way.
You eliminate whatever comes my way.

You eliminate any betrayal that comes my way.
You eliminate my bad memories.
You eliminate my bad experiences.
You eliminate my frowns and replace them with a smile.

You eliminate my emotions that drag me down and you lift my spirits.
You eliminate my darkest days and brighten them up.
You eliminate my darkest moments and light it up like no other.
You eliminate my inner crisis and help me defy them.
You eliminate the long rollercoaster I have been on.
You eliminate the long road I walk down.

Take Me Under Your Wing

You take me under your wing when I look back at my fragile past.
You take me under your wing when I face my lifelong fears.
You take me under my wing when I'm down.
You take me under your wing when I need you the most.

You take me under your wing to keep me on the straight and narrow.
You take me under your wing when I have nowhere to turn.
You take me under your wing when no one else understands me but you.
You take me under your wing when I go into a destructive mode.

You take me under your wing when no one else gives me a fair chance.
You take me under your wing when I feel like I'm hitting rock bottom.
You take me under your wing when I go through tough times.
You take me under your wing when I feel broken.

You take me under your wing when I feel like I'm lost.
You take me under your wing when I feel rejection from people around me.
You take me under your wing when I feel rage about to come out of me.
You take me under your wing and never let me face anything alone.
You take me under you wing to keep me smiling when no one else can.

You take me under your wing when I feel my life is going down a destructive road.
You take me under your wing when I feel let down by others around me.

You take me under your wing when I feel hurt.
You take me under your wing when I feel unnoticed.

You take me under your wing when I feel like I'm breaking into a thousand pieces.
You take me under your wing to prove to people I am worthy of being.
You take me under your wing when I feel abandoned.
You take under your wing to show people I can bring out the true me.

You take me under your wing as you bring out the best in me.
You take me under your wing as you believe in me when no one else did.
You take me under your wing to keep me from rebellion.
You take me under your wing as you stand by me no matter what.

You take me under your wing when you see me in my hour of need.
You take me under your wing when you see me at my weakest.
You take me under your wing when you see me at my lowest.
You take me under your wing when you see me in denial.

Approach

I can approach my fragile past in a different way as you stand by me.
I can approach my lifelong fears in a different way as you stand by me.
I can approach my pain in a different way as you stand by me.
I can approach my hurt in a different way as you stand by me.

I can approach my difficulties in a different way as you stand by me.
I can approach my traumas in a different way as you stand by me.
I can approach my darkest days in a different way as you stand by me.
I can approach my abandonment issues in a different way as you stand by me.

I can stay on the straight and narrow as you stand by me.
I can approach my hour of need in a different way as you stand by me.
I can approach my chances in a different way as you stand by me.
I can approach my rejections in a different way as you stand by me.

I can approach taking risks in a different way as you stand by me.
I can face anything and everything in a different way as you stand by me.
I can approach my battles in a different way as you stand by me.
I can approach denial in a different way as you stand by me.

I can approach my doubts in a different way as you stand by me.

I can approach bringing the true me to the surface as you stand by me.
I can approach challenges that come my way in a different way as you stand by me.
I can achieve my goals in a different way as you stand by me.

I can be me in a different way as you stand by me.
I can approach my reality in a different way as you stand by me.
I can approach the feeling of feeling broken in a different way as you stand by me.
I can approach my loneliness in a different way as you stand by me.

I can approach finding myself in a different way as you stand by me.
I can approach hearing hateful words in a different way as you stand by me.
I can approach being dragged down a destructive road in a different way as you stand by me.
I can approach going into a destructive mode in a different way as you stand by me.
I can approach the cruelty in this world in a different way as you stand by me.
I can approach being as strong as I can be in a different way as you stand by me.
I can approach being as brave as I can be in a different way as you stand by me.
I can approach turning to the people I care about in a different way as you stand by me.

I can approach knowing I have a flood of people around me in a different way as you stand by me.
I can approach dangerous areas in a different way as you stand by me.
I can approach facing danger in a different way as you stand by me.
I can approach the consequences of my actions good or bad in a different way as you stand by me.
I can approach my backlashes in a different way as you stand by me.
I can approach my own way of life in a different way as you stand by me.

Living Proof

Living proof of my fragile past.
Living proof of my lifelong fears.
Living proof of my underlying issues.
Living proof of my pain.

Living proof of my heartbreak.
Living proof of my darkest days.

Living proof of my rage.
Living proof that I can make dreams a reality.

Living proof that I can change my life for the better.
Living proof I can take a chance on things.
Living proof I can take a risk on things.
Living proof I can control what life throws my way.

Living proof that even though I had a difficult start in life I can make something of myself.
Living proof I have a flood of people around me to lean on.
Living proof I can make a u turn
Living proof I can change the outcome on my life.

Living proof I have people in my life that want me for me.
Living proof I have people in my life that care about me
Living proof I have people in my life when I need them the most.
Living proof I am never alone.

Living proof I have someone to always turn to.
Living proof that I have people in my life that will make me smile when I am down
Living proof I have people in my life that will be there for me through thick and thin.
Living proof I have people who will be there for me no matter what.

Living proof I have people in my life that will be there for me in my hour of need.
Living proof I have people in my life that will be there for me in my darkest of days.
Living proof I have people in my life that will be there for me when I need to escape my reality.
Living proof I have people in my life that will be there for me when I need to scream.
Living proof I have people in my life that will be there for me when I want to let out rage.
Living proof I have people in my life that will be there for me when I am sad.
Living proof I have people in my life as and when I want to vent.
Living proof I have people in my life that will cheer me up when I need it.
Living proof I have people in my life that will be there for me when I need a laugh.

Living proof I have people in my life that will be there for me when I need to talk any time.
Living proof I have people in my life that will be there for me when I need a shoulder to cry on.
Living proof I have people in my life that will be there for me when I have a meltdown.
Living proof I have people in my life that will be there for me when I have a breakdown.

Living proof I have people in my life that will be there for me and not let me walk alone and will walk beside me.
Living proof I have people in my life that will be there for me when I feel broken
Living proof I have people in my life that will be there for me when I feel rejected
Living proof I have people in my life that will be there for me when I don't feel valued by others.
Living proof I have people in my life that will be there for me when I feel let down by others around me.
Living proof I have people in my life that will be there for me when I lead my own life in my own unique way.

I Unlock

I unlock my fragile past as I look into it with you beside me.
I unlock my lifelong fears that terrorise me to no end with you beside me.
I unlock my pain with you beside me.
I unlock m reality as I stumble upon it with you beside me.

I unlock my deepest secrets which don't have a hold over me with you beside me.
I unlock my uniqueness of me with you beside me.
I unlock my rage as everything gets the better of me.
I unlock my thoughts in my head with you beside me.

I unlock my loneliness as it tries to take hold of me with you beside me.
I unlock my hatred to try and release it with you beside me.
I unlock my heart to let those who care about me in with you beside me.
I unlock my tears that stream down my face with you beside me.
I unlock ur shoulder as you let me wipe my tears on you with you beside me.

I unlock my reasons behind my emotion for only you to see and know with you beside me.
I unlock my dilemmas that creep up on me without notice with you beside me.
I unlock the way I strain myself with you beside me.
I unlock my rejection and release it into the open with you beside me.
I unlock my guilt that overwhelms me with you beside me.
I unlock a way for you to always make me smile any way you can.
I unlock the hateful words I hear and I release them into the open air with you beside me.

Against Me

You never hold my past against me
You never hold my lifelong fears tat terrorise me to no end against me.
You never hold my fragile state against me.
You never hold my hurt against me.

You never hold the fact that I am not perfect against me.
You never hold my pain against me.
You never hold me accountable for what life throws my way.
You never hold the fact that I am different in my own way against me.
You never hold the fact that I can bring out the true me against me.
You never judge the person I am meant to be.

Rise Above It

As I look back at my fragile past you help me rise above it.
As my lifelong fears terrorise me to no end you help me rise above it.
As an ugly side of me comes firing out at me you help me rise above it.
As my state of mind comes back to trigger something in me you help me rise above it.

As my rage tries to take hold of me you pull me out and help me rise above it.
As the anger in me comes to light you help me rise above it.
With my hour of need lurking around you help me rise above it.
As my battles make a u turn from the back of my mind you help me rise above the beasts and beat them.

As my loneliness takes its toil on me you come crashing in and help me rise above it.

As my mood changes from happy to dark you help me rise above it.
As I feel down you lift my mood and help me rise above it.
As I feel broken you patch me back together and help me rise above it.
As I feel lost you bring me back from a world that isn't for me and you help me rise above it.
When my walls crack wide open you come racing in and help me rise above it.

Heal Me

You heal my fragile past.
You heal my fragile heart.
You heal my heartache.
You heal my pain.

You heal my troubles that follow me.
You heal my lifelong traumas.
You heal my disbelief.
You heal my denial.

You heal my hurt
You heal the way I am.
You heal the energetic demons.
You heal my loneliness.
You heal my need for revenge.
You heal my need for vengeance.
You heal my need to succeed.
You heal the need to fix wonky me.

Light Me Up

When I look back at my fragile past you light me up.
When I face my lifelong fears that terrorise me to no end you light me up.
When I try and break my lifelong issues that affect me you light me up.
When I try and overcome my loneliness you light me up.

When unruly things happen, it happens in true unforgettable style and you light me up.
When you find me down you find a way to light me up.
As you find me broken you never leave me until you light me up.
When you find me in a dark place you take me aside and light me up.

When you find me struggling you sit beside me and talk with me until you light me up.
When my inner cries take its toil on me you light me up.
When I don't feel strong enough you light me up.
When I don't feel brave enough you light me up.

When I feel low you light me up.
When I feel lost you light me up.
When I want to cry you give me your shoulder to wipe my tears on and you light me up.
When I don't feel good enough you light me up.

When I say nothing, you know and you do everything you can to light me up.
When I feel like an outsider you light me up.
When I feel rejected you light me up.
When I feel like giving up you turn it around and light me up.

When I feel unwanted you light me up.
When I feel worthless you light me up.
When I walk into a trap you pull me out and light me up.
When I feel like I'm in denial you light me up.

When I have nowhere to turn you light me up.
When I don't have the courage to fight you light me up.
When I feel insecure you light me up.
When I feel guilt, you know how to make me smile and you light me up.
As you are my lifelong friend you light me up.
As I trust in you, you light me up.
When I feel tired you keep me going and you light me up.
When you take a risk on me you light me up.
When you take a chance on me you light me up.
When I am around you, you light me up.
When I go through challenging days you light me up.
When I go into a destructive mode you light me up.

When I feel alone you appear and light me up.
When I walk down a long road you walk beside me and light me up.
When I feel wonky you patch me up and light me up
You light up my life.
You light up my world.
When I am not myself you light me up any way you can.

Tear Me Apart

I won't let my fragile past tear me apart as long as I've got you.
I won't let my lifelong fears that terrorise me to no end tear me apart as long as I've got you.
I won't let my loneliness take its toll on me tear me apart as long as I've got you.
I won't let my rage that comes out of me tear me apart as long as I've got you.

I won't let my lifelong issues that affect me tear me apart as long as I've got you.
When you find me down, I won't let it tear me apart as long as I've got you.
When you find me broken, I won't let it tear me apart as long as I've got you,
When you find me in a dark place, I won't let it tear me apart as long as I've got you.

When you find me struggling, I won't let it tear me apart as long as I've got you,
When my inner cries take its toll on me, I won't let it tear me apart as long as I've got you.
When I don't feel strong enough, I won't let it tear me apart as long as I've got you.
When I don't feel brave enough, I won't let it tear me apart as long as I've got you.

When I feel low, I won't let it tear me apart as long as I've got you.
When I feel lost I wont let it tear me apart as long as I've got you.
When I wanna cry I won't let it tear me apart as long as I've got you.
When I don't feel good enough, I won't let it tear me apart as long as I've got you.

When I feel like an outsider, I won't let it tear me apart as long as I've got you.
When I feel rejected, I won't let it tear me apart as long as I've got you.
When I feel like giving up, I won't let it tear me apart as long as I've got you.
When I feel hurt, I won't let it tear me apart as long as I've got you.

When I feel damaged, I won't let it tear me apart as long as I've got you.
When I like there's a hole in me, I won't let it tear me apart as long as I've got you.
When I am not myself, I won't let it tear me apart as long as I've got you.
When I need you the most, I will call out and I won't let it tear me apart as long as I've got you.
When I feel torn, I won't let it tear me apart as long as I've got you.

Reach Out To Me

When you look back at your fragile past you can reach out to me.
When you face your lifelong fears, you can reach out to me,
When you try and break your lifelong issues that affect you, you can reach out to me,
When you try and overcome the loneliness you feel you can reach out to me.

When you feel down you can reach out to me.
If and when you feel broken you can reach out to me.
When you feel like you're in a dark place you can reach out to me.
When you feel like you're struggling you can reach out to me.

When your inner cries take its toll on you, you can reach out to me.
When you don't feel strong enough you can reach out to me.
When you don't feel brave enough you can reach out to me.
When you feel low you can reach out to me.

When you feel lost in any way you can reach out to me.
When you need a shoulder to cry on you can reach out to me.
If and when you don't feel good enough you can reach out to me.
When you feel like an outsider you can reach out to me.

If and when you feel rejected you can reach out to me.
When you feel like giving up you can reach out to me.
If and when you feel unwanted you can reach out to me.
If and when you feel worthless you can reach out to me.

When you feel like your entering an unknown trap you can reach out to me.
When you feel like you're in denial you can reach out to me.
If and when you have nowhere to turn you can reach out to me.
If and when you don't feel you have the courage to fight you can reach out to me.

If and when you feel insecure you can reach out to me.
If and when you feel guilt you can reach out to me.
When you need me the most you can reach out to me.
When you are not yourself you can reach out to me.
When you feel alone you can reach out to me.
When you face challenging days, I will walk alongside you and you can reach out to me.
If and when you need to vent you can reach out to me.

Lean On Me

When you look back at your fragile past you can lean on me.
When you face your lifelong fears, you can lean on me.
When you try and break your lifelong issues that affect you, you can lean on me.
When you try and overcome the loneliness you feel you can lean on me.

When you feel down you can lean on me.
If and when you feel broken you can lean on me.
When you feel like you're in a dark place you can lean on me.
When you feel like you're struggling you can lean on me.

When your inner cries take its toll on you, you can lean on me.
When you don't feel strong enough you can lean on me.
When you don't feel brave enough you can lean on me.
When you feel low you can lean on me.

When you feel lost in any way you can lean on me.
When you need a shoulder to cry on you can lean on me.
If and when you don't feel good enough you can lean on me.
When you feel like an outsider you can lean on me.

If and when you feel rejected you can lean on me.
When you feel like giving up you can lean on me.
If and when you feel unwanted you can lean on me.
If and when you feel worthless you can lean on me.

When you feel like you're entering an unknown trap you can lean on me.
When you feel like you're in denial you can lean on me.
If and when you have nowhere to turn you can lean on me.
If and when you don't feel you have the courage to fight you can lean on me.

If and when you feel insecure you can lean on me.
If and when you feel guilt you can lean on me.
When you need me the most you can lean on me.
When you are not yourself you can lean on me.
When you feel alone you can lean on me
When you face challenging days, I will walk alongside you and you can lean on me.
If and when you need to vent you can lean on me.

Vent To Me

When you look back at your fragile past you can vent to me.
When you face your lifelong fears, you can vent to me.
When you try and break your lifelong issues that affect you, you can vent to me.
When you try and overcome the loneliness you feel you can vent to me.

When you feel down you can vent to me.
If and when you feel broken you can vent to me.
When you feel like you're in a dark place you can vent to me.
When you feel like you're struggling you can vent to me.

When your inner cries take its toll on you, you can vent to me.
When you don't feel strong enough you can vent to me.
When you don't feel brave enough you can vent to me.
When you feel low you can vent to me.

When you feel lost in any way you can vent to me.
When you need a shoulder to cry on you can vent to me.
If and when you don't feel good enough you can vent to me.
When you feel like an outsider you can vent to me.

If and when you feel rejected you can vent to me.
When you feel like giving up you can vent to me.
If and when you feel unwanted you can vent to me.
If and when you feel worthless you can vent to me.

When you feel like you're entering an unknown trap you can vent to me.
When you feel like you're in denial you can vent to me.
If and when you have nowhere to turn you can vent to me.
If and when you don't feel you have the courage to fight you can vent to me.

If and when you feel insecure you can vent to me.
If and when you feel guilt you can vent to me.
When you need me the most you can vent to me.
When you are not yourself you can vent to me.

When you feel alone you can vent to me.
When you face challenging days,
I will walk alongside you and you can vent to me.
If and when you need to vent you can vent to me.

Count On Me

When you look back at your fragile past you can count on me
When you face your lifelong fears, you can count on me.
When you try and break your lifelong issues that affect you, you can count on me.
When you try and overcome the loneliness you feel you can count on me.

When you feel down you can count on me.
If and when you feel broken you can count on me.
When you feel like you're in a dark place you can count on me.
When you feel like you're struggling you can count on me.

When your inner cries take its toll on you, you can count on me.
When you don't feel strong enough you can count on me.
When you don't feel brave enough you can count on me.
When you feel low you can count on me.

When you feel lost in any way you can count on me.
When you need a shoulder to cry on you can count on me.
If and when you don't feel good enough you can count on me.
When you feel like an outsider you can count on me.

If and when you feel rejected you can count on me.
When you feel like giving up you can count on me.
If and when you feel unwanted you can count on me.
If and when you feel worthless you can count on me.

When you feel like you're entering an unknown trap you can count on me.
When you feel like you're in denial you can count on me.
If and when you have nowhere to turn you can count on me.
If and when you don't feel you have the courage to fight you can count on me.

If and when you feel insecure you can count on me.
If and when you feel guilt you can count on me.
When you are not yourself you can count on me

When you feel alone you can count on me.
When you face challenging days, I will walk alongside you and you can count on me.
If and when you need to vent you can count on me.

Have Your Back

When you look back at your fragile past, I will have your back.
When you face your lifelong fears, I will have your back.
When you try and break your lifelong issues that affect you, I will have your back.
When you try and overcome the loneliness you feel I will have your back.

When you feel down, I will have your back.
If and when you feel broken, I will have your back.
When you feel like you're in a dark place I will have your back.
When you feel like you're struggling I will have your back.

When your inner cries take its toll on you, I will have your back.
When you don't feel strong enough, I will have your back.
When you don't feel brave enough, I will have your back.
When you feel low, I will have your back.

When you feel lost in any way, I will have your back
When you need a shoulder to cry on, I will have your back.
If and when you don't feel good enough, I will have your back.
When you feel like an outsider, I will have your back.

If and when you feel rejected, I will have your back.
When you feel like giving up, I will have your back.
If and when you feel unwanted, I will have your back.
If and when you feel worthless, I will have your back.

When you feel like you're entering an unknown trap, I will have your back.
When you feel like you're in denial, I will have your back.
If and when you have nowhere to turn, I will have your back.
If and when you don't feel you have the courage to fight, I will have your back.

If and when you feel insecure, I will have your back.
If and when you feel guilt, I will have your back,
When you need me the most, I will have your back.
When you are not yourself, I will have your back.

When you feel alone, I will have your back.
When you face challenging days, I will walk alongside you and I will have your back.
If and when you need to vent, I will have your back.

Be Your Rock

When you look back at your fragile past, I will be your rock.
When you face your lifelong fears, I will be your rock.
When you try and break your lifelong issues that affect you, I will be your rock.
When you try and overcome the loneliness you feel I will be your rock.

When you feel down, I will be your rock.
If and when you feel broken, I will be your rock.
When you feel like you're in a dark place I will be your rock.
When you feel like you're struggling I will be your rock.

When your inner cries take its toll on you, I will be your rock,
When you don't feel strong enough, I will be your rock.
When you don't feel brave enough, I will be your rock.
When you feel low, I will be your rock.

When you feel lost in any way, I will be your rock.
When you need a shoulder to cry on, I will be your rock.
If and when you don't feel good enough, I will be your rock,
When you feel like an outsider, I will be your rock.

If and when you feel rejected, I will be your rock.
When you feel like giving up, I will be your rock.
If and when you feel unwanted, I will be your rock.
If and when you feel worthless, I will be your rock.

When you feel like you're entering an unknown trap, I will be your rock.
When you feel like you're in denial, I will be your rock.
If and when you have nowhere to turn, I will be your rock,
If and when you don't feel you have the courage to fight, I will be your rock,
If and when you feel insecure, I will be your rock
If and when you feel guilt, I will be your rock.
When you need me the most, I will be your rock.
When you are not yourself, I will be your rock.
When you feel alone, I will be your rock.
When you face challenging days, I will walk alongside you and I will be your rock.
If and when you need to vent, I will be your rock.

Rely On Me

When you look back at your fragile past, you can always rely on me.
When you face your lifelong fears, you can always rely on me.
When you try and break your lifelong issues that affect you, you can always rely on me.
When you try and overcome the loneliness you feel, you can always rely on me.

When you feel down, you can always rely on me.
If and when you feel broken, you can always rely on me.
When you feel like you're in a dark place, you can always rely on me;
When you feel like you're struggling, you can always rely on me.

When your inner cries take its toll on you, you can always rely on me.
When you don't feel strong enough, you can always rely on me.
When you don't feel brave enough, you can always rely on me.
When you feel low, you can always rely on me.

When you feel lost in any way, you can always rely on me.
When you need a shoulder to cry on, you can always rely on me.
If and when you don't feel good enough, you can always rely on me.
When you feel like an outsider, you can always rely on me.

If and when you feel rejected, you can always rely on me.
When you feel like giving up, you can always rely on me.
If and when you feel unwanted, you can always rely on me.
If and when you feel worthless, you can always rely on me.

When you feel like you're entering an unknown trap, you can always rely on me.
When you feel like you're in denial, you can always rely on me.
If and when you have nowhere to turn, you can always rely on me.
If and when you don't feel you have the courage to fight, you can always rely on me.

If and when you feel insecure, you can always rely on me.
If and when you feel guilt, you can always rely on me.
When you need me the most, you can always rely on me.

When you are not yourself, you can always rely on me.
When you feel alone you can always rely on me.
When you face challenging days, I will walk alongside you and
you can always rely on me.
If and when you need to vent, you can always rely on me,

Won't Let You Fall

When you look back at your fragile past, I won't let you fall.
When you face your lifelong fears, I won't let you fall
When you try and break your lifelong issues that affect you, I won't let you fall.
When you try and overcome the loneliness you feel, I won't let you fall.

When you feel down, I won't let you fall.
If and when you feel broken, I won't let you fall.
When you feel like you're in a dark place, I won't let you fall.
When you feel like you're struggling, I won't let you fall.

When your inner cries take its toll on you, I won't let you fall.
When you don't feel strong enough, I won't let you fall.
When you don't feel brave enough, I won't let you fall.
When you feel low, I won't let you fall.

When you feel lost in any way, I won't let you fall.
When you need a shoulder to cry on, I won't let you fall.
If and when you don't feel good enough, I won't let you fall.
When you feel like an outsider, I won't let you fall.

If and when you feel rejected, I won't let you fall.
When you feel like giving up, I won't let you fall.
If and when you feel unwanted, I won't let you fall.
If and when you feel worthless, I won't let you fall.

When you feel like you're entering an unknown trap, I won't let you fall.
When you feel like you're in denial, I won't let you fall.
If and when you have nowhere to turn, I won't let you fall.
If and when you don't feel you have the courage to fight, I won't let you fall.

If and when you feel insecure, I won't let you fall.
If and when you feel guilt, I won't let you fall.
When you need me the most, I won't let you fall.

When you are not yourself, I won't let you fall.
When you feel alone, I won't let you fall.
When you face challenging days, I will walk alongside you, and I won't let you fall.
If and when you need to vent, I won't let you fall.

Won't Turn You Away

When you look back at your fragile past, I won't turn you away.
When you face your lifelong fears, I won't turn you away.
When you try and break your lifelong issues that affect you, I won't turn you away.
When you try and overcome the loneliness you feel, I won't turn you away.

When you feel down, I won't turn you away.
If and when you feel broken, I won't turn you away.
When you feel like you're in a dark place, I won't turn you away.
When you feel like you're struggling, I won't turn you away.

When your inner cries take its toll on you, I won't turn you away.
When you don't feel strong enough, I won't turn you away.
When you don't feel brave enough, I won't turn you away.
When you feel low, I won't turn you away.

When you feel lost in any way, I won't turn you away.
When you need a shoulder to cry on, I won't turn you away.
If and when you don't feel good enough, I won't turn you away.
When you feel like an outsider, I won't turn you away.

If and when you feel rejected, I won't turn you away.
When you feel like giving up, I won't turn you away.
If and when you feel unwanted, I won't turn you away.
If and when you feel worthless, I won't turn you away.

When you feel like you're entering an unknown trap, I won't turn you away.
When you feel like you're in denial, I won't turn you away.
If and when you have nowhere to turn, I won't turn you away.
If and when you don't feel you have the courage to fight, I won't turn you away.

If and when you feel insecure, I won't turn you away.
If and when you feel guilt, I won't turn you away.
When you need me the most, I won't turn you away.

When you are not yourself, I won't turn you away.
When you feel alone, I won't turn you away.
When you face challenging days, I will walk alongside you, and I won't turn you away.
If and when you need to vent, I won't turn you away.

Always Have Me

When you look back at your fragile past, you will always have me.
When you face your lifelong fears, you will always have me.
When you try and break your lifelong issues that affect you, you will always have me.
When you try and overcome the loneliness you feel, you will always have me.

When you feel down, you will always have me.
If and when you feel broken, you will always have me
When you feel like you're in a dark place, you will always have me.
When you feel like you're struggling, you will always have me.

When your inner cries take its toll on you, you will always have me.
When you don't feel strong enough, you will always have me.
When you don't feel brave enough, you will always have me.
When you feel low, you will always have me.

When you feel lost in any way, you will always have me.
When you need a shoulder to cry on, you will always have me.
 If and when you don't feel good enough, you will always have me.
When you feel like an outsider, you will always have me.

If and when you feel rejected, you will always have me.
When you feel like giving up, you will always have me.
If and when you feel unwanted, you will always have me.
If and when you feel worthless, you will always have me.

When you feel like you're entering an unknown trap, you will always have me.
When you feel like you're in denial, you will always have me.
If and when you have nowhere to turn, you will always have me.
If and when you don't feel you have the courage to fight, you will always have me.

If and when you feel insecure, you will always have me.
If and when you feel guilt, you will always have me.
When you need me the most, you will always have me.
When you are not yourself, you will always have me.
When you feel alone, you will always have me.
When you face challenging days, I will walk alongside you, and you will always have me.
If and when you need to vent, you will always have me.

Hear You Call

When you look back at your fragile past, I hear you call.
When you face your lifelong fears, I hear you call.
When you try and break your lifelong issues that affect you, I hear you call.
When you try and overcome the loneliness you feel, I hear you call,

When you feel down, I hear you call.
If and when you feel broken, I hear you call.
When you feel like you're in a dark place, I hear you call.
When you feel like you're struggling, I hear you call.

When your inner cries take its toll on you, I hear you call.
When you don't feel strong enough, I hear you call.
When you don't feel brave enough, I hear you call.
When you feel low, I hear you call.

When you feel lost in any way, I hear you call.
When you need a shoulder to cry on, I hear you call.
 If and when you don't feel good enough, I hear you call.
When you feel like an outsider, I hear you call.

If and when you feel rejected, I hear you call.
When you feel like giving up, I hear you call.
If and when you feel unwanted, I hear you call.
If and when you feel worthless, I hear you call.

When you feel like you're entering an unknown trap, I hear you call.
When you feel like you're in denial, I hear you call.
If and when you have nowhere to turn, I hear you call.
If and when you don't feel you have the courage to fight, I hear you call.

If and when you feel insecure, I hear you call.
If and when you feel guilt, I hear you call,
When you need me the most, I hear you call.
When you are not yourself, I hear you call.
When you feel alone, I hear you call.
When you face challenging days, I will walk alongside you, and I hear you call.
If and when you need to vent, I hear you call.

Look My Way

When you look back at your fragile past, always look my way.
When you face your lifelong fears, always look my way
When you try and break your lifelong issues that affect you, always look my way.
When you try and overcome the loneliness you feel, always look my way.

When you feel down, always look my way.
If and when you feel broken, always look my way.
When you feel like you're in a dark place, always look my way.
When you feel like you're struggling, always look my way.

When your inner cries take its toll on you, always look my way.
When you don't feel strong enough, always look my way.
When you don't feel brave enough, always look my way.
When you feel low, always look my way.

When you feel lost in any way, always look my way.
When you need a shoulder to cry on, always look my way.
If and when you don't feel good enough, always look my way
When you feel like an outsider, always look my way.

If and when you feel rejected, always look my way.
When you feel like giving up, always look my way.
If and when you feel unwanted, always look my way.
If and when you feel worthless, always look my way.

When you feel like you're entering an unknown trap always look my way.
When you feel like you're in denial, always look my way.
If and when you have nowhere to turn, always look my way.
If and when you don't feel you have the courage to fight, always look my way.

If and when you feel insecure, always look my way.
If and when you feel guilt, always look my way,
When you need me the most, always look my way.
When you are not yourself, always look my way.
When you feel alone, always look my way.
When you face challenging days, I will walk alongside you, and   always look my way.
If and when you need to vent, always look my way.

Trust In Me

When you look back at your fragile past, know you can trust in me.
When you face your lifelong fears, know you can trust in me.
When you try and break your lifelong issues that affect you, know you can trust in me.
When you try and overcome the loneliness you feel, know you can trust in me.

When you feel down, know you trust in me.
If and when you feel broken, know you can trust in me.
When you feel like you're in a dark place, know you can trust in me
When you feel like you're struggling, know you can trust in me.

When your inner cries take its toll on you, know you can trust in me.
When you don't feel strong enough, know you can trust in me.
When you don't feel brave enough, know you can trust in me.
When you feel low, know you can trust in me.

When you feel lost in any way, know you can trust in me.
When you need a shoulder to cry on, know you can trust in me.
If and when you don't feel good enough, know you can trust in me.
When you feel like an outsider, know you can trust in me.

If and when you feel rejected, know you can trust in me.
When you feel like giving up, know you can trust in me.
If and when you feel unwanted, know you can trust in me.
If and when you feel worthless, know you can trust in me.

When you feel like your entering an unknown trap, know you can trust in me.
When you feel like you're in denial, know you can trust in me.
If and when you have nowhere to turn, know you can trust in me.
If and when you don't feel you have the courage to fight, know you can trust in me.

If and when you feel insecure, know you can trust in me.
If and when you feel guilt, know you can trust in me.
When you need me the most, know you can trust in me.
When you are not yourself, know you can trust in me.
When you feel alone, know you can trust in me.
When you face challenging days, I will walk alongside you, and know you can trust in me
If and when you need to vent, know you can trust in me

Turn To Me

When you look back at your fragile past, know you can turn to me.
When you face your lifelong fears, know you can turn to me.
When you try and break your lifelong issues that affect you, know you can turn to me.
When you try and overcome the loneliness you feel, know you can turn to me.

When you feel down, know you turn to me.
If and when you feel broken, know you can turn to me.
When you feel like you're in a dark place, know you can turn to me
When you feel like you're struggling, know you can turn to me.

When your inner cries take its toll on you, know you can turn to me.
When you don't feel strong enough, know you can turn to me.
When you don't feel brave enough, know you can turn to me
When you feel low, know you can turn to me.

When you feel lost in any way, know you can turn to me.
When you need a shoulder to cry on, know you can turn to me.
If and when you don't feel good enough, know you can turn to me.
When you feel like an outsider, know you can turn to me.

If and when you feel rejected, know you can turn to me.
When you feel like giving up, know you can turn to me.
If and when you feel unwanted, know you can turn to me.
If and when you feel worthless, know you can turn to me.

When you feel like you're entering an unknown trap, know you can turn to me.
When you feel like you're in denial, know you can turn to me.
If and when you have nowhere to turn, know you can turn to me.
If and when you don't feel you have the courage to fight, know you can turn to me,

If and when you feel insecure, know you can turn to me.
If and when you feel guilt, know you can turn to me.
When you need me the most, know you can turn to me
When you are not yourself, know you can turn to me.
When you feel alone, know you can turn to me.
When you face challenging days, I will walk alongside you, and know you can turn to me.
If and when you need to vent, know you can turn to me.

Never Leave Your Side

When you look back at your fragile past, know I will never leave your side.
When you face your lifelong fears, know I will never leave your side.
When you try and break your lifelong issues that affect you, know I will never leave your side.
When you try and overcome the loneliness you feel, know I will never leave your side.

When you feel down, know I will never leave your side.
If and when you feel broken, know I will never leave your side.
When you feel like you're in a dark place, know I will never leave your side.
When you feel like you're struggling, know I will never leave your side.

When your inner cries take its toll on you, know I will never leave your side.
When you don't feel strong enough, know I will never leave your side.
When you don't feel brave enough, know I will never leave your side.
When you feel low, know I will never leave your side.

When you feel lost in any way, know I will never leave your side.
When you need a shoulder to cry on, know I will never leave your side.
If and when you don't feel good enough, know I will never leave your side.
When you feel like an outsider, know I will never leave your side.

If and when you feel rejected, know I will never leave your side.
When you feel like giving up, know I will never leave your side.
If and when you feel unwanted, know I will never leave your side.
If and when you feel worthless, know I will never leave your side.

When you feel like you're entering an unknown trap, know I will never leave your side.
When you feel like you're in denial, know I will never leave your side.
If and when you have nowhere to turn, know I will never leave your side.
If and when you don't feel you have the courage to fight, know I will never leave your side.

If and when you feel insecure, know I will never leave your side.
If and when you feel guilt, know I will never leave your side.
When you need me the most, know I will never leave your side.
When you are not yourself, know I will never leave your side,
When you feel alone, know I will never leave your side.
When you face challenging days, I will walk alongside you, and know I will never leave your side.
If and when you need to vent, know I will never leave your side.

Never Let You Down

When you look back at your fragile past, know I will never let you down.
When you face your lifelong fears, know I will never let you down.
When you try and break your lifelong issues that affect you, know I will never let you down.
When you try and overcome the loneliness you feel, know I will never let you down.

When you feel down, know I will never let you down.
If and when you feel broken, know I will never let you down.
When you feel like you're in a dark place, know I will never let you down.
When you feel like you're struggling, know I will never let you down.

When your inner cries take its toll on you, know I will never let you down.
When you don't feel strong enough, know I will never let you down.
When you don't feel brave enough, know I will never let you down.
When you feel low, know I will never let you down.

When you feel lost in any way, know I will never let you down.
When you need a shoulder to cry on, know I will never let you down.
If and when you don't feel good enough, know I will never let you down.
When you feel like an outsider, know I will never let you down.

If and when you feel rejected, know I will never let you down.
When you feel like giving up, know I will never let you down.
If and when you feel unwanted, know I will never let you down.
If and when you feel worthless, know I will never let you down.

When you feel like you're entering an unknown trap, know I will never let you down.
When you feel like you're in denial, know I will never let you down
if and when you have nowhere to turn, know I will never let you down.
If and when you feel you don't have the courage to fight, know I will never let you down.

If and when you feel insecure, know I will never let you down.
If and when you feel guilt, know I will never let you down.
When you need me the most, know I will never let you down.
When you are not yourself, know I will never let you down.
When you feel alone, know I will never let you down.
When you face challenging days, I will walk alongside you and know I will never let you down.
If and when you need to vent know I will never let you down.

Glue You Back Together

When you look back at your fragile past, know I will glue you back together.
When you face your lifelong fears, know I will glue you back together.
When you try and break your lifelong issues that affect you, know I will glue you back together.
When you try and overcome the loneliness you feel, know I will glue you back together.

When you feel down, know I will glue you back together.
When you feel broken, know I will glue you back together.
When you feel like you're in a dark place, know I will glue you back together.
When you feel like you're struggling, know I will glue you back together.

When your inner cries take its toll on you, know I will glue you back together,
When you don't feel strong enough, know I will glue you back together.
When you don't feel brave enough, know I will glue you back together.
When you feel low, know I will glue you back together.

When you feel lost in any way, know I will glue you back together.
When you need a shoulder to cry on, know I will glue you back together.
If and when you don't feel good enough, know I will glue you back together.
When you feel like an outsider, know I will glue you back together.

If and when you feel rejected, know I will glue you back together.
When you feel like giving up, know I will glue you back together.
If and when you feel unwanted, know I will glue you back together.
If and when you feel worthless, know I will glue you back together.

When you feel like you're entering an unknown trap, know I will glue you back together.
When you feel like you're in denial, know I will glue you back together.
If and when you have nowhere to turn, know I will glue you back together.
If and when you feel you don't have the courage to fight, know I will glue you back together.

If and when you feel insecure, know I will glue you back together.
If and when you feel guilt, know I will glue you back together.
When you need me the most, know I will glue you back together.
When you are not yourself, know I will glue you back together.

When you feel alone, know I will glue you back together.
When face challenging days, know I will glue you back together.
If and when you need to vent, know I will glue you back together.

Hurt You

When you look back at your fragile past, know I will make sure no one hurts you.
When you face your lifelong fears, know I will make sure no one hurts you.
When you try and break your lifelong issues that affect you, know I will make sure no one hurts you.
When you try and overcome the loneliness you feel, know I will make sure no one hurts you.

When you feel down, know I will make sure no one hurts you.
When you feel broken, know I will make sure no one hurts you.
When you feel like you're in a dark place, know I will make sure no one hurts you
When you feel like you're struggling, know I will make sure no one hurts you.

When your inner cries take its toll on you, know I will make sure no one hurts you.
When you don't feel strong enough, know I will make sure no one hurts you.
When you don't feel brave enough, know I will make sure no one hurts you.
When you feel low, know I will make sure no one hurts you.

When you feel lost in any way, know I will make sure no one hurts you.
When you need a shoulder to cry on, know I will make sure no one hurts you..
If and when you don't feel good enough, know I will make sure no one hurts you.
When you feel like an outsider, know I will make sure no one hurts you.

If and when you feel rejected, know I will make sure no one hurts you.
When you feel like giving up, know I will make sure no one hurts you.
If and when you feel unwanted, know I will make sure no one hurts you.
If and when you feel worthless, know I will make sure no one hurts you.

When you feel like you're entering an unknown trap, know I will make sure no one hurts you.
When you feel like you're in denial, know I will make sure no one hurts you.
If and when you have nowhere to turn, know I will make sure no one hurts you.
If and when you feel you don't have the courage to fight, know I will make sure no one hurts you.

If and when you feel insecure, know I will make sure no one hurts you.
If and when you feel guilt, know I will make sure no one hurts you.

When you need me the most, know I will make sure no one hurts you.
When you are not yourself, know I will make sure no one hurts you.

When you feel alone, know I will make sure no one hurts you.
When face challenging days, know I will make sure no one hurts you.
If and when you need to vent, know I will make sure no one hurts you.

Blink Of An Eye

When you look back at your fragile past, know I will appear in a blink of an eye.
When you face your lifelong fears, know I will appear in a blink of an eye.
When you try and break your lifelong issues that affect you, know I will appear in a blink of an eye.
When you try and overcome the loneliness you feel, know I will appear in a blink of an eye

When you feel down, know I will appear in a blink of an eye.
When you feel broken, know I will appear in a blink of an eye.
When you feel like you're in a dark place, know I will appear in a blink of an eye.
When you feel like you're struggling, know I will appear in a blink of an eye.

When your inner cries take its toll on you, know I will appear in a blink of an eye.
When you don't feel strong enough, know I will appear in a blink of an eye.
When you don't feel brave enough, know I will appear in a blink of an eye.
When you feel low, know I will appear in a blink of an eye.

When you feel lost in any way, know I will appear in a blink of an eye.
When you need a shoulder to cry on, know I will appear in a blink of an eye.
If and when you don't feel good enough, know I will appear in a blink of an eye.
When you feel like an outsider, know I will appear in a blink of an eye.

If and when you feel rejected, know I will appear in a blink of an eye.
When you feel like giving up, know I will appear in a blink of an eye.
If and when you feel unwanted, know I will appear in a blink of an eye.
If and when you feel worthless, know I will appear in a blink of an eye.

When you feel like you're entering an unknown trap, know I will appear in a blink of an eye.
When you feel like you're in denial, know I will appear in a blink of an eye.

If and when you have nowhere to turn, know I will appear in a blink of an eye.
If and when you feel you don't have the courage to fight, know I will appear in a blink of an eye.

If and when you feel insecure, know I will appear in a blink of an eye.
If and when you feel guilt, know I will appear in a blink of an eye.
When you need me the most, know I will appear in a blink of an eye.
When you are not yourself, know I will appear in a blink of an eye.

When you feel alone, know I will appear in a blink of an eye.
When face challenging days, know I will appear in a blink of an eye.
If and when you need to vent, know I will appear in a blink of an eye

In Your Corner

When you look back at your fragile past, know I will always be in your corner.
When you face your lifelong fears, know I will always be in your corner.
When you try and break your lifelong issues that affect you, know I will always be in your corner.
When you try and overcome the loneliness you feel, know I will always be in your corner.

When you feel down, know I will always be in your corner.
When you feel broken, know I will always be in your corner.
When you feel like you're in a dark place, know I will always be in your corner.
When you feel like you're struggling, know I will always be in your corner.

When your inner cries take its toll on you, know I will always be in your corner.
When you don't feel strong enough, know I will always be in your corner.
When you don't feel brave enough, know I will always be in your corner.
When you feel low, know I will always be in your corner.

When you feel lost in any way, know I will always be in your corner.
When you need a shoulder to cry on, know I will always be in your corner.
If and when you don't feel good enough, know I will always be in your corner.
When you feel like an outsider, know I will always be in your corner.

If and when you feel rejected, know I will always be in your corner.
When you feel like giving up, know I will always be in your corner.
If and when you feel unwanted, know I will always be in your corner.
If and when you feel worthless, know I will always be in your corner.

When you feel like you're entering an unknown trap, know I will always be in your corner.
When you feel like you're in denial, know I will always be in your corner.
If and when you have nowhere to turn, know I will always be in your corner.
If and when you feel you don't have the courage to fight, know I will always be in your corner.

If and when you feel insecure, know I will always be in your corner.
If and when you feel guilt, know I will always be in your corner.
When you need me the most, know I will always be in your corner.
When you are not yourself, know I will always be in your corner.

When you feel alone, know I will always be in your corner.
When face challenging days, know I will always be in your corner.
If and when you need to vent, know I will always be in your corner.

When You Need Me

When you look back at your fragile past, I will know when you need me.
When you face your lifelong fears, I will know when you need me.
When you try and break your lifelong issues that affect you, I will know when you need me.
When you try and overcome the loneliness you feel, I will know when you need me.

When you feel down, I will know when you need me.
When you feel broken, I will know when you need me.
When you feel like you're in a dark place, I will know when you need me.
When you feel like you're struggling, I will know when you need me.

When your inner cries take its toll on you, I will know when you need me.
When you don't feel strong enough, I will know when you need me.
When you don't feel brave enough, I will know when you need me.
When you feel low, I will know when you need me.

When you feel lost in any way, I will know when you need me.
When you need a shoulder to cry on, I will know when you need me.
If and when you don't feel good enough, I will know when you need me.
When you feel like an outsider, I will know when you need me.

If and when you feel rejected, I will know when you need me.
When you feel like giving up, I will know when you need me.

If and when you feel unwanted, I will know when you need me.
If and when you feel worthless, I will know when you need me

When you feel like you're entering an unknown trap, I will know when you need me.
When you feel like you're in denial, I will know when you need me.
If and when you have nowhere to turn, I will know when you need me.
If and when you feel you don't have the courage to fight, I will know when you need me.

If and when you feel insecure, I will know when you need me.
If and when you feel guilt, I will know when you need me.
When you need me the most, I will know when you need me.
When you are not yourself, I will know when you need me.
When you feel alone, I will know when you need me.
When face challenging days, I will know when you need me.
If and when you need to vent, I will know when you need me.

In The Flesh

When you look back at your fragile past, know I will always appear in the flesh
When you face you your lifelong fears, know I will always appear in the flesh.
When you try and break your lifelong issues that affect you, know I will always appear in the flesh.
When you try and overcome the loneliness you feel, know I will always appear in the flesh.

When you feel down, know I will always appear in the flesh.
If and when you feel broken, know I will always appear in the flesh.
When you feel like you're in a dark place, know I will always appear in the flesh.
When you feel like you're struggling, know I will always appear in the flesh.

When your inner cries take its toll on you, know I will always appear in the flesh.
When you don't feel strong enough, know I will always appear in the flesh.
When you don't feel brave enough, know I will always appear in the flesh.
When you feel low, know I will always appear in the flesh.

When you feel lost in any way, know I will always appear in the flesh.
When you need a shoulder to cry on, know I will always appear in the flesh.

If and when you don't feel good enough, know I will always appear in the flesh.
When you feel like an outsider, know I will always appear in the flesh.

If and when you feel rejected, know I will always appear in the flesh.
When you feel like giving up, know I will always appear in the flesh.
If and when you feel unwanted, know I will always appear in the flesh.
If and when you feel worthless, know I will always appear in the flesh.

When you feel like you are entering an unknown trap, know I will appear in the flesh.
When you feel like you're in denial, know I will always appear in the flesh.
If and when you have nowhere to turn, know I will always appear in the flesh.
If and when you don't feel you have the courage to fight, know I will always appear in the flesh.

If and when you feel insecure, know I will always appear in the flesh.
If and when you feel guilt in any way, know I will always appear in the flesh.
When you need me the most, know I will always appear in the flesh.
When you are not yourself, know I will always appear in the flesh.
When you feel alone, know I will always appear in the flesh.
When you face challenging days, I will walk alongside you and know I will always appear in the flesh.
If and when you need to vent, know I will always appear in the flesh.

Blink Of A Light

When you look back at your fragile past, know I will always be there in a blink of light.
When you face you your lifelong fears, know I will always be there in a blink of light.
When you try and break your lifelong issues that affect you, know I will always be there in a blink of light.
When you try and overcome the loneliness you feel, know I will always be there in a blink of light.

When you feel down, know I will always be there in a blink of light.
If and when you feel broken, know I will always be there in a blink of light.
When you feel like you're in a dark place, know I will always be there in a blink of light.
When you feel like you're struggling, know I will always be there in a blink of light.

When your inner cries take its toll on you, know I will always be there in a blink of light.
When you don't feel strong enough, know I will always be there in a blink of light.
When you don't feel brave enough, know I will always be there in a blink of light.
When you feel low, know I will always be there in a blink of light.

When you feel lost in any way, know I will always be there in a blink of light.
When you need a shoulder to cry on, know I will always be there in a blink of light.
If and when you don't feel good enough, know I will always be there in a blink of light.
When you feel like an outsider, know I will always be there in a blink of light.

If and when you feel rejected, know I will always be there in a blink of light.
When you feel like giving up, know I will always be there in a blink of light.
If and when you feel unwanted, know I will always be there in a blink of light.
If and when you feel worthless, know I will always be there in a blink of light.

When you feel like you are entering an unknown trap, know I will always be there in a blink of light.
When you feel like you're in denial, know I will always be there in a blink of light.
If and when you have nowhere to turn, know I will always be there in a blink of light.
If and when you don't feel you have the courage to fight, know I will always be there in a blink of light.
If and when you feel insecure, know I will always be there in a blink of light.
If and when you feel guilt in any way, know I will always be there in a blink of light.
When you need me the most, know I will always be there in a blink of light.
When you are not yourself, know I will always be there in a blink of light.
When you feel alone, know I will always be there in a blink of light.
When you face challenging days, I will walk alongside you and know I will always be there in a blink of light.
If and when you need to vent, know I will always be there in a blink of light.

Won't Walk Away

When you look back at your fragile past, know I won't walk away.
When you face you your lifelong fears, know I won't walk away.
When you try and break your lifelong issues that affect you, know I won't walk away.
When you try and overcome the loneliness you feel, know I won't walk away.

When you feel down, know I won't walk away.
If and when you feel broken, know I won't walk away.
When you feel like you're in a dark place, know I won't walk away.
When you feel like you're struggling, know I won't walk away.

When your inner cries take its toll on you, know I won't walk away.
When you don't feel strong enough, know I won't walk away.
When you don't feel brave enough, know I won't walk away.
When you feel low, know I won't walk away.

When you feel lost in any way, know I won't walk away.
When you need a shoulder to cry on, know I won't walk away.
If and when you don't feel good enough, know I won't walk away.
When you feel like an outsider, know I won't walk way.

If and when you feel rejected, know I won't walk away.
When you feel like giving up, know I won't walk away.
If and when you feel unwanted, know I won't walk away.
If and when you feel worthless, know I won't walk away.

When you feel like you are entering an unknown trap, know I won't walk away.
When you feel like you're in denial, know I won't walk away.
If and when you have nowhere to turn, know I won't walk away.
If and when you don't feel you have the courage to fight, know I won't walk away.

If and when you feel insecure, know I won't walk away.
If and when you feel guilt in any way, know I won't walk away.
When you need me the most, know I won't walk away.
When you are not yourself, know I won't walk away.
When you feel alone, know I won't walk away
When you face challenging days, I will walk alongside you and know I won't walk away.
If and when you need to vent, know I won't walk away.

Free You

When you look back at your fragile past, know I will always free you.
When you face you your lifelong fears, know I will always free you.
When you try and break your lifelong issues that affect you, know I will always free you.
When you try and overcome the loneliness you feel, know I will always free you.

When you feel down, know I will always free you.
If and when you feel broken, know I will always free you.
When you feel like you're in a dark place, know I will always free you.
When you feel like you're struggling, know I will always free you.

When your inner cries take its toll on you, know I will always free you.
When you don't feel strong enough, know I will always free you.
When you don't feel brave enough, know I will always free you
When you feel low, know I will always free you.

When you feel lost in any way, know I will always free you.
When you need a shoulder to cry on, know I will always free you.
If and when you don't feel good enough, know I will always free you.
When you feel like an outsider, know I will always free you.

If and when you feel rejected, know I will always free you.
When you feel like giving up, know I will always free you.
If and when you feel unwanted, know I will always free you.
If and when you feel worthless, know I will always free you.

When you feel like you are entering an unknown trap, know I will always free you.
When you feel like you're in denial, know I will always free you.
If and when you have nowhere to turn, know I will always free you.
If and when you don't feel you have the courage to fight, know I will always free you.

If and when you feel insecure, know I will always free you.
If and when you feel guilt in any way, know I will always free you.
When you need me the most, know I will always free you.
When you are not yourself, know I will always free you.
When you feel alone, know I will always free you
When you face challenging days, I will walk alongside you and know I will always free you.
If and when you need to vent, know I will always free you.

Knock You Down

When you look back at your fragile past, know I won't let anyone knock you down.
When you face you your lifelong fears, know I won't let anyone knock you down.
When you try and break your lifelong issues that affect you, know I won't let anyone knock you down
When you try and overcome the loneliness you feel, know I won't let anyone knock you down.

When you feel down, know I won't let anyone knock you down.
If and when you feel broken, know I won't let anyone knock you down.
When you feel like you're in a dark place, know I won't let anyone knock you down.
When you feel like you're struggling, know I won't let anyone knock you down.

When your inner cries take its toll on you, know I won't let anyone knock you down.
When you don't feel strong enough, know I won't let anyone knock you down.
When you don't feel brave enough, know I won't let anyone knock you down.
When you feel low, know I won't let anyone knock you down.

When you feel lost in any way, know I won't let anyone knock you down.
When you need a shoulder to cry on, know I won't let anyone knock you down.
If and when you don't feel good enough, know I won't let anyone knock you down.
When you feel like an outsider, know I won't let anyone knock you down.

If and when you feel rejected, know I won't let anyone knock you down.
When you feel like giving up, know I won't let anyone knock you down.
If and when you feel unwanted, know I won't let anyone knock you down.
If and when you feel worthless, know I won't let anyone knock you down.

When you feel like you are entering an unknown trap, know I won't let anyone knock you down.
When you feel like you're in denial, know I won't let anyone knock you down.
If and when you have nowhere to turn, know I won't let anyone knock you down.
If and when you don't feel you have the courage to fight, know I won't let anyone knock you down
If and when you feel insecure, know I won't let anyone knock you down.

If and when you feel guilt in any way, know I won't let anyone knock you down.
When you need me the most, know I won't let anyone knock you down.
When you are not yourself, know I won't let anyone knock you down.
When you feel alone, know I won't let anyone knock you down.
When you face challenging days, I will walk alongside you and know I won't let anyone knock you down.
If and when you need to vent, know I won't let anyone knock you down.

Look For Me

When you look back at your fragile past, know you can always look for me.
When you face you your lifelong fears, know you can always look for me.
When you try and break your lifelong issues that affect you, know you can always look for me.
When you try and overcome the loneliness you feel, know you can always look for me.

When you feel down, know you can always look for me.
If and when you feel broken, know you can always look for me.
When you feel like you're in a dark place, know you can always look for me.
When you feel like you're struggling, know you can always look for me.

When your inner cries take its toll on you, know you can always look for me.
When you don't feel strong enough, know you can always look for me.
When you don't feel brave enough, know you can always look for me.
When you feel low, know you can always look for me

When you feel lost in any way, know you can always look for me.
When you need a shoulder to cry on, know you can always look for me.
If and when you don't feel good enough, know you can always look for me.
When you feel like an outsider, know you can always look for me.

If and when you feel rejected, know you can always look for me.
When you feel like giving up, know you can always look for me.
If and when you feel unwanted, know you can always look for me.
If and when you feel worthless, know you can always look for me.

When you feel like you are entering an unknown trap, know you can always look for me.
When you feel like you're in denial, know you can always look for me.
If and when you have nowhere to turn, know you can always look for me.

If and when you don't feel you have the courage to fight, know you can always look for me.

If and when you feel insecure, know you can always look for me.
If and when you feel guilt in any way, know you can always look for me.
When you need me the most, know you can always look for me.
When you are not yourself, know you can always look for me.
When you feel alone, know you can always look for me.
When you face challenging days, I will walk alongside you and know you can always look for me.
If and when you need to vent, know you can always look for me.

Cave In

When you look back at your fragile past, know I won't let you cave in.
When you face your lifelong fears, know I won't let you cave in.
When you try and break your lifelong issues that affect you, know I won't let you cave in.
When you try and overcome the loneliness you feel, know I won't let you cave in.

When you feel down, know I won't let you cave in.
If and when you feel broken, know I won't let you cave in.
When you feel like you're in a dark place, know I won't let you cave in.
When you feel like you're struggling, know I won't let you cave in.

When your inner cries take its toll on you, know I won't let you cave in.
When you don't feel strong enough, know I won't let you cave in.
When you don't feel brave enough, know I won't let you cave in.
When you feel low, know I won't let you cave in.

When you feel lost in any way, know I won't let you cave in.
When you need a shoulder to cry on, know I won't let you cave in.
If and when you don't feel good enough, know I won't let you cave in.
When you feel like an outsider, know I won't let you cave in.

If and when you feel rejected, know I won't let you cave in.
When you feel like giving up, know I won't let you cave in.
If and when you feel unwanted, know I won't let you cave in.
If and when you feel worthless, know I won't let you cave in.

When you feel like you are entering an unknown trap, know I won't let you cave in.
When you feel like you're in denial, know I won't let you cave in.
If and when you have nowhere to turn, know I won't let you cave in.
If and when you don't feel you have the courage to fight, know I won't let you cave in.

If and when you feel insecure, know I won't let you cave in.
If and when you feel guilt in any way, know I won't let you cave in.
When you need me the most, know I won't let you cave in.
When you are not yourself, know I won't let you cave in.
When you feel alone, know I won't let you cave in.
When you face challenging days, I will walk alongside you and know I won't let you cave in.
If and when you need to vent, know I won't let you cave in.

Care For You

When you look back at your fragile past, know I will always care for you.
When you face you your lifelong fears, know I will always care for you.
When you try and break your lifelong issues that affect you, know I will always care for you.
When you try and overcome the loneliness you feel, know I will always care for you.

When you feel down, know I will always care for you.
If and when you feel broken, know I will always care for you.
When you feel like you're in a dark place, know I will always care for you.
When you feel like you're struggling, know I will always care for you.

When your inner cries take its toll on you, know I will always care for you.
When you don't feel strong enough, know I will always care for you.
When you don't feel brave enough, know I will always care for you.
When you feel low, know I will always care for you.

When you feel lost in any way, know I will always care for you.
When you need a shoulder to cry on, know I will always care for you.
If and when you don't feel good enough, know I will always care for you.
When you feel like an outsider, know I will always care for you.

If and when you feel rejected, know I will always care for you.

When you feel like giving up, know I will always care for you.
If and when you feel unwanted, know I will always care for you.
If and when you feel worthless, know I will always care for you.

When you feel like you are entering an unknown trap, know I will always care for you.
When you feel like you're in denial, know I will always care for you.
If and when you have nowhere to turn, know I will always care for you.
If and when you don't feel you have the courage to fight, know I will always care for you.

If and when you feel insecure, know I will always care for you.
If and when you feel guilt in any way, know I will always care for you.
When you need me the most, know I will always care for you.
When you are not yourself, know I will always care for you.
When you feel alone, know I will always care for you.
When you face challenging days, I will walk alongside you and know I will always care for you.
If and when you need to vent, know I will always care for you

Look Out For You

When you look back at your fragile past, know I will always look out for you.
When you face you your lifelong fears, know I will always look out for you.
When you try and break your lifelong issues that affect you, know I will always look out for you.
When you try and overcome the loneliness you feel, know I will always look out for you.

When you feel down, know I will always look out for you.
If and when you feel broken, know I will always look out for you.
When you feel like you're in a dark place, know I will always look out for you.
When you feel like you're struggling, know I will always look out for you.

When your inner cries take its toll on you, know I will always look out for you.
When you don't feel strong enough, know I will always look out for you.
When you don't feel brave enough, know I will always look out for you.
When you feel low, know I will always look out for you.

When you feel lost in any way, know I will always look out for you.
When you need a shoulder to cry on, know I will always look out for you.

If and when you don't feel good enough, know I will always look out for you.
When you feel like an outsider, know I will always look out for you.

If and when you feel rejected, know I will always look out for you.
When you feel like giving up, know I will always look out for you.
If and when you feel unwanted, know I will always look out for you.
If and when you feel worthless, know I will always look out for you.

When you feel like you are entering an unknown trap, know I will always look out for you.
When you feel like you're in denial, know I will always look out for you.
If and when you have nowhere to turn, know I will always look out for you.
If and when you don't feel you have the courage to fight, know I will always look out for you.

If and when you feel insecure, know I will always look out for you.
If and when you feel guilt in any way, know I will always look out for you.
When you need me the most, know I will always look out for you.
When you are not yourself, know I will always look out for you.
When you feel alone, know I will always look out for you.
When you face challenging days, I will walk alongside you and know I will always look out for you.
If and when you need to vent, know I will always look out for you.

Loyal To You For Life

When you look back at your fragile past, know I will always be loyal to you for life.
When you face you your lifelong fears, know I will always be loyal to you for life.
When you try and break your lifelong issues that affect you, know I will always be loyal to you for life.
When you try and overcome the loneliness you feel, know I will always be loyal to you for life.

When you feel down, know I will always be loyal to you for life.
If and when you feel broken, know I will always be loyal to you for life.
When you feel like you're in a dark place, know I will always be loyal to you for life.
When you feel like you're struggling, know I will always be loyal to you for life.

When your inner cries take its toll on you, know I will always be loyal to you for life.
When you don't feel strong enough, know I will always be loyal to you for life.
When you don't feel brave enough, know I will always be loyal to you for life.
When you feel low, know I will always be loyal to you for life.

When you feel lost in any way, know I will always be loyal to you for life.
When you need a shoulder to cry on, know I will always be loyal to you for life.
If and when you don't feel good enough, know I will always be loyal to you for life.
When you feel like an outsider, know I will always be loyal to you for life.

If and when you feel rejected, know I will always be loyal to you for life.
When you feel like giving up, know I will always be loyal to you for life.
If and when you feel unwanted, know I will always be loyal to you for life.
If and when you feel worthless, know I will always be loyal to you for life.

When you feel like you are entering an unknown trap, know I will always be loyal to you for life.
When you feel like you're in denial, know I will always be loyal to you for life.
If and when you have nowhere to turn, know I will always be loyal to you for life.
If and when you don't feel you have the courage to fight, know I will always be loyal to you for life
If and when you feel insecure, know I will always be loyal to you for life.
If and when you feel guilt in any way, know I will always be loyal to you for life.
When you need me the most, know I will always be loyal to you for life.
When you are not yourself, know I will always be loyal to you for life.
When you feel alone, know I will always be loyal to you for life.
When you face challenging days, I will walk alongside you and know I will always be loyal to you for life.
If and when you need to vent, know I will always be loyal to you for life.

In A Flash

When you look back at your fragile past, know I will always appear in a flash.
When you face you your lifelong fears, know I will always appear in a flash.
When you try and break your lifelong issues that affect you, know I will always appear in a flash.

When you try and overcome the loneliness you feel, know I will always appear in a flash.

When you feel down, know I will always appear in a flash.
If and when you feel broken, know I will always appear in a flash.
When you feel like you're in a dark place, know I will always appear in a flash.
When you feel like you're struggling, know I will always appear in a flash.

When your inner cries take its toll on you, know I will always appear in a flash.
When you don't feel strong enough, know I will always appear in a flash.
When you don't feel brave enough, know I will always appear in a flash.
When you feel low, know I will always appear in a flash.

When you feel lost in any way, know I will always appear in a flash.
When you need a shoulder to cry on, know I will always appear in a flash.
If and when you don't feel good enough, know I will always appear in a flash.
When you feel like an outsider, know I will always appear in a flash.

If and when you feel rejected, know I will always appear in a flash.
When you feel like giving up, know I will always appear in a flash.
If and when you feel unwanted, know I will always appear in a flash.
If and when you feel worthless, know I will always appear in a flash.

When you feel like you are entering an unknown trap, know I will appear in a flash.
When you feel like you're in denial, know I will always appear in a flash.
If and when you have nowhere to turn, know I will always appear in a flash.
If and when you don't feel you have the courage to fight, know I will always appear in a flash.

If and when you feel insecure, know I will always appear in a flash.
If and when you feel guilt in any way, know I will always appear in a flash.
When you need me the most, know I will always appear in a flash.
When you are not yourself, know I will always appear in a flash
When you feel alone, know I will always appear in a flash
When you face challenging days, I will walk alongside you and know I will always appear in a flash
If and when you need to vent, know I will always appear in a flash

Believe In You

When you look back at your fragile past, know I will always believe in you.
When you face you your lifelong fears, know I will always believe in you.
When you try and break your lifelong issues that affect you, know I will always believe in you.
When you try and overcome the loneliness you feel, know I will always believe in you.

When you feel down, know I will always believe in me.
If and when you feel broken, know I will always believe in you.
When you feel like you're in a dark place, know I will always believe in you.
When you feel like you're struggling, know I will always believe in you.

When your inner cries take its toll on you, know I will always believe in you.
When you don't feel strong enough, know I will always believe in you.
When you don't feel brave enough, know I will always believe in you.
When you feel low, know I will always believe in you.

When you feel lost in any way, know I will always believe in you.
When you need a shoulder to cry on, know I will always believe in you.
If and when you don't feel good enough, know I will always believe in you.
When you feel like an outsider, know I will always believe in you.

If and when you feel rejected, know I will always believe in you.
When you feel like giving up, know I will always believe in you.
If and when you feel unwanted, know I will always believe in you.
If and when you feel worthless, know I will always believe in you.

When you feel like you are entering an unknown trap, know I will always believe in you.
When you feel like you're in denial, know I will always believe in you.
If and when you have nowhere to turn, know I will always believe in you.
If and when you don't feel you have the courage to fight, know I will always believe in you.

If and when you feel insecure, know I will always believe in you.
If and when you feel guilt in any way, know I will always believe in you.
When you need me the most, know I will always believe in you.
When you are not yourself, know I will always believe in you.
When you feel alone, know I will always believe in you.
When you face challenging days, I will walk alongside you and know I will always believe in you.
If and when you need to vent, know I will always believe in you.

Never Let You Face Anything Alone

When you look back at your fragile past, know I will never let you face anything alone.
When you face you your lifelong fears, know I will never let you face anything alone.
When you try and break your lifelong issues that affect you, know I will never let you face anything alone.
When you try and overcome the loneliness you feel, know I will never let you face anything alone.

When you feel down, know I will never let you face anything alone.
If and when you feel broken, know I will never let you face anything alone.
When you feel like you're in a dark place, know I will never let you face anything alone.
When you feel like you're struggling, know I will never let you face anything alone.

When your inner cries take its toll on you, know I will never let you face anything alone.
When you don't feel strong enough, know I will never let you face anything alone.
When you don't feel brave enough, know I will never let you face anything alone.
When you feel low, know I will never let you face anything alone.

When you feel lost in any way, know I will never let you face anything alone.
When you need a shoulder to cry on, know I will never let you face anything alone.
If and when you don't feel good enough, know I will never let you face anything alone.
When you feel like an outsider, know I will never let you face anything alone.

If and when you feel rejected, know I will never let you face anything alone.
When you feel like giving up, know I will never let you face anything alone.
If and when you feel unwanted, know I will never let you face anything alone.
If and when you feel worthless, know I will never let you face anything alone.

When you feel like you are entering an unknown trap, know I will never let you face anything alone.
When you feel like you're in denial, know I will never let you face anything alone.

If and when you have nowhere to turn, know I will never let you face anything alone
If and when you don't feel you have the courage to fight, know I will never let you face anything alone.
If and when you feel insecure, know I will never let you face anything alone.
If and when you feel guilt in any way, know I will never let you face anything alone.
When you need me the most, know I will never let you face anything alone.
When you are not yourself, know I will never let you face anything alone.
When you feel alone, know I will never let you face anything alone.
When you face challenging days, I will walk alongside you and know I will never let you face anything alone.
If and when you need to vent, know I will never let you face anything alone.

Take You Aside And Make You Smile

When you look back at your fragile past, know I will always take you aside and make you smile.
When you face you your lifelong fears, know I will always take you aside and make you smile.
When you try and break your lifelong issues that affect you, know I will always take you aside and make you smile.
When you try and overcome the loneliness you feel, know I will always take you aside and make you smile.

When you feel down, know I will always take you aside and make you smile.
If and when you feel broken, know I will always take you aside and make you smile.
When you feel like you're in a dark place, know I will always take you aside and make you smile
When you feel like you're struggling, know I will always take you aside and make you smile.

When your inner cries take its toll on you, know I will always take you aside and make you smile.
When you don't feel strong enough, know I will always take you aside and make you smile
When you don't feel brave enough, know I will always take you aside and make you smile.
When you feel low, know I will always take you aside and make you smile.

When you feel lost in any way, know I will always take you aside and make you smile.
When you need a shoulder to cry on, know I will always take you aside and make you smile.
If and when you don't feel good enough, know I will always take you aside and make you smile.
When you feel like an outsider, know I will always take you aside and make you smile.

If and when you feel rejected, know I will always take you aside and make you smile.
When you feel like giving up, know I will always take you aside and make you smile.
If and when you feel unwanted, know I will always take you aside and make you smile
If and when you feel worthless, know I will always take you aside and make you smile.

When you feel like you are entering an unknown trap, know I will always take you aside and make you smile.
When you feel like you're in denial, know I will always take you aside and make you smile.
If and when you have nowhere to turn, know I will always take you aside and make you smile.
If and when you don't feel you have the courage to fight, know I will always take you aside and make you smile.
If and when you feel insecure, know I will always take you aside and make you smile.
If and when you feel guilt in any way, know I will always take you aside and make you smile.
When you need me the most, know I will always take you aside and make you smile.
When you are not yourself, know I will always take you aside and make you smile.
When you feel alone, know I will always take you aside and make you smile.
When you face challenging days, I will walk alongside you and know I will always take you aside and make you smile.
If and when you need to vent, know I will always take you aside and make you smile.

Drag You Down

When you look back at your fragile past, know I will never let anyone drag you down.
When you face you your lifelong fears, know I will never let anyone drag you down.
When you try and break your lifelong issues that affect you, know I will never let anyone drag you down.
When you try and overcome the loneliness you feel, know I will never let anyone drag you down.

When you feel down, know I will never let anyone drag you down.
If and when you feel broken, know I will never let anyone drag you down.
When you feel like you're in a dark place, know I will never let anyone drag you down.
When you feel like you're struggling, know I will never let anyone drag you down.

When your inner cries take its toll on you, know I will never let anyone drag you down.
When you don't feel strong enough, know I will never let anyone drag you down.
When you don't feel brave enough, know I will never let anyone drag you down.
When you feel low, know I will never let anyone drag you down.

When you feel lost in any way, know I will never let anyone drag you down.
When you need a shoulder to cry on, know I will never let anyone drag you down.
If and when you don't feel good enough, know I will never let anyone drag you down.
When you feel like an outsider, know I will never let anyone drag you down.

If and when you feel rejected, know I will never let anyone drag you down.
When you feel like giving up, know I will never let anyone drag you down.
If and when you feel unwanted, know I will never let anyone drag you down.
If and when you feel worthless, know I will never let anyone drag you down.

When you feel like you are entering an unknown trap, know I will never let anyone drag you down.
When you feel like you're in denial, know I will never let anyone drag you down.

If and when you have nowhere to turn, know I will never let anyone drag you down.
If and when you don't feel you have the courage to fight, know I will never let anyone drag you down.
If and when you feel insecure, know I will never let anyone drag you down.
If and when you feel guilt in any way, know I will never let anyone drag you down.
When you need me the most, know I will never let anyone drag you down.
When you are not yourself, know I will never let anyone drag you down.
When you feel alone, know I will never let anyone drag you down.
When you face challenging days, I will walk alongside you and know I will never let anyone drag you down.
If and when you need to vent, know I will never let anyone drag you down.

I Give You

I give you my heart.
I give you my soul.
I give you my honesty.
I give you my strength.
I give you my energy.
I give you my hope.
I give you my loyalty.
I give you my bravery.
I give you my fearless ways of being.
I give you my confidence.
I give you the real me
I give you the true me.
I give you my vision of life.

Brave Face

When you look back at your fragile past, know you don't always have to put on a brave face in front of me.
When you face you your lifelong fears, know you don't always have to put on a brave face in front of me.
When you try and break your lifelong issues that affect you, know you don't always have to put on a brave face in front of me.
When you try and overcome the loneliness you feel, know you don't always have to put on a brave face in front of me.

When you feel down, know you don't always have to put on a brave face in front of me.
If and when you feel broken, know you don't always have to put on a brave face in front of me.
When you feel like you're in a dark place, know you don't always have to put on a brave face in front of me.
When you feel like you're struggling, know you don't always have to put on a brave face in front of me.

When your inner cries take its toll on you, know you don't always have to put on a brave face in front of me
When you don't feel strong enough, know you don't always have to put on a brave face in front of me.
When you don't feel brave enough, know you don't always have to put on a brave face in front of me.
When you feel low, know you don't always have to put on a brave face in front of me.

When you feel lost in any way, know you don't always have to put on a brave face in front of me.
When you need a shoulder to cry on, know you don't always have to put on a brave face in front of me.
If and when you don't feel good enough, know you don't always have to put on a brave face in front of me.
When you feel like an outsider, know you don't always have to put on a brave face in front of me.

If and when you feel rejected, know you don't always have to put on a brave face in front of me.
When you feel like giving up, know you don't always have to put on a brave face in front of me.
If and when you feel unwanted, know you don't always have to put on a brave face in front of me.
If and when you feel worthless, know you don't always have to put on a brave face in front of me.
When you feel like you are entering an unknown trap, know you don't always have to put on a brave face in front of me.
When you feel like you're in denial, know you don't always have to put on a brave face in front of me.
If and when you have nowhere to turn, know you don't always have put on a brave face in front of me.

If and when you don't feel you have the courage to fight, know you don't always have to put on a brave face in front of me.
If and when you feel insecure, know you don't always have to put on a brave face in front of me.
If and when you feel guilt in any way, know you don't always have to put on a brave face in front of me.
When you need me the most, know you don't always have to put on a brave face in front of me.
When you are not yourself, know you don't always have to put on a brave face in front of me.
When you feel alone, know you don't always have to put on a brave face in front of me.
When you face challenging days, know you don't always have to put on a brave face in front of me.
If and when you need to vent, know you don't always have to put on a brave face in front of me.

Fake Smile

When you look back at your fragile past, know you don't always have to fake a smile around me.
When you face you your lifelong fears, know you don't always have to fake a smile around me.
When you try and break your lifelong issues that affect you, know you don't always have to fake a smile around me.
When you try and overcome the loneliness you feel, know you don't always have to fake a smile around me.
When you feel down, know you don't always have to fake a smile around me.
If and when you feel broken, know you don't always have to fake a smile around me.
When you feel like you're in a dark place, know you don't always have to fake a smile around me.
When you feel like you're struggling, know you don't always have to fake a smile around me.

When your inner cries take its toll on you, know you don't always have to fake a smile around me.
When you don't feel strong enough, know you don't always have to fake a smile around me.
When you don't feel brave enough, know you don't always have to fake a smile around me.

When you feel low, know you don't always have to fake a smile around me.

When you feel lost in any way, know you don't always have to fake a smile around me.
When you need a shoulder to cry on, know you don't always have to fake a smile around me.
If and when you don't feel good enough, know you don't always have to fake a smile around me.
When you feel like an outsider, know you don't always have to fake a smile around me.

If and when you feel rejected, know you don't always have to fake a smile around me.
When you feel like giving up, know you don't always have to fake a smile around me.
If and when you feel unwanted, know you don't always have to fake a smile around me.
If and when you feel worthless, know you don't always have to fake a smile around me.

When you feel like you are entering an unknown trap, know you don't always have to fake a smile around me.
When you feel like you're in denial, know you don't always have to fake a smile around me.
If and when you have nowhere to turn, know you don't always have to fake a smile around me.
If and when you don't feel you have the courage to fight, know you don't always have to fake a smile around me.
If and when you feel insecure, know you don't always have to fake a smile around me.
If and when you feel guilt in any way, know you don't always have to fake a smile around me.
When you need me the most, know you don't always have to fake a smile around me.
When you are not yourself, know you don't always have to fake a smile around me.
When you feel alone, know you don't always have to fake a smile around me.
When you face challenging days, I will walk alongside you and know you don't always have to fake a smile around me.
If and when you need to vent, know you don't always have to fake a smile around me.

Put On An Act

When you look back at your fragile past, know you don't always have to put on an act around me.
When you face you your lifelong fears, know you don't always have to put on an act around me.
When you try and break your lifelong issues that affect you, know you don't always have to put on an act around me.
When you try and overcome the loneliness you feel, know you don't always have to put on an act around me.

When you feel down, know you don't always have to put on an act around me.
If and when you feel broken, know you don't always have to put on an act around me.
When you feel like you're in a dark place, know you don't always have to put on an act around me.
When you feel like you're struggling, know you don't always have to put on an act around me.

When your inner cries take its toll on you, know you don't always have to put on an act around me.
When you don't feel strong enough, know you don't always have to put on an act around me.
When you don't feel brave enough, know you don't always have to put on an act around me.
When you feel low, know you don't always have to put on an act around me.

When you feel lost in any way, know you don't always have to put on an act around me.
When you need a shoulder to cry on, know you don't always have to put on an act around me.
If and when you don't feel good enough, know you don't always have to put on an act around me.
When you feel like an outsider, know you don't always have to put on an act around me.

If and when you feel rejected, know you don't always have to put on an act around me.
When you feel like giving up, know you don't always have to put on an act around me.
If and when you feel unwanted, know you don't always have to put on an act around me.

If and when you feel worthless, know you don't always have to put on an act around me.
When you feel like you are entering an unknown trap, know you don't always have to put on an act around me.
When you feel like you're in denial, know you don't always have to put on an act around me.
If and when you have nowhere to turn, know you don't always have to put on an act around me.
If and when you don't feel you have the courage to fight, know you don't always have to put on an act around me.
If and when you feel insecure, know you don't always have to put on an act around me.
If and when you feel guilt in any way, know you don't always have to put on an act around me.
When you need me the most, know you don't always have to put on an act around me.
When you are not yourself, know you don't always have to put on an act around me.
When you feel alone, know you don't always have to put on an act around me.
When you face challenging days, I will walk alongside you and know you don't always have to put on an act around me.
If and when you need to vent, know you don't always have to put on an act around me.

You Can Be Yourself

When you look back at your fragile past, know you can always be yourself around me.
When you face you your lifelong fears, know you can always be yourself around me.
When you try and break your lifelong issues that affect you, know you can always be yourself around me.
When you try and overcome the loneliness you feel, know you can always be yourself around me.

When you feel down, know you can always be yourself around me.
If and when you feel broken, know you can always be yourself around me.
When you feel like you're in a dark place, know you can always be yourself around me.
When you feel like you're struggling, know you can always be yourself around me.

When your inner cries take its toll on you, know you can always be yourself around me.
When you don't feel strong enough, know you can always be yourself around me.
When you don't feel brave enough, know you can always be yourself around me.
When you feel low, know you can always be yourself around me.

When you feel lost in any way, know you can always be yourself around me.
When you need a shoulder to cry on, know you can always be yourself around me.
If and when you don't feel good enough, know you can always be yourself around me.
When you feel like an outsider, know you can always be yourself around me.

If and when you feel rejected, know you can always be yourself around me.
When you feel like giving up, know you can always be yourself around me.
If and when you feel unwanted, know you can always be yourself around me.
If and when you feel worthless, know you can always be yourself around me
When you feel like you are entering an unknown trap, know you can always be yourself around me.
When you feel like you're in denial, know you can always be yourself around me.
If and when you have nowhere to turn, know you can always be yourself around me.
If and when you don't feel you have the courage to fight, know you can always be yourself around me.
If and when you feel insecure, know you can always be yourself around me.
If and when you feel guilt in any way, know you can always be yourself around me.
When you need me the most, know you can always be yourself around me.
When you are not yourself, know you can always be yourself around me.
When you feel alone, know you can always be yourself around me.
When you face challenging days, I will walk alongside you and know you can always be yourself around me.
If and when you need to vent, know you can always be yourself around me.

Shed A Teardrop On Me

When you look back at your fragile past, know you can shed a teardrop on me.
When you face you your lifelong fears, know you can shed a teardrop on me.
When you try and break your lifelong issues that affect you, know you can shed a teardrop on me.
When you try and overcome the loneliness you feel, know you can shed a teardrop on me.

When you feel down, know you can shed a teardrop on me.
If and when you feel broken, know you can shed a teardrop on me.
When you feel like you're in a dark place, know you can shed a teardrop on me.
When you feel like you're struggling, know you can shed a teardrop on me.

When your inner cries take its toll on you, know you can shed a teardrop on me.
When you don't feel strong enough, know you can shed a teardrop on me.
When you don't feel brave enough, know you can shed a teardrop on me.
When you feel low, know you can shed a teardrop on me.

When you feel lost in any way, know you can shed a teardrop on me.
When you need a shoulder to cry on, know you can shed a teardrop on me.
If and when you don't feel good enough, know you can shed a teardrop on me.
When you feel like an outsider, know you can shed a teardrop on me.

If and when you feel rejected, know you can shed a teardrop on me.
When you feel like giving up, know you can shed a teardrop on me.
If and when you feel unwanted, know you can shed a teardrop on me.
If and when you feel worthless, know you can shed a teardrop on me.

When you feel like you are entering an unknown trap, know you can shed a teardrop on me.
When you feel like you're in denial, know you can shed a teardrop on me.
If and when you have nowhere to turn, know you can shed a teardrop on me.
If and when you don't feel you have the courage to fight, know you can shed a teardrop on me.

If and when you feel insecure, know you can shed a teardrop on me.
If and when you feel guilt in any way, know you can shed a teardrop on me.
When you need me the most, know you can shed a teardrop on me.
When you are not yourself, know you can shed a teardrop on me.
When you feel alone, know you can shed a teardrop on me.

When you face challenging days, I will walk alongside you and know you can shed a teardrop on me.
If and when you need to vent, know you can shed a teardrop on me.

Inseparable For Life

When you look back at your fragile past, know we will always be inseparable for life.
When you face you your lifelong fears, know we will always be inseparable for life.
When you try and break your lifelong issues that affect you, know we will always be inseparable for life.
When you try and overcome the loneliness you feel, know we will always be inseparable for life.

When you feel down, know we will always be inseparable for life.
If and when you feel broken, know we will always be inseparable for life.
When you feel like you're in a dark place, know we will always be inseparable for life.
When you feel like you're struggling, know we will always be inseparable for life.

When your inner cries take its toll on you, know we will always be inseparable for life.
When you don't feel strong enough, know we will always be inseparable for life
When you don't feel brave enough, know we will always be inseparable for life.
When you feel low, know we will always be inseparable for life.

When you feel lost in any way, know we will always be inseparable for life.
When you need a shoulder to cry on, know we will always be inseparable for life.
If and when you don't feel good enough, know we will always be inseparable for life.
When you feel like an outsider, know we will always be inseparable for life.

If and when you feel rejected, know we will always be inseparable for life.
When you feel like giving up, know we will always be inseparable for life.
If and when you feel unwanted, know we will always be inseparable for life.
If and when you feel worthless, know we will always be inseparable for life.

When you feel like you are entering an unknown trap, know we will always be inseparable for life.
When you feel like you're in denial, know we will always be inseparable for life.
If and when you have nowhere to turn, know we will always be inseparable for life.
If and when you don't feel you have the courage to fight, know we will be inseparable for life.
If and when you feel insecure, know we will always be inseparable for life.
If and when you feel guilt in any way, know we will always be inseparable for life.
When you need me the most, know we will always be inseparable for life.
When you are not yourself, know we will always be inseparable for life.
When you feel alone, know we will always be inseparable for life.
When you face challenging days, I will walk alongside you and know we will always be inseparable for life.
If and when you need to vent, know we will always be inseparable for life.

Close By

When you look back at your fragile past, know I will always be close by.
When you face you your lifelong fears, know I will always be close by.
When you try and break your lifelong issues that affect you, know I will always be close by.
When you try and overcome the loneliness you feel, know I will always be close by.

When you feel down, know I will always be close by.
If and when you feel broken, know I will always be close by.
When you feel like you're in a dark place, know I will always be close by.
When you feel like you're struggling, know I will always be close by.

When your inner cries take its toll on you, know I will always be close by.
When you don't feel strong enough, know I will always be close by.
When you don't feel brave enough, know I will always be close by.
When you feel low, know I will always be close by.

When you feel lost in any way, know I will always be close by.
When you need a shoulder to cry on, know I will always be close by.
If and when you don't feel good enough, know I will always be close by.
When you feel like an outsider, know I will always be close by.

If and when you feel rejected, know I will always be close by.

When you feel like giving up, know I will always be close by.
If and when you feel unwanted, know I will always be close by.
If and when you feel worthless, know I will always be close by.

When you feel like you are entering an unknown trap, know I will always be close by.
When you feel like you're in denial, know I will always be close by.
If and when you have nowhere to turn, know I will always be close by.
If and when you don't feel you have the courage to fight, know I will always be close by.
If and when you feel insecure, know I will always be close by.
If and when you feel guilt in any way, know I will always be close by.
When you need me the most, know I will always be close by.
When you are not yourself, know I will always be close by.
When you feel alone, know I will always be close by.
When you face challenging days, I will walk alongside you and know I will always be close by.
If and when you need to vent, know I will always be close by.

Stick By My Word

When you look back at your fragile past, know I will always stick by my word.
When you face you your lifelong fears, know I will always stick by my word.
When you try and break your lifelong issues that affect you, know I will always stick by my word.
When you try and overcome the loneliness you feel, know I will always stick by my word.

When you feel down, know I will always stick by my word.
If and when you feel broken, know I will always stick by my word.
When you feel like you're in a dark place, know I will always stick by my word
When you feel like you're struggling, know I will always stick by my word.

When your inner cries take its toll on you, know I will always stick by my word.
When you don't feel strong enough, know I will always stick by my word.
When you don't feel brave enough, know I will always stick by my word.
When you feel low, know I will always stick by my word.

When you feel lost in any way, know I will always stick by my word.
When you need a shoulder to cry on, know I will always stick by my word.
If and when you don't feel good enough, know I will always stick by my word.
When you feel like an outsider, know I will always stick by my word.

If and when you feel rejected, know I will always stick by my word.
When you feel like giving up, know I will always stick by my word.
If and when you feel unwanted, know I will always stick by my word.
If and when you feel worthless, know I will always stick by my word.

When you feel like you are entering an unknown trap, know I will always stick by my word.
When you feel like you're in denial, know I will always stick by my word.
If and when you have nowhere to turn, know I will always stick by my word.
If and when you don't feel you have the courage to fight, know I will always stick by my word.
If and when you feel insecure, know I will always stick by my word.
If and when you feel guilt in any way, know I will always stick by my word.
When you need me the most, know I will always stick by my word.
When you are not yourself, know I will always stick by my word.
When you feel alone, know I will always stick by my word.
When you face challenging days, I will walk alongside you and know I will always stick by my word.
If and when you need to vent, know I will always stick by my word.

Untangle You

When you look back at your fragile past, know I will always untangle you.
When you face you your lifelong fears, know I will always untangle you.
When you try and break your lifelong issues that affect you, know I will always untangle you.
When you try and overcome the loneliness you feel, know I will always untangle you.

When you feel down, know I will always untangle you.
If and when you feel broken, know I will always untangle you.
When you feel like you're in a dark place, know I will always untangle you.
When you feel like you're struggling, know I will always untangle you.

When your inner cries take its toll on you, know I will always untangle you.
When you don't feel strong enough, know I will always untangle you.
When you don't feel brave enough, know I will always untangle you.
When you feel low, know I will always untangle you.

When you feel lost in any way, know I will always untangle you.

When you need a shoulder to cry on, know I will always untangle you.
If and when you don't feel good enough, know I will always untangle you.
When you feel like an outsider, know I will always untangle you.

If and when you feel rejected, know I will always untangle you.
When you feel like giving up, know I will always untangle you.
If and when you feel unwanted, know I will always untangle you.
If and when you feel worthless, know I will always untangle you.
When you feel like you are entering an unknown trap, know I will untangle you.
When you feel like you're in denial, know I will always untangle you.
If and when you have nowhere to turn, know I will always untangle you.
If and when you don't feel you have the courage to fight, know I will always untangle you.
If and when you feel insecure, know I will always untangle you.
If and when you feel guilt in any way, know I will always untangle you.
When you need me the most, know I will always untangle you.
When you are not yourself, know I will always untangle you.
When you feel alone, know I will always untangle you.
When you face challenging days, I will walk alongside you and know I will always untangle you.
If and when you need to vent, know I will always untangle you.

Lead You Astray

When you look back at your fragile past, know I will always make sure no one leads you astray.
When you face your lifelong fears, know I will always make sure no one leads you astray.
When you try and break your lifelong issues that affect you, know I will always make sure no one leads you astray.
When you try and overcome the loneliness you feel, know I will always make sure no one leads you astray.

When you feel down, know I will always make sure no one leads you astray.
If and when you feel broken, know I will always make sure no one leads you astray.
When you feel like you're in a dark place, know I will always make sure no one leads you astray.
When you feel like you're struggling, know I will always make sure no one leads you astray.

When your inner cries take its toll on you, know I will always make sure no one leads you astray.
When you don't feel strong enough, know I will always make sure no one leads you astray.
When you don't feel brave enough, know I will always make sure no one leads you astray.
When you feel low, know I will always make sure none leads you astray.

When you feel lost in any way, know I will always make sure no one leads you astray.
When you need a shoulder to cry on, know I will always make sure no one leads you astray.
If and when you don't feel good enough, know I will always make sure no one leads you astray.
When you feel like an outsider, know I will always make sure no one leads you astray.

If and when you feel rejected, know I will always make sure no one leads you astray.
When you feel like giving up, know I will always make sure no one leads you astray.
If and when you feel unwanted, know I will always make sure no one leads you astray.
If and when you feel worthless, know I will always make sure no one leads you astray.
When you feel like you are entering an unknown trap, know I will always make sure no one leads you astray.
When you feel like you're in denial, know I will always make sure no one leads you astray.
If and when you have nowhere to turn, know I will always make sure no one leads you astray.
If and when you don't feel you have the courage to fight, know I will always make sure no one leads you astray.
If and when you feel insecure, know I will always make sure no one leads you astray.
If and when you feel guilt in any way, know I will always make sure no one leads you astray.
When you need me the most, know I will always make sure no one leads you astray.
When you are not yourself, know I will always make sure no one leads you astray.
When you feel alone, know I will always make sure no one leads you astray.

When you face challenging days, I will walk alongside you and know I will always make sure no one leads you astray.
If and when you need to vent, know I will always make sure no one leads you astray.

Look Up To You

When you look back at your fragile past, know I will always look up to you.
When you face your lifelong fears, know I will always look up to you.
When you try and break your lifelong issues that affect you, know I will always look up to you.
When you try and overcame the loneliness you feel, know I will always look up to you.

When you feel down, know I will always look up to you.
If and when you feel broken, know I will always look up to you.
When you feel like you're in a dark place, know I will always look up to you.
When you feel like you're struggling, know I will always look up to you.

When your inner cries take its toll on you, know I will always look up to you.
When you don't feel strong enough, know I will always look up to you.
When you don't feel brave enough, know I will always look up to you.
When you feel low, know I will always look up to you.

When you feel lost in any way, know I will always look up to you.
When you need a shoulder to cry on, know I will always look up to you.
If and when you don't feel good enough, know I will always look up to you.
When you feel like an outsider, know I will always look up to you.

If and when you feel rejected, know I will always look up to you.
When you feel like giving up, know I will always look up to you.
If and when you feel unwanted, know I will always look up to you.
If and when you feel worthless, know I will always look up to you.

When you feel like you're entering an unknown trap, know I will always look up to you.
When you feel like you're in denial, know I will always
If and when you have nowhere to turn, know I will always look up to you.
If and when you feel you don't have the courage to fight, know I will always look up to you.

If and when you feel insecure, know I will always look up to you.
If and when you feel guilt in any way, know I will always look up to you.

When you need me the most, know I will always look up to you.
When you are not yourself, know I will always look up to you.
When you feel alone, know I will always look up to you.
When you face challenging days, I will walk alongside you and know I will always look up to you.
If and when you need to vent, know I will always look up to you.

Look Up To Me

When you look back at your fragile past, know you can always look up to me.
When you face your lifelong fears, know you can always look up to me.
When you try and break your lifelong issues that affect you, know you can always look up to you.
When you try and overcame the loneliness you feel, know you can always look up to me.

When you feel down, know you can always look up to me.
If and when you feel broken, know you can always look up to me.
When you feel like you're in a dark place, know you can always look up to me.
When you feel like you're struggling, know you can always look up to me.

When your inner cries take its toll on you, know you can always look up to me.
When you don't feel strong enough, know you can always look up to me.
When you don't feel brave enough, know you can always look up to me.
When you feel low, know you can always look up to me.

When you feel lost in any way, know you can always look up to me.
When you need a shoulder to cry on, know you can always look up to me.
If and when you don't feel good enough, know you can always look up to me.
When you feel like an outsider, know you can always look up to me.

If and when you feel rejected, know you can always look up to me.
When you feel like giving up, know you can always look up to me.
If and when you feel unwanted, know you can always look up to me.
If and when you feel worthless, know you can always look up to me.

When you feel like your entering an unknown trap, know you can always look up to me.
When you feel like you're in denial, know you can always look up to me.
If and when you have nowhere to turn, know you can always look up to me.
If and when you feel you don't have the courage to fight, know you can always look up to me.

If and when you feel insecure, know you can always look up to me.
If and when you feel guilt in any way, know you can always look up to me.
When you need me the most, know you can always look up to me.
When you are not yourself, know you can always look up to me.
When you feel alone, know you can always look up to me.
When you face challenging days, I will walk alongside you and know you can always look up to me.
If and when you need to vent, know you can always look up to me.

Bring You Out Of Your Shell

When you look back at your fragile past, know I will always try and bring you out of your shell.
When you face your lifelong fears, know I will always try and bring you out of your shell.
When you try and break your lifelong issues that affect you, know I will always try and bring you out of your shell.
When you try and overcame the loneliness you feel, know I will always try and bring you out of your shell.

When you feel down, know I will always try and bring you out of your shell.
If and when you feel broken, know I will always try and bring you out of your shell.
When you feel like you're in a dark place, know I will always try and bring you out of your shell.
When you feel like you're struggling, know I will always try and bring you out of your shell.

When your inner cries take its toll on you, know I will always try and bring you out of your shell.
When you don't feel strong enough, know I will always try and bring you out of your shell.
When you don't feel brave enough, know I will always try and bring you out of your shell.
When you feel low, know I will always try and bring you out of your shell.

When you feel lost in any way, know I will always try and bring you out of your shell.
When you need a shoulder to cry on, know I will always try and bring you out of your shell.

If and when you don't feel good enough, know I will always try and bring you out of your shell.
When you feel like an outsider, know I will always try and bring you out of your shell.

If and when you feel rejected, know I will always try and bring you out of your shell.
When you feel like giving up, know I will always try and bring you out of your shell.
If and when you feel unwanted, know I will always try and bring you out of your shell.
If and when you feel worthless, know I will always try and bring you out of your shell.

When you feel like you're entering an unknown trap, know I will always try and bring you out of your shell.
When you feel like you're in denial, know I will always try and bring you out of your shell.
If and when you have nowhere to turn, know I will always try and bring you out of your shell.
If and when you feel you don't have the courage to fight, know I will always try and bring you out of your shell.
If and when you feel insecure, know I will always try and bring you out of your shell.
If and when you feel guilt in any way, know I will always try and bring you out of your shell.
When you need me the most, know I will always try and bring you out of your shell.
When you are not yourself, know I will always try and bring you out of your shell.
When you feel alone, know I will always try always try and bring you out of your shell.
When you face challenging days, I will walk alongside you and know I will always try and bring you out of your shell.
If and when you need to vent, know I will always try and bring you out of your shell.

Admire You

When you look back at your fragile past, know I will always admire you.
When you face your lifelong fears, know I will always admire you.
When you try and break your lifelong issues that affect you, know I will always admire you.
When you try and overcame the loneliness you feel, know I will always admire you.

When you feel down, know I will always admire you.
If and when you feel broken, know I will always admire you.
When you feel like you're in a dark place, know I will always admire you.
When you feel like you're struggling, know I will always admire you.

When your inner cries take its toll on you, know I will always admire you.
When you don't feel strong enough, know I will always admire you.
When you don't feel brave enough, know I will always admire you
When you feel low, know I will always admire you.

When you feel lost in any way, know I will always admire you.
When you need a shoulder to cry on, know I will always admire you.
If and when you don't feel good enough, know I will always admire you.
When you feel like an outsider, know I will always admire you.

If and when you feel rejected, know I will always admire you.
When you feel like giving up, know I will always admire you.
If and when you feel unwanted, know I will always admire you.
If and when you feel worthless, know I will always admire you

When you feel like your entering an unknown trap, know I will always admire you.
When you feel like you're in denial, know I will always admire you.
If and when you have nowhere to turn, know I will always admire you.
If and when you feel you don't have the courage to fight, know I will always admire you.
If and when you feel insecure, know I will always admire you.
If and when you feel guilt in any way, know I will always admire you.
When you need me the most, know I will always admire you.
When you are not yourself, know I will always admire you.
When you feel alone, know I will always admire you.
When you face challenging days, I will walk alongside you and know I will always admire you.
If and when you need to vent, know I will always admire you.

Bring Out The Warrior In You

When you look back at your fragile past, know I will always bring out the warrior in you.
When you face your lifelong fears, know I will always bring out the warrior in you.
When you try and break your lifelong issues that affect you, know I will always bring out the warrior in you.
When you try and overcame the loneliness you feel, know I will always bring out the warrior in you.

When you feel down, know I will always bring out the warrior in you.
If and when you feel broken, know I will always bring out the warrior in you.
When you feel like you're in a dark place, know I will always bring out the warrior in you.
When you feel like you're struggling, know I will always bring out the warrior in you.

When your inner cries take its toll on you, know I will always bring out the warrior in you.
When you don't feel strong enough, know I will always bring out the warrior in you.
When you don't feel brave enough, know I will always bring out the warrior in you.
When you feel low, know I will always bring out the warrior in you.

When you feel lost in any way, know I will always bring out the warrior in you.
When you need a shoulder to cry on, know I will always bring out the warrior in you.
If and when you don't feel good enough, know I will always bring out the warrior in you.
When you feel like an outsider, know I will always bring out the warrior in you.

If and when you feel rejected, know I will always bring out the warrior in you.
When you feel like giving up, know I will always bring out the warrior in you.
If and when you feel unwanted, know I will always bring out the warrior in you.
If and when you feel worthless, know I will always bring out the warrior in you.

When you feel like you're entering an unknown trap, know I will always bring out the warrior in you.
When you feel like you're in denial, know I will always bring out the warrior in you.

If and when you have nowhere to turn, know I will always bring out the warrior in you.
If and when you feel you don't have the courage to fight, know I will always bring out the warrior in you.
If and when you feel insecure, know I will always bring out the warrior in you.
If and when you feel guilt in any way, know I will always bring out the warrior in you.
When you need me the most, know I will always bring out the warrior in you.
When you are not yourself, know I will always bring out the warrior in you.
When you feel alone, know I will always bring out the warrior in you.
When you face challenging days, I will walk alongside you and know I will always bring out the warrior in you.
If and when you need to vent, know I will always bring out the warrior in you.

Screw You Over

When you look back at your fragile past, know I will never let anyone screw you over.
When you face your lifelong fears, know I will never let anyone screw you over.
When you try and break your lifelong issues that affect you, know I will never let anyone screw you over.
When you try and overcame the loneliness you feel, know I will never let anyone screw you over.

When you feel down, know I will never let anyone screw you over.
If and when you feel broken, know I will never let anyone screw you over.
When you feel like you're in a dark place, know I will never let anyone screw you over.
When you feel like you're struggling, know I will never let anyone screw you over.

When your inner cries take its toll on you, know I will never let anyone screw you over.
When you don't feel strong enough, know I will never let anyone screw you over.
When you don't feel brave enough, know I will never let anyone screw you over.
When you feel low, know I will never let anyone screw you over.

When you feel lost in any way, know I will never let anyone screw you over.
When you need a shoulder to cry on, know I will never let anyone screw you over.

If and when you don't feel good enough, know I will never let anyone screw you over.
When you feel like an outsider, know I will never let anyone screw you over.

If and when you feel rejected, know I will never let anyone screw you over
When you feel like giving up, know I will never let anyone screw you over.
If and when you feel unwanted, know I will never let anyone screw you over.
If and when you feel worthless, know I will never let anyone screw you over.

When you feel like your entering an unknown trap, know I will never let anyone screw you over.
When you feel like you're in denial, know I will never let anyone screw you over.
If and when you have nowhere to turn, know I will never let anyone screw you over.
If and when you feel you don't have the courage to fight, know I will never let anyone screw you over.

If and when you feel insecure, know I will never let anyone screw you over.
If and when you feel guilt in any way, know I will never let anyone screw you over.
When you need me the most, know I will never let anyone screw you over.
When you are not yourself, know I will never let anyone screw you over.
When you feel alone, know I will never let anyone screw you over.
When you face challenging days, I will walk alongside you and know I will never let anyone screw you over.
If and when you need to vent, know I will never let anyone screw you over.

Bring Out The Best In You

When you look back at your fragile past, know I will always bring out the best in you.
When you face your lifelong fears, know I will always bring out the best in you.
When you try and break your lifelong issues that affect you, know I will always bring out the best in you.
When you try and overcame the loneliness you feel, know I will always bring out the best in you.

When you feel down, know I will always bring out the best in you.
If and when you feel broken, know I will always bring out the best in you.

When you feel like you're in a dark place, know I will always bring out the best in you.
When you feel like you're struggling, know I will always bring out the best in you.

When your inner cries take its toll on you, know I will always bring out the best in you.
When you don't feel strong enough, know I will always bring out the best in you.
When you don't feel brave enough, know I will always bring out the best in you.
When you feel low, know I will always bring out the best in you.

When you feel lost in any way, know I will always bring out the best in you.
When you need a shoulder to cry on, know I will always bring out the best in you.
If and when you don't feel good enough, know I will always bring out the best in you.
When you feel like an outsider, know I will always bring out the best in you.

If and when you feel rejected, know I will always bring out the best in you.
When you feel like giving up, know I will always bring out the best in you.
If and when you feel unwanted, know I will always bring out the best in you.
If and when you feel worthless, know I will always bring out the best in you.

When you feel like you're entering an unknown trap, know I will always bring out the best in you.
When you feel like you're in denial, know I will always bring out the best in you.
If and when you have nowhere to turn, know I will always bring out the best in you.
If and when you feel you don't have the courage to fight, know I will always bring out the best in you.

If and when you feel insecure, know I will always bring out the best in you.
If and when you feel guilt in any way, know I will always bring out the best in you.
When you need me the most, know I will always bring out the best in you.
When you are not yourself, know I will always bring out the best in you.
When you feel alone, know I will always bring out the best in you.
When you face challenging days, I will walk alongside you and know I will always bring out the best in you.
If and when you need to vent, know I will always bring out the best in you.

Perfect To Me

When you look back at your fragile past, know you are perfect to me.
When you face your lifelong fears, know you are perfect to me.
When you try and break your lifelong issues that affect you, know you are perfect to me.
When you try and overcame the loneliness you feel, know you are perfect to me.

When you feel down, know you are perfect to me.
If and when you feel broken, know you are perfect to me.
When you feel like you're in a dark place, know you are perfect to me.
When you feel like you're struggling, know you are perfect to me.

When your inner cries take its toll on you, know you are perfect to me.
When you don't feel strong enough, know you are perfect to me.
When you don't feel brave enough, know you are perfect to me.
When you feel low, know you are perfect to me.
When you feel lost in any way, know you are perfect to me.
When you need a shoulder to cry on, know you are perfect to me.
If and when you don't feel good enough, know you are perfect to me.
When you feel like an outsider, know you are perfect to me.

If and when you feel rejected, know you are perfect to me.
When you feel like giving up, know you are perfect to me.
If and when you feel unwanted, know you are perfect to me.
If and when you feel worthless, know you are perfect to me.

When you feel like you're entering an unknown trap, know you are perfect to me
When you feel like you're in denial, know you are perfect to me.
If and when you have nowhere to turn, know you are perfect to me.
If and when you feel you don't have the courage to fight, know you are perfect to me.
if and when you feel insecure, know you are perfect to me.
If and when you feel guilt in any way, know you are perfect to me.
When you need me the most, know you are perfect to me.
When you are not yourself, know you are perfect to me.
When you feel alone, know you are perfect to me.
When you face challenging days, I will walk alongside you and know you are perfect to me.
If and when you need to vent, know you are perfect to me.

Reality

Reality is not simple.
Reality is not easy.
Reality is far from the truth.
Reality is hard to accept.
Reality is hard to face.
Reality is not straightforward.
Reality can be cruel
Reality is not knowing the back story
Reality can affect those who have to get through it.
Reality is true
Reality is real
Reality is not a world someone makes up in their minds.
Reality is making it happen.
Reality is accepting

Walk All Over You

When you look back at your fragile past, know I will never let anyone walk all over you.
When you face your lifelong fears, know I will never let anyone walk all over you.
When you try and break your lifelong issues that affect you, know I will never let anyone walk all over you.
When you try and overcame the loneliness you feel, know I will never let anyone walk all over you.

When you feel down, know I will never let anyone walk all over you.
If and when you feel broken, know I will never let anyone walk all over you.
When you feel like you're in a dark place, know I will never let anyone walk all over you.
When you feel like you're struggling, know I will never let anyone walk all over you.

When your inner cries take its toll on you, know I will never let anyone walk all over you.
When you don't feel strong enough, know I will never let anyone walk all over you.
When you don't feel brave enough, know I will never let anyone walk all over you.

When you feel low, know I will never let anyone walk all over you.

When you feel lost in any way, know I will never let anyone walk all over you.
When you need a shoulder to cry on, know I will never let anyone walk all over you.
If and when you don't feel good enough, know I will never let anyone walk all over you.
When you feel like an outsider, know I will never let anyone walk all over you.

If and when you feel rejected, know I will never let anyone walk all over you.
When you feel like giving up, know I will never let anyone walk all over you.
If and when you feel unwanted, know I will never let anyone walk all over you.
If and when you feel worthless, know I will never let anyone walk all over you.

When you feel like your entering an unknown trap, know I will never let anyone walk all over you.
When you feel like you're in denial, know I will never let anyone walk all over you.
If and when you have nowhere to turn, know I will never let anyone walk all over you.
If and when you feel you don't have the courage to fight, know I will never let anyone walk all over you.
If and when you feel insecure, know I will never let anyone walk all over you.
If and when you feel guilt in any way, know I will never let anyone walk all over you.
When you need me the most, know I will never let anyone walk all over you.
When you are not yourself, know I will never let anyone walk all over you.
When you feel alone, know I will never let anyone walk all over you.
When you face challenging days, I will walk alongside you and know I will never let anyone walk all over you.
If and when you need to vent, know I will never let anyone walk all over you.

Bring Out The Worst In You

When you look back at your fragile past, know I will never let anyone bring out the worst in you.
When you face your lifelong fears, know I will never let anyone bring out the worst in you.
When you try and break your lifelong issues that affect you, know I will never let anyone bring out the worst in you.

When you try and overcame the loneliness you feel, know I will never let anyone bring out the worst in you.

When you feel down, know I will never let anyone bring out the worst in you.
If and when you feel broken, know I will never let anyone bring out the worst in you.
When you feel like you're in a dark place, know I will never let anyone bring out the worst in you.
When you feel like you're struggling, know I will never let anyone bring out the worst in you.

When your inner cries take its toll on you, know I will never let anyone bring out the worst in you.
When you don't feel strong enough, know I will never let anyone bring out the worst in you.
When you don't feel brave enough, know I will never let anyone bring out the worst in you.
When you feel low, know I will never let anyone bring out the worst in you.

When you feel lost in any way, know I will never let anyone bring out the worst in you.
When you need a shoulder to cry on, know I will never let anyone bring out the worst in you.
If and when you don't feel good enough, know I will never let anyone bring out the worst in you.
When you feel like an outsider, know I will never let anyone bring out the worst in you.

If and when you feel rejected, know I will never let anyone bring out the worst in you.
When you feel like giving up, know I will never let anyone bring out the worst in you.
If and when you feel unwanted, know I will never let anyone bring out the worst in you.
If and when you feel worthless, know I will never let anyone bring out the worst in you.

When you feel like your entering an unknown trap, know I will never let anyone bring out the worst in you
When you feel like you're in denial, know I will never let anyone bring out the worst in you.

If and when you have nowhere to turn, know I will never let anyone bring out the worst in you.
If and when you feel you don't have the courage to fight, know I will never let anyone bring out the worst in you.
If and when you feel insecure, know I will never let anyone bring out the worst in you.
If and when you feel guilt in any way, know I will never let anyone bring out the worst in you.
When you need me the most, know I will never let anyone bring out the worst in you
When you are not yourself, know I will never let anyone bring out the worst in you.
When you feel alone, know I will never let anyone bring out the worst in you.
When you face challenging days, I will walk alongside you and know I will never let anyone bring out the worst in you.
If and when you need to vent, know I will never let anyone bring out the worst in you.

Walk On Fire For You

When you look back at your fragile past, know I will always walk on fire for you.
When you face your lifelong fears, know I will always walk on fire for you.
When you try and break your lifelong issues that affect you, know I will always walk on fire for you.
When you try and overcame the loneliness you feel, know I will always walk on fire for you.

When you feel down, know I will always walk on fire for you.
If and when you feel broken, know I will always walk on fire for you.
When you feel like you're in a dark place, know I will always walk on fire for you.
When you feel like you're struggling, know I will always walk on fire for you.

When your inner cries take its toll on you, know I will always walk on fire for you.
When you don't feel strong enough, know I will always walk on fire for you.
When you don't feel brave enough, know I will always walk on fire for you
When you feel low, know I will always walk on fire for you.

When you feel lost in any way, know I will always walk on fire for you.

When you need a shoulder to cry on, know I will always walk on fire for you.
If and when you don't feel good enough, know I will always walk on fire for you.
When you feel like an outsider, know I will always walk on fire for you.

If and when you feel rejected, know I will always walk on fire for you.
When you feel like giving up, know I will always walk on fire for you.
If and when you feel unwanted, know I will always walk on fire for you.
If and when you feel worthless, know I will always walk on fire for you.

When you feel like your entering an unknown trap, know I will always walk on fire for you.
When you feel like you're in denial, know I will always walk on fire for you
If and when you have nowhere to turn, know I will always walk on fire for you.
If and when you feel you don't have the courage to fight, know I will always walk on fire for you.
If and when you feel insecure, know I will always walk on fire for you.
If and when you feel guilt in any way, know I will always walk on fire for you.
When you need me the most, know I will always walk on fire for you.
When you are not yourself, know I will always walk on fire for you.
When you feel alone, know I will always walk on fire for you.
When you face challenging days, I will walk alongside you and know I will always walk on fire for you.
If and when you need to vent, know I will always walk on fire for you.

Never Run A Mile

When you look back at your fragile past, know I will never run a mile.
When you face your lifelong fears, know I will never run a mile.
When you try and break your lifelong issues that affect you, know I will never run a mile.
When you try and overcame the loneliness you feel, know I will never run a mile.

When you feel down, know I will never run a mile.
If and when you feel broken, know I will never run a mile.
When you feel like you're in a dark place, know I will never run a mile.
When you feel like you're struggling, know I will never run a mile.

When your inner cries take its toll on you, know I will never run a mile.
When you don't feel strong enough, know I will never run a mile.
When you don't feel brave enough, know I will never run a mile.

When you feel low, know I will never run a mile.

When you feel lost in any way, know I will never run a mile.
When you need a shoulder to cry on, know I will never run a mile.
If and when you don't feel good enough, know I will never run a mile.
When you feel like an outsider, know I will never run a mile.

If and when you feel rejected, know I will never run a mile.
When you feel like giving up, know I will never run a mile.
If and when you feel unwanted, know I will never run a mile.
If and when you feel worthless, know I will never run a mile.

When you feel like your entering an unknown trap, know I will never run a mile.
When you feel like you're in denial, know I will never run a mile.
If and when you have nowhere to turn, know I will never run a mile.
If and when you feel you don't have the courage to fight, know I will never run a mile.

If and when you feel insecure, know I will never run a mile.
If and when you feel guilt in any way, know I will never run a mile.
When you need me the most, know I will never run a mile.
When you are not yourself, know I will never run a mile.
When you feel alone, know I will never run a mile.
When you face challenging days, I will walk alongside you and know I will never run a mile.
If and when you need to vent, know I will never run a mile.

Go That Extra Mile For You

When you look back at your fragile past, know I will go that extra mile for you.
When you face your lifelong fears, know I will go that extra mile for you.
When you try and break your lifelong issues that affect you, know I will go that extra mile for you.
When you try and overcame the loneliness you feel, know I will go that extra mile for you

When you feel down, know I will go that extra mile for you.
If and when you feel broken, know I will go that extra mile for you.
When you feel like you're in a dark place, know I will go that extra mile for you.
When you feel like you're struggling, know I will go that extra mile for you.

When your inner cries take its toll on you, know I will go that extra mile for you.

When you don't feel strong enough, know I will go that extra mile for you.
When you don't feel brave enough, know I will go that extra mile for you.
When you feel low, know I will go that extra mile for you.

When you feel lost in any way, know I will go that extra mile for you.
When you need a shoulder to cry on, know I will go that extra mile for you.
If and when you don't feel good enough, know I will go that extra mile for you.
When you feel like an outsider, know I will go that extra mile for you.

If and when you feel rejected, know I will go that extra mile for you.
When you feel like giving up, know I will go that extra mile for you.
If and when you feel unwanted, know I will go that extra mile for you.
If and when you feel worthless, know I will go that extra mile for you.

When you feel like your entering an unknown trap, know I will go that extra mile for you.
When you feel like you're in denial, know I will go that extra mile for you.
If and when you have nowhere to turn, know I will go that extra mile for you.
If and when you feel you don't have the courage to fight, know I will go that extra mile for you.

If and when you feel insecure, know I will go that extra mile for you.
If and when you feel guilt in any way, know I will go that extra mile for you.
When you need me the most, know I will go that extra mile for you.
When you are not yourself, know I will go that extra mile for you
When you feel alone, know I will go that extra mile for you.
When you face challenging days, I will walk alongside you and know I will go that extra mile for you.
If and when you need to vent, know I will go that extra mile for you.

Best Intentions

When you look back at your fragile past, know I will always have the best intentions for you.
When you face your lifelong fears, know I will always have the best intentions for you.
When you try and break your lifelong issues that affect you, know I will always have the best intentions for you.
When you try and overcame the loneliness you feel, know I will always have the best intentions for you.

When you feel down, know I will always have the best intentions for you.
If and when you feel broken, know I will always have the best intentions for you.
When you feel like you're in a dark place, know I will always have the best intentions for you.
When you feel like you're struggling, know I will always have the best intentions for you.

When your inner cries take its toll on you, know I will always have the best intentions for you.
When you don't feel strong enough, know I will always have the best intentions for you.
When you don't feel brave enough, know I will always have the best intentions for you.
When you feel low, know I will always have the best intentions for you.

When you feel lost in any way, know I will always have the best intentions for you.
When you need a shoulder to cry on, know I will always have the best intentions for you.
If and when you don't feel good enough, know I will always have the best intentions for you.
When you feel like an outsider, know I will always have the best intentions for you.

If and when you feel rejected, know I will always have the best intentions for you.
When you feel like giving up, know I will always have the best intentions for you.
If and when you feel unwanted, know I will always have the best intentions for you.
If and when you feel worthless, know I will always have the best intentions for you.

When you feel like you're entering an unknown trap, know I will always have the best intentions for you.
When you feel like you're in denial, know I will always have the best intentions for you.
If and when you have nowhere to turn, know I will always have the best intentions for you.
If and when you feel you don't have the courage to fight, know I will always have the best intentions for you.

If and when you feel insecure, know I will always have the best intentions for you.
If and when you feel guilt in any way, know I will always have the best intentions for you.
When you need me the most, know I will always have the best intentions for you.
When you are not yourself, know I will always have the best intentions for you
When you feel alone, know I will always have the best intentions for you.
When you face challenging days, I will walk alongside you and know I will always have the best intentions for you.
If and when you need to vent, know I will always have the best intentions for you.

Best Interest

When you look back at your fragile past, know I will always have your best interest at heart.
When you face your lifelong fears, know I will always have your best interest at heart.
When you try and break your lifelong issues that affect you, know I will always have your best interest at heart.
When you try and overcame the loneliness you feel, know I will always have your best interest at heart.

When you feel down, know I will always have your best interest at heart.
If and when you feel broken, know I will always have your best interest at heart.
When you feel like you're in a dark place, know I will always have your best interest at heart.
When you feel like you're struggling, know I will always have your best interest at heart.

When your inner cries take its toll on you, know I will always have your best interest at heart.
When you don't feel strong enough, know I will always have your best interest at heart.
When you don't feel brave enough, know I will always have your best interest at heart.
When you feel low, know I will always have your best interest at heart.

When you feel lost in any way, know I will always have your best interest at heart.

When you need a shoulder to cry on, know I will always have your best interest at heart.
If and when you don't feel good enough, know I will always have your best interest at heart.
When you feel like an outsider, know I will always have your best interest at heart.

If and when you feel rejected, know I will always have your best interest at heart.
When you feel like giving up, know I will always have your best interest at heart.
If and when you feel unwanted, know I will always have your best interest at heart.
If and when you feel worthless, know I will always have your best interest at heart.

When you feel like you're entering an unknown trap, know I will always have your best interest at heart.
When you feel like you're in denial, know I will always have your best interest at heart.
If and when you have nowhere to turn, know I will always have your best interest at heart.
If and when you feel you don't have the courage to fight, know I will always have your best interest at heart.
If and when you feel insecure, know I will always have your best interest at heart.
If and when you feel guilt in any way, know I will always have your best interest at heart.
When you need me the most, know I will always have your best interest at heart.
When you are not yourself, know I will always have your best interest at heart.
When you feel alone, know I will always have your best interest at heart.
When you face challenging days, I will walk alongside you and know I will always have your best interest at heart.
If and when you need to vent, know I will always have your best interest at heart.

When I'm Around You

When I'm around you I feel blessed.
When I'm around you I feel like I don't have to hide the true me.
When I'm around you, you make me feel alive in any way you can.
When I'm around you I know I can be open.

When I'm around you I feel like I can be me.

When I'm around you I know I'll never be alone.
When I'm around you I find I am happiest of all.
When I'm around you, you make me feel like I'm good enough.

When I'm around you I know you have the best intentions for me.
When I'm around you I know I feel valued.
When I'm around you I know I wouldn't trade you for anything.
When I'm around you I feel inspired.

When I'm around you I feel brave to achieve everything I ever wanted
When I'm around you I know you won't let me down in any way.
When I'm around you I feel have someone to turn to when I need to.
When I'm around you nothing ever gets me down.

When I'm around you I know you will always be there for me when I need you the most.
When I'm around you, you make me smile in any way you can.
When I'm around you I don't have to hide my emotions.
When I'm around you I know I will never walk alone.

Defeat You

I won't let your fragile past defeat you in any way.
I won't let your fears that terrorise you to no end defeat you in any way.
I won't let your troubles that follow you defeat you in any way.
I won't let you doubt your awesome abilities in any way.

I won't let demons over take you in any way.
Whatever life throws ur way I won't let you face it alone
and we will always face it together.
I won't let anything ever come between us
When you need me, I will always come to your aid.

When we are together you always make me feel free from my reality.
When we are together you always make me feel like an incredible sister.
Without you I don't know what I'd do.
You keep me going any way possible.

When I am apart from you there isn't a day, minute, hour, second, I don't think about you.
I wish I could be around and with you 24/7.
When we are together I never wanna leave your side.

When we are together you make me feel like I don't have a care in the world.

You mean everything to me and I will always be apart of you no matter what.
When we are together you make me feel happier then when I'm not around you.
When I cry, I cry because it indicates that I miss you when we are thousands of miles apart and I hate it.
When I'm around you, you make me feel good enough in myself.

When we are together you make me the proudest sister ever.
When we are together you make me feel braver then I could ever be.
When we are together you make me feel stronger than ever.
I know if I didn't have you in my life I wouldn't have got as far as I have.
When we are together you make my life so much better in so many ways.
When we are together you always have the best intentions for me.
You are perfect to me in every way.
I wouldn't trade you for the world.

You Shield Me

You shield me from my fragile past.
You shield me from the fears that terrorise me to no end.
You shield me from the pain I feel.
You shield me from the coldest of this dark winter.

You shield me from the hurt I feel.
You shield me from the cruelty of this world.
You shield me from the hatred I feel within.
You shield me from the true intentions of this world we live in.
You shield me from breaking my heart into a thousand pieces.

You shied me from the toughest of times.
You shield me from my darkest of days.
You shield me from feeling rejected.
You shield me from feeling worthless.

You shield me from feeling like a nobody.
You shield me from the betrayal I feel from others.
You shield me from the false hope I sometimes feel.
You shield me from my demons that try and scare me in to not facing them.

Dreams

Never let your fragile past determine your dream.
Never let your fears that terrorise you to no end determine your dream.
Never let the darkness of your inner world sway you from achieving your dreams.
Never let the cruelty of this world stop you achieving what you want in life.

If you want to leave a mark on this world go chase the dream of a lifetime.
When you work hard it will always pay off in the end result.
Never let anyone stop you believing in yourself and the dream you so badly want to achieve.
Surround yourself with good vibes and the dream will fall into place.
Be proud of your achievements and keep the dream alive in so many ways.
Never doubt your abilities and capabilities and chase the dram and prove that you are original.
Make your dreams a reality and prove them who didn't believe in you wrong.

Bring You Down

When you look back at your fragile past, know I will always make sure no one brings you down.
When you face your lifelong fears, know I will always make sure no one brings you down.
When you try and break your lifelong issues that affect you, know I will always make sure no one brings you down.
When you try and overcame the loneliness you feel, know I will always make sure no one brings you down.

When you feel down, know I will always make sure no one brings you down.
If and when you feel broken, know I will always make sure no one brings you down.
When you feel like you're in a dark place, know I will always make sure no one brings you down.
When you feel like you're struggling, know I will always make sure no one brings you down.

When your inner cries take its toll on you, know I will always make sure no one brings you down.
When you don't feel strong enough, know I will always make sure no one brings you down.

When you don't feel brave enough, know I will always make sure no one brings you down.
When you feel low, know I will always make sure no one brings you down.

When you feel lost in any way, know I will always make sure no one brings you down.
When you need a shoulder to cry on, know I will always make sure no one brings you down.
If and when you don't feel good enough, know I will always make sure no one brings you down.
When you feel like an outsider, know I will always make sure no one brings you down.

If and when you feel rejected, know I will always make sure no one brings you down.
When you feel like giving up, know I will always make sure no one brings you down.
If and when you feel unwanted, know I will always make sure no one brings you down.
If and when you feel worthless, know I will always make sure no one brings you down.
When you feel like you're entering an unknown trap, know I will always make sure no one brings you down.
When you feel like you're in denial, know I will always make sure no one brings you down.
If and when you have nowhere to turn, know I will always make sure no one brings you down.
If and when you feel you don't have the courage to fight, know I will always make sure no one brings you down.
If and when you feel insecure, know I will always make sure no one brings you down.
If and when you feel guilt in any way, know I will always make sure no one brings you down.
When you need me the most, know I will always make sure no one brings you down.
When you are not yourself, know I will always make sure no one brings you down.

When you feel alone, know I will always make sure no one brings you down.
When you face challenging days, I will walk alongside you and know I will always make sure no one brings you down.

If and when you need to vent, know I will always make sure no one brings you down.

Never Question

Never question your fragile past as your past is only a reminder.
Never question how you reach your dreams in your own unique way.
Never question the way your life runs as life itself takes you on a journey of a lifetime.
Never question the value of yourself.

Never question how strong you can be.
Never question how brave you are.
Never question your abilities and capabilities within yourself.
Never question the outcome of your life as it will lead you down the right path in the end.

Never question the battles you face as they show how far you have come to get where you are.
Never question that someone n matter where they are will always be there to give you the hope, strength and courage you need.
Never question the determination you have to focus on the good things that come your way.

Take You Underground

When you look back at your fragile past, know I will always take you underground.
When you face your lifelong fears, know I will always take you underground.
When you try and break your lifelong issues that affect you, know I will always take you underground.
When you try and overcame the loneliness you feel, know I will always take you underground.

When you feel down, know I will always take you underground.
If and when you feel broken, know I will always take you underground.
When you feel like you're in a dark place, know I will always take you underground.
When you feel like you're struggling, know I will always take you underground.

When your inner cries take its toll on you, know I will always take you underground.
When you don't feel strong enough, know I will always take you underground.
When you don't feel brave enough, know I will always take you underground.
When you feel low, know I will always take you underground.

When you feel lost in any way, know I will always take you underground.
When you need a shoulder to cry on, know I will always take you underground.
If and when you don't feel good enough, know I will always take you underground.
When you feel like an outsider, know I will always take you underground.

If and when you feel rejected, know I will always take you underground.
When you feel like giving up, know I will always take you underground.
If and when you feel unwanted, know I will always take you underground.
If and when you feel worthless, know I will always take you underground.

When you feel like you're entering an unknown trap, know I will always take you underground.
When you feel like you're in denial, know I will always take you underground.
If and when you have nowhere to turn, know I will always take you underground.
If and when you feel you don't have the courage to fight, know I will always take you underground.

If and when you feel insecure, know I will always take you underground.
If and when you feel guilt in any way, know I will always take you underground.
When you need me the most, know I will always take you underground.
When you are not yourself, know I will always take you underground.
When you feel alone, know I will always take you underground.
When you face challenging days, I will walk alongside you and know I will always take you underground.
If and when you need to vent, know I will always take you underground.

Vision Impairment

I never let my vision impairment define me as a person.
I never let my vision impairment break me.
I never let my vision impairment stop me hiding away.
I never let my vision impairment impact my emotions.

I never let my vision impairment dictate my outlook on life.
I never let my vision impairment lose a battle as I win every one of them.
I never let my vision impairment define who I am in myself.
I never let my vision impairment stop me achieving my goals in life.

I never let my vision impairment determine the way I should be.
I never let my vision impairment stop me chasing long awaited dreams and turning them into reality
I never let my vision impairment being stronger than I've ever been.
I never let my vision impairment keep me down.
I never let my vision impairment stop me being braver than ever before.
I never let my vision impairment change me
I never let my vision impairment determine my abilities and capabilities.

Backstab You

When you look back at your fragile past, know I will never let anyone backstab you.
When you face you your lifelong fears, know I will never let anyone backstab you.
When you try and break your lifelong issues that affect you, know I will never let anyone backstab you.
When you try and overcome the loneliness you feel, know I will never let anyone backstab you.
When you feel down, know I will never let anyone backstab you.
If and when you feel broken, know I will never let anyone backstab you.
When you feel like you're in a dark place, know I will never let anyone backstab you.
When you feel like you're struggling, know I will never let anyone backstab you.

When your inner cries take its toll on you, know I will never let anyone backstab you.
When you don't feel strong enough, know I will never let anyone backstab you.
When you don't feel brave enough, know I will never let anyone backstab you.
When you feel low, know I will never let anyone backstab you.

When you feel lost in any way, know I will never let anyone backstab you.
When you need a shoulder to cry on, know I will never let anyone backstab you.
If and when you don't feel good enough, know I will never let anyone backstab you.
When you feel like an outsider, know I will never let anyone backstab you.

If and when you feel rejected, know I will never let anyone backstab you.
When you feel like giving up, know I will never let anyone backstab you.
If and when you feel unwanted, know I will never let anyone backstab you.
If and when you feel worthless, know I will never let anyone backstab you.

When you feel like you are entering an unknown trap, know I will never let anyone backstab you.
When you feel like you're in denial, know I will never let anyone backstab you.
If and when you have nowhere to turn, know I will never let anyone backstab you.
If and when you don't feel you have the courage to fight, know I will never let anyone backstab you.

If and when you feel insecure, know I will never let anyone backstab you.
If and when you feel guilt in any way, know I will never let anyone backstab you.
When you need me the most, know I will never let anyone backstab you.
When you are not yourself, know I will never let anyone backstab you.
When you feel alone, know I will never let anyone backstab you.
When you face challenging days, I will walk alongside you and know I will never let anyone backstab you.
If and when you need to vent, know I will never let anyone backstab you.

Take Advantage Of You

When you look back at your fragile past, know I will never let anyone take advantage of you.
When you face you your lifelong fears, know I will never let anyone take advantage of you.
When you try and break your lifelong issues that affect you, know I will never let anyone take advantage of you.
When you try and overcome the loneliness you feel, know I will never let anyone take advantage of you.

When you feel down, know I will never let anyone take advantage of you.
If and when you feel broken, know I will never let anyone take advantage of you.
When you feel like you're in a dark place, know I will never let anyone take advantage of you.

When you feel like you're struggling, know I will never let anyone take advantage of you.

When your inner cries take its toll on you, know I will never let anyone take advantage of you.
When you don't feel strong enough, know I will never let anyone take advantage of you.
When you don't feel brave enough, know I will never let anyone take advantage of you.
When you feel low, know I will never let anyone take advantage of you.

When you feel lost in any way, know I will never let anyone take advantage of you.
When you need a shoulder to cry on, know I will never let anyone take advantage of you.
If and when you don't feel good enough, know I will never let anyone take advantage of you.
When you feel like an outsider, know I will never let anyone take advantage of you.

If and when you feel rejected, know I will never let anyone take advantage of you.
When you feel like giving up, know I will never let anyone take advantage of you.
If and when you feel unwanted, know I will never let anyone take advantage of you.
If and when you feel worthless, know I will never let anyone take advantage of you.

When you feel like you are entering an unknown trap, know I will never let anyone take advantage of you.
When you feel like you're in denial, know I will never let anyone take advantage of you.
If and when you have nowhere to turn, know I will never let anyone take advantage of you.
If and when you don't feel you have the courage to fight, know I will never let anyone take advantage of you.
If and when you feel insecure, know I will never let anyone take advantage of you.
If and when you feel guilt in any way, know I will never let anyone take advantage of you.

When you need me the most, know I will never let anyone take advantage of you.
When you are not yourself, know I will never let anyone take advantage of you.
When you feel alone, know I will never let anyone take advantage of you.
When you face challenging days, I will walk alongside you and know I will never let anyone take advantage of you
If and when you need to vent, know I will never let anyone take advantage of you.

Betray You In Any Way

When you look back at your fragile past, know I will never let anyone betray you in any way.
When you face you your lifelong fears, know I will never let anyone betray you in any way.
When you try and break your lifelong issues that affect you, know I will never let anyone betray you in any way.
When you try and overcome the loneliness you feel, know I will never let anyone betray you in any way.

When you feel down, know I will never let anyone betray you in way.
If and when you feel broken, know I will never let anyone betray you in any way.
When you feel like you're in a dark place, know I will never let anyone betray you in any way.
When you feel like you're struggling, know I will never let anyone betray you in any way.

When your inner cries take its toll on you, know I will never let anyone betray you in any way.
When you don't feel strong enough, know I will never let anyone betray you in any way.
When you don't feel brave enough, know I will never let anyone betray you in any way.
When you feel low, know I will never let anyone betray you in any way.

When you feel lost in any way, know I will never let anyone betray you in any way.
When you need a shoulder to cry on, know I will never let anyone betray you in any way.

If and when you don't feel good enough, know I will never let anyone betray you in any way
When you feel like an outsider, know I will never let anyone betray you in any way.

If and when you feel rejected, know I will never let anyone betray you in any way.
When you feel like giving up, know I will never let anyone betray you.
If and when you feel unwanted, know I will never let anyone betray you in any way.
If and when you feel worthless, know I will never let anyone betray you in any way.

When you feel like you are entering an unknown trap, know I will never let anyone betray you in any way.
When you feel like you're in denial, know I will never let anyone betray you in any way.
If and when you have nowhere to turn, know I will never let anyone betray you in any way.
If and when you don't feel you have the courage to fight, know I will never let anyone betray you in any way.
If and when you feel insecure, know I will never let anyone betray you in any way.
If and when you feel guilt in any way, know I will never let anyone betray you in any way.
When you need me the most, know I will never let anyone betray you in any way.
When you are not yourself, know I will never let anyone betray you in any way.
When you feel alone, know I will never let anyone betray you in any way.
When you face challenging days, I will walk alongside you and know I will never let anyone betray you in any way.
If and when you need to vent, know I will never let anyone betray you in any way.

Hit A Brick Wall

When you look back at your fragile past, know I will never let you hit a brick wall.
When you face you your lifelong fears, know I will never let you hit a brick wall.
When you try and break your lifelong issues that affect you, know I will never let you hit a brick wall.

When you try and overcome the loneliness you feel, know I will never let you hit a brick wall.

When you feel down, know I will never let you hit a brick wall.
If and when you feel broken, know I will never let you hit a brick wall.
When you feel like you're in a dark place, know I will never let you hit a brick wall.
When you feel like you're struggling, know I will never let you hit a brick wall.

When your inner cries take its toll on you, know I will never let you hit a brick wall.
When you don't feel strong enough, know I will never let you hit a brick wall.
When you don't feel brave enough, know I will never let you hit a brick wall.
When you feel low, know I will never let you hit a brick wall.

When you feel lost in any way, know I will never let you hit a brick wall.
When you need a shoulder to cry on, know I will never let you hit a brick wall.
If and when you don't feel good enough, know I will never let you hit a brick wall.
When you feel like an outsider, know I will never let you hit a brick wall.

If and when you feel rejected, know I will never let you hit a brick wall.
When you feel like giving up, know I will never let you hit a brick wall.
If and when you feel unwanted, know I will never let you hit a brick wall.
If and when you feel worthless, know I will never let you hit a brick wall.

When you feel like you are entering an unknown trap, know I will never let you hit a brick wall.
When you feel like you're in denial, know I will never let you hit a brick wall.
If and when you have nowhere to turn, know I will never let you hit a brick wall.
If and when you don't feel you have the courage to fight, know I will never let you hit a brick wall.
If and when you feel insecure, know I will never let you hit a brick wall.
If and when you feel guilt in any way, know I will never let you hit a brick wall.
When you need me the most, know I will never let you hit a brick wall.
When you are not yourself, know I will never let you hit a brick wall.
When you feel alone, know I will never let you hit a brick wall.
When you face challenging days, I will walk alongside you and know I will never let you hit a brick wall.
If and when you need to vent, know I will never let you hit a brick wall.

Doubt Yourself

When you look back at your fragile past, know I will never let you doubt yourself.
When you face you your lifelong fears, know I will never let you doubt yourself.
When you try and break your lifelong issues that affect you, know I will never let you doubt yourself.
When you try and overcome the loneliness you feel, know I will never let you doubt yourself.

When you feel down, know I will never let you doubt yourself.
If and when you feel broken, know I will never let you doubt yourself.
When you feel like you're in a dark place, know I will never let you doubt yourself.
When you feel like you're struggling, know I will never let you doubt yourself.

When your inner cries take its toll on you, know I will never let you doubt yourself.
When you don't feel strong enough, know I will never let you doubt yourself.
When you don't feel brave enough, know I will never let you doubt yourself.
When you feel low, know I will never let you doubt yourself.

When you feel lost in any way, know I will never let you doubt yourself.
When you need a shoulder to cry on, know I will never let you doubt yourself.
If and when you don't feel good enough, know I will never let you doubt yourself.
When you feel like an outsider, know I will never let you doubt yourself.

If and when you feel rejected, know I will never let you doubt yourself.
When you feel like giving up, know I will never let you doubt yourself.
If and when you feel unwanted, know I will never let you doubt yourself.
If and when you feel worthless, know I will never let you doubt yourself.

When you feel like you are entering an unknown trap, know I will never let you doubt yourself.
When you feel like you're in denial, know I will never let you doubt yourself.
If and when you have nowhere to turn, know I will never let you doubt yourself.
If and when you don't feel you have the courage to fight, know I will never let you doubt yourself.
If and when you feel insecure, know I will never let you doubt yourself.
If and when you feel guilt in any way, know I will never let you doubt yourself.
When you need me the most, know I will never let you doubt yourself.

When you are not yourself, know I will never let you doubt yourself.
When you feel alone, know I will never let you doubt yourself.
When you face challenging days, I will walk alongside you and know I will never let you doubt yourself.
If and when you need to vent, know I will never let you doubt yourself.

You Mean The Absolute World To Me

When you look back at your fragile past, know you mean the absolute world to me.
When you face you your lifelong fears, know you mean the absolute world to me.
When you try and break your lifelong issues that affect you, know you mean the absolute world to me.
When you try and overcome the loneliness you feel, know you mean the absolute world to me.

When you feel down, know you mean the absolute world to me.
If and when you feel broken, know you mean the absolute world to me.
When you feel like you're in a dark place, know you mean the absolute world to me.
When you feel like you're struggling, know you mean the absolute word to me.

When your inner cries take its toll on you, know you mean the absolute world to me.
When you don't feel strong enough, know you mean the absolute world to me.
When you don't feel brave enough, know you mean the absolute world to me.
When you feel low, know you mean the absolute world to me.

When you feel lost in any way, know you mean the absolute world to me.
When you need a shoulder to cry on, know you mean the absolute world to me.
If and when you don't feel good enough, know you mean the absolute world to me.
When you feel like an outsider, know you mean the absolute world to me.

If and when you feel rejected, know you mean the absolute world to me.
When you feel like giving up, know you mean the absolute world to me.
If and when you feel unwanted, know you mean the absolute world to me.
If and when you feel worthless, know you mean the absolute world to me.

When you feel like you are entering an unknown trap, know you mean the absolute world to me.
When you feel like you're in denial, know you mean the absolute world to me.
If and when you have nowhere to turn, know you mean the absolute world to me.
If and when you don't feel you have the courage to fight, know you mean the absolute world to me.

If and when you feel insecure, know you mean the absolute world to me.
If and when you feel guilt in any way, know you mean the absolute world to me.
When you need me the most, know you mean the absolute world to me.
When you are not yourself, know you mean the absolute world to me.
When you feel alone, know you mean the absolute world to me.
When you face challenging days, I will walk alongside you and know you mean the absolute world to me.
If and when you need to vent, know you mean the absolute world to me.

Never Change You

When you look back at your fragile past, know I would never change you for who you are.
When you face you your lifelong fears, know I would never change you for who you are.
When you try and break your lifelong issues that affect you, know I would never change you for who you are.
When you try and overcome the loneliness you feel, know I would never change you for who you are.
When you feel down, know I would never change you for who you are.
If and when you feel broken, know I would never change you for who you are.
When you feel like you're in a dark place, know I would never change you for who you are.
When you feel like you're struggling, know I would never change you for who you are.

When your inner cries take its toll on you, know I would never change you for who you are.
When you don't feel strong enough, know I would never change you for who you are.
When you don't feel brave enough, know I would never change you for who you are.
When you feel low, know I would never change you for who you are.

When you feel lost in any way, know I would never change you for who you are.
When you need a shoulder to cry on, know I would never change you for who you are.
If and when you don't feel good enough, know I would never change you for who you are.
When you feel like an outsider, know I would never change you for who you are.

If and when you feel rejected, know I would never change you for who you are.
When you feel like giving up, know I would never change you for who you are.
If and when you feel unwanted, know I would never change you for who you are.
If and when you feel worthless, know I would never change you for who you are.

When you feel like you are entering an unknown trap, know I would never change you for who you are.
When you feel like you're in denial, know I would never change you for who you are.
If and when you have nowhere to turn, know I would never change you for who you are.
If and when you don't feel you have the courage to fight, know I would never change you for who you are.
If and when you feel insecure, know I would never change you for who you are.
If and when you feel guilt in any way, know I would never change you for who you are.
When you need me the most, know I would never change you for who you are.
When you are not yourself, know I would never change you for who you are.
When you feel alone, know I would never change you for who you are.
When you face challenging days, I will walk alongside you and know I would never change you for who you are.
If and when you need to vent, know I would never change you for who you are.

Revenge

Revenge is never simple
Revenge is never a last-minute thing
Revenge is never okay to inflict on others without good reason
Revenge can leave lives tainted in many ways.

Revenge can result in devastation within the lives of the victims loved ones.
Revenge is never an easy decision to make without knowing the full circumstances of the situation.

Revenge is never a solution to forget the real reason behind why you want to take revenge.
Revenge can lead to dangerous outcomes without thinking,

Revenge can lead to hurtful consequences.
Revenge can lead to the victim having lifelong issues that they will carry around with them forever.
Revenge can leave the victim scared of their own shadow.
Revenge is careless
Revenge is cruel as no one deserves to be treated unfairly.

Positive Impression On Me

You leave a positive impression on my fragile past
You leave a positive impression on a way to release my lifelong fears.
You leave a positive impression on the secrets I hold within.
You leave a positive lasting impression on me when I need you the most.

You leave me with a positive impression giving me strength when I need it.
You leave me with a positive impression of how I can be.
You leave me with a positive impression on my life and the way I want it to be.
You leave a positive impression on me when I know I have you in my life.

You leave a positive impression on me when I feel let down by others.
You leave a positive impression on me when I feel down.
You leave a positive impression on me to keep me smiling.
You leave a positive impression on me when I feel broken.

You leave a positive impression on me when I'm sad.
You leave a positive impression on me when I need a helping hand.
You leave a positive impression on me as you set me free from my reality.
You leave a positive impression on me when I need a shoulder to cry on.

You leave a positive impression on me when no one can uplift me but you.
You leave a positive impression on me when I know you see the best in me.
You leave a positive impression on me when I know I will never walk alone.

Looking In The Mirror

When my fragile past is a reminder of who I was as I look in the mirror.
Looking in the mirror is never knowing what you're going to find.
Looking in the mirror is never knowing how you are going to feel emotionally.
Looking in the mirror is never knowing how the world you're in got so cruel.

Looking in the mirror is not knowing what your evaluating within yourself.
Looking in the mirror is allowing you to realize who is there for you & who is not.
Looking in the mirror is making you realize who is true to you & who is not.
Looking in the mirror is knowing who will stick by you through thick & thin.

Looking in the mirror will allow you to witness who will stand by you no matter what.
Looking in the mirror is knowing that the people in your life will always look out for you.
Looking in the mirror will determine who will stick around for you.
Looking in the mirror is knowing you have a flood of people around you that will never leave your side throughout the good & bad experiences.

Looking in the mirror lets you figure out who to trust & who not to trust.
Looking in the mirror is knowing that the people around you will take you as you are and not expect you to be someone you're not.
Looking in the mirror is knowing that the people you have in your life will never run a mile.
Looking in the mirror is knowing that the scars & bruises on you don't define you or rule what those around you think about you.
Looking in the mirror is knowing that people around you will take you for the real you and not expect to be someone who is not original and unique
Looking in the mirror is knowing that the scars, burns, bruises, battles & pain you face explains that whatever you went through you survived and the journey you're on continues.

Blinded

Blinded by your fragile past as it shows you what you did.
Blinded by lifelong fears that terrorise you to no end but it shows you the fears that you had to overcome.
Blinded by reality that isn't what you expected it to be.
Blinded by regret that you so truly wish wasn't.

Blinded by expectations of what others want from you but realizing its not what you want.
Blinded by the cruelty of this world that surrounds us.
Blinded by the traitors that betray you
Blinded by the true extant of your situation or circumstances that you are in.

Regrets

Regrets are never simple.
Regrets are never straight forward.
Regrets are never easy to forget.
Regrets are never easy to turn around.

Regrets are never easy to come back from.
Regrets are never an easy decision to make.
Once regrets are committed there is no turning back.
Regrets are never easy to forgive.

Regrets stay with you forever.
Regrets can rip you apart.
Regrets can hurt others around you.
Regrets can have outcomes you don't expect.

Never Be Ashamed

When I look into my fragile past never be ashamed as it's only a light reminder.
When I look into my lifelong fears that terrorise me never be ashamed as its not long term.
When I try and break my lifelong issues that affect me never be ashamed for having issues that you can fix. `
When I try and overcome the loneliness, I feel never be ashamed as all I have to think is it won't last forever.

When I feel down never feel ashamed to feel this way until someone comes along & makes my day.
When I feel broken never feel ashamed as I won't be for long as I know I have a flood of people around me who care about me.
When I don't feel strong enough never feel ashamed as I know I will be once again with the encouragement of people around me.

When I don't feel good enough never feel ashamed, I know with the support I have in my life I will find a way to feel good enough within myself.

When I don't feel brave enough never feel ashamed to admit your scared as I know I will be again.
When I feel unwanted never feel ashamed as I know I will be wanted by people I chose to be around.
When I feel rejected never feel ashamed as the people I chose to have around me will never reject me.
When I feel like a nobody never feel ashamed because I know I am a somebody to the people I chose to be around.

When I feel low never feel ashamed to ask for a helping hand from someone close to you as they show you, you are never to feel this way with them around you.
When I feel alone never feel ashamed to say I'm lonely because it will show people around you that you are reaching out to them.
When I need you the most never feel ashamed to say you need them when they know they will do whatever it takes to make you not feel this way.
When I need someone to make me smile never feel ashamed to say the reason behind why you need them to make you smile and you won't feel this way & it will be because of that person you smile.

Push In The Right Direction

Looking into my fragile past is never simple but you give me a push in the right direction.
Looking for a way to overcome the lifelong fears that terrorise me to no end I know I wouldn't have been able to do that without a push from you in the right direction.
When I try and break the lifelong issues that affect me you direct me with a push in the right direction.
When I try and overcome the loneliness, I feel you help me realize it won't last long with a push in the right direction.

When I feel down you help me realize that I won't be down for long with a push in the right direction.
When something tries to bring out the devil in me, I know people around me will not let that happen to me with a push in the right direction.
When I don't feel strong enough with a push in the right direction, I know I will be stronger than ever before.

When I feel broken with a push in the right direction, I won't break into a thousand tiny pieces.

When I don't feel brave enough with a push in the right direction, I know I will face whatever made me feel this way.
When I feel unwanted with a push in the right direction, I will know I am wanted by people I chose to have in my life.
When I feel rejected with a push in the right direction, I know that I won't feel this way again as the people I chose to be around won't reject me.
When I feel like I'm struggling with a pus in the right direction I know I won't struggle to face whatever it is as I have people around me to lead me to the right option.

When I feel low with a push in the right direction, I know I won't feel this way when I have people to talk it out with.
When I feel alone with a push in the right direction, I know I have a flood of people in my life I can reach out to.
When I need you the most with a push in the right direction, I know I can call out.
When I need you to make me smile with a push in the right direction you can say the reason behind why you need to smile.

Echoes

When my fragile past echoes through the doors.
When my lifelong fears that terrorise me to no end echoes through my mind.
When I try and break my lifelong issues that affect me it echoes like a reminding sound.
When I don't feel good enough it echoes through me that it truly hurts to be me.

When things get on top of me it echoes to the point I run.
When I feel low it voices echoes as it tells me what to think.
When I feel like a nobody it echoes loudly but you remind me, I am somebody.
When I don't feel brave enough it echoes through to the other side.

When I don't feel strong enough it echoes through the walls.
When I feel like I'm struggling it echoes through me the words you say and I believe I won't be this way for long.
When I feel like a burden it echoes far out and you catch it to release it.
When hateful or hurtful words come firing at me it echoes through me, I am not that person.

Its Ok To Admit

When I look into my fragile past its ok to admit that it's just a window of misdeeds.
When I face my lifelong fears that terrorise me to no end its ok to admit as I know it's not real and it can be solved when I try and confront it head on.
When I try and break my lifelong issues its ok to admit as I know they do not define me.
When I don't feel strong enough its ok to admit I need think of a way that made me feel this way and it is telling me that I will be stronger than ever before.
When I don't feel good enough its ok to admit as it's a way of reassuring yourself and those close to you and around you that you are good enough.
When I don't feel brave enough its ok to admit that as it shows you are being honest with yourself and those around you.
When I have good days its ok to admit as it shows those around you that you are coping with what the good days throw you way.
When I have bad days its ok to admit as it shows those around you that you a finding it a little difficult to cope with things that you usually do without any trouble arising.
When I need you the most its ok to admit as you call out and tell the people around you that you need them.
When I feel down its ok to admit to someone how down you feel and why because it allows them to understand me better as a person.
When I feel low its ok to admit as I ask for someone to hold me as I figure out the reasons as to why I feel low in myself.
When I am not myself its ok to admit that as it gives those around me a better chance of finding a way to help me find out who I am in myself.
When I feel like I'm struggling its ok to admit that I need a helping hand from those close to and around me.

Imprint

You leave an imprint on my fragile past which is a never ending nightmare I face.
You leave an imprint as my lifelong fears that terrorise me to no end come to surface.
You leave an imprint as I try and break the ongoing issues that affect me within a second of them coming to ahead.
When I don't feel strong enough you leave an imprint to allow me to realise how strong I can be.

When I don't feel good enough you leave an imprint to tell me I am good enough and I shouldn't let what others think of me deflect me from being good enough.
When I don't feel brave enough you leave an imprint to tell me I am braver than I think and not to worry as you know you are braver in your unique way.
When I feel like I'm struggling you leave an imprint telling me as I struggle it will find a way to resolve itself.
When I feel low, you leave an imprint telling me I won't feel this way forever as it will turn into something you won't see coming.
When I feel alone you leave an imprint on my life as you have a massive impact on me and how my life plays out.
When I feel down, you leave an imprint on my life as you make a massive difference in me and my life that I become someone I didn't think I had within me.
When I feel lost in myself you leave an imprint on my life telling me I will find a way out of this mess.

Words

When I look into my fragile past, the words you say ring out.
When I face my lifelong fears that terrorise me to no end, the words you say always allow me to stay afloat.
When I try & break my lifelong issues that affect me, the words you say always allow me to know I can do this.
When I don't feel strong enough, the words you say help me realize I can be as strong as ever before.
When I don't feel good enough, the words you say never leave me.
When I don't feel brave enough, the words you say always take me further than I was before.
When I feel low, the words you say trigger within me.
When I feel emotionally drained, the words you say allow me to realize that this is not the way I wanna be.
When I am not myself, the words you say allow me to keep an open mind & I can be me.
When I feel alone, the words you say always reassure me that I am not in this alone.

Different Side Of Me

When I look into my fragile past, you see a glimpse of a different side of me.
When I face my lifelong fears that terrorise me to no end, you see a glimpse of different me.
When I try & break my lifelong issues that affect me, you see a glimpse of something you haven't seen before.
When I don't feel good enough, you see s glimpse of a closed door within me.
When I don't feel strong enough, you see a side of me that don't have the strength to continue sometimes.
When I feel low, you see a side of me as I let you in & I break.
When I feel down, you see a side of me that drags me to the ground.
When I feel broken, you see a side of me that you always fix me with just by being around & apart of my life & just by being you.

Confidence

You give me the confidence to face my fragile past.
You give me the confidence to face my lifelong fears that terrorise me to no end.
You give me the confidence to face my lifelong issues that affect me.
You give me the confidence to face the hard times I endure.
You give me the confidence to face the dark times I so truly feel I can't escape.

You give me the confidence to feel strong in any way I can.
You give me the confidence to feel brave as I can be.
You give me confidence to prove to those who did not believe in me
You give me confidence to be who I wanna be.

You give me confidence to reach out to those who are around me.
You give me the confidence to follow my lifetime dreams I so truly deserve.
You give me the confidence to keep an open mind.
You give me the confidence to look at myself and think this isn't who I wanna be.

You give me the confidence to prove that I am worth the risk.
You give me the confidence to be me.
You give me the confidence to know I never walk alone.

Until You Came Into My Life

No one ever made me feel I could ever get past my fragile past until you came into my life.
No one ever made me feel I could ever get past my lifelong fears that terrorise me to no end until you came into my life.
No one ever made me feel I could get to the bottom of the lifelong issues that affect me until you came into my life.
No one ever made me feel like I existed until you came into my life.

No one ever made me feel valued until you came into my life.
No one ever made me feel I was someone they would take a risk on until you came into my life.
No one ever made me feel I was someone they would take a chance on until you came into my life.
No one ever made time to get to know me until you came into my life.

No one ever lifted my sprits until you come into my life.
No one ever believed in me until you came into my life.
No one wanted to see me progress until you came into my life.
No one wanted to see me as me until you come into my life.

No one wanted to take me under their wing until you come into my life.
No one wanted to see the best in me until you came into my life.
No one wanted to give me a helping hand until you came into my life.
No one wanted to see the talent I have within me until you came into my life.
No one ever looked at me like I was worth it until you came into my life.

No one could see past the disappointment I put on them until you came into my life.
No one could see past the shame I put on them until you came into my life.
No one could see past the misdeeds I did until you come into my life.
No one could see past the guilt I felt until you came into my life.
No one could see that given a chance I can make something of myself until you came into my life.
No one could see that even I have a breaking point until you came into my life.
No one could see how much I am capable of until you came into my life.

I Don't Wanna Be Overlooked

I don't wanna be overlooked because of my fragile past.
I don't wanna be overlooked because of my lifelong fears that terrorise me to no end.
I don't wanna be overlooked because of my lifelong issues that affect me.
I don't wanna be overlooked because of rejection.

I don't wanna be overlooked because of being different.
I don't wanna be overlooked because of the difficulties I face.
I don't wanna be overlooked because of feeling insecure.
I don't wanna be overlooked because of who I was

I don't wanna be overlooked because of my situations.
I don't wanna be overlooked because of my abilities
I don't wanna be overlooked because some people don't wanna know me.
I don't wanna be overlooked because of something someone overhears about me.
I don't wanna be overlooked because I am someone who takes whatever life throws at me and wins.

I don't wanna be overlooked for the way I do things that's easier for me.
I don't wanna be overlooked for the way life is for me.
I don't wanna be overlooked for being myself in front of those I care about.
I don't wanna be overlooked for being someone who needs a helping hand from time to time.

I don't wanna be overlook for being someone who turns to those I care about.
I don't wanna be overlooked for taking control of my life in my own way.
I don't wanna be overlooked for having a breaking point.
I don't wanna be overlooked for who I am.
I don't wanna be overlooked because of those who never believed in me.
I don't wanna be overlooked because I follow my own path in life.
I don't wanna be overlooked because I will prove I am good enough.
I don't wanna be overlooked because I know I am worth the risk.
I don't wanna be overlooked because I know I am stronger than ever before.
I don't wanna be overlooked because I know I am braver than ever before.
I don't wanna be overlooked because I know I will achieve everything I wanted through determination and hard work.
I don't wanna be overlooked because I know I will come out on top regardless of what people think about me.

Reasons

There are always reasons behind my fragile past only you can see.
There are always reasons behind my lifelong fears only you can see.
There are always reasons behind my lifelong issues that affect me only you can see.
There are always reasons behind my hurt only you can see.

There are always reasons behind why I am the way I am only you can see.
There are always reasons behind my dark moods only you can see.
There are always reasons behind the rejection I feel only you can see.
There are always reasons behind the hatred I feel only you can see.

There are always reasons behind when I don't feel strong enough only you can see.
There are always reasons behind the scars I try & hide from everyone else but you.
There are always reasons you are the only one that sets me free from my reality.
There are always reasons behind why I mess up only you can see.

There are always reasons behind why I protect those I care about only you can see.
There are always reasons behind the rage I hold within only you can see.
There are always reasons behind the anger I hold on to only you can see.
There are always reasons behind the choices and decisions I make only you can see.

There are always reasons behind how I respond to situations in a certain way only you can see.
There are always reasons behind why I feel I don't exist only you can see.
There are always reasons behind why I feel I don't belong only you can see.
There are always reasons behind the loneliness I feel only you can see.

There are always reasons behind why I feel unwanted only you can see.
There are always reasons behind why I don't feel valued only you can see.
There are always reasons behind why I feel trapped only you can see.
There are reasons behind why I never feel good enough only you can see.
There are always reasons behind the dramas I get myself into only you can see.

Found My Way

When I go down a dark path, I've finally found my way
When I go down the wrong path, I've finally found my way.
When I take the wrong direction, I've finally found my way
When I take a wrong turn, I've finally found my way
When I go into a dark place, I know I've finally found my way.
When I feel empty within, I know I've finally found my way.
When I feel a part of me is missing, I know I've finally found my way.
When there is no way back, I know I've finally found my way.
When there is no truth in why I'm here I know I've finally found my way.
When no one in family notices me I know I've finally found my way.
When I've gone off the rails, I know I've finally found my way.
When people make me feel really bad, I know I've finally found my way.
When family makes me feel guilty, I know I've finally found my way.
When everything goes wrong for me I know I've finally found my way.
When I'm ignored, I know I've finally found my way.
When no one acknowledges me, I feel I've finally found my way.

Someone Understands Me

Someone finally understands what I'm all about.
Someone finally understands the emptiness I feel.
Someone finally understands my weakness.
Someone finally understands my thinking the way I do.

Someone understands the real reason behind it all x4

Someone finally understands how I feel in myself.
Someone finally understands the betrayal I feel.
Someone finally understands the hurt I feel.
Someone finally understands the pain I feel.
Someone finally understands the guilt I feel.
Someone finally understands the heartache I feel.
Someone finally understands the rejection I feel.

Someone finally understands the reasons behind my smile.

Someone finally understands why I'm always alone.
Someone finally understands me.
Someone finally understands the real me.

Someone finally understands who I am.
Someone finally understands the reasons behind my silence.
Someone finally understands the reasons behind the tears I cry.
Someone finally understands the anger I feel.
Someone finally understands the hatred I feel.
Someone finally understands the loneliness I feel.
Someone finally understands the reasons behind the darkness I am in.
Someone finally understands what went wrong.

I Can

I can finally face the past I've ruined.
I can finally face who I have become.
I can finally face the people around me.
I can finally face the heartache I've caused.
I can finally face the pain I feel
I can finally face the hurt I feel within.
I can finally face being alone.
I can finally face every tear I cry over you.
I can finally face the silence in me.
I can finally face the fact I will never be without you in my life
I can finally face struggling though my days.
I can finally face the outside world without a smile.
I can finally face that I won't be breaking on the inside anymore.
I can finally face the pain I have created.

Release

I can finally release the past in a way I know how.
I can finally release my experiences in a way I know how.
I can finally release my fears in a way I know how.
I can finally release the dark side of me in a way I know how.
I can finally release my shadows in a way I know how.
I can finally release my disagreements in a way I know how.
I can finally release my secrets in a way I know how.
I can finally release my true self in a way I know how.
I can finally release my heartbreak in a way I know how.
I can finally release the scars I have in a way I know how.
I can finally release the real me that turned cold and become warm for those close to and round me.

I can finally release the reality I so truly see in a way I know how.
I can finally release the reason I become in a way I know how
I can finally release the person I was in a way I know how.
I can finally release the person I am today in a way I know how.
I can finally release everyone around me and watch them come closer then ever before in a way only I know.
I can finally release what I believe in a way I know how.
I can finally release myself bit by bit in a way I know how.
I can finally release why I disappeared in a way I know how.
I can finally release everything about me in a way I know how.
I can finally release every situation I am in or was in in a way I know how.
I can finally be me and not worry about fading as I release the tension I had.

At A Standstill

I don't wanna be someone who's at a standstill too exhausted to look into my past.
I don't wanna be someone who's at a standstill and finding it tough to face my experiences.
I don't wanna be someone who's at a standstill touring myself over my fears that terrorize me to no end.
I don't wanna be someone who's at a standstill that can't find a side of me that I can finally be proud of.
 I don't wanna be someone who's at a standstill too fragile to face a hard time.
I don't wanna be someone who's at a standstill and can't face the old me.
I don't wanna be someone who's at a standstill that makes mistakes but can't take on board that they are a way of learning.
I don't wanna be someone who's at a standstill not able to chase my troubles away.
I don't wanna be someone who's at a standstill to terrified to know what this unknown world is all about.
I don't wanna be someone who's at a standstill not able to face my bad memories straight away.
I don't wanna be someone who's at a standstill not knowing the answers I so truly aim to get.
I don't wanna be someone who's at a standstill not knowing what my inner self has in store for me.
I don't wanna be someone who's at a standstill not knowing what the outside world has waiting for me to find.
I don't wanna be someone who's at a standstill not knowing my true feelings towards things.

I don't wanna be someone who's at a standstill not knowing what to make of my own unknown future.
I don't wanna be someone who's at a standstill too scared to face failure in order to make myself even better than I was before.
I don't wanna be someone who is at a standstill who gives up or in so easily.
I don't wanna be someone who is at a standstill trying to hide from things that are hard to face.
I don't wanna be someone who's at a standstill too scared to face the world.
I don't wanna be someone who's at a standstill I wanna stare lighting in the face.
I don't wanna be someone who's at a standstill I want to stare storms in the face.

I Don't Wanna Be Awake

I don't wanna be awake at night thinking what my past could have been like.
I don't wanna be awake at night thinking what my fears could have been like if I didn't have them.
I don't wanna be awake at night thinking what my lifelong issues could have been if I solved them.
I don't wanna be awake at night thinking about why I was the way I was.
I don't wanna be awake thinking what opportunities I could have had if I went after them.
I don't wanna be awake at night thinking what I would do if I shut the door on my dream.
I don't wanna be awake at night thinking what life has thrown my way.
I don't wanna be awake at night worried about what obstructions get in my way.
I don't wanna be awake thinking about the pain I caused.
I don't wanna be awake thinking about the hurt I felt.
I don't wanna be awake thinking what truths I hide from.
I don't wanna be awake thinking how life would be different for me if I didn't have the health issues I have.
I don't wanna be awake thinking about what if I didn't stand up for what I believe.
I don't wanna be awake at night thinking what if I wasn't strong.
I don't wanna be awake at night thinking what obstacles I have had to become to get where I am today.
I don't wanna be awake at night thinking what regrets I have.

You Reassure Me

When I feel torn about my fragile past, you reassure me
When I feel torn about my lifelong fears that terrorize me to no end, you reassure me.
When I feel torn about my lifelong issues that affect me, you reassure me.
When I feel torn about who I am, you reassure me.
When I feel torn about who I was, you reassure me.
When I feel torn about feeling down, you reassure me.
When I feel torn about being different to others, you reassure me.
When I feel torn about the way people treat me, you reassure me.
When I feel torn about the battles I face, you reassure me.
When I feel torn about who to trust, you reassure me.
When I feel torn about the way I turned out, you reassure me.
When I feel torn about the way I learned differently to others, you reassured me
When I feel torn about how to go about confronting those who didn't believe in me, you reassured me.
When I feel torn about the scars & bruises, I have, you reassure me.
When I feel torn about who will be there for me when I need them the most, you reassure me.
When I feel torn about who will stick by me when I don't expect it, you reassure me.
When I feel torn about feeling unwanted, you reassure me.
When I feel torn about feeling ripped apart, you reassure me.

Close Chapter

I close the chapter of my fragile past as I know I now don't need to keep guessing.
I close the chapter of my lifelong fears as I know I am no long terrified to face them.
I close the chapter of my lifelong issues that use to affect me as I try and solve them straight away.
I close the chapter on the hurt I felt before as I know I will never let anything hurt me again.
I close the chapter on the people who didn't believe in me from the start as I know I have the people who believe in me in my life.
I close the chapter of feeling rejected as I don't wanna let it get to me and let whoever says it win.

I close the chapter of the feeling of never being able to please other people accept those who are close to me, in my life and by my side and finally being able to please myself.
I close the chapter of never having a perfect life because I am unique there is no such thing as perfect as long as I am happy with my life that's all that should matter.
I close the chapter of having the wrong people in my life, as I know I have finally found the people who I want in my life that care about me and will be there when I need them.
I close the chapter on the guilt I felt all this time as I know I have nothing to feel guilty about.
I close the chapter of never feeling strong enough as I know I can be strong as I want to be when I want to be.
I close the chapter of never feeling brave enough as I know I am brave and I don't need to prove it to anyone outside of my life and close inner circle.
I close the chapter of feeling lost as I know I won't be for long as I have my way of finding a way out.
I close the chapter of failing as I know I will make something of myself with the people around me to get me through it.
I close the chapter of never being alone as I know I have a flood of people around me that care about me and will be there for me no matter what.
I close the chapter of never finding the right way of being as I know I am different and I have people I know I can be myself around and I know they accept me for me.

Dictate

I don't wanna let my past dictate my life.
I don't wanna let my lifelong fears dictate my life.
I don't wanna let my lifelong issues dictate my life.
I don't wanna let my pain dictate my life.
I don't wanna let my hurt dictate my life.
I don't want my troubles that follow me around dictate my life.
I don't want the fact I wasn't strong enough to dictate my life.
I don't want the fact I wasn't brave enough to dictate my life.
I don't want my failures to dictate my life.
I don't want the fact I never felt good enough to dictate my life.
I don't want the fact I am different from others to dictate my life
I don't want the fact I know I have a flood of people around me that care about me to dictate my life.
I don't want who I aim to be to dictate my life.

I don't want what I've had to overcome in order to get where I am today to dictate my life

I'll Find The Truth

I know I will find the truth to the fragile past I have.
I know I will find the truth to my lifelong fears
I know I will find the truth to the pain I feel
I know I will find the truth to the hurt I feel
I know I will find the truth to the worry I have within me.
I know I will find the truth to the mess I got myself into.
I know I will find the truth to the bravery I try and face.
I know I will find the truth to the back story of my life.
I know I will find the truth to why I became so anxious
I know I will find the truth as to why some people pull away from me.
I know I will find the truth to the bruises and scars I have.
I know I will find the truth to why I run to get away.
I know I will find the truth to why some people say hurtful things to me.
I know I will find the truth to why people use to look at me as if I wasn't worth the risk.
I know I will find the truth to why i felt so alone.
I know I will find the truth as to why I felt rejected .
I know I will find the truth as to why I felt unwanted.
I know I will find the truth as to why I felt like a black sheep.
 I know I will find the truth as to why I felt I wasn't important enough.
I know I will find the truth as to why I felt like I didn't belong.
I know I will find the truth as to why I felt let down in so many ways.
I know I will find the truth as to why I couldn't turn to the people around me.
I know I will find the truth as to why I felt guilty for things that weren't my doing.
I know I will find the truth to who I am now.
I know I will find the truth as to why I felt so low
I know I will find the truth as to why I felt so broken
I know I will find the truth as to why I felt like I didn't exist

Didn't Know

People didn't know what I'm all about.
People didn't know the full existent of my life.
People didn't know how to appreciate me as me.

People didn't know how to be around me because I was someone they disregarded as someone they didn't wanna like or be around.
People didn't take kindly to the fact I wasn't the same as them.
People didn't know how to act around me.
People didn't come to me to ask questions instead they spread nasty rumours about me that I felt I shouldn't be.
People thought I was a nobody and stayed as far away from me as they possibly could.
People thought I wasn't worth the risk.
People thought I wasn't strong enough to stand up to them.
People thought I wasn't brave enough to cope with the hateful words I heard.
People thought I wasn't good enough to get through the hard times, tough times, dark times, bad times, fragile times.
People thought I wasn't valuable enough to be important
People thought I was a disease that they would never let me explain and they thought if they got close enough, I would explode.

Because Of You

Because of you I know I excel.
Because of you I know I never struggle as much as I did.
Because of you I know I am worth the risk.
Because of you I stay on the straight and narrow.
Because of you I am stronger than ever before.
Because of you I am braver than ever before.
Because of you I am who I wanna be
Because of you I let out the true me.
Because of you I let out the real me.
Because of you I don't have to pretend.
Because of you i don't feel drained anymore.
Because of you I face my demons without being drawn in.
Because of you I look at myself and think I am more than I thought I could be.
Because of you I don't have to hide anymore.
Because of you I feel wanted.
Because of you I feel valued.
Because of you I know I can achieve what I have always wanted.
Because of you I know I am good enough for the people around me.
Because of you I know I have a flood of people around me.
Because of you I know I have a purpose.
Because of you I see the people who I have and who I don't.
Because of you I found myself.

Because of you I don't feel ashamed to put myself out there for the world to see my talent just like you did.
Because of you I have a different way of being.
Because of you I look at my life difficultly.
Because of you I am the person I am.
Because of you I got this far.
Because of you I believe in myself.
Because of you I have hope.
Because of you I have strength.
Because of you I have confidence

Bite

I bite my fragile past from reoccurring
I bite my lifelong fears that terrorize me to no end from drenching up.
I bite the hatred I feel from people I feel hate me.
I bite the hateful words I hear from reaching my head and twisting the truth.
I bite the way I hurt stopping the hurtful things people say about me.
I bite the bullshit I have to deal with as I know I have the people around me to give me the support and encouragement I so truly need.
I bite the burning sensation of the truth that one day will come out when I least expect it.
I bite the dark moods I sometimes let out with the people around me giving me the confidence I need
I bite the dramas I got myself into without thinking.
I bite the rejection I feel to outsmart the ones who say it.
I bite the fact I don't feel good enough because I try not to let it affect me.
I bite the fact I don't feel brave enough to face the world with my close inner circle surrounding me.
I bite the fact I don't feel strong enough to stand tall at every chance I get.
I bite the fact I failed in order to make a success of what I put my mind to.
I bite the fact I felt let down by those who made me think I wasn't going to rise again.
I bite the battles I face to prove I can win them.

To The Back Of My Mind

I put my past to the back of my mind.
I put my lifelong fears that terrorize me to no end to the back of my mind.
I put my demons to the back of my mind.

I put the people who treated me unfairly to the back of my mind.
I put the hater who hate me to the back of my mind.
I put the tears that fall down my face to the back of my mind.
I put the conscious I have to the back of my mind.
I put the guilt I felt to the back of my mind.
I put the worn out me to the back of my mind.
I put the dark me to the back of my mind.
I put the scars and bruises I have to the back of my mind.
I put the hateful words I hears to the back of my mind.
I put the feelings of not being wanted to the back of my mind.
I put the fragile me to the back of my mind.
When I didn't feel good enough, I put it to the back of my mind.
When I didn't feel strong enough, I put it to the back of my mind.
When I felt low, I put it to the back of my mind.
When I felt I didn't exist I put it to the back of my mind.
I put my emotional strain to the back of my mind.
I put my baggage to the back of my mind.
I put my tension to the back of my mind.
I put the freaked out me to the back of my mind.
I put the empty me to the back of my mind.
I put the negative me to the back of my mind.
I put the pain I feel to the back of my mind.
I put the hurt I feel to the back of my mind.
I put the fact I am never alone to the back of my mind.
I put the fact I won't face anything without those around me to the back of my mind.
I put the fact I know I have a flood of people that care about me to the back of my mind.
I put my misdeeds to the back of my mind.
I put the fact I never felt important enough to people who would put me down to the back of my mind.
I put the fact I felt let down by those who wanted to see me fail to the back of my mind.
I put the fact that those who didn't see me as me, see the best in me, wanted to see me fail, didn't want to see me excel to the back of my mind.
Stick the people who care about you, will take you as you are, will be with you no matter what, as it shows who you have and who you don't.

Confide In You

I confide in you about my fragile past.
I confide in you about my lifelong fears that terrorize me to no end.
I confide in you about my lifelong issues that affect me.
I confide in you about the hateful things I have to deal with.
I confide in you when I don't feel strong enough.
I confide in you when I don't feel brave enough.
I confide in you because I trust you totally.
I confide in you when I feel low.
I confide in you when I feel broken.
I confide in you when I don't feel like myself.
I confide in you about things I can't tell anyone else.
I confide in you when I feel unwanted.
I confide in you when I feel scared.
I confide in you when I feel let down by others.
I confide in you when I feel I can't keep my tears from rolling down my face.
I confide in you when I don't feel important enough.
I confide in you when I don't feel good enough.
I confide in you because you're the only one I feel able to talk to.
I confide in you when I feel damaged.
I confide in you because I know I am never alone.
I confide in you because I know I can be me when I'm around you
I confide in you when I need you the most.
I confide in you during my dark times
I confide in you during my hour of need.
I confide in you during my darkest points in life.
I confide in you when there is no other way.
I confide in you because you see what others don't
I confide in you because we are lifelong friends and inseparable for life.

Block Out

I know I can block out my fragile past.
I know I can block out my lifelong fears that terrorize ne to no end.
I know I can block out my lifelong issues that affect me.
I know I can block out my demons.
I know I can block out my bad experiences
I know I can block out the feeling of not being wanted
I know I can block out the hateful words I hear.
I know I can block out the hurt I feel.

I know I can block out the emotional strain that I have.
I know I can block out the rejection I feel.
I know I can block out the feeling of feeling down.
I know I can block out the feeling of feeling low.
I know I can block out when I don't feel brave enough
I know I can block out when I don't feel strong enough
I know I can block out when I don't feel good enough
I know I can block out when I don't feel important enough
I know I can block out when I feel lost.

Don't Hold It In

When you look back at your fragile past, don't hold it in.
When you face your lifelong fears, don't hold it in.
When you try and break your lifelong issues that affect you, don't hold it in.
When you try and overcome the loneliness you feel, don't hold it in.

When you feel down, don't hold it in.
If and when you feel broken, don't hold it in.
When you feel like you're in a dark place, don't hold it in.
When you feel like you're struggling, don't hold it in.

When your inner cries take its toll on you, don't hold it in.
When you don't feel strong enough, don't hold it in.
When you don't feel brave enough, don't hold it in
When you feel low, don't hold it in.

When you feel lost in any way, don't hold it in.
When you need a shoulder to cry on, don't hold it in.
If and when you don't feel good enough, don't hold it in.
When you feel like an outsider, don't hold it in.

If and when you feel rejected, don't hold it in.
When you feel like giving up, don't hold it in.
If and when you feel unwanted, don't hold it in.
If and when you feel worthless, don't hold it in.

When you feel like you are entering an unknown trap don't hold it in.
When you feel like you're in denial, don't hold it in.
If and when you have nowhere to turn, don't hold it in.
If and when you don't feel you have the courage to fight, don't hold it in.

If and when you feel insecure, don't hold it in.
If and when you feel guilt in any way, don't hold it in.
When you need me the most, don't hold it in.
When you are not yourself, don't hold it in.
When you feel alone, don't hold it in.
When you face challenging days, I will walk alongside you and know you don't have to hold it in.
If and when you need to vent, don't hold it in.

Twist The Truth

When you look back at your fragile past, know I will not let anyone twist the truth.
When you face your lifelong fears, know I will not let anyone twist the truth.
When you try and break your lifelong issues that affect you, know I will not let anyone twist the truth.
When you try and overcome the loneliness you feel, know I will not let anyone twist the truth.

When you feel down, know I will not let anyone twist the truth.
If and when you feel broken, know I will not let anyone twist the truth.
When you feel like you're in a dark place, know I will not let anyone twist the truth.
When you feel like you're struggling, know I will not let anyone twist the truth.

When your inner cries take its toll on you, know I will not let anyone twist the truth.
When you don't feel strong enough, know I will not let anyone twist the truth.
When you don't feel brave enough, know I will not let anyone twist the truth.
When you feel low, know I will not let anyone twist the truth.

When you feel lost in any way, know I will not let anyone twist the truth.
When you need a shoulder to cry on, know I will not let anyone twist the truth.
If and when you don't feel good enough, know I will not let anyone twist the truth.
When you feel like an outsider, know I will not let anyone twist the truth.

If and when you feel rejected, know I will not let anyone twist the truth.
When you feel like giving up, know I will not let anyone twist the truth.
If and when you feel unwanted, know I will not let anyone twist the truth.
If and when you feel worthless, know I will not let anyone twist the truth.

When you feel like you are entering an unknown trap, know I will not let anyone twist the truth.
When you feel like you're in denial, know I will not let anyone twist the truth.
If and when you have nowhere to turn, know I will not let anyone twist the truth.
If and when you don't feel you have the courage to fight, know I will not let anyone twist the truth.

If and when you feel insecure, know I will not let anyone twist the truth.
If and when you feel guilt in any way, know I will not let anyone twist the truth.
When you need me the most, know I will not let anyone twist the truth.
When you are not yourself, know I will not let anyone twist the truth.
When you feel alone, know I will not let anyone twist the truth.
When you face challenging days, I will walk alongside you and know I will not let anyone twist the truth.
If and when you need to vent, know I will not let anyone twist the truth.

The Weight On Ur Shoulders

When you look back at your fragile past, know I will not let you carry the weight on ur shoulders.
When you face your lifelong fears, know I will not let you carry the weight on ur shoulders.
When you try and break your lifelong issues that affect you, know I will not let you carry the weight on ur shoulders.
When you try and overcome the loneliness you feel, know I will not let you carry the weight on ur shoulders.
When you feel down, know I will not let you carry the weight on ur shoulders.
If and when you feel broken, know I will not let you carry the weight on ur shoulders.
When you feel like you're in a dark place, know I will not let you carry the weight on ur shoulders.
When you feel like you're struggling, know I will not let you carry the weight on ur shoulders.

When your inner cries take its toll on you, know I will not let you carry the weight on ur shoulders.
When you don't feel strong enough, know I will not let you carry the weight on ur shoulders.
When you don't feel brave enough, know I will not let you carry the weight on ur shoulders.

When you feel low, know I will not let you carry the weight on ur shoulders.

When you feel lost in any way, know I will not let you carry the weight on ur shoulders.
When you need a shoulder to cry on, know I will not let you carry the weight on ur shoulders.
If and when you don't feel good enough, know I will not let you carry the weight on ur shoulders.
When you feel like an outsider, know I will not let you carry the weight on ur shoulders.

If and when you feel rejected, know I will not let you carry the weight on ur shoulders.
When you feel like giving up, know I will not let you carry the weight on ur shoulders.
If and when you feel unwanted, know I will not let you carry the weight on ur shoulders.
If and when you feel worthless, know I will not let you carry the weight on ur shoulders.
When you feel like you are entering an unknown trap, know I will not let you carry the weight on ur shoulders.
When you feel like you're in denial, know I will not let you carry the weight on ur shoulders.
If and when you have nowhere to turn, know I will not let you carry the weight on ur shoulders.
If and when you don't feel you have the courage to fight, know I will not let you carry the weight on ur shoulders.
If and when you feel insecure, know I will not let you carry the weight on ur shoulders.
If and when you feel guilt in any way, know I will not let you carry the weight on ur shoulders.
When you need me the most, know I will not let you carry the weight on ur shoulders.
When you are not yourself, know I will not let you carry the weight on ur shoulders.
When you feel alone, know I will not let you carry the weight on ur shoulders.
When you face challenging days, I will walk alongside you and know I will not let you carry the weight on ur shoulders.
If and when you need to vent, know I will not let you carry the weight on ur shoulders.

Build A Wall Around You

When you look back at your fragile past, know I will build a wall around you
When you face your lifelong fears, know I will build a wall around you.
When you try and break your lifelong issues that affect you, know I will build a wall around you.
When you try and overcome the loneliness you feel, know I will build a wall around you.

When you feel down, know I will build a wall around you.
If and when you feel broken, know I will build a wall around you.
When you feel like you're in a dark place, know I will build a wall around you.
When you feel like you're struggling, know I will build a wall around you.

When your inner cries take its toll on you, know I will build a wall around you.
When you don't feel strong enough, know I will build a wall around you.
When you don't feel brave enough, know I will build a wall around you.
When you feel low, know I will build a wall around you.

When you feel lost in any way, know I will build a wall around you.
When you need a shoulder to cry on, know I will build a wall around you.
If and when you don't feel good enough, know I will build a wall around you.
When you feel like an outsider, know I will build a wall around you.

If and when you feel rejected, know I will build a wall around you.
When you feel like giving up, know I will build a wall around you.
If and when you feel unwanted, know I will build a wall around you.
If and when you feel worthless, know I will build a wall around you.

When you feel like you are entering an unknown trap, know I will build a wall around you.
When you feel like you're in denial, know I will build a wall around you.
If and when you have nowhere to turn, know I will build a wall around you.
If and when you don't feel you have the courage to fight, know I will build a wall around you.
If and when you feel insecure, know I will build a wall around you.
If and when you feel guilt in any way, know I will build a wall around you.
When you need me the most, know I will build a wall around you.
When you are not yourself, know I will build a wall around you.
When you feel alone, know I will build a wall around you.
When you face challenging days, I will walk alongside you and know I build a wall around you.
If and when you need to vent, know I will build a wall around you.

Come & Find Me

When you look back at your fragile past know all you have to do is come and find me
When you face your lifelong fears. You know I will always chase away your fears.
When you try and break your lifelong issues that affect you, you know I will never scatter your issues
When you try and overcome the loneliness you feel know I will never let you be lonely.

when you feel down all you have to do is shout and I will surface.
If and when you feel broken. You know I won't be far
 when you feel like you're in a dark place and you can't get out. And you know I will be here
When you feel like you're struggling, and you feel no one is around you know I will be.

When your inner cries take its toll on you, know I will keep your inner cries from escaping.
When you don't feel strong enough know that I know you can be as strong as you want to be.
When you don't feel brave enough know that I know you will be brave once again.
When you feel low know I will never let you stumble to the ground.

When you feel lost in any way, know I will never let you fear the worst as I retrace your steps to find you.
 When you need a shoulder to cry on, know I will never let you sob away and I will be the one to stop you sobbing.
when you don't feel good enough, know I will always reassure you that you are good enough.
When you feel like an outsider, know I will never leave you out in the cold.

when you feel rejected, know I will never let you think that you are a reject as you are not.
When you feel like giving up, know I will never let you give up on anything.
when you feel unwanted, know I will always reassure you that you are wanted.
when you feel worthless, know I will always reassure you that you are worth it in every way.
When you feel like you are entering an unknown trap know that I will never let you fall in to the trap
When you feel like you're in denial, know that denial will never stop you
when you have nowhere to turn, know you will have somewhere always.

when you don't feel you have the courage to fight, know I will give you the courage to fight

when you feel insecure, know you will always be secure
when you feel guilt in any way, know I won't let you feel guilty for something you haven't done.
When you need me the most, know all you have to do is call on me.
When you are not yourself, know I will keep you from going down under.
When you feel alone, know I will never let you be alone as I will always be your sidekick.
When you face challenging days, I will walk alongside you and know I will face every challenge with you.
If and when you need to vent, know you can tell me anything

You Are Good Enough

When you look back at your fragile past know you are good enough.
When you face your lifelong fears, know you are good enough.
When you try and break your lifelong issues that affect you, know you are good enough.
When you try and overcome the loneliness you feel know you are good enough.
When you feel down know you are good enough.
If and when you feel broken know you are good enough.
When you feel like you're in a dark place know you are good enough.
When you feel like you're struggling know you are good enough.

When your inner cries take its toll on you, know you are good enough.
When you don't feel strong enough know you are good enough.
When you don't feel brave enough know you are good enough.
When you feel low know you are good enough.

When you feel lost in any way know you are good enough.
When you need a shoulder to cry on know you are good enough.
If and when you don't feel good enough know you are good enough.
When you feel like an outsider know you are good enough.

If and when you feel rejected know you are good enough.
When you feel like giving up know you are good enough.
If and when you feel unwanted know you are good enough.
If and when you feel worthless know you are good enough.

When you feel like you're entering an unknown trap know you are good enough.
When you feel like you're in denial know you are good enough.
If and when you have nowhere to turn know you are good enough.
If and when you don't feel you have the courage to fight know you are good enough.
If and when you feel insecure know you are good enough.
If and when you feel guilt know you are good enough.
When you need me the most know you are good enough.
When you are not yourself know you are good enough.
When you feel alone know you are good enough.
When you face challenging days, I will walk alongside you and know you are good enough.
If and when you need to vent know you are good enough.

Important To Me

When you look back at your fragile past know you are very important to me
When you face your lifelong fears, know you are very important to me.
When you try and break your lifelong issues that affect you, know you are very important to me.
When you try and overcome the loneliness you feel know you are very important to me.
When you feel down know you are very important to me.
If and when you feel broken know you are very important to me.
When you feel like you're in a dark place know you are very important to me.
When you feel like you're struggling know you are very important to me.

When your inner cries take its toll on you, know you are very important to me.
When you don't feel strong enough know you are very important to me.
When you don't feel brave enough know you are very important to me.
When you feel low know you are very important to me.

When you feel lost in any way know you are very important to me.
When you need a shoulder to cry on know you are very important to me.
If and when you don't feel good enough know you are very important to me.
When you feel like an outsider know you are very important to me.

If and when you feel rejected know you are very important to me.
When you feel like giving up know you are very important to me.
If and when you feel unwanted know you are very important to me.
If and when you feel worthless know you are very important to me.

When you feel like your entering an unknown trap know you are very important to me.
When you feel like you're in denial know you are very important to me.
If and when you have nowhere to turn know you are very important to me.
If and when you don't feel you have the courage to fight know you are very important to me.

If and when you feel insecure know you are very important to me.
If and when you feel guilt know you are very important to me.
When you need me, the most know you are very important to me
When you are not yourself know you are very important to me.
When you feel alone know you are very important to me.
When you face challenging days, I will walk alongside you and know you are very important to me.
If and when you need to vent know you are very important to me.

As I Go Under

When I look back at my fragile past as I go under you bring me back up.
When I face my lifelong fears, as I go under you bring me back up.
When I try and break my lifelong issues that affect me, as I go under you bring me back up.
When I try and overcome the loneliness I feel as I go under you bring me back up.

When I feel down as I go under you bring me back up.
If and when I feel broken as I go under you bring me back up.
When I feel like I'm in a dark place as I go under you bring me back up.
When I feel like I'm struggling as I go under you bring me back up.

When my inner cries take its toll on me, as I go under you bring me back up.
When I don't feel strong enough, as I go under you bring me back up.
When I don't feel brave enough, as I go under you bring me back up.
When I feel low, as I go under you bring me back up.

When I feel lost in any way, as I go under you bring me back up.
When I need a shoulder to cry on, as I go under you bring me back up.
If and when I don't feel good enough, as I go under you bring me back up.
When I feel like an outsider, as I go under you bring me back up.

If and when I feel rejected, as I go under you bring me back up
When I feel like giving up, as I go under you bring me back up.
If and when I feel unwanted, as I go under you bring me back up.

If and when I feel worthless, as I go under you bring me back up.

When I feel like I'm entering an unknown trap, as I go under you bring me back up.
When I feel like I'm in denial, as I go under you bring me back up,
If and when I have nowhere to turn, as I go under you bring me back up.
If and when I don't feel you have the courage to fight, as I go under you bring me back up.

If and when I feel insecure, as I go under you bring me back up.
If and when I feel guilt, as I go under you bring me back up.
When I need you the most, as I go under you bring me back up.
When I am not myself, as I go under you bring me back up.
When I feel alone, as I go under you bring me back up.
When I face challenging days, you will walk alongside me and as I go under you bring me back up.
If and when I need to vent as I go under you bring me back up.

I'd Take A Risk On You

When you look back at your fragile past know I'd take a risk on you.
When you face your lifelong fears, know I'd take a risk on you.
When you try and break your lifelong issues that affect you, know I'd take a risk on you.
When you try and overcome the loneliness you feel, know I'd take a risk on you.

When you feel down, know I'd take a risk on you.
If and when you feel broken, know I'd take a risk on you.
When you feel like you're in a dark place, know I'd take a risk ion you.
When you feel like you're struggling, know I'd take a risk on you.

When your inner cries take its toll on you, know I'd take a risk on you.
When you don't feel strong enough, know I'd take a risk on you.
When you don't feel brave enough, know I'd take a risk on you
When you feel low, know I'd take a risk on you.

When you feel lost in any way, know I'd take a risk on you.
When you need a shoulder to cry on, know I'd take a risk on you.
If and when you don't feel good enough, know I'd take a risk on you.
When you feel like an outsider, know I'd take a risk on you.

If and when you feel rejected, know I'd take a risk on you.

When you feel like giving up, know I'd take a risk on you.
If and when you feel unwanted, know I'd take a risk on you.
If and when you feel worthless, know I'd take a risk on you.

When you feel like your entering an unknown trap, know I'd take a risk on you.
When you feel like you're in denial, know I'd take a risk on you.
If and when you have nowhere to turn, know I'd take a risk on you.
If and when you don't feel you have the courage to fight, know I'd take a risk on you.

If and when you feel insecure, know I'd take a risk on you.
If and when you feel guilt, know I'd take a risk on you.
When you are not yourself, know I'd take a risk on you.

When you feel alone, know I'd take a risk on you.
When you face challenging days, I will walk alongside you and know I'd take a risk on you.
If and when you need to vent, know I'd take a risk on you.

Pick Up The Pieces

When you look back at your fragile past know I'd pick up the pieces.
When you face your lifelong fears, know I'd pick up the pieces.
When you try and break your lifelong issues that affect you, know I'd pick up the pieces.
When you try and overcome the loneliness you feel, know I'd pick up the pieces.

When you feel down, know I'd pick up the pieces.
If and when you feel broken, know I'd pick up the pieces.
When you feel like you're in a dark place, know I'd pick up the pieces.
When you feel like you're struggling, know I'd pick up the pieces.

When your inner cries take its toll on you, know I'd pick up the pieces.
When you don't feel strong enough, know I'd pick up the pieces.
When you don't feel brave enough, know I'd pick up the pieces.
When you feel low, know I'd pick up the pieces.

When you feel lost in any way, know I'd pick up the pieces.
When you need a shoulder to cry on, know I'd pick up the pieces.
If and when you don't feel good enough, know I'd pick up the pieces.
When you feel like an outsider, know I'd pick up the pieces.

If and when you feel rejected, know I'd pick up the pieces.
When you feel like giving up, know I'd pick up the pieces.
If and when you feel unwanted, know I'd pick up the pieces.
If and when you feel worthless, know I'd pick up the pieces

When you feel like your entering an unknown trap, know I'd pick up the pieces
When you feel like you're in denial, know I'd pick up the pieces.
If and when you have nowhere to turn, know I'd pick up the pieces.
If and when you don't feel you have the courage to fight, know I'd pick up the pieces.

If and when you feel insecure, know I'd pick up the pieces.
If and when you feel guilt, know I'd pick up the pieces.
When you are not yourself, know I'd pick up the pieces.
When you feel alone, know I'd pick up the pieces.
When you face challenging days, I will walk alongside you and pick up the pieces.
If and when you need to vent, know I'd pick up the pieces.

I'd Take A Bullet For You

When you look back at your fragile past know I'd take a bullet for you.
When you face your lifelong fears, know I'd take a bullet for you.
When you try and break your lifelong issues that affect you, know I'd take a bullet for you.
When you try and overcome the loneliness you feel,
know I'd take a bullet for you.

When you feel down, know I'd take a bullet for you.
If and when you feel broken, know I'd take a bullet for you.
When you feel like you're in a dark place, know I'd take a bullet for you.
When you feel like you're struggling, know I'd take a bullet for you.

When your inner cries take its toll on you, know I'd take a bullet for you.
When you don't feel strong enough, know I'd take a bullet for you.
When you don't feel brave enough, know I'd take a bullet for you
When you feel low, know I'd take a bullet for you.

When you feel lost in any way, know I'd take a bullet for you.
When you need a shoulder to cry on, know I'd take a bullet for you.
If and when you don't feel good enough, know I'd take a bullet for you

When you feel like an outsider, know I'd take a bullet for you.

If and when you feel rejected, know I'd take a bullet for you
When you feel like giving up, know I'd take a bullet for you.
If and when you feel unwanted, know I'd take a bullet for you.
If and when you feel worthless, know I'd take a bullet for you.

When you feel like your entering an unknown trap, know I'd take a bullet for you.
When you feel like you're in denial, know I'd take a bullet for you.
If and when you have nowhere to turn, know I'd take a bullet for you.
If and when you don't feel you have the courage to fight, know I'd take a bullet for you.

If and when you feel insecure, know I'd take a bullet for you.
If and when you feel guilt, know I'd take a bullet for you.
When you are not yourself, know I'd take a bullet for you.
When you feel alone, know I'd take a bullet for you.
When you face challenging days, I will walk alongside you and know I'd take a bullet for you. If and when you need to vent, know I'd take a bullet for you.

Be Ur Sidekick

When you look back at your fragile past know I'd be ur sidekick.
When you face your lifelong fears, know I'd be ur sidekick.
When you try and break your lifelong issues that affect you, know I'd be ur sidekick.
When you try and overcome the loneliness you feel, know I'd be ur sidekick.

When you feel down, know I'd be ur sidekick.
If and when you feel broken, know I'd be ur sidekick.
When you feel like you're in a dark place, know I'd be ur sidekick.
When you feel like you're struggling, know I'd be ur sidekick.

When your inner cries take its toll on you, know I'd be ur sidekick.
When you don't feel strong enough, know I'd be ur sidekick.
When you don't feel brave enough, know I'd be ur sidekick.
When you feel low, know I'd be ur sidekick.

When you feel lost in any way, know I'd be ur sidekick.
When you need a shoulder to cry on, know I'd be ur sidekick.
If and when you don't feel good enough, know I'd be ur sidekick.

When you feel like an outsider, know I'd be ur sidekick.

If and when you feel rejected, know I'd be ur sidekick.
When you feel like giving up, know I'd be ur sidekick.
If and when you feel unwanted, know I'd be ur sidekick.
If and when you feel worthless, know I'd be ur sidekick.

When you feel like your entering an unknown trap, know I'd be ur sidekick.
When you feel like you're in denial, know I'd be ur sidekick.
If and when you have nowhere to turn, know I'd be ur sidekick.
If and when you don't feel you have the courage to fight, know I'd be ur sidekick.

If and when you feel insecure, know I'd be ur sidekick.
If and when you feel guilt, know I'd be ur sidekick.
When you are not yourself, know I'd be ur sidekick.
When you feel alone, know I'd be ur sidekick.
When you face challenging days, I will walk alongside you and know I'd be ur sidekick.
If and when you need to vent, know I'd be ur sidekick.

I'd Jump To Ur Defence

When you look back at your fragile past, I'd jump to ur defence.
When you face your lifelong fears, I'd jump to ur defence.
When you try and break your lifelong issues that affect you, I'd jump to ur defence.
When you try and overcome the loneliness you feel, I'd jump to ur defence.

When you feel down, I'd jump to ur defence.
If and when you feel broken, I'd jump to ur defence.
When you feel like you're in a dark place, I'd jump to ur defence.
When you feel like you're struggling, I'd jump to ur defence.

When your inner cries take its toll on you, I'd jump to ur defence.
When you don't feel strong enough, I'd jump to ur defence.
When you don't feel brave enough, I'd jump to ur defence.
When you feel low, I'd jump to ur defence.

When you feel lost in any way, I'd jump to ur defence.
When you need a shoulder to cry on, I'd jump to ur defence.

If and when you don't feel good enough, I'd jump to ur defence.
When you feel like an outsider, I'd jump to ur defence.

If and when you feel rejected, I'd jump to ur defence.
When you feel like giving up, I'd jump to ur defence.
If and when you feel unwanted, I'd jump to ur defence.
If and when you feel worthless, I'd jump to ur defence.

When you feel like you're entering an unknown trap, I'd jump to ur defence.
When you feel like you're in denial, I'd jump to ur defence.
If and when you have nowhere to turn, I'd jump to ur defence.
If and when you don't feel you have the courage to fight, I'd jump to ur defence.

If and when you feel insecure, I'd jump to ur defence.
If and when you feel guilt, I'd jump to ur defence.
When you are not yourself, I'd jump to ur defence.
When you feel alone, I'd jump to ur defence.
When you face challenging days, I will walk alongside you and I'd jump to ur defence.
If and when you need to vent, I'd jump to ur defence

Won't Let You Feel Rejected

When you look back at your fragile past know I won't let you feel rejected.
When you face your lifelong fears, know I won't let you feel rejected.
When you try and break your lifelong issues that affect you, know I won't let you feel rejected.
When you try and overcome the loneliness you feel, know I won't let you feel rejected.
When you feel down, know I won't let you feel rejected.
If and when you feel broken, know I won't let you feel rejected.
When you feel like you're in a dark place, know I won't let you feel rejected.
When you feel like you're struggling, know I won't let you feel rejected.

When your inner cries take its toll on you, know I won't let you feel rejected.
When you don't feel strong enough, know I won't let you feel rejected.
When you don't feel brave enough, know I won't let you feel rejected.
When you feel low, know I won't let you feel rejected.

When you feel lost in any way, know I won't let you feel rejected.
When you need a shoulder to cry on, know I won't let you feel rejected.
If and when you don't feel good enough, know I won't let you feel rejected.

When you feel like an outsider, know I won't let you feel rejected.

If and when you feel rejected, know I won't let you feel rejected.
When you feel like giving up, know I won't let you feel rejected.
If and when you feel unwanted, know I won't let you feel rejected.
If and when you feel worthless, know I won't let you feel rejected.

When you feel like your entering an unknown trap, know I won't let you feel rejected.
When you feel like you're in denial, know I won't let you feel rejected.
If and when you have nowhere to turn, know I won't let you feel rejected.
If and when you don't feel you have the courage to fight, know I won't let you feel rejected.

If and when you feel insecure, know I won't let you feel rejected.
If and when you feel guilt, know I won't let you feel rejected.
When you are not yourself, know I won't let you feel rejected.

When you feel alone, know I won't let you feel rejected.
When you face challenging days, I will walk alongside you and know I won't let you feel rejected
If and when you need to vent, know I won't let you feel rejected.

Only You Can

Only you can give me hope
Only you can give me strength
Only you can keep me on the straight and narrow
Only you can see when I feel down
Only you can see when I don't feel strong enough
Only you can see the strain I put on myself
only you can get me to do things I don't usually do or try
Only you can get me to open up
Only you can see when I'm not myself
Only you can inspire me like you do
Only you can read my mind
Only you know the way I hurt
Only you know how to make my day
Only you know how to make me smile
Only you know how to get me out of my comfort zone
Only you know that being around you I am the happiest I've ever been
Only you know when I need you
Only you know the pain I endured

Only you know the battles I face
Only you know that I turn my life around because you showed me I can
Only you know the dreams I achieve
Only you know how much I want to prove to the people that didn't want to take a risk on me that I am worth the risk
Only you know how much I struggled
Only you know how much I've had to overcame to get this far
Only you know the dark times I've been through
Only you know the way I thrive
Only you know how determined I am to get what I want
Only you know I will do what I have to get heard

It's Hard To Admit

When I look back at your fragile past, it's hard to admit.
When I face my lifelong fears, it's hard to admit.
When I try and break my lifelong issues that affect me. It's hard to admit.
When I try and overcome the loneliness I feel, it's hard to admit.

When I feel down, it's hard to admit.
If and when I feel broken, it's hard to admit.
When I feel like I'm in a dark place, it's hard to admit.
When I feel like I'm struggling, it's hard to admit.

When my inner cries take its toll on me, it's hard to admit.
When I don't feel strong enough, it's hard to admit.
When I don't feel brave enough, it's hard to admit.
When I feel low, it's hard to admit.

When I feel lost in any way, it's hard to admit.
When I need a shoulder to cry on, it's hard to admit.
If and when I don't feel good enough, it's hard to admit.
When I feel like an outsider, it's hard to admit.

If and when I feel rejected, it's hard to admit.
When I feel like giving up, it's hard to admit.
If and when I feel unwanted, it's hard to admit.
If and when I feel worthless, it's hard to admit.

When I feel like I'm entering an unknown trap, it's hard to admit.
When I feel like I'm in denial, it's hard to admit.

If and when I have nowhere to turn, it's hard to admit.
If and when I don't feel I have the courage to fight, it's hard to admit.

If and when I feel insecure, it's hard to admit.
If and when I feel guilt, it's hard to admit.
When I need you the most, it's hard to admit.
When I am not myself, it's hard to admit.
When I feel alone, it's hard to admit.
When I face challenging days, you will walk alongside me and it's hard to admit.
If and when I need to vent, it's hard to admit.

Bring Me Back From The Edge

When I look back at my fragile past, you bring me back from the edge.
When I face my lifelong fears, you bring me back from the edge.
When I try and break my lifelong issues that affect me. You bring me back from the edge.
When I try and overcome the loneliness I feel, you bring me back from the edge.

When I feel down, you bring me back from the edge.
If and when I feel broken, you bring me back from the edge.
When I feel like I'm in a dark place, you bring me back from the edge.
When I feel like I'm struggling, you bring me back from the edge.

When my inner cries take its toll on me, you bring me back from the edge.
When I don't feel strong enough, you bring me back from the edge.
When I don't feel brave enough, you bring me back from the edge.
When I feel low, you bring me back from the edge.

When I feel lost in any way, you bring me back from the edge.
 When I need a shoulder to cry on, you bring me back from the edge.
If and when I don't feel good enough, you bring me back from the edge.
When I feel like an outsider, you bring me back from the edge.

If and when I feel rejected, you bring me back from the edge.
When I feel like giving up, you bring me back from the edge.
If and when I feel unwanted, you bring me back from the edge.
If and when I feel worthless, you bring me back from the edge.

When I feel like I'm entering an unknown trap, you bring me back from the edge.

When i feel like I'm in denial, you bring me back from the edge.
If and when I have nowhere to turn, you bring me back from the edge.
If and when I don't feel I have the courage to fight, you bring me back from the edge.

If and when I feel insecure, you bring me back from the edge.
If and when I feel guilt, you bring me back from the edge.
When I need you the most, you bring me back from the edge.
When I am not myself, you bring me back from the edge.
When I feel alone, you bring me back from the edge.
When I face challenging days, you will walk alongside me and you bring me back from the edge.
If and when I need to vent, you bring me back from the edge.

Don't Have To Say A Word I'll Know

When you look back at your fragile past, you don't have to say a word I'll know.
When you face your lifelong fears, you don't have to say a word I'll know.
When you try and break your lifelong issues that affect you. You don't have to say a word I'll know.
When you try and overcome the loneliness you feel, you don't have to say a word I'll know.

When you feel down, you don't have to say a word I'll know.
If and when you feel broken, you don't have to say a word I'll know.
When you feel like you're in a dark place, you don't have to say a word I'll know.
When you feel like you're struggling, you don't have to say a word I'll know.

When your inner cries take its toll on you, you don't have to say a word I'll know.
When you don't feel strong enough, you don't have to say a word I'll know.
When you don't feel brave enough, you don't have to say a word I'll know.
When you feel low, you don't have to say a word I'll know.

When you feel lost in any way, you don't have to say a word I'll know
When you need a shoulder to cry on, you don't have to say a word I'll know
If and when you don't feel good enough, you don't have to say a word I'll know.
When you feel like an outsider, you don't have to say a word I'll know.
If and when you feel rejected, you don't have to say a word I'll know.
When you feel like giving up, you don't have to say a word I'll know.

If and when you feel unwanted, you don't have to say a word I'll know.
If and when you feel worthless, you don't have to say a word I'll know.

When you feel like you're entering an unknown trap, you don't have to say a word I'll know.
When you feel like you're in denial, you don't have to say a word I'll know.
If and when you have nowhere to turn, you don't have to say a word I'll know.
If and when you don't feel you have the courage to fright, you don't have to say a word I'll know.

If and when you feel insecure, you don't have to say a word I'll know.
If and when you feel guilt, you don't have to say a word I'll know.
When you need me the most, you don't have to say a word I'll know.
When you are not yourself, you don't have to say a word I'll know.
When you feel alone, you don't have to say a word I'll know
When you face challenging days, I will walk alongside YOU and you don't have to say a word I'll know.
If and when you need to vent, you don't have to say a word I'll know.

You Are Not Invisible To Me

When you look back at your fragile past, you are not invisible to me
When you face your lifelong fears, you are not invisible to me.
When you try and break your lifelong issues that affect you. You are not invisible to me.
When you try and overcome the loneliness you feel, you are not invisible to me.

When you feel down, you are not invisible to me.
If and when you feel broken, you are not invisible to me.
When you feel like you're in a dark place you are not invisible to me.
When you feel like you're struggling, you are not invisible to me.

When your inner cries take its toll on you, you are not invisible to me.
When you don't feel strong enough, you are not invisible to me.
When you don't feel brave enough, you are not invisible to me
When you feel low, you are not invisible to me.

When you feel lost in any way, you are not invisible to me.
When you need a shoulder to cry on, you are not invisible to me.
If and when you don't feel good enough, you are not invisible to me.
When you feel like an outsider, you are not invisible to me.

If and when you feel rejected, you are not invisible to me.
When you feel like giving up, you are not invisible to me.
If and when you feel unwanted, you are not invisible to me.
If and when you feel worthless, you are not invisible to me.

When you feel like you're entering an unknown trap, you are not invisible to me.
When you feel like you're in denial, you are not invisible to me.
If and when you have nowhere to turn, you are not invisible to me.
If and when you don't feel you have the courage to fright, you are not invisible to me.

If and when you feel insecure, you are not invisible to me.
If and when you feel guilt, you are not invisible to me.
When you need me the most, you are not invisible to me.
When you are not yourself, you are not invisible to me.
When you feel alone, you are not invisible to me.
When you face challenging days, I will walk alongside you and you are not invisible to me
If and when you need to vent, you are not invisible to me.

Give In

When you look back at your fragile past, I won't let you give in.
When you face your lifelong fears, I won't let you give in.
When you try and break your lifelong issues that affect you. I won't let you give in.
When you try and overcome the loneliness you feel, I won't let you give in.

When you feel down, I won't let you give in.
If and when you feel broken, I won't let you give in,
When you feel like you're in a dark place, I won't let you give in.
When you feel like you're struggling, I won't let you give in.

When your inner cries take its toll on you, I won't let you give in.
When you don't feel strong enough, I won't let you give in.
When you don't feel brave enough, I won't let you give in.
When you feel low, I won't let you give in.

When you feel lost in any way, I won't let you give in,
When you need a shoulder to cry on, I won't let you give in.
If and when you don't feel good enough, I won't let you give in.

When you feel like an outsider, I won't let you give in.
If and when you feel rejected, I won't let you give in.
When you feel like giving up, I won't let you give in.
If and when you feel unwanted, I won't let you give in.
If and when you feel worthless, I won't let you give in.

When you feel like you're entering an unknown trap, I won't let you give in.
When you feel like you're in denial, I won't let you give in.
If and when you have nowhere to turn, I won't let you give in.
If and when you don't feel you have the courage to fright, I won't let you give in.

If and when you feel insecure, I won't let you give in.
If and when you feel guilt, I won't let you give in,
When you need me the most, I won't let you give in.
When you are not yourself, I won't let you give in.
When you feel alone, I won't let you give in,
When you face challenging days, I will walk alongside you and I won't let you give in.
If and when you need to vent, I won't let you give in.

Won't Leave You Out In The Cold

When you look back at your fragile past, I won't leave you out in the cold.
When you face your lifelong fears, I won't leave you out in the cold.
When you try and break your lifelong issues that affect you. I won't leave you out in the cold.
When you try and overcome the loneliness you feel, I won't leave you out in the cold.

When you feel down, I won't leave you out in the cold.
If and when you feel broken, I won't leave you out in the cold.
When you feel like you're in a dark place, I won't leave you out In the cold.
When you feel like you're struggling, I won't leave you out in the cold.

When your inner cries take its toll on you, I won't leave you out in the cold.
When you don't feel strong enough, I won't leave you out in the cold.
When you don't feel brave enough, I won't leave you out in the cold.
When you feel low, I won't leave you out in the cold.

When you feel lost in any way, I won't leave you out in the cold.
When you need a shoulder to cry on, I won't leave you out in the cold.
If and when you don't feel good enough, I won't leave you out in the cold.

When you feel like an outsider, I won't leave you out in the cold.
If and when you feel rejected, I won't leave you out in the cold
When you feel like giving up, I won't leave you out in the cold.
If and when you feel unwanted, I won't leave you out in the cold.
If and when you feel worthless, I won't leave you out in the cold.

When you feel like you're entering an unknown trap, I won't leave you out in the cold.
When you feel like you're in denial, I won't leave you out in the cold.
If and when you have nowhere to turn, I won't leave you out in the cold.
If and when you don't feel you have the courage to fright, I won't leave you out in the cold.

If and when you feel insecure, I won't leave you out in the cold.
If and when you feel guilt, I won't leave you out in the cold.
When you need me the most, I won't leave you out in the cold.
When you are not yourself, I won't leave you out in the cold.
When you feel alone, I won't leave you out in the cold.
When you face challenging days, I will walk alongside you and I won't leave you out in the cold.
If and when you need to vent, I won't leave you out in the cold.

I'll Be Ur Safe Place

When you look back at your fragile past, I'll be your safe place.
When you face your lifelong fears, I'll be your safe place.
When you try and break your lifelong issues that affect you, I'll l be your safe place.
When you try and overcome the loneliness you feel, I'll be your safe place.

When you feel down, I'll be your safe place.
If and when you feel broken, I'll be your safe place.
When you feel like you're in a dark place, I'll be your safe place.
When you feel like you're struggling, I'll be your safe place.

When your inner cries take its toll on you, I'll be your safe place.
When you don't feel strong enough, I'll be your safe place.
When you don't feel brave enough, I'll be your safe place.
When you feel low, I'll be your safe place.

When you feel lost in any way, I'll be your safe place.
When you need a shoulder to cry on, I'll be your safe place.

If and when you don't feel good enough, I'll be your safe place.
When you feel like an outsider, I'll be your safe place.
If and when you feel rejected, I'll be your safe place.
When you feel like giving up, I'll be your safe place.
If and when you feel unwanted, I'll be your safe place.
If and when you feel worthless, I'll be your safe place.

When you feel like you're entering an unknown trap, I'll be your safe place.
When you feel like you're in denial, I'll be your safe place.
If and when you have nowhere to turn, I'll be your safe place.
If and when you don't feel you have the courage to fright, I'll be your safe place.
If and when you feel insecure, I'll be your safe place.
If and when you feel guilt, I'll be your safe place.
When you need me the most, I'll be your safe place.
When you are not yourself, I'll be your safe place.
When you feel alone, I'll be your safe place.
When you face challenging days, I will walk alongside you and I'll be your safe place.
If and when you need to vent, I'll be your safe place.

I'll Be Ur Lifeline

When you look back at your fragile past, I'll be your lifeline.
When you face your lifelong fears, I'll be your lifeline.
When you try and break your lifelong issues that affect you. I'll be your lifeline.
When you try and overcome the loneliness you feel, I'll be your lifeline.

When you feel down, I'll be your lifeline.
If and when you feel broken, I'll be your lifeline.
When you feel like you're in a dark place, I'll be your lifeline.
When you feel like you're struggling, I'll be your lifeline.

When your inner cries take its toll on you, I'll be your lifeline.
When you don't feel strong enough, I'll be your lifeline.
When you don't feel brave enough, I'll be your lifeline.
When you feel low, I'll be your lifeline.

When you feel lost in any way, I'll be your lifeline.
When you need a shoulder to cry on, I'll be your lifeline.
If and when you don't feel good enough, I'll be your lifeline.
When you feel like an outsider, I'll be your lifeline.

If and when you feel rejected, I'll be your lifeline.
When you feel like giving up, I'll be your lifeline.
If and when you feel unwanted, I'll be your lifeline.
If and when you feel worthless, I'll be your lifeline.

When you feel like you're entering an unknown trap, I'll be your lifeline.
When you feel like you're in denial, I'll be your lifeline.
If and when you have nowhere to turn, I'll be your lifeline.
If and when you don't feel you have the courage to fright, I'll be your lifeline.
If and when you feel insecure, I'll be your lifeline.
If and when you feel guilt, I'll be your lifeline.
When you need me the most, I'll be your lifeline.
When you are not yourself, I'll be your lifeline.
When you feel alone, I'll be your lifeline.
When you face challenging days, I will walk alongside you and I'll be your lifeline.
If and when you need to vent, I'll be your lifeline

Give Up

When you look back at your fragile past, I won't let you give up.
When you face your lifelong fears, I won't let you give up.
When you try and break your lifelong issues that affect you. I won't let you give up.
When you try and overcome the loneliness you feel, I won't let you give up.

When you feel down, I won't let you give up.
If and when you feel broken, I won't let you give up.
When you feel like you're in a dark place, I won't let you give up.
When you feel like you're struggling, I won't let you give up.

When your inner cries take its toll on you, I won't let you give up.
When you don't feel strong enough, I won't let you give up.
When you don't feel brave enough, I won't let you give up.
When you feel low, I won't let you give up.

When you feel lost in any way, I won't let you give up.
When you need a shoulder to cry on, I won't let you give up.
If and when you don't feel good enough, I won't let you give up.
When you feel like an outsider, I won't let you give up.
If and when you feel rejected, I won't let you give up.

When you feel like giving up, I won't let you give up.
If and when you feel unwanted, I won't let you give up.
If and when you feel worthless, I won't let you give up.

When you feel like you're entering an unknown trap, I won't let you give up.
When you feel like you're in denial, I won't let you give up.
If and when you have nowhere to turn, I won't let you give up.
If and when you don't feel you have the courage to fright, I won't let you give up.
If and when you feel insecure, I won't let you give up.
If and when you feel guilt, I won't let you give up.
When you need me the most, I won't let you give up.
When you are not yourself, I won't let you give up.
When you feel alone, I won't let you give up.
When you face challenging days, I will walk alongside you and I won't let you give up.
If and when you need to vent, I won't let you give up.

I'll Be Ur U Turn

When you look back at your fragile past, I'll be your u turn,
When you face your lifelong fears, I'll be your u turn,
When you try and break your lifelong issues that affect you. I'll be your u turn.
When you try and overcome the loneliness you feel, I'll be your u turn

When you feel down, I'll be your u turn.
If and when you feel broken, I'll be your u turn.
When you feel like you're in a dark place, I'll be your u turn
When you feel like you're struggling, I'll be your u turn.

When your inner cries take its toll on you, I'll be your u turn.
When you don't feel strong enough, I'll be your u turn,
When you don't feel brave enough, I'll be your u turn.
When you feel low, I'll be your u turn.

When you feel lost in any way, I'll be your u turn.
When you need a shoulder to cry on, I'll be your u turn.
If and when you don't feel good enough, I'll be your u turn.
When you feel like an outsider, I'll be your u turn.
If and when you feel rejected, I'll be your u turn
When you feel like giving up, I'll be your u turn.
If and when you feel unwanted, I'll be your u turn.

If and when you feel worthless, I'll be your u turn.

When you feel like you're entering an unknown trap, I'll be your u turn.
When you feel like you're in denial, I'll be your u turn.
If and when you have nowhere to turn, I'll be your u turn.
If and when you don't feel you have the courage to fright, I'll be your u turn.
If and when you feel insecure, I'll be your u turn.
If and when you feel guilt, I'll be your u turn.
When you need me the most, I'll be your u turn.
When you are not yourself, I'll be your u turn.
When you feel alone, I'll be your u turn.
When you face challenging days, I will walk alongside you and I'll be your u turn.
If and when you need to vent, I'll be your u turn

Won't Be Far

When you look back at your fragile past, I won't be far.
When you face your lifelong fears, I won't be far.
When you try and break your lifelong issues that affect you. I won't be far.
When you try and overcome the loneliness you feel, I won't be far.

When you feel down, I won't be far.
If and when you feel broken, I won't be far.
When you feel like you're in a dark place, I won't be far.
When you feel like you're struggling, I won't be far.

When your inner cries take its toll on you, I won't be far.
When you don't feel strong enough, I won't be far.
When you don't feel brave enough, I won't be far.
When you feel low, I won't be far.

When you feel lost in any way, I won't be far.
When you need a shoulder to cry on, I won't be far.
If and when you don't feel good enough, I won't be far.
When you feel like an outsider, I won't be far.
If and when you feel rejected, I won't be far.
When you feel like giving up, I won't be far.
If and when you feel unwanted, I won't be far.
If and when you feel worthless, I won't be far.

When you feel like you're entering an unknown trap, I won't be far.
When you feel like you're in denial, I won't be far.
If and when you have nowhere to turn, I won't be far.
If and when you don't feel you have the courage to fright, I won't be far.
If and when you feel insecure, I won't be far.
If and when you feel guilt, I won't be far.
When you need me the most, I won't be far.
When you are not yourself, I won't be far.
When you feel alone, I won't be far.
When you face challenging days, I will walk alongside you and I won't be far.
If and when you need to vent, I won't be far.

I'll Be With You Every Step Of The Way

When you look back at your fragile past, I'll be with you every step of the way.
When you face your lifelong fears, I'll be with you every step of the way.
When you try and break your lifelong issues that affect you. I'll be with you every step of the way.
When you try and overcome the loneliness you feel, I'll be with you every step of the way.

When you feel down, I'll be with you every step of the way.
If and when you feel broken, I'll be with you every step of the way.
When you feel like you're in a dark place, I'll be with you every step of the way,
When you feel like you're struggling, I'll be with you every step of the way.

When your inner cries take its toll on you, I'll be with you every step of the way.
When you don't feel strong enough, I'll be with you every step of the way,
When you don't feel brave enough, I'll be with you every step of the way.
When you feel low, I'll be with you every step of the way.

When you feel lost in any way, I'll be with you every step of the way.
When you need a shoulder to cry on, I'll be with you every step of the way.
If and when you don't feel good enough, I'll be with you every step of the way.
When you feel like an outsider, I'll be with you every step of the way.
If and when you feel rejected, I'll be with you every step of the way.
When you feel like giving up, I'll be with you every step of the way.
If and when you feel unwanted, I'll be with you every step of the way.
If and when you feel worthless, I'll be with you every step of the way.

When you feel like you're entering an unknown trap, I'll be with you every step of the way.
 When you feel like you're in denial, I'll be with you every step of the way.
If and when you have nowhere to turn, I'll be with you every step of the way.
If and when you don't feel you have the courage to fright, I'll be with you every step of the way.
If and when you feel insecure, I'll be with you every step of the way.
If and when you feel guilt, I'll be with you every step of the way.
When you need me the most, I'll be with you every step of the way.
When you are not yourself, I'll be with you every step of the way.
When you feel alone, I'll be with you every step of the way.
When you face challenging days, I will walk alongside you I'll be with you every step of the way.
If and when you need to vent, I'll be with you every step of the way.

Won't Let You Quit

When you look back at your fragile past, I won't let you quit.
When you face your lifelong fears, I won't let you quit.
When you try and break your lifelong issues that affect you. I won't let you quit.
When you try and overcome the loneliness you feel, I won't let you quit

When you feel down, I won't let you quit.
If and when you feel broken, I won't let you quit.
When you feel like you're in a dark place, I won't let you quit.
When you feel like you're struggling, I won't let you quit.

When your inner cries take its toll on you, I won't let you quit.
When you don't feel strong enough, I won't let you quit.
When you don't feel brave enough, I won't let you quit.
When you feel low, I won't let you quit.

When you feel lost in any way, I won't let you quit.
When you need a shoulder to cry on, I won't let you quit.
If and when you don't feel good enough, I won't let you quit.
When you feel like an outsider, I won't let you quit.
If and when you feel rejected, I won't let you quit.
When you feel like giving up, I won't let you quit.
If and when you feel unwanted, I won't let you quit.
If and when you feel worthless, I won't let you quit.

When you feel like you're entering an unknown trap, I won't let you quit.
When you feel like you're in denial, I won't let you quit.
If and when you have nowhere to turn, I won't let you quit.
If and when you don't feel you have the courage to fright, I won't let you quit.
If and when you feel insecure, I won't let you quit.
If and when you feel guilt, I won't let you quit.
When you need me the most, I won't let you quit.
When you are not yourself, I won't let you quit.
When you feel alone, I won't let you quit.
When you face challenging days, I will walk alongside you and I won't let you quit.
If and when you need to vent, I won't let you quit.

VBBS

The VBBS is amazing
The VBBS is incredible
The VBBS is brilliant
The VBBS is out of this world
The VBBS is fabulous
The VBBS is remarkable
The VBBS is simply the best
The VBBS is tremendous
The VBBS is spectacular
The VBBS is terrific
The VBBS is fantastic
The VBBS is extremely extraordinary
The VBBS is joyful
The VBBS is wonderful
The VBBS is marvellous
The VBBS is the highlight of my mornings & days
The VBBS is great
The VBBS is one in a million
The VBBS always makes my day
The VBBS is Awesome
The VBBS is magnificent
The VBBS is extremely exceptional
The VBBS is so legendary
The VBBS is so breath taking
The VBBS is so sensational

The VBBS outstanding
The VBBS is a thousand times better than any other show
The VBBS is so superb
The VBBS is so uplifting
The VBBS sometimes leaves me speechless
The VBBS is so upbeat
The VBBS is so energetic
The VBBS is so epic
The VBBS amazes me.

I Know

I know I'm fragile
I know I'm messed up
I know I'm not as strong as I make out
I know I'm not as brave as I make out
I know I feel like not worth the risk
I know I feel rejected
I know I feel unwanted
I know I don't feel good enough
I know I'm damaged
I know I'm a disappointment
I know I am not perfect
I know I am not going to turn out the way you want
I know you are ashamed of me
I know I'm invisible to you
I know I don't belong in your eyes
I know I don't exist in your eyes.
I know I feel like a nobody
I know I am not the daughter you see as your child
I know I am not the person you thought I'd be.
I know you don't want to see me thrive
I know you don't want to see the best in me
I know I feel ignored as if I am not there
I know I am not important to you
I know all I feel is hurt
I know all I feel is pain on the inside
I know I feel like I've been stabbed in the back
by those who don't care about me
I know I let out a side of me that you hate seeing

but its coz you made me this way
I know you don't care about me.
I know I feel broken on the inside
I know I have a dark side of me that I show to only people who let me down,

Good In Me Only You Can See

When I look back at my fragile past know there is good in me and ur the only one that sees it in me.
When I face my lifelong fears, know there is good in me and ur the only one that sees it in me.
When I try and break my lifelong issues that affect me, know there is good in me and ur the only one that sees it in me.
When I try and overcome the loneliness I feel, know there is good in me and ur the only one that sees it in me.
When I feel down know there is good in me and ur the only one that sees it in me.
If and when I feel broken know there is good in me and ur the only one that sees it in me.
When I feel like I'm in a dark place know there is good in me and ur the only one that sees it in me.
When I feel like I'm struggling know there is good in me and ur the only one that see it in me.

When my inner cries take its toll on me, know there is good in me and ur the only one that sees it in me.
When I don't feel strong enough know there is good in me and ur the only one that sees it in me.
When I don't feel brave enough know there is good in me and ur the only one that sees it in me.
When I feel low know there is good in me and ur the only one that sees it in me.

When I feel lost in any way know there is good in me and ur the only one that sees it in me.
When I need a shoulder to cry on know there is good in me and ur the only one that sees it in me.
If and when I don't feel good enough know there is good in me and ur the only one that sees it in me.
When I feel like an outsider know there is good in me and ur the only one that sees it in me.

If and when I feel rejected know there is good in me and ur the only one that sees it in me.
When I feel like giving up know there is good in me and ur the only one that sees it in me.
If and when I feel unwanted know there is good in me and ur the only one that sees it in me.
If and when I feel worthless know there is good in me and ur the only one that sees it in me.
When I feel like I'm entering an unknown trap know there is good in me and ur the only one that sees it in me.
When I feel like I'm in denial know there is good in me and ur the only one that sees it in me.
If and when I have nowhere to turn know there is good in me and ur the only one that sees it in me.
If and when I don't feel I have the courage to fight know there is good in me and ur the only one that sees it in me.
If and when I feel insecure know there is good in me and ur the only one that sees it in me.
If and when I feel guilt know there is good in me and ur the only one that sees it in me.
When I need you the most know there is good in me and ur the only one that sees it in me.
When I am not myself know there is good in me and ur the only one that sees it in me.
When I feel alone know there is good in me and ur the only one that sees it in me.
When I face challenging days, you will walk alongside me and know there is good in me and ur the only one that sees it in me.
If and when I need to vent know there is good in me and ur the only one that sees it in me.

Open With You

When I look back at my fragile past, I know I can be open with you.
When I face my lifelong fears, I know I can be open with you.
When I try and break my lifelong issues that affect me, I know I can be open with you.
When I try and overcome the loneliness I feel, I know I can be open with you.

When I feel down, I know I can be open with you.
If and when I feel broken, I know I can be open with you.

When I feel like I'm in a dark place, I know I can be open with you.
When I feel like I'm struggling, I know I can be open with you.

When my inner cries take its toll on me, I know I can be open with you.
When I don't feel strong enough, I know I can be open with you.
When I don't feel brave enough, I know I can open with you.
When I feel low, I know I can be open with you.

When I feel lost in any way, I know I can be open with you.
When I need a shoulder to cry on, I know I can be open with you.
If and when I don't feel good enough, I know I can be open with you.
When I feel like an outsider, I know I can be open with you.
If and when I feel rejected, I know I can be open with you.
When I feel like giving up, I know I can be open with you.
If and when I feel unwanted, I know I can be open with you.
If and when I feel worthless, I know I can be open with you.

When I feel like I am entering an unknown trap I know I can be open with you.
When I feel like I'm in denial, I know I can be open with you.
If and when I have nowhere to turn, I know I can be open with you.
If and when I don't feel I have the courage to fight, I know I can be open with you.
If and when I feel insecure, I know I can be open with you.
If and when I feel guilt in any way, I know I can be open with you.
When I need you the most, I know I can be open with you.
When I am not myself, I know I can be open with you.
When I feel alone, I know I can be open with you.
When I face challenging days, you will walk alongside me and know I can be open with you
If and when I need to vent, I know I can be open with you.

Open With Me

When you look back at your fragile past, know you can be open with me.
When you face your lifelong fears, know you can be open with me.
When you try and break your lifelong issues that affect you, know you can be open with me.
When you try and overcome the loneliness you feel, know you can be open with me.

When you feel down, know you can be open with me.

If and when you feel broken, know you can be open with me.
When you feel like you're in a dark place, know you can be open with me.
When you feel like you're struggling, know you can be open with me.

When your inner cries take its toll on you, know you can be open with me.
When you don't feel strong enough, know you can be open with me.
When you don't feel brave enough, you can be open with me.
When you feel low, know you can be open with me.

When you feel lost in any way, know you can be open with me.
When you need a shoulder to cry on, know you can be open with me.
If and when you don't feel good enough, know you can be open with me.
When you feel like an outsider, know you can be open with me.

If and when you feel rejected, know you can be open with me.
When you feel like giving up, know you can be open with me.
If and when you feel unwanted, know you can be open with me.
If and when you feel worthless, know you can be open with me.
When you feel like you are entering an unknown trap know you can be open with me.
When you feel like you're in denial, know you can be open with me.
If and when you have nowhere to turn, know you can be open with me.
If and when you don't feel you have the courage to fight, know you can be open with me.
If and when you feel insecure, know you can be open with me.
If and when you feel guilt in any way, know you can be open with me.
When you need me the most, know you can be open with me.
When you are not yourself, know you can be open with me.
When you feel alone, know you can be open with me.
When you face challenging days, I will walk alongside you and know you can be open with me.
If and when you need to vent, know you can be open with me.

Keep You On The Straight & Narrow

When you look back at your fragile past, I will keep you on the straight and narrow
When you face your lifelong fears, I will keep you on the straight and narrow.
When you try and break your lifelong issues that affect you, I will keep you on the straight and narrow.

When you try and overcome the loneliness you feel, I will keep you on the straight and narrow.

When you feel down, I will keep you on the straight and narrow.
If and when you feel broken, I will keep you on the straight and narrow.
When you feel like you're in a dark place, I will keep you on the straight and narrow.
When you feel like you're struggling, I will keep you on the straight and narrow.

When your inner cries take its toll on you, I will keep you on the straight and narrow.
When you don't feel strong enough, I will keep you on the straight and narrow.
When you don't feel brave enough, I will keep you on the straight and narrow.
When you feel low, I will keep you on the straight and narrow.

When you feel lost in any way, I will keep you on the straight and narrow.
When you need a shoulder to cry on, I will keep you on the straight and narrow.
If and when you don't feel good enough, I will keep you on the straight and narrow.
When you feel like an outsider, I will keep you on the straight and narrow.

If and when you feel rejected, I will keep you on the straight and narrow.
When you feel like giving up, I will keep you on the straight and narrow.
If and when you feel unwanted, I will keep you on the straight and narrow.
If and when you feel worthless, I will keep you on the straight and narrow.
When you feel like you are entering an unknown trap, I will keep you on the straight and narrow.
When you feel like you're in denial, I will keep you on the straight and narrow.
If and when you have nowhere to turn, I will keep you on the straight and narrow.
If and when you don't feel you have the courage to fight, I will keep you on the straight and narrow.
If and when you feel insecure, I will keep you on the straight and narrow.
If and when you feel guilt in any way, I will keep you on the straight and narrow.
When you need me the most, I will keep you on the straight and narrow.
When you are not yourself, I will keep you on the straight and narrow.
When you feel alone, I will keep you on the straight and narrow.
When you face challenging days, I will walk alongside you and know I will keep you on the straight and narrow.
If and when you need to vent, I will keep you on the straight and narrow.

Keep Me On The Straight & Narrow

When I look back at my fragile past, you keep me on the straight and narrow.
When I face my lifelong fears, you keep me on the straight and narrow.
When I try and break my lifelong issues that affect me, you keep me on the straight and narrow.
When I try and overcome the loneliness I feel, you keep me on the straight and narrow.

When I feel down, you keep me on the straight and narrow.
If and when I feel broken, you keep me on the straight and narrow.
When I feel like I'm in a dark place, you keep me on the straight and narrow.
When I feel like I'm struggling, you keep me on the straight and narrow.

When my inner cries take its toll on me, you keep me on the straight and narrow.
When I don't feel strong enough, you keep me on the straight and narrow.
When I don't feel brave enough, you keep me on the straight and narrow.
When I feel low, you keep me on the straight and narrow.

When I feel lost in any way, you keep me on the straight and narrow.
When I need a shoulder to cry on, you keep me on the straight and narrow.
If and when I don't feel good enough, you keep me on the straight and narrow.
When I feel like an outsider, you keep me on the straight and narrow.

If and when I feel rejected, you keep me on the straight and narrow.
When I feel like giving up, you keep me on the straight and narrow.
If and when I feel unwanted, you keep me on the straight and narrow.
If and when I feel worthless, you keep me on the straight and narrow.

When I feel like I am entering an unknown trap, you keep me on the straight and narrow.
When I feel like I'm in denial, you keep me on the straight and narrow.
If and when I have nowhere to turn, you keep me on the straight and narrow.
If and when I don't feel I have the courage to fight, you keep me on the straight and narrow.
If and when I feel insecure, you keep me on the straight and narrow.
If and when I feel guilt in any way, you keep me on the straight and narrow.
When I need you the most, you keep me on the straight and narrow.
When I am not myself, you keep me on the straight and narrow.
When I feel alone, you keep me on the straight and narrow.
When I face challenging days, you will walk alongside me and you keep me on the straight and narrow.

If and when I need to vent, you keep me on the straight and narrow.

Free Me

When I look back at my fragile past, you know I always feel free as ur the only one that can free me.
When I face my lifelong fears, you know I always feel free as ur the only one that can free me.
When I try and break my lifelong issues that affect me, you know I always feel free as ur the only one that can free me.
When I try and overcome the loneliness I feel, you know I always feel free as ur the only one that can free me.

When I feel down, you know I always feel free as ur the only one that can free me.
If and when I feel broken, you know I always feel free as ur the only one that can free me.
When I feel like I'm in a dark place, you know I always feel free as ur the only one that can free me
When I feel like I'm struggling, you know I always feel free as ur the only one that can free me.

When my inner cries take its toll on me, you know I always feel free as ur the only one that can free me.
When I don't feel strong enough, you know I always feel free as ur the only one that can free me.
When I don't feel brave enough, you know I always feel free as ur the only one that can free me.
When I feel low, you know I always feel free as ur the only one that can free me.

When I feel lost in any way, you know I always feel free as ur the only one that can free me.
When I need a shoulder to cry on, you know I always feel free as ur the only one that can free me.
If and when I don't feel good enough, you know I always feel free as ur the only one that can free me.
When I feel like an outsider, you know I always feel free as ur the only one that can free me.

If and when I feel rejected, you know I always feel free as ur the only one that can free me.

When I feel like giving up, you know I always feel free as ur the only one that can free me.
If and when I feel unwanted, you know I always feel free as ur the only one that can free me.
If and when I feel worthless, you know I always feel free as ur the only one that can free me.
When I feel like I am entering an unknown trap you know I always feel free as ur the only one that can free me
When I feel like I'm in denial, you know I always feel free as ur the only one that can free me.
If and when I have nowhere to turn, you know I always feel free as ur the only one that can free me.
If and when I don't feel I have the courage to fight, you know I always feel free as ur the only one that can free me.
If and when I feel insecure, you know I always feel free as ur the only one that can free me.
If and when I feel guilt in any way, you know I always feel free as ur the only one that can free me.
When I need you the most, you know I always feel free as ur the only one that can free me.
When I am not myself, you know I always feel free as ur the only one that can free me.
When I feel alone, you know I always feel free as ur the only one that can free me.
When I face challenging days, you will walk alongside me and know I always feel free as ur the only one that can free me.
If and when I need to vent, you know I always feel free as ur the only one that can free me

You Are My Rock

When I look back at my fragile past, you are my rock
When I face my lifelong fears, you are my rock.
When I try and break my lifelong issues that affect me, you are my rock
When I try and overcome the loneliness I feel, you are my rock

When I feel down, you are my rock.
If and when I feel broken, you are my rock
When I feel like I'm in a dark place, you are my rock.
When I feel like I'm struggling, you are my rock.

When my inner cries take its toll on me, you are my rock
When I don't feel strong enough, you are my rock.
When I don't feel brave enough, you are my rock.
When I feel low, you are my rock.

When I feel lost in any way, you are my rock.
When I need a shoulder to cry on, you are my rock.
If and when I don't feel good enough, you are my rock.
When I feel like an outsider, you are my rock.

If and when I feel rejected, you are my rock.
When I feel like giving up, you are my rock.
If and when I feel unwanted, you are my rock.
If and when I feel worthless, you are my rock.

When I feel like I am entering an unknown trap you are my rock.
When I feel like I'm in denial, you are my rock.
If and when I have nowhere to turn, you are my rock.
If and when I don't feel I have the courage to fight, you are my rock.
If and when I feel insecure, you are my rock.
If and when I feel guilt in any way, you are my rock.
When I need you the most, you are my rock.
When I am not myself, you are my rock.
When I feel alone, you are my rock.
When I face challenging days, you will walk alongside me and know you are my rock
If and when I need to vent, you are my rock.

Ur Faith In Me

When I look back at my fragile past, I know ur faith in me tells me all I need to know.
When I face my lifelong fears, I know ur faith in me tells me all I need to know.
When I try and break my lifelong issues that affect me, I know ur faith in me tells me all I need to know.
When I try and overcome the loneliness I feel, I know ur faith in me tells me all I need to know.

When I feel down, I know ur faith in me tells me all I need to know.
If and when I feel broken, I know ur faith in me tells me all I need to know.

When I feel like I'm in a dark place, I know ur faith in me tells me all I need to know.
When I feel like I'm struggling, I know ur faith in me tells me all I need to know.
When my inner cries take its toll on me, I know ur faith in me tells me all I need to know
When I don't feel strong enough, I know ur faith in me tells me all I need to know.
When I don't feel brave enough, I know ur faith in me tells me all I need to know.
When I feel low, I know ur faith in me tells me all I need to know.

When I feel lost in any way, I know ur faith in me tells me all I need to know.
When I need a shoulder to cry on, I know ur faith in me tells me all I need to know.
If and when I don't feel good enough, I know ur faith in me tells me all I need to know.
When I feel like an outsider, I know ur faith in me tells me all I need to know.

If and when I feel rejected, I know ur faith in me tells me all I need to know
When I feel like giving up, I know ur faith in me tells me all I need to know.
If and when I feel unwanted, I know ur faith in me tells me all I need to know.
If and when I feel worthless, I know ur faith in me tells me all I need to know

When I feel like I am entering an unknown trap I know ur faith in me tells me all I need to know.
When I feel like I'm in denial, I know ur faith in me tells me all I need to know.
If and when I have nowhere to turn, I know ur faith in me tells me all I need to know.
If and when I don't feel I have the courage to fight, I know ur faith in me tells me all I need to know.
If and when I feel insecure, I know ur faith in me tells me all I need to know.
If and when I feel guilt in any way, I know ur faith in me tells me all I need to know.
When I need you the most, I know ur faith in me tells me all I need to know.
When I am not myself, I know ur faith in me tells me all I need to know.
When I feel alone, I know ur faith in me tells me all I need to know.
When I face challenging days, you will walk alongside me and know ur faith in me tells me all I need to know.
If and when I need to vent, I know ur faith in me tells me all I need to know.

Don't Have To Cry On The Inside

When I look back at my fragile past, I know when ur around I don't have to cry on the inside.
When I face my lifelong fears, I know when ur around I don't have to cry on the inside
When I try and break my lifelong issues that affect me, I know when ur around I don't have to cry on the inside.
When I try and overcome the loneliness I feel, I know when ur around I don't have to cry on the inside.

When I feel down, I know when ur around I don't have to cry on the inside.
If and when I feel broken, I know when ur around I don't have to cry on the inside.
When I feel like I'm in a dark place, I know when ur around I don't have to cry on the inside.
When I feel like I'm struggling, I know when ur around I don't have to cry on the inside.

When my inner cries take its toll on me, I know when ur around I don't have to cry on the inside.
When I don't feel strong enough, I know when ur around I don't have to cry on the inside.
When I don't feel brave enough, I know when ur around I don't have to cry on the inside.
When I feel low, I know when ur around I don't have to cry on the inside.

When I feel lost in any way, I know when ur around I don't have to cry on the inside
When I need a shoulder to cry on, I know when ur around I don't have to cry on the inside.
If and when I don't feel good enough, I know when ur around I don't have to cry on the inside.
When I feel like an outsider, I know when ur around I don't have to cry on the inside.

If and when I feel rejected, I know when ur around I don't have to cry on the inside.
When I feel like giving up, I know when ur around I don't have to cry on the inside.
If and when I feel unwanted, I know when ur around I don't have to cry on the inside.

If and when I feel worthless, I know when ur around I don't have to cry on the inside.

When I feel like I am entering an unknown trap I know when ur around I don't have to cry on the inside.
When I feel like I'm in denial, I know when ur around I don't have to cry on the inside.
If and when I have nowhere to turn, I know when ur around I don't have to cry on the inside.
If and when I don't feel I have the courage to fight, I know when ur around I don't have to cry on the inside.
If and when I feel insecure, I know when ur around I don't have to cry on the inside.
If and when I feel guilt in any way, I know when ur around I don't have to cry on the inside.
When I need you the most, I know when ur around I don't have to cry on the inside.
When I am not myself, I know when ur around I don't have to cry on the inside.
When I feel alone, I know when ur around I don't have to cry on the inside.
When I face challenging days, you will walk alongside me and know when ur around I don't have to cry on the inside.
If and when I need to vent, I know when ur around I don't have to cry on the inside.

My Emotional Strain

When I look back at my fragile past, I know you will take away my emotional strain.
When I face my lifelong fears, I know you will take away my emotional strain.
When I try and break my lifelong issues that affect me, I know you will take away my emotional strain.
When I try and overcome the loneliness I feel, I know you will take away my emotional strain.

When I feel down, I know you will take away my emotional strain.
If and when I feel broken, I know you will take away my emotional strain.
When I feel like I'm in a dark place, I know you will take away my emotional strain.
When I feel like I'm struggling, I know you will take away my emotional strain.

When my inner cries take its toll on me, I know you will take away my emotional strain.
When I don't feel strong enough, I know you will take away my emotional strain.
When I don't feel brave enough, I know you will take away my emotional strain.
When I feel low, I know you will take away my emotional strain.

When I feel lost in any way, I know you will take away my emotional strain.
When I need a shoulder to cry on, I know you will take away my emotional strain.
If and when I don't feel good enough, I know you will take away my emotional strain.
When I feel like an outsider, I know you will take away my emotional strain.

If and when I feel rejected, I know you will take away my emotional strain.
When I feel like giving up, I know you will take away my emotional strain.
If and when I feel unwanted, I know you will take away my emotional strain.
If and when I feel worthless, I know you will take away my emotional strain.

When I feel like I am entering an unknown trap I know you will take away my emotional strain.
When I feel like I'm in denial, I know you will take away my emotional strain.
If and when I have nowhere to turn, I know you will take away my emotional strain.
If and when I don't feel I have the courage to fight, I know you will take away my emotional strain.
If and when I feel insecure, I know you will take away my emotional strain.
If and when I feel guilt in any way, I know you will take away my emotional strain.
When I need you the most, I know you will take away my emotional strain.
When I am not myself, I know you will take away my emotional strain.
When I feel alone, I know you will take away my emotional strain.
When I face challenging days, you will walk alongside me and know you will take away my emotional strain.
If and when I need to vent, I know you will take away my emotional strain.

Won't Leave My Side

When I look back at my fragile past, I know you won't leave my side.
When I face my lifelong fears, I know you won't leave my side.
When I try and break my lifelong issues that affect me, I know you won't leave my side.
When I try and overcome the loneliness I feel, I know you won't leave my side.

When I feel down, I know you won't leave my side.
If and when I feel broken, I know you won't leave my side.
When I feel like I'm in a dark place, I know you won't leave my side.
When I feel like I'm struggling, I know you won't leave my side.

When my inner cries take its toll on me, I know you won't leave my side.
When I don't feel strong enough, I know you won't leave my side.
When I don't feel brave enough, I know you won't leave my side.
When I feel low, I know you won't leave my side.

When I feel lost in any way, I know you won't leave my side.
When I need a shoulder to cry on, I know you won't leave my side.
If and when I don't feel good enough, I know you won't leave my side.
When I feel like an outsider, I know you won't leave my side.

If and when I feel rejected, I know you won't leave my side.
When I feel like giving up, I know you won't leave my side.
If and when I feel unwanted, I know you won't leave my side.
If and when I feel worthless, I know you won't leave my side.

When I feel like I am entering an unknown trap I know you won't leave my side.
When I feel like I'm in denial, I know you won't leave my side.
If and when I have nowhere to turn, I know you won't leave my side.
If and when I don't feel I have the courage to fight, I know you won't leave my side.
If and when I feel insecure, I know you won't leave my side.
If and when I feel guilt in any way, I know you won't leave my side.
When I need you the most, I know you won't leave my side.
When I am not myself, I know you won't leave my side.
When I feel alone, I know you won't leave my side.
When I face challenging days, you will walk alongside me and know you won't leave my side.
If and when I need to vent, I know you won't leave my side.

Help Me Find Purpose

When I look back at my fragile past, you help me find purpose.
When I face my lifelong fears, you help me find purpose.
When I try and break my lifelong issues that affect me, you help me find purpose.
When I try and overcome the loneliness I feel, you help me find purpose.

When I feel down, you help me find purpose.
If and when I feel broken, you help me find purpose.
When I feel like I'm in a dark place, you help me find purpose.
When I feel like I'm struggling, you help me find purpose.

When my inner cries take its toll on me, you help me find purpose.
When I don't feel strong enough, you help me find purpose.
When I don't feel brave enough, you help me find purpose.
When I feel low, you help me find purpose.

When I feel lost in any way, you help me find purpose.
When I need a shoulder to cry on, you help me find purpose.
If and when I don't feel good enough, you help me find purpose.
When I feel like an outsider, you help me find purpose.

If and when I feel rejected, you help me find purpose.
When I feel like giving up, you help me find purpose.
If and when I feel unwanted, you help me find purpose.
If and when I feel worthless, you help me find purpose.
When I feel like I am entering an unknown trap you help me find purpose.
When I feel like I'm in denial, you help me find purpose.
If and when I have nowhere to turn, you help me find purpose.
If and when I don't feel I have the courage to fight, you help me find purpose.
If and when I feel insecure, you help me find purpose.
If and when I feel guilt in any way, you help me find purpose.
When I need you the most, you help me find purpose.
When I am not myself, you help me find purpose.
When I feel alone, you help me find purpose.
When I face challenging days, you will walk alongside me and know you help me find purpose.
If and when I need to vent, you help me find purpose.

Help Me Find My True Calling

When I look back at my fragile past, you help me find my true calling.
When I face my lifelong fears, you help me find my true calling.
When I try and break my lifelong issues that affect me, you help me find my true calling.
When I try and overcome the loneliness I feel, you help me find my true calling.

When I feel down, you help me find my true calling.
If and when I feel broken, you help me find my true calling.
When I feel like I'm in a dark place, you help me find my true calling.
When I feel like I'm struggling, you help me find my true calling.

When my inner cries take its toll on me, you help me find my true calling.
When I don't feel strong enough, you help me find my true calling.
When I don't feel brave enough, you help me find my true calling.
When I feel low, you help me find my true calling.

When I feel lost in any way, you help me find my true calling.
When I need a shoulder to cry on, you help me find my true calling.
If and when I don't feel good enough, you help me find my true calling.
When I feel like an outsider, you help me find my true calling.

If and when I feel rejected, you help me find my true calling.
When I feel like giving up, you help me find my true calling.
If and when I feel unwanted, you help me find my true calling.
If and when I feel worthless, you help me find my true calling.

When I feel like I am entering an unknown trap you help me find my true calling.
When I feel like I'm in denial, you help me find my true calling.
If and when I have nowhere to turn, you help me find my true calling.
If and when I don't feel I have the courage to fight, you help me find my true calling.
If and when I feel insecure, you help me find my true calling.
If and when I feel guilt in any way, you help me find my true calling.
When I need you the most, you help me find my true calling.
When I am not myself, you help me find my true calling.
When I feel alone, you help me find my true calling.
When I face challenging days, you will walk alongside me and you help me find my true calling.
If and when I need to vent, you help me find my true calling.

Proud Of Me No Matter What

When I look back at my fragile past, I know you will always be proud of me no matter what.
When I face my lifelong fears, I know you will always be proud of me no matter what.
When I try and break my lifelong issues that affect me, I know you will always be proud of me no matter what.
When I try and overcome the loneliness I feel, I know you will always be proud of me no matter what.

When I feel down, I know you will always be proud of me no matter what.
If and when I feel broken, I know you will always be proud of me no matter what.
When I feel like I'm in a dark place, I know you will always be proud of me no matter what.
When I feel like I'm struggling, I know you will always be proud of me no matter what.

When my inner cries take its toll on me, I know you will always be proud of me no matter what.
When I don't feel strong enough, I know you will always be proud of me no matter what.
When I don't feel brave enough, I know you will always be proud of me no matter what.
When I feel low, I know you will always be proud of me no matter what.

When I feel lost in any way, I know you will always be proud of me no matter what.
When I need a shoulder to cry on, I know you will always be proud of me no matter what.
If and when I don't feel good enough, I know you will always be proud of me no matter what.
When I feel like an outsider, I know you will always be proud of me no matter what.

If and when I feel rejected, I know you will always be proud of me no matter what.
When I feel like giving up, I know you will always be proud of me no matter what.
If and when I feel unwanted, I know you will always be proud of me no matter what.

If and when I feel worthless, I know you will always be proud of me no matter what.
When I feel like I am entering an unknown trap I know you will always be proud of me no matter what.
When I feel like I'm in denial, I know you will always be proud of me no matter what.
If and when I have nowhere to turn, I know you will always be proud of me no matter what.
If and when I don't feel I have the courage to fight, I know you will always be proud of me no matter what.
If and when I feel insecure, I know you will always be proud of me no matter what.
If and when I feel guilt in any way, I know you will always be proud of me no matter what.
When I need you the most, I know you will always be proud of me no matter what.
When I am not myself, I know you will always be proud of me no matter what.
When I feel alone, I know you will always be proud of me no matter what.
When I face challenging days, you will walk alongside me and know you will always be proud of me no matter what.
If and when I need to vent, I know you will always be proud of me no matter what.

Always Be My Lookout

When I look back at my fragile past, I know you will always be my lookout.
When I face my lifelong fears, I know you will always be my lookout.
When I try and break my lifelong issues that affect me, I know you will always be my lookout.
When I try and overcome the loneliness I feel, I know you will always be my lookout.

When I feel down, I know you will always be my lookout.
If and when I feel broken, I know you will always be my lookout.
When I feel like I'm in a dark place, I know you will always be my lookout.
When I feel like I'm struggling, I know you will always be my lookout.

When my inner cries take its toll on me, I know you will always be my lookout.
When I don't feel strong enough, I know you will always be my lookout.
When I don't feel brave enough, I know you will always be my lookout.
When I feel low, I know you will always be my lookout.

When I feel lost in any way, I know you will always be my lookout.
When I need a shoulder to cry on, I know you will always be my lookout.
If and when I don't feel good enough, I know you will always be my lookout.
When I feel like an outsider, I know you will always be my lookout.

If and when I feel rejected, I know you will always be my lookout.
When I feel like giving up, I know you will always be my lookout.
If and when I feel unwanted, I know you will always be my lookout.
If and when I feel worthless, I know you will always be my lookout.

When I feel like I am entering an unknown trap I know you will always be my lookout.
When I feel like I'm in denial, I know you will always be my lookout.
If and when I have nowhere to turn, I know you will always be my lookout.
If and when I don't feel I have the courage to fight, I know you will always be my lookout.
If and when I feel insecure, I know you will always be my lookout.
If and when I feel guilt in any way, I know you will always be my lookout.
When I need you the most, I know you will always be my lookout.
When I am not myself, I know you will always be my lookout.
When I feel alone, I know you will always be my lookout.
When I face challenging days, you will walk alongside me and know you will always be my lookout.
If and when I need to vent, I know you will always be my lookout.

Proud Of You No Matter What

When you look back at your fragile past, know I will always be proud of you no matter what.
When you face your lifelong fears, know I will always be proud of you no matter what.
When you try and break your lifelong issues that affect you, know I will always be proud of you no matter what.
When you try and overcome the loneliness you feel, know I will always be proud of you no matter what.

When you feel down, know I will always be proud of you no matter what.
If and when you feel broken, know I will always be proud of you no matter what.
When you feel like you're in a dark place, know I will always be proud of you no matter what.

When you feel like you're struggling, know I will always be proud of you no matter what.

When your inner cries take its toll on you, know I will always be proud of you no matter what.
When you don't feel strong enough, know I will always be proud of you no matter what.
When you don't feel brave enough, know I will always be proud of you no matter what.
When you feel low, know I will always be proud off you no matter what.

When you feel lost in any way, know I will always be proud of you no matter what.
When you need a shoulder to cry on, know I will always be proud of you no matter what.
If and when you don't feel good enough, know I will always be proud of you no matter what.
When you feel like an outsider, know I will always be proud of you no matter what.

If and when you feel rejected, know I will always be proud of you no matter what.
When you feel like giving up, know I will always be proud of you no matter what.
If and when you feel unwanted, know I will always be proud of you no matter what.
If and when you feel worthless, know I will always be proud of you no matter what.

When you feel like you are entering an unknown trap know I will always be proud of you no matter what.
When you feel like I'm in denial, know I will always be proud of you no matter what.
If and when you have nowhere to turn, know I will always be proud of you no matter what.
If and when you don't feel you have the courage to fight, know I will always be proud of you no matter what.
If and when you feel insecure, know I will always be proud of you no matter what.
If and when you feel guilt in any way, know I will always be proud of you no matter what

When you need me the most, know I will always be proud of you no matter what.
When you are not yourself, know I will always be proud of you no matter what.
When you feel alone, know I will always be proud of you no matter what.
When you face challenging days, i will walk alongside you and know I will always be proud of you no matter what.
If and when you need to vent, know I will always be proud of you no matter what.

Know Me Inside Out

When I look back at my fragile past, I know I don't have to prove anything to you as you know me inside out.
When I face my lifelong fears, I know I don't have to prove anything to you as you know me inside out.
When I try and break my lifelong issues that affect me, I know I don't have to prove anything to you as you know me inside out.
When I try and overcome the loneliness I feel, I know I don't have to prove anything to you as you know me inside out.

When I feel down, I know I don't have to prove anything to you as you know me inside out.
If and when I feel broken, I know I don't have to prove anything to you as you know me inside out.
When I feel like I'm in a dark place, I know I don't have to prove anything to you as you know me inside out.
When I feel like I'm struggling, I know I don't have to prove anything to you as you know me inside out.

When my inner cries take its toll on me, I know I don't have to prove anything to you as you know me inside out.
When I don't feel strong enough, I know I don't have to prove anything to you as you know me inside out.
When I don't feel brave enough, I know I don't have to prove anything to you as you know me inside out.
When I feel low, I know I don't have to prove anything to you as you know me inside out.

When I feel lost in any way, I know I don't have to prove anything to you as you know me inside out.

When I need a shoulder to cry on, I know I don't have to prove anything to you as you know me inside out.
If and when I don't feel good enough, I know I don't have to prove anything to you as you know me inside out.
When I feel like an outsider, I know I don't have to prove anything to you as you know me inside out.

If and when I feel rejected, I know I don't have to prove anything to you as you know me inside out.
When I feel like giving up, I know I don't have to prove anything to you as you know me inside out.
If and when I feel unwanted, I know I don't have to prove anything to you as you know me inside out.
If and when I feel worthless, I know I don't have to prove anything to you as you know me inside out.
When I feel like I am entering an unknown trap I know I don't have to prove anything to you as you know me inside out.
When I feel like I'm in denial, I know I don't have to prove anything to you as you know me inside out.
If and when I have nowhere to turn, I know I don't have to prove anything to you as you know me inside out.
If and when I don't feel I have the courage to fight, I know I don't have to prove anything to you as you know me inside out.
If and when I feel insecure, I know I don't have to prove anything to you as you know me inside out.
If and when I feel guilt in any way, I know I don't have to prove anything to you as you know me inside out.
When I need you the most, I know I don't have to prove anything to you as you know me inside out.
When I am not myself, I know I don't have to prove anything to you as you know me inside out.
When I feel alone, I know I don't have to prove anything to you as you know me inside out.
When I face challenging days, you will walk alongside me and know I don't have to prove anything to you as you know me inside out.
If and when I need to vent, I know I don't have to prove anything to you as you know me inside out.

Rashma Mehta

Won't Let Me Struggle

When I look back at my fragile past, I know you won't let me struggle.
When I face my lifelong fears, I know you won't let me struggle.
When I try and break my lifelong issues that affect me. I know you won't let me struggle.
When I try and overcome the loneliness I feel, I know you won't let me struggle.

When I feel down, I know you won't let me struggle
If and when I feel broken, I know you won't let me struggle.
When I feel like I'm in a dark place, I know you won't let me Struggle.
When I feel like I'm struggling, I know you won't let me struggle.

When my inner cries take its toll on me, I know you won't let me struggle.
When I don't feel strong enough, I know you won't let me struggle.
When I don't feel brave enough, I know you won't let me struggle.
When I feel low, I know you won't let me struggle.

When I feel lost in any way, I know you won't let me struggle.
When I need a shoulder to cry on, I know you won't let me struggle.
If and when I don't feel good enough, I know you won't let me struggle.
When I feel like an outsider, I know you won't let me struggle.
If and when I feel rejected, I know you won't let me struggle.
When I feel like giving up, I know you won't let me struggle.
If and when I feel unwanted, I know you won't let me struggle.
If and when I feel worthless, I know you won't let me struggle.

When I feel like I'm entering an unknown trap, I know you won't let me struggle.
When I feel like I'm in denial, I know you won't let me struggle.
If and when I have nowhere to turn, I know you won't let me struggle.
If and when I don't feel I have the courage to fright, I know you won't let me struggle.

If and when I feel insecure, I know you won't let me struggle.
If and when I feel guilt, I know you won't let me struggle.
When I need you the most, I know you won't let me struggle.
When I am not myself, I know you won't let me struggle.
When i feel alone, I know you won't let me struggle.
When I face challenging days, you will walk alongside me and I know you won't let me struggle.
If and when I need to vent, I know you won't let me struggle.

Won't Abandon Me

When I look back at my fragile past, I know you will never abandon me
When I face my lifelong fears, I know you will never abandon me
When I try and break my lifelong issues that affect me, I know you will never abandon me
When I try and overcome the loneliness I feel, I know you will never abandon me
When I feel down, I know you will never abandon me
If and when I feel broken, I know you will never abandon me
When I feel like I'm in a dark place, I know you will never abandon me
When I feel like I'm struggling, I know you will never abandon me
When my inner cries take its toll on me, I know you will never abandon me
When I don't feel strong enough, I know you will never abandon me
When I don't feel brave enough, I know you will never abandon me
When I feel low, I know you will never abandon me.
When I feel lost in any way, I know you will never abandon me
When I need a shoulder to cry on, I know you will never abandon me.
If and when I don't feel good enough, I know you will never abandon me

When I feel like an outsider, I know you will never abandon me
If and when I feel rejected, I know you will never abandon me
When I feel like giving up, I know you will never abandon me
If and when I feel unwanted, I know you will never abandon me
If and when I feel worthless, I know you will never abandon me
When I feel like I am entering an unknown trap, I know you will never abandon me.
When I feel like I'm in denial, I know you will never abandon me
If and when I have nowhere to turn, I know you will never abandon me
If and when I don't feel I have the courage to fight, I know you will never abandon me
When I feel insecure, I know you will never abandon me.
If and when I feel guilt in any way, I know you will never abandon me
When I need you the most, I know you will never abandon me
When I am not myself, I know you will never abandon me
When I feel alone, I know you will never abandon me
When I face challenging days, I know you will never abandon me
If and when I need to vent, I know you will never abandon me

Stick By Me Through Thick & Thin

When I look back at my fragile past, I know you will always stick by me through thick & thin.
When I face my lifelong fears, I know you will always stick by me through thick & thin.
When I try and break my lifelong issues that affect me, I know you will always stick by me through thick & thin.
When I try and overcome the loneliness I feel, I know you will always stick by me through thick & thin.
When I feel down, I know you will always stick by me through thick & thin.
If and when I feel broken, I know you will always stick by me through thick & thin.
When I feel like I'm in a dark place, I know you will always stick by me through thick & thin.
When I feel like I'm struggling, I know you will always stick by me through thick & thin.
When my inner cries take its toll on me, I know you will always stick by me through thick & thin.
When I don't feel strong enough, I know you will always stick by me through thick & thin.
When I don't feel brave enough, I know you will always stick by me through thick & thin.
When I feel low, I know you will always stick by me through thick & thin.
When I feel lost in any way, I know you will always stick by me through thick & thin.
When I need a shoulder to cry on, I know you will always stick by me through thick & thin.
If and when I don't feel good enough, I know you will always stick by me through thick & thin.

When I feel like an outsider, I know you will always stick by me through thick & thin.
If and when I feel rejected, I know you will always stick by me through thick & thin.
When i feel like giving up, I know you will always stick by me through thick & thin.
If and when I feel unwanted, I know you will always stick by me through thick & thin.
If and when I feel worthless, I know you will always stick by me through thick & thin.

When I feel like I am entering an unknown trap, I know you will always stick by me through thick & thin.
When I feel like I'm in denial, I know you will always stick by me through thick & thin.
If and when I have nowhere to turn, I know you will always stick by me through thick & thin.
If and when I don't feel I have the courage to fight, I know you will always stick by me through thick & thin.
When I feel insecure, I know you will always stick by me through thick & thin.
If and when I feel guilt in any way, I know you will always stick by me through thick & thin.
When I need you the most, I know you will always stick by me through thick & thin.
When I am not myself, I know you will always stick by me through thick & thin.
When I feel alone, I know you will always stick by me through thick & thin.
When I face challenging days, I know you will always stick by me through thick & thin.
If and when I need to vent, I know you will always stick by me through thick & thin.

Give Me Hope

When I look back at my fragile past, I know you will always give me hope.
When I face my lifelong fears, I know you will always give me hope.
When I try and break my lifelong issues that affect me, I know you will always give me hope.
When I try and overcome the loneliness I feel, I know you will always give me hope.
When I feel down, I know you will always give me hope.
If and when I feel broken, I know you will always give me hope.
When I feel like I'm in a dark place, I know you will always give me hope.
When I feel like I'm struggling, I know you will always give me hope.
When my inner cries take its toll on me, I know you will always give me hope.
When I don't feel strong enough, I know you will always give me hope.
When I don't feel brave enough, I know you will always give me hope.
When I feel low, I know you will always give me hope.
When I feel lost in any way, I know you will always give me hope.
When I need a shoulder to cry on, I know you will always give me hope.
If and when I don't feel good enough, I know you will always give me hope.

When I feel like an outsider, I know you will always give me hope.

If and when I feel rejected, I know you will always give me hope
When I feel like giving up, I know you will always give me hope.
If and when I feel unwanted, I know you will always give me hope,
If and when I feel worthless, I know you will always give me hope.
When I feel like I am entering an unknown trap, I know you will always give me hope.
When I feel like I'm in denial, I know you will always give me hope.
If and when I have nowhere to turn, I know you will always give me hope.
If and when I don't feel I have the courage to fight, I know you will always give me hope.
When I feel insecure, I know you will always give me hope.
If and when I feel guilt in any way, I know you will always give me hope.
When I need you the most, I know you will always give me hope,
When I am not myself, I know you will always give me hope.
When I feel alone, I know you will always give me hope.
When I face challenging days, I know you will always give me hope.
If and when I need to vent, I know you will always give me hope

Give Me Strength

When I look back at my fragile past, I know you will always give me strength.
When I face my lifelong fears, I know you will always give me strength.
When I try and break my lifelong issues that affect me, I know you will always give me strength.
When I try and overcome the loneliness I feel, I know you will always give me strength.
When I feel down, I know you will always give me strength.
If and when I feel broken, I know you will always give me strength.
When I feel like I'm in a dark place, I know you will always give me strength.
When I feel like I'm struggling, I know you will always give me strength.
When my inner cries take its toll on me, I know you will always give me strength.
When I don't feel strong enough, I know you will always give me strength.
When I don't feel brave enough, I know you will always give me strength.
When I feel low, I know you will always give me strength.
When I feel lost in any way, I know you will always give me strength.
When I need a shoulder to cry on, I know you will always give me strength.
If and when I don't feel good enough, I know you will always give me strength.

When I feel like an outsider, I know you will always give me strength.
If and when I feel rejected, I know you will always give me strength.

When I feel like giving up, I know you will always give me strength.
If and when I feel unwanted, I know you will always give me strength.
If and when I feel worthless, I know you will always give me strength.
When I feel like I am entering an unknown trap, I know you will always give me strength.
When I feel like I'm in denial, I know you will always give me strength.
If and when I have nowhere to turn, I know you will always give me strength.
If and when I don't feel I have the courage to fight, I know you will always give me strength.
When I feel insecure, I know you will always give me strength.
If and when I feel guilt in any way, I know you will never abandon me
When I need you the most, I know you will always give me strength.
When I am not myself, I know you will always give me strength.
When I feel alone, I know you will always give me strength.
When I face challenging days, I know you will always give me strength.
If and when I need to vent, I know you will always give me strength

Stand By You Through Thick & Thin

When you look back at your fragile past, know I will always stand by you through thick & thin.
When you face your lifelong fears, know I will always stand by you through thick & thin.
When you try and break your lifelong issues that affect you, know I will always stand by you through thick & thin.
When you try and overcome the loneliness you feel, know I will always stand by you through thick & thin.
When you feel down, know I will always stand by you through thick & thin.
If and when you feel broken, know I will always stand by you through thick & thin.
When you feel like you're in a dark place, know I will always stand by you through thick & thin.
When you feel like you're struggling, know I will always stand by you through thick & thin.
When your inner cries take its toll on you, know I will always stand by you through thick & thin.
When you don't feel strong enough, know I will always stand by you through thick & thin.
When you don't feel brave enough, know I will always stand by you through thick & thin.
When you feel low, know I will always stand by you through thick & thin.

When you feel lost in any way, know I will always stand by you through thick & thin.
When you need a shoulder to cry on, know I will always stand by you through thick & thin.
If and when you don't feel good enough, know I will always stand by you through thick & thin.

When you feel like an outsider, know I will always stand by you through thick & thin.
If and when you feel rejected, know I will always stand by you through thick & thin.
When you feel like giving up, know I will always stand by you through thick & thin.
If and when you feel unwanted, know I will always stand by you through thick & thin.
If and when you feel worthless, know I will always stand by you through thick & thin.
When you feel like you are entering an unknown trap, know I will always stand by you through thick & thin.
When you feel like you're in denial, know I will always stand by you through thick & thin.
If and when you have nowhere to turn, know I will always stand by you through thick & thin.
If and when you don't feel you have the courage to fight, know I will always stand by you through thick & thin.
When you feel insecure, know I will always stand by you through thick & thin.
If and when you feel guilt in any way, know I will always stand by you through thick & thin.
When you need me the most, know I will always stand by you through thick & thin.
When you are not yourself, know I will always stand by you through thick & thin.
When you feel alone, know I will always stand by you through thick & thin.
When you face challenging days, know I will always stand by you through thick & thin.
If and when you need to vent, know I will always stand by you through thick & thin.

Make Me Feel Like Somebody

When I look back at my fragile past, I know you always make me feel like somebody.
When I face my lifelong fears, I know you always make me feel like somebody.
When I try and break my lifelong issues that affect me, I know you always make me feel like somebody.
When I try and overcome the loneliness I feel, I know you always make me feel like somebody.
When I feel down, I know you always make me feel like a somebody.
If and when I feel broken, I know you always make me feel like somebody.
When I feel like I'm in a dark place, I know you always make me feel like somebody.
When I feel like I'm struggling, I know you always make me feel like somebody.
When my inner cries take its toll on me, I know you always make me feel like somebody.
When I don't feel strong enough, I know you always make me feel like somebody.
When I don't feel brave enough, I know you always make me feel like somebody.
When I feel low, I know you always make me feel like somebody.
When I feel lost in any way, I know you always make me feel like somebody.
When I need a shoulder to cry on, I know you always make me feel like somebody.
If and when I don't feel good enough, I know you always make me feel like somebody.

When I feel like an outsider, I know you always make me feel like somebody.
If and when I feel rejected, I know you always make me feel like somebody.
When I feel like giving up, I know you always make me feel like somebody.
If and when I feel unwanted, I know you always make me feel like somebody.
If and when I feel worthless, I know you always make me feel like somebody.
When I feel like I am entering an unknown trap, I know you always make me feel like somebody.
When I feel like I'm in denial, I know you always make me feel like somebody.
If and when I have nowhere to turn, I know you always make me feel like somebody.
If and when I don't feel I have the courage to fight, I know you always make me feel like somebody.
When I feel insecure, I know you always make me feel like somebody.
If and when I feel guilt in any way, I know you always make me feel like somebody.

When I need you the most, I know you always make me feel like somebody.
When I am not myself, I know you always make me feel like somebody.
When I feel alone, I know you always make me feel like somebody.
When I face challenging days, I know you always make me feel like somebody.
If and when I need to vent, I know you always make me feel like somebody.

Make Me Feel Valued

When I look back at my fragile past, I know you always make me feel valued.
When I face my lifelong fears, I know you always make me feel valued.
When I try and break my lifelong issues that affect me, I know you always make me feel valued.
When I try and overcome the loneliness I feel, I know you always make me feel valued.
When I feel down, I know you always make me feel valued.
If and when I feel broken, I know you always make me feel valued.
When I feel like I'm in a dark place, I know you always make me feel valued.
When I feel like I'm struggling, I know you always make me feel valued.
When my inner cries take its toll on me, I know you always make me feel valued.
When I don't feel strong enough, I know you always make me feel valued
When I don't feel brave enough, I know you always make me feel valued.
When I feel low, I know you always make me feel valued.
When I feel lost in any way, I know you always make me feel valued.
When I need a shoulder to cry on, I know you always make me feel valued.
If and when I don't feel good enough, I know you always make me feel valued.

When I feel like an outsider, I know you always make me feel valued.
If and when I feel rejected, I know you always make me feel valued.
When I feel like giving up, I know you always make me feel valued.
If and when I feel unwanted, I know you always make me feel valued.
If and when I feel worthless, I know you always make me feel valued.
When I feel like I am entering an unknown trap, I know you always make me feel valued.
When I feel like I'm in denial, I know you always make me feel valued.
If and when I have nowhere to turn, I know you always make me feel valued.
If and when I don't feel I have the courage to fight, I know you always make me feel valued.
When I feel insecure, I know you always make me feel valued.
If and when I feel guilt in any way, I know you always make me feel valued.
When I need you the most, I know you always make me feel valued.

When I am not myself, I know you always make me feel valued.
When I feel alone, I know you always make me feel valued.
When I face challenging days, I know you always make me feel valued.
If and when I need to vent, I know you always make me feel valued.

Always Take Me As Me

When I look back at my fragile past, I know you will always take me as me.
When I face my lifelong fears, I know you will always take me as me.
When I try and break my lifelong issues that affect me, I know you will always take me as me.
When I try and overcome the loneliness I feel, I know you will always take me as me
When I feel down, I know you will always take me as me.
If and when I feel broken, I know you will always take me as me.
When I feel like I'm in a dark place, I know you will always take me as me.
When I feel like I'm struggling, I know you will always take me as me.
When my inner cries take its toll on me, I know you will always take me as me.
When I don't feel strong enough, I know you will always take me as me.
When I don't feel brave enough, I know you will always take me as me.
When I feel low, I know you will always take me as me.
When I feel lost in any way, I know you will always take me as me.
When I need a shoulder to cry on, I know you will always take me as me.
If and when I don't feel good enough, I know you will always take me as me.

When I feel like an outsider, I know you will always take me as me.
If and when I feel rejected, I know you will always take me as me.
When I feel like giving up, I know you will always take me as me.
If and when I feel unwanted, I know you will always take me as me.
If and when I feel worthless, I know you will always take me as me.
When I feel like I am entering an unknown trap, I know you will always take me as me.
When I feel like I'm in denial, I know you will always take me as me.
If and when I have nowhere to turn, I know you will always take me as me.
If and when I don't feel I have the courage to fight, I know you will always take me as me.
When I feel insecure, I know you will always take me as me.
If and when I feel guilt in any way, I know you will always take me as me.
When I need you the most, I know you will always take me as me,
When I am not myself, I know you will always take me as me.
When I feel alone, I know you will always take me as me.

When I face challenging days, I know you will always take me as me.
If and when I need to vent, I know you will always take me as me.

My World In Tatters

When I look back at my fragile past, I know my world is in tatters.
When I face my lifelong fears, I know my world is in tatters.
When I try and break my lifelong issues that affect me, I know my world is in tatters.
When I try and overcome the loneliness I feel, I know my world is in tatters.
When I feel down, I know my world is in tatters.
If and when I feel broken, I know my world is in tatters.
When I feel like I'm in a dark place, I know my world is in tatters.
When I feel like I'm struggling, I know my world is in tatters.
When my inner cries take its toll on me, I know my world is in tatters.
When I don't feel strong enough, I know my world is in tatters.
When I don't feel brave enough, I know my world is in tatters.
When I feel low, I know my world is in tatters.
When I feel lost in any way, I know my world will be in tatters.
When I need a shoulder to cry on, I know my world is in tatters.
If and when I don't feel good enough, I know my world is in tatters.

When I feel like an outsider, I know my world is in tatters.
If and when I feel rejected, I know my world is in tatters.
When I feel like giving up, I know my world is in tatters.
If and when I feel unwanted, I know my world is in tatters.
If and when I feel worthless, I know my world is in tatters
When I feel like I am entering an unknown trap, I know my world is in tatters.
When I feel like I'm in denial, I know my world is in tatters.
If and when I have nowhere to turn, I know my world is in tatters.
If and when I don't feel I have the courage to fight, I know my world is in tatters.
When I feel insecure, I know my world is in tatters.
If and when I feel guilt in any way, I know my world is in tatters.
When I need you the most, I know my world is in tatters.
When I am not myself, I know my world is in tatters.
When I feel alone, I know my world is in tatters.
When I face challenging days, I know my world is in tatters.
If and when I need to vent, I know my world is in tatters.

Make Me Feel Like I Belong

When I look back at my fragile past, you always make me feel like I belong.
When I face my lifelong fears, you always make me feel like I belong.
When I try and break my lifelong issues that affect me, you always make me feel like I belong.
When I try and overcome the loneliness I feel, you always make me feel like I belong.
When I feel down, you always make me feel like I belong.
If and when I feel broken, you always make me feel like I belong.
When I feel like I'm in a dark place, you always make me feel like I belong.
When I feel like I'm struggling, you always make me feel like I belong.
When my inner cries take its toll on me, you always make me feel like I belong.
When I don't feel strong enough, you always make me feel like I belong.
When I don't feel brave enough, you always make me feel like I belong.
When I feel low, you always make me feel like I belong.
When I feel lost in any way, you always make me feel like I belong.
When I need a shoulder to cry on, you always make me feel like I belong.
If and when I don't feel good enough, you always make me feel like I belong.

When I feel like an outsider, you always make me feel like I belong.
If and when I feel rejected, you always make me feel like I belong.
When I feel like giving up, you always make me feel like I belong.
If and when I feel unwanted, you always make me feel like I belong.
If and when I feel worthless, you always make me feel like I belong.
When I feel like I am entering an unknown trap, you always make me feel like I belong.
When I feel like I'm in denial, you always make me feel like I belong.
If and when I have nowhere to turn, you always make me feel like I belong.
If and when I don't feel I have the courage to fight, you always make me feel like I belong.
When I feel insecure, you always make me feel like I belong.
If and when I feel guilt in any way, you always make me feel like I belong
When I need you the most, you always make me feel like I belong.
When I am not myself, you always make me feel like I belong.
When I feel alone, you always make me feel like I belong.
When I face challenging days, you always make me feel like I belong.
If and when I need to vent, you always make me feel like I belong.

True Friends Like You Are Hard To Find

When I look back at my fragile past, I know true friends like you are hard to find.
When I face my lifelong fears, I know true friends like you are hard to find.
When I try and break my lifelong issues that affect me, I know true friends like you are hard to find.
When I try and overcome the loneliness I feel, I know true friends like you are hard to find.
When I feel down, I know true friends like you are hard to find.
If and when I feel broken, I know true friends like you are hard to find.
When I feel like I'm in a dark place, I know true friends like you are hard to find.
When I feel like I'm struggling, I know true friends like you are hard to find
When my inner cries take its toll on me, I know true friends like you are hard to find.
When I don't feel strong enough, I know true friends like you are hard to find.
When I don't feel brave enough, I know true friends like you are hard to find.
When I feel low, I know true friends like you are hard to find.
When I feel lost in any way, I know true friends like you are hard to find.
When I need a shoulder to cry on, I know true friends like you are hard to find.
If and when I don't feel good enough, I know true friends are hard to find.

When I feel like an outsider, I know true friends like you are hard to find.
If and when I feel rejected, I know true friends like you are hard to find.
When I feel like giving up, I know true friends like you are hard to find.
If and when I feel unwanted, I know true friends like you are hard to find.
If and when I feel worthless, I know true friends like you are hard to find.
When I feel like I am entering an unknown trap, I know true friends like you are hard to find.
When I feel like I'm in denial, I know true friends like you are hard to find.
If and when I have nowhere to turn, I know true friends like you are hard to find.
If and when I don't feel I have the courage to fight, I know true friends like you are hard to find.
When I feel insecure, I know true friends like you are hard to find.
If and when I feel guilt in any way, I know true friends like you are hard to find.
When I need you the most, I know true friends like you are hard to find.
When I am not myself, I know true friends like you are hard to find.
When I feel alone, I know true friends like you are hard to find.
When I face challenging days, I know true friends like you are hard to find.
If and when I need to vent, I know true friends like you are hard to find.

My Hour Of Need

When I look back at my fragile past, I know you will always be around in my hour of need.
When I face my lifelong fears, I know you will always be around in my hour of need.
When I try and break my lifelong issues that affect me, I know you will always be around in my hour of need.
When I try and overcome the loneliness I feel, I know you will always be around in my hour of need.
When I feel down, I know you will always be around in my hour of need.
If and when I feel broken, I know you will always be around in my hour of need.
When I feel like I'm in a dark place, I know you will always be around in my hour of need.
When I feel like I'm struggling, I know you will always be around in my hour of need.
When my inner cries take its toll on me, I know you will always be around in my hour of need.
When I don't feel strong enough, I know you will always be around in my hour of need.
When I don't feel brave enough, I know you will always be around in my hour of need.
When I feel low, I know you will always be around in my hour of need.
When I feel lost in any way, I know you will always be around in my hour of need.
When I need a shoulder to cry on, I know you will always be around in my hour of need.
If and when I don't feel good enough, I know you will always be around in my hour of need.

When I feel like an outsider, I know you will always be around in my hour of need.
If and when I feel rejected, I know you will always be around in my hour of need.
When I feel like giving up, I know you will always be around in my hour of need.
If and when I feel unwanted, I know you will always be around in my hour of need.
If and when I feel worthless, I know you will always be around in my hour of need.
When I feel like I am entering an unknown trap, I know you will always be around in my hour of need.

When I feel like I'm in denial, I know you will always be around in my hour of need.
If and when I have nowhere to turn, I know you will always be around in my hour of need.
If and when I don't feel I have the courage to fight, I know you will always be around in my hour of need.
When I feel insecure, I know you will always be around in my hour of need.
If and when I feel guilt in any way, I know you will always be around in my hour of need.
When I need you the most, I know you will always be around in my hour of need.
When I am not myself, I know you will always be around in my hour of need.
When I feel alone, I know you will always be around in my hour of need.
When I face challenging days, I know you will always be around in my hour of need.
If and when I need to vent, I know you will always be around in my hour of need

Make A Massive Difference To Me & My Life.

When I look back at my fragile past, you always make a massive difference to me & my life.
When I face my lifelong fears, you always make a massive difference to me & my life
When I try and break my lifelong issues that affect me, you always make a massive difference to me & my life.
When I try and overcome the loneliness I feel, you always make a massive difference to me & my life.
When I feel down, you always make a massive difference to me & my life.
If and when I feel broken, you always make a massive difference to me & my life.
When I feel like I'm in a dark place, you always make a massive difference to me & my life.
When I feel like I'm struggling, you always make a massive difference to me & my life.
When my inner cries take its toll on me, you always make a massive difference to me & my life.
When I don't feel strong enough, you always make a massive difference to me & my life.
When I don't feel brave enough, you always make a massive difference to me & my life.
When I feel low, you always make a massive difference to me & my life

When I feel lost in any way, you always make a massive difference to me & my life.
When I need a shoulder to cry on, you always make a massive difference to me & my life.
If and when I don't feel good enough, you always make a massive difference to me & my life.

When I feel like an outsider, you always make a massive difference to me & my life.
If and when I feel rejected, you always make a massive difference to me & my life.
When I feel like giving up, you always make a massive difference to me & my life.
If and when I feel unwanted, you always make a massive difference to me & my life.
If and when I feel worthless, you always make a massive difference to me & my life.
When I feel like I am entering an unknown trap, you always make a massive difference to me & my life.
When I feel like I'm in denial, you always make a massive difference to me & my life.
If and when I have nowhere to turn, you always make a massive difference to me & my life.
If and when I don't feel I have the courage to fight, you always make a massive difference to me & my life.
When I feel insecure, you always make a massive difference to me & my life.
If and when I feel guilt in any way, you always make a massive difference to me & my life.
When I need you the most, you always make a massive difference to me & my life.
When I am not myself, you always make a massive difference to me & my life.
When I feel alone, you always make a massive difference to me & my life.
When I face challenging days, you always make a massive difference to me & my life.
If and when I need to vent, you always make a massive difference to me & my life.

Make My Day

When I look back at my fragile past, you always make my day.
When I face my lifelong fears, you always make my day.
When I try and break my lifelong issues that affect me, you always make my day.
When I try and overcome the loneliness I feel, you always make my day.
When I feel down, you always make my day.
If and when I feel broken, you always make my day.
When I feel like I'm in a dark place, you always make my day.
When I feel like I'm struggling, you always make my day.
When my inner cries take its toll on me, you always make my day.
When I don't feel strong enough, you always make my day.
When I don't feel brave enough, you always make my day.
When I feel low, you always make my day.
When I feel lost in any way, you always make my day.
When I need a shoulder to cry on, you always make my day.
If and when I don't feel good enough, you always make my day.

When I feel like an outsider, you always make my day.
If and when I feel rejected, you always make my day.
When I feel like giving up, you always make my day.
If and when I feel unwanted, you always make my day.
If and when I feel worthless, you always make my day.
When I feel like I am entering an unknown trap, you always make my day.
When I feel like I'm in denial, you always make my day.
If and when I have nowhere to turn, you always make my day.
If and when I don't feel I have the courage to fight, you always make my day
When I feel insecure, you always make my day.
If and when I feel guilt in any way, you always make my day.
When I need you the most, you always make my day.
When I am not myself, you always make my day.
When I feel alone, you always make my day.
When I face challenging days, you always make my day.
If and when I need to vent, you always make my day.

Give Me Stability

When I look back at my fragile past, you always give me stability.
When I face my lifelong fears, you always give me stability.
When I try and break my lifelong issues that affect me, you always give me stability.
When I try and overcome the loneliness I feel, you always give me stability.
When I feel down, you always give me stability.
If and when I feel broken, you always give me stability.
When I feel like I'm in a dark place, you always give me stability.
When I feel like I'm struggling, you always give me stability.
When my inner cries take its toll on me, you always give me stability.
When I don't feel strong enough, you always give me stability.
When I don't feel brave enough, you always give me stability.
When I feel low, you always give me stability.
When I feel lost in any way, you always give me stability.
When I need a shoulder to cry on, you always give me stability.
If and when I don't feel good enough, you always give me stability.

When I feel like an outsider, you always give me stability.
If and when I feel rejected, you always give me stability.
When I feel like giving up, you always give me stability.
If and when I feel unwanted, you always give me stability.
If and when I feel worthless, you always give me stability.
When I feel like I am entering an unknown trap, you always give me stability.
When I feel like I'm in denial, you always give me stability.
If and when I have nowhere to turn, you always give me stability.
If and when I don't feel I have the courage to fight, you always give me stability.
When I feel insecure, you always give me stability.
If and when I feel guilt in any way, you always give me stability.
When I need you the most, you always give me stability.
When I am not myself, you always give me stability.
When I feel alone, you always give me stability.
When I face challenging days, you always give me stability.
If and when I need to vent, you always give me stability

Won't Let Me Down

When I look back at my fragile past, I know you won't let me down.
When I face my lifelong fears, I know you won't let me down.

When I try and break my lifelong issues that affect me, I know you won't let me down.
When I try and overcome the loneliness I feel, I know you won't let me down.
When I feel down, I know you won't let me down.
If and when I feel broken, I know you won't let me down.
When I feel like I'm in a dark place, I know you won't let me down.
When I feel like I'm struggling, I know you won't let me down.
When my inner cries take its toll on me, I know you won't let me down.
When I don't feel strong enough, I know you won't let me down.
When I don't feel brave enough, I know you won't let me down.
When I feel low, I know you won't let me down.
When I feel lost in any way, I know you won't let me down.
When I need a shoulder to cry on, I know you won't let me down.
If and when I don't feel good enough, I know you won't let me down.

When I feel like an outsider, I know you won't let me down.
If and when I feel rejected, I know you won't let me down.
When I feel like giving up, I know you won't let me down.
If and when I feel unwanted, I know you won't let me down.
If and when I feel worthless, I know you won't let me down.
When I feel like I am entering an unknown trap, I know you won't let me down.
When I feel like I'm in denial, I know you won't let me down.
If and when I have nowhere to turn, I know you won't let me down.
If and when I don't feel I have the courage to fight, I know you won't let me down.
When I feel insecure, I know you won't let me down.
If and when I feel guilt in any way, I know you won't let me down.
When I need you the most, I know you won't let me down.
When I am not myself, I know you won't let me down.
When I feel alone, I know you won't let me down.
When I face challenging days, I know you won't let me down.
If and when I need to vent, I know you won't let me down.

Take You Under My Wing

When you look back at your fragile past, know I will take you under my wing.
When you face your lifelong fears, know I will take you under my wing.
When you try and break your lifelong issues that affect you, know I will take you under my wing.
When you try and overcome the loneliness you feel, know I will take you under my wing,

When you feel down, know I will take you under my wing.
If and when you feel broken, know I will take you under my wing,
When you feel like you're in a dark place, know I will take you under my wing,
When you feel like you're struggling, know I will take you under my wing.
When your inner cries take its toll on you, know I will take you under my wing.
When you don't feel strong enough, know I will take you under my wing.
When you don't feel brave enough, know I will take you under my wing.
When you feel low, know I will take you under my wing.
When you feel lost in any way, know I will take you under my wing.
When you need a shoulder to cry on, know I will take you under my wing.
If and when you don't feel good enough, know I will take you under my wing.

When you feel like an outsider, know I will take you under my wing.
If and when you feel rejected, know I will take you under my wing.
When you feel like giving up, know I will take you under my wing.
If and when you feel unwanted, know I will take you under my wing.
If and when you feel worthless, know I will take you under my wing.
When you feel like you are entering an unknown trap, know I will take you under my wing.
When you feel like you're in denial, know I will take you under my wing.
If and when you have nowhere to turn, know I will take you under my wing.
If and when you don't feel you have the courage to fight, know I will take you under my wing.
When you feel insecure, know I will take you under my wing.
If and when you feel guilt in any way, know I will take you under my wing.
When you need me the most, know I will take you under my wing.
When you are not yourself, know I will take you under my wing.
When you feel alone, know I will take you under my wing.
When you face challenging days, know I will take you under my wing.
If and when you need to vent, know I will take you under my wing.

Hold Back My Tears

When I look back at my fragile past, I know I don't have to hold back my tears in front of you.
When I face my lifelong fears, I know I don't have to hold back my tears in front of you.
When I try and break my lifelong issues that affect me, I know I don't have to hold back my tears in front of you.
When I try and overcome the loneliness I feel, I know I don't have to hold back my tears in front of you.

When I feel down, I know I don't have to hold back my tears in front of you.
If and when I feel broken, I know I don't have to hold back my tears in front of you.
When I feel like I'm in a dark place, I know I don't have to hold back my tears in front of you.
When I feel like I'm struggling, I know I don't have to hold back my tears in front of you.
When my inner cries take its toll on me, I know I don't have to hold back my tears in front of you.
When I don't feel strong enough, I know I don't have to hold back my tears in front of you.
When I don't feel brave enough, I know I don't have to hold back my tears in front of you.
When I feel low, I know I don't have to hold back my tears in front of you.
When I feel lost in any way, I know I don't have to hold back my tears in front of you.
When I need a shoulder to cry on, I know I don't have to hold back my tears in front of you.
If and when I don't feel good enough, I know I don't have to hold back my tears in front of you.

When I feel like an outsider, I know I don't have to hold back my tears in front of you.
If and when I feel rejected, I know I don't have to hold back my tears in front of you.
When I feel like giving up, I know I don't have to hold back my tears in front of you.
If and when I feel unwanted, I know I don't have to hold back my tears in front of you.
If and when I feel worthless, I know I don't have to hold back my tears in front of you.
When I feel like I am entering an unknown trap, I know I don't have to hold back my tears in front of you.
When I feel like I'm in denial, I know I don't have to hold back my tears in front of you.
If and when I have nowhere to turn, I know I don't have to hold back my tears in front of you.
If and when I don't feel I have the courage to fight, I know I don't have to hold back my tears in front of you.
When I feel insecure, I know I don't have to hold back my tears in front of you.
If and when I feel guilt in any way, I know I don't have to hold back my tears in front of you.

When I need you the most, I know I don't have to hold back my tears in front of you.
When I am not myself, I know I don't have to hold back my tears in front of you.
When I feel alone, I know I don't have to hold back my tears in front of you.
When I face challenging days, I know I don't have to hold back my tears in front of you.
If and when I need to vent, I know I don't have to hold back my tears in front of you.

Hold Back My Pain

When I look back at my fragile past, I know I know I don't have to hold back my pain in front of you.
When I face my lifelong fears, I know I don't have to hold back my pain in front of you.
When I try and break my lifelong issues that affect me, I know I don't have to hold back my pain in front of you.
When I try and overcome the loneliness I feel, I know I don't have to hold back my pain in front of you.
When I feel down, I know I don't have to hold back my pain in front of you.
If and when I feel broken, I know I don't have to hold back my pain in front of you.
When I feel like I'm in a dark place, I know I don't have to hold back my pain in front of you.
When I feel like I'm struggling, I know I don't have to hold back my pain in front of you.
When my inner cries take its toll on me, I know I don't have to hold back my pain in front of you.
When I don't feel strong enough, I know I don't have to hold back my pain in front of you.
When I don't feel brave enough, I know I don't have to hold back my pain in front of you.
When I feel low, I know I don't have to hold back my pain in front of you.
When I feel lost in any way, I know I don't have to hold back my pain in front of you.
When I need a shoulder to cry on, I know I don't have to hold back my pain in front of you.
If and when I don't feel good enough, I know I don't have to hold back my pain in front of you.

When I feel like an outsider, I know I don't have to hold back my pain in front of you.
If and when I feel rejected, I know I don't have to hold back my pain in front of you.
When I feel like giving up, I know I don't have to hold back my pain in front of you.
If and when I feel unwanted, I know I don't have to hold back my pain in front of you.
If and when I feel worthless, I know I don't have to hold back my pain in front of you.
When I feel like I am entering an unknown trap, I know I don't have to hold back my pain in front of you.
When I feel like I'm in denial, I know I don't have to hold back my pain in front of you.
If and when I have nowhere to turn, I know I don't have to hold back my pain in front of you.
If and when I don't feel I have the courage to fight, I know I don't have to hold back my pain in front of you.
When I feel insecure, I know I don't have to hold back my pain in front of you.
If and when I feel guilt in any way, I know I don't have to hold back my pain in front of you.
When I need you the most, I know I don't have to hold back my pain in front of you.
When I am not myself, I know I don't have to hold back my pain in front of you.
When I feel alone, I know I don't have to hold back my pain in front of you.
When I face challenging days, I know I don't have to hold back my pain in front of you.
If and when I need to vent, I know I don't have to hold back my pain in front of you.

Hear Me

When I look back at my fragile past, I know all I have to do is call out for you & you will hear me.
When I face my lifelong fears, I know all I have to do is call out for you & you will hear me.
When I try and break my lifelong issues that affect me, I know all I have to do is call out for you & you will hear me.
When I try and overcome the loneliness I feel, I know all I have to do is call out for you & you will hear me.
When I feel down, I know all I have to do is call out for you & you will hear me.

If and when I feel broken, I know all I have to do is call out for you & you will hear me.
When I feel like I'm in a dark place, I know all I have to do is call out for you & you will hear me.
When I feel like I'm struggling, I know all I have to do is call out for you & you will hear me.
When my inner cries take its toll on me, I know all I have to do is call out for you & you will hear me.
When I don't feel strong enough, I know all I have to do is call out for you & you will hear me.
When I don't feel brave enough, I know all I have to do is call out for you & you will hear me.
When I feel low, I know all I have to do is call out for you & you will hear me.
When I feel lost in any way, I know all I have to do is call out for you & you will hear me.
When I need a shoulder to cry on, I know all I have to do is call out for you & you will hear me.
If and when I don't feel good enough, I know all I have to do is call out for you & you will hear me.

When I feel like an outsider, I know all I have to do is call out for you & you will hear me.
If and when I feel rejected, I know all I have to do is call out for you & you will hear me.
When I feel like giving up, I know all I have to do is call out for you & you will hear me.
If and when I feel unwanted, I know all I have to do is call out for you & you will hear me.
If and when I feel worthless, I know all I have to do is call out for you & you will hear me.
When I feel like I am entering an unknown trap, I know all I have to do is call out for you & you will hear me.
When I feel like I'm in denial, I know all I have to do is call out for you & you will hear me.
If and when I have nowhere to turn, I know all I have to do is call out or you & you will hear me.
If and when I don't feel I have the courage to fight, I know all I have to do is call out for you & you will hear me.
When I feel insecure, I know all I have to do is call you for you & you will hear me.
If and when I feel guilt in any way, I know all I have to do is call out for you & you will hear me.

When I need you the most, I know all I have to do is call out for you & you will hear me.
When I am not myself, I know all I have to do is call out for you & you will hear me.
When I feel alone, I know all I have to do is call out for you & you will hear me.
When I face challenging days, I know all I have to do is call out for you & you will hear me.
If and when I need to vent, I know all I have to do is call out for you & you will hear me.

Hold Back My Hurt

When I look back at my fragile past, I know I don't have to hold back my hurt in front of you.
When I face my lifelong fears, I know I don't have to hold back my hurt in front of you.
When I try and break my lifelong issues that affect me, I know I don't have to hold back my hurt in front of you.
When I try and overcome the loneliness I feel, I know I don't have to hold back my hurt in front of you.
When I feel down, I know I don't have to hold back my hurt in front of you.
If and when I feel broken, I know I don't have to hold back my hurt in front of you.
When I feel like I'm in a dark place, I know I don't have to hold back my hurt in front of you.
When I feel like I'm struggling, I know I don't have to hold back my hurt in front of you.
When my inner cries take its toll on me, I know I don't have to hold back my hurt in front of you.
When I don't feel strong enough, I know I don't have to hold back my hurt in front of you.
When I don't feel brave enough, I know I don't have to hold back my hurt in front of you.
When I feel low, I know I don't have to hold back my hurt in front of you.
When I feel lost in any way, I know I don't have to hold back my hurt in front of you.
When I need a shoulder to cry on, I know I don't have to hold back my hurt in front of you.
If and when I don't feel good enough, I know I don't have to hold back my hurt in front of you.

When I feel like an outsider, I know I don't have to hold back my hurt in front of you.
If and when I feel rejected, I know I don't have to hold back my hurt in front of you.
When I feel like giving up, I know I don't have to hold back my hurt in front of you.
If and when I feel unwanted, I know I don't have to hold back my hurt in front of you.
If and when I feel worthless, I know I don't have to hold back my hurt in front of you.
When I feel like I am entering an unknown trap, I know I don't have to hold back my hurt in front of you.
When I feel like I'm in denial, I know I don't have to hold back my hurt in front of you.
If and when I have nowhere to turn, I know I don't have to hold back my hurt in front of you.
If and when I don't feel I have the courage to fight, I know I don't have to hold back my hurt in front of you.
When I feel insecure, I know I don't have to hold back my hurt in front of you.
If and when I feel guilt in any way, I know I don't have to hold back my hurt in front of you.
When I need you the most, I know I don't have to hold back my hurt in front of you.
When I am not myself, I know I don't have to hold back -my hurt in front of you.
When I feel alone, I know I don't have to hold back hurt in front of you.
When I face challenging days, I know I don't have to hold back my hurt in front of you.
If and when I need to vent, I know I don't have to hold back my hurt in front of you.

Don't Have To Be Ashamed Of My Scars & Burns

When I look back at my fragile past, I know I don't have to be ashamed of my scars & burns in front of you.
When I face my lifelong fears, I know I don't have to be ashamed of my scars & burns in front of you.
When I try and break my lifelong issues that affect me, I know I don't have to be ashamed of my scars & burns in front of you.
When I try and overcome the loneliness I feel, I know I don't have tobe ashamed of my scars & burns in front of you.

When I feel down, I know I don't have to be ashamed of my scars & burns in front of you.
If and when I feel broken, I know I don't have to be ashamed of my scars & burns in front of you.
When I feel like I'm in a dark place, I know I don't have to be ashamed of my scars & burns in front of you.
When I feel like I'm struggling, I know I don't have to be ashamed of my scars & burns in front of you.
When my inner cries take its toll on me, I know I don't have to be ashamed of my scars & burns in front of you.
When I don't feel strong enough, I know I don't have to be ashamed of my scars & burns in front of you.
When I don't feel brave enough, I know I don't have to be ashamed of my scars & burns in front of you.
When I feel low, I know I don't have to be ashamed of my scars & burns in front of you.
When I feel lost in any way, I know I don't have to be ashamed of my scars & burns in front of you.
When I need a shoulder to cry on, I know I don't have to be ashamed of my scars & burns in front of you.
If and when I don't feel good enough, I know I don't have to be ashamed of my scars & burns in front of you.

When I feel like an outsider, I know I don't have to be ashamed of my scars & burns in front of you.
If and when I feel rejected, I know I don't have to be ashamed of my scars & burns in front of you.
When I feel like giving up, I know I don't have to be ashamed of my scars &burns in front of you.
If and when I feel unwanted, I know I don't have to be ashamed of my scars & burns in front of you.
If and when I feel worthless, I know I don't have to be ashamed of my scars & burns in front of you.
When I feel like I am entering an unknown trap, I know I don't have to be ashamed of my scars & burns in front of you.
When I feel like I'm in denial, I know I don't have to be ashamed of my scars & burns in front of you.
If and when I have nowhere to turn, I know I don't have to be ashamed of my scars & burns in front of you.
If and when I don't feel I have the courage to fight, I know I don't have to be ashamed of my scars & burns in front of you.

When I feel insecure, I know I don't have to be ashamed of my scars & burns in front of you.
If and when I feel guilt in any way, I know I don't have to be ashamed of my scars & burns in front of you.
When I need you the most, I know I don't have to be ashamed of my scars & burns in front of you.
When I am not myself, I know I don't have to be ashamed of my scars & burns in front of you.
When I feel alone, I know I don't have to be ashamed of my scars & burns in front of you.
When I face challenging days, I know I don't have to hold back my scars & burns in front of you.
If and when I need to vent, I know I don't have be ashamed of my scars & burns in front of you.

Don't Have To Be Ashamed Of My Disability

When I look back at my fragile past, I know I don't have to be ashamed of my disability as I am proud to be unique
When I face my lifelong fears, I know I don't have to be ashamed of my disability as I am proud to be unique.
When I try and break my lifelong issues that affect me, I know I don't have to be ashamed of my disability as I am proud to be unique.
When I try and overcome the loneliness I feel, I know I don't have to be ashamed of my disability as I am proud to be unique.
When I feel down, I know I don't have to be ashamed of my disability as I am proud to be unique.
If and when I feel broken, I know I don't have to be ashamed of my disability as I am proud to be unique.
When I feel like I'm in a dark place, I know I don't have to be ashamed of my disability as I am proud to be unique.
When I feel like I'm struggling, I know I don't have to be ashamed of my disability as I am proud to be unique.
When my inner cries take its toll on me, I know I don't have to be ashamed of my disability as I am proud to be unique.
When I don't feel strong enough, I know I don't have to be ashamed of my disability as I am proud to be unique.
When I don't feel brave enough, I know I don't have to be ashamed of my disability as I am proud to be unique.
When I feel low, I know I don't have to be ashamed of my disability as I am proud to be unique.

When I feel lost in any way, I know I don't have to be ashamed of my disability as I am proud to be unique.
When I need a shoulder to cry on, I know I don't have to be ashamed of my disability I am proud to be unique.
If and when I don't feel good enough, I know I don't have to be ashamed of my disability as I am proud to be unique.

When I feel like an outsider, I know I don't have to be ashamed of my disability as I am proud to be unique.
If and when I feel rejected, I know I don't have to be ashamed of my disability as I am proud to be unique.
When I feel like giving up, I know I don't have to be ashamed of my disability as I am proud to be unique.
If and when I feel unwanted, I know I don't have to be ashamed of my disability as I am proud to be unique.
If and when I feel worthless, I know I don't have to be ashamed of my disability as I am proud to be unique.
When I feel like I am entering an unknown trap, I know I don't have to be ashamed of my disability as I am proud to be unique.
When I feel like I'm in denial, I know I don't have to be ashamed of my disability as I am proud to be unique.
If and when I have nowhere to turn, I know I don't have to be ashamed of my disability as I am proud to be unique.
If and when I don't feel I have the courage to fight, I know I don't have to be ashamed of my disability as I am proud to be unique.
When I feel insecure, I know I don't have to be ashamed of my disability as I am proud to be unique.
If and when I feel guilt in any way, I know I don't have to be ashamed of my disability as I am proud to be unique.
When I need you the most, I know I don't have to be ashamed of my disability as I am proud to be unique.
When I am not myself, I know I don't have to be ashamed of my disability as I am proud to be unique.
When I feel alone, I know I don't have to be ashamed of my disability as I am proud to be unique.
When I face challenging days, I know I don't have to be ashamed of my disability as I am proud to be unique.
If and when I need to vent, I know I don't have to be ashamed of my disability as I am proud to be unique.

Hold Back My Honesty

When I look back at my fragile past, I know I don't have to hold back my honesty in front of you.
When I face my lifelong fears, I know I don't have to hold back my honesty in front of you.
When I try and break my lifelong issues that affect me, I know I don't have to hold back my honesty in front of you.
When I try and overcome the loneliness I feel, I know I don't have to hold back my honesty in front of you.
When I feel down, I know I don't have to hold back my honesty in front of you.
If and when I feel broken, I know I don't have to hold back my honesty in front of you.
When I feel like I'm in a dark place, I know I don't have to hold back my honesty in front of you.
When I feel like I'm struggling, I know I don't have to hold back my honesty in front of you.
When my inner cries take its toll on me, I know I don't have to hold back my honesty in front of you.
When I don't feel strong enough, I know I don't have to hold back my honesty in front of you.
When I don't feel brave enough, I know I don't have to hold back my honesty n in front of you.
When I feel low, I know I don't have to hold back my honesty in front of you.
When I feel lost in any way, I know I don't have to hold back my honesty in front of you.
When I need a shoulder to cry on, I know I don't have to hold back my honesty in front of you.
If and when I don't feel good enough, I know I don't have to hold back my honesty in front of you.

When I feel like an outsider, I know I don't have to hold back my honesty in front of you.
If and when I feel rejected, I know I don't have to hold back my honesty in front of you.
When I feel like giving up, I know I don't have to hold back my honesty in front of you.
If and when I feel unwanted, I know I don't have to hold back my honesty in front of you.
If and when I feel worthless, I know I don't have to hold back my honesty in front of you.

When I feel like I am entering an unknown trap, I know I don't have to hold back my honesty in front of you.
When I feel like I'm in denial, I know I don't have to hold back my honesty in front of you.
If and when I have nowhere to turn, I know I don't have to hold back my honesty in front of you.
If and when I don't feel I have the courage to fight, I know I don't have to hold back my honesty in front of you.
When I feel insecure, I know I don't have to hold back my honesty in front of you.
If and when I feel guilt in any way, I know I don't have to hold back my honesty in front of you.
When I need you the most, I know I don't have to hold back my honesty in front of you.
When I am not myself, I know I don't have to hold back my honesty in front of you.
When I feel alone, I know I don't have to hold back my honesty in front of you.
When I face challenging days, I know I don't have to hold back my honestly in front of you.
If and when I need to vent, I know I don't have to hold back my honesty in front of you.

Give me courage

When I look back at my fragile past, I know you will always give me courage.
When I face my lifelong fears, I know you will always give me courage.
When I try and break my lifelong issues that affect me, I know you will always give me courage.
When I try and overcome the loneliness I feel, I know you will always give me courage.
When I feel down, I know you will always give me courage.
If and when I feel broken, I know you will always give me courage.
When I feel like I'm in a dark place, I know you will always give me courage.
When I feel like I'm struggling, I know you will always give me courage.
When my inner cries take its toll on me, I know you will always give me courage.
When I don't feel strong enough, I know you will always give me courage.
When I don't feel brave enough, I know you will always give me courage.
When I feel low, I know you will always give me courage.
When I feel lost in any way, I know you will always give me courage.
When I need a shoulder to cry on, I know you will always give me courage.

If and when I don't feel good enough, I know you will always give me courage.

When I feel like an outsider, I know you will always give me courage.
If and when I feel rejected, I know you will always give me courage.
When I feel like giving up, I know you will always give me courage.
If and when I feel unwanted, I know you will always give me courage.
If and when I feel worthless, I know you will always give me courage.
When I feel like I am entering an unknown trap, I know you will always give me courage.
When I feel like I'm in denial, I know you will always give me courage.
If and when I have nowhere to turn, I know you will always give me courage,
If and when I don't feel I have the courage to fight, I know you will always give me courage.
When I feel insecure, I know you will always give me courage.
If and when I feel guilt in any way, I know you will always give me courage.
When I need you the most, I know you will always give me courage.
When I am not myself, I know you will always give me courage.
When I feel alone, I know you will always give me courage.
When I face challenging days, I know you will always give me courage.
If and when I need to vent, I know you will always give me courage

Best In Me

When I look back at my fragile past, I know you will always see the best in me.
When I face my lifelong fears, I know you will always see the best in me
When I try and break my lifelong issues that affect me, I know you will always see the best in me.
When I try and overcome the loneliness I feel, I know you will always see the best in me.
When I feel down, I know you will always see the best in me.
If and when I feel broken, I know you will always see the best in me.
When I feel like I'm in a dark place, I know you will always see the best in me.
When I feel like I'm struggling, I know you will always see the best in me.
When my inner cries take its toll on me, I know you will always see the best in me.
When I don't feel strong enough, I know you will always see the best in me.
When I don't feel brave enough, I know you will always see the best in me.
When I feel low, I know you will always see the best in me.
When I feel lost in any way, I know you will always see the best in me.
When I need a shoulder to cry on, I know you will always see the best in me.
If and when I don't feel good enough, I know you will always see the best in me.

When I feel like an outsider, I know you will always see the best in me.
If and when I feel rejected, I know you will always see the best in me.
When I feel like giving up, I know you will always see the best in me.
If and when I feel unwanted, I know you will always see the best in me.
If and when I feel worthless, I know you will always see the best in me.
When I feel like I am entering an unknown trap, I know you will always see the best in me.
When I feel like I'm in denial, I know you will always see the best in me.
If and when I have nowhere to turn, I know you will always see the best in me.
If and when I don't feel I have the courage to fight, I know you will always see the best in me.
When I feel insecure, I know you will always see the best in me.
If and when I feel guilt in any way, I know you will always see the best in me.
When I need you the most, I know you will always see the best in me.
When I am not myself, I know you will always see the best in me.
When I feel alone, I know you will always see the best in me.
When I face challenging days, I know you will always see the best in me.
If and when I need to vent, I know you will always see the best in me.

I Don't Have To Put On A Brave Face

When I look back at my fragile past, I know I don't have to put on a brave face in front of you.
When I face my lifelong fears, I know I don't have to put on a brave face in front of you.
When I try and break my lifelong issues that affect me, I know I don't have to put on a brave face in front of you.
When I try and overcome the loneliness I feel, I know I don't have to put on a brave face in front of you.
When I feel down, I know I don't have to put on a brave face in front of you.
If and when I feel broken, I know I don't have to put on a brave face in front of you.
When I feel like I'm in a dark place, I know I don't have to put on a brave face in front of you.
When I feel like I'm struggling, I know I don't have to put on a brave face in front of you.
When my inner cries take its toll on me, I know I don't have to put on a brave face in front of you.
When I don't feel strong enough, I know I don't have to put on a brave face in front of you.

When I don't feel brave enough, I know I don't have to put on a brave face in front of you.
When I feel low, I know I don't have to put on a brave in front of you.
When I feel lost in any way, I know I don't have to put on a brave face in front of you.
When I need a shoulder to cry on, I know I don't have to put on a brave face in front of you.
If and when I don't feel good enough, I know I don't have to put on a brave face in front of you.

When I feel like an outsider, I know I don't have to put on a brave face in front of you.
If and when I feel rejected, I know I don't have to put on a brave face in front of you.
When I feel like giving up, I know I don't have to put on a brave face in front of you.
If and when I feel unwanted, I know I don't have to put on a brave face in front of you.
If and when I feel worthless, I know I don't have to put on a brave face in front of you.
When I feel like I am entering an unknown trap, I know I don't have to put on a brave face in front of you.
When I feel like I'm in denial, I know I don't have to put on a brave face in front of you.
If and when I have nowhere to turn, I know I don't have to put on a brave face in front of you.
If and when I don't feel I have the courage to fight, I know I don't have to put on a brave face in front of you.
When I feel insecure, I know I don't have to put on a brave face in front of you.
If and when I feel guilt in any way, I know I don't have to put on a brave face in front of you.
When I need you the most, I know I don't have to put on a brave face in front of you.
When I am not myself, I know I don't have to put on a brave face in front of you.
When I feel alone, I know I don't have to put on a brave face in front of you.
When I face challenging days, I know I don't have to put on a brave face in front of you.
If and when I need to vent, I know I don't have to put on a brave face in front of you.

When I Question Myself

When I look back at my fragile past, you know when I start to question myself.
When I face my lifelong fears, you know when I start to question myself.
When I try and break my lifelong issues that affect me, you know when I start to question myself.
When I try and overcome the loneliness I feel, you know when I start to question myself.
When I feel down, you know when I start to question myself.
If and when I feel broken, you know when I start to question myself.
When I feel like I'm in a dark place, you know when I start to question myself.
When I feel like I'm struggling, you know when I start to question myself.
When my inner cries take its toll on me, you know when I start to question myself.
When I don't feel strong enough, you know when I start to question myself.
When I don't feel brave enough, you know when I start to question myself.
When I feel low, you know when I start to question myself.
When I feel lost in any way, you know when I start to question myself.
When I need a shoulder to cry on, you know when I start to question myself.
If and when I don't feel good enough, you know when I start to question myself.

When I feel like an outsider, you know when I start to question myself.
If and when I feel rejected, you know when I start to question myself
When I feel like giving up, you know when I start to question myself.
If and when I feel unwanted, you know when I start to question myself.
If and when I feel worthless, you know when I start to question myself.
When I feel like I am entering an unknown trap, you know when I start to question myself.
When I feel like I'm in denial, you know when I start to question myself.
If and when I have nowhere to turn, you know when I start to question myself.
If and when I don't feel I have the courage to fight, you know when I start to question myself.
When I feel insecure, you know when I start to question myself.
If and when I feel guilt in any way, you know when I start to question myself.
When I need you the most, you know when I start to question myself.
When I am not myself, you know when I start to question myself.
When I feel alone, you know when I start to question myself.
When I face challenging days, you know when I start to question myself.
If and when I need to vent, you know when I start to question myself.

Stuck by me

When I look back at my fragile past, you have stuck by me no matter what.
When I face my lifelong fears, you have stuck by me no matter what.
When I try and break my lifelong issues that affect me, you have stuck by me no matter what.
When I try and overcome the loneliness I feel, you have stuck by me no matter what.
When I feel down, you have stuck by me no matter what.
If and when I feel broken, you have stuck by me no matter what.
When I feel like I'm in a dark place, you have stuck by me no matter what.
When I feel like I'm struggling, you have stuck by me no matter what.
When my inner cries take its toll on me, you have stuck by me no matter what.
When I don't feel strong enough, you have stuck by me no matter what.
When I don't feel brave enough, you have stuck by me no matter what
When I feel low, you have stuck by me no matter what.
When I feel lost in any way, you have stuck by me no matter what.
When I need a shoulder to cry on, you have stuck by me no matter what.
If and when I don't feel good enough, you have stuck by me no matter what.

When I feel like an outsider, you have stuck by me no matter what.
If and when I feel rejected, you have stuck by me no matter what.
When I feel like giving up, you have stuck by me no matter what.
If and when I feel unwanted, you have stuck by me no matter what.
If and when I feel worthless, you have stuck by me no matter what.
When I feel like I am entering an unknown trap, you have stuck by me no matter what.
When I feel like I'm in denial, you have stuck by me no matter what.
If and when I have nowhere to turn, you have stuck by me no matter what.

If and when I don't feel I have the courage to fight, you have stuck by me no matter what.
When I feel insecure, you have stuck by me no matter what.
If and when I feel guilt in any way, you have stuck by me no matter what.
When I need you the most, you have stuck by me no matter what.
When I am not myself, you have stuck by me no matter what.
When I feel alone, you have stuck by me no matter what.
When I face challenging days, you have stuck by me no matter what.
If and when I need to vent, you have stuck by me no matter what

Appreciate You

When I look back at my fragile past, I appreciate you so much more than you know.
When I face my lifelong fears, I appreciate you so much more than you know.
When I try and break my lifelong issues that affect me, I appreciate you so much more than you know.
When I try and overcome the loneliness I feel, I appreciate you so much more than you know.
When I feel down, I appreciate you so much more than you know.
If and when I feel broken, I appreciate you so much more than you know.
When I feel like I'm in a dark place, I appreciate you so much more than you know.
When I feel like I'm struggling, I appreciate you so much more than you know.
When my inner cries take its toll on me, I appreciate you so much more than you know.
When I don't feel strong enough, I appreciate you so much more than you know.
When I don't feel brave enough, I appreciate you so much more than you know.
When I feel low, I appreciate you so much more than you know.
When I feel lost in any way, I appreciate you so much more than you know.
When I need a shoulder to cry on, I appreciate you so much more than you know.
If and when I don't feel good enough, I appreciate you so much more than you know.

When I feel like an outsider, I appreciate you so much more than you know.
If and when I feel rejected, I appreciate you so much more than you know.
When I feel like giving up, I appreciate you so much more than you know.
If and when I feel unwanted, I appreciate you so much more than you know.
If and when I feel worthless, I appreciate you so much more than you know.
When I feel like I am entering an unknown trap, I appreciate you so much more than you know.
When I feel like I'm in denial, I appreciate you so much more than you know.
If and when I have nowhere to turn, I appreciate you so much more than you know.
If and when I don't feel I have the courage to fight, I appreciate you so much more than you know.
When I feel insecure, I appreciate you so much more than you know.
If and when I feel guilt in any way, I appreciate you so much more than you know.
When I need you the most, I appreciate you so much more than you know.
When I am not myself, I appreciate you so much more than you know.

When I feel alone, I appreciate you so much more than you know.
When I face challenging days, I appreciate you so much more than you know.
If and when I need to vent, I appreciate you so much more than you know.

When I Am A Wreck

When I look back at my fragile past, you know when I am a wreck.
When I face my lifelong fears, you know when I am a wreck.
When I try and break my lifelong issues that affect me, you know when I am a wreck.
When I try and overcome the loneliness I feel, you know when I am a wreck.
When I feel down, you know when I am a wreck.
If and when I feel broken, you know when I am a wreck.
When I feel like I'm in a dark place, you know when I am a wreck.
When I feel like I'm struggling, you know when I am a wreck.
When my inner cries take its toll on me, you know when I am a wreck.
When I don't feel strong enough, you know when I am a wreck.
When I don't feel brave enough, you know when I am a wreck.
When I feel low, you know when I am a wreck.
When I feel lost in any way, you told when I am a wreck.
When I need a shoulder to cry on, you know when I am a wreck.
If and when I don't feel good enough, you know when I am a wreck.

When I feel like an outsider, you know when I am a wreck.
If and when I feel rejected, you know when I am a wreck.
When I feel like giving up, you know when I am a wreck.
If and when I feel unwanted, you know when I am a wreck
If and when I feel worthless, you know when I am a wreck.
When I feel like I am entering an unknown trap, you know when I am a wreck.
When I feel like I'm in denial, you know when I am a wreck.
If and when I have nowhere to turn, you know when I am a wreck.
If and when I don't feel I have the courage to fight, you know when I am a wreck.
When I feel insecure, you know when I am a wreck.
If and when I feel guilt in any way, you know when I am a wreck.
When I need you the most, you know when I am a wreck.
When I am not myself, you know when I am a wreck.
When I feel alone, you know when I am a wreck.
When I face challenging days, you know when I am a wreck.
If and when I need to vent, you know when I am a wreck.

Never Judge Me

When I look back at my fragile past, you never judge me.
When I face my lifelong fears, you never judge me.
When I try and break my lifelong issues that affect me, you never judge me
When I try and overcome the loneliness I feel, you never judge me.
When I feel down, you never judge me.
If and when I feel broken, you never judge me.
When I feel like I'm in a dark place, you never judge me.
When I feel like I'm struggling, you never judge me.
When my inner cries take its toll on me, you never judge me.
When I don't feel strong enough, you never judge me.
When I don't feel brave enough, you never judge me.
When I feel low, you never judge me.
When I feel lost in any way, you never judge me.
When I need a shoulder to cry on, you never judge me.
If and when I don't feel good enough, you never judge me.

When I feel like an outsider, you never judge me.
If and when I feel rejected, you never judge me.
When I feel like giving up, you never judge me.
If and when I feel unwanted, you never judge me.
If and when I feel worthless, you never judge me.
When I feel like I am entering an unknown trap, you never judge me.
When I feel like I'm in denial, you never judge me.
If and when I have nowhere to turn, you never judge me.
If and when I don't feel I have the courage to fight, you never judge me.
When I feel insecure, you never judge me.
If and when I feel guilt in any way, you never judge me.
When I need you the most, you never judge me.
When I am not myself, you never judge me.
When I feel alone, you never judge me.
When I face challenging days, you never judge me.
If and when I need to vent, you never judge me

Take Me On A Lifetime Journey

When I look back at my fragile past, you take me on a lifetime journey.
When I face my lifelong fears, you take me on a lifetime journey.
When I try and break my lifelong issues that affect me, you take me on a lifetime journey.

When I try and overcome the loneliness I feel, you take me on a lifetime journey.
When I feel down, you take me on a lifetime journey.
If and when I feel broken, you take me on a lifetime journey.
When I feel like I'm in a dark place, you take me on a lifetime journey.
When I feel like I'm struggling, you take me on a lifetime journey.
When my inner cries take its toll on me, you take me on a lifetime journey.
When I don't feel strong enough, you take me on a lifetime journey.
When I don't feel brave enough, you take me on a lifetime journey.
When I feel low, you take me on a lifetime journey.
When I feel lost in any way, you take me on a lifetime journey.
When I need a shoulder to cry on, you take me on a lifetime journey.
If and when I don't feel good enough, you take me on a lifetime journey.

When I feel like an outsider, you take me on a lifetime journey.
If and when I feel rejected, you take me on a lifetime journey.
When I feel like giving up, you take me on a lifetime journey.
If and when I feel unwanted, you take me on a lifetime journey.
If and when I feel worthless, you take me on a lifetime journey.
When I feel like I am entering an unknown trap, you take me on a lifetime journey.
When I feel like I'm in denial, you take me on a lifetime journey.
If and when I have nowhere to turn, you take me on a lifetime journey.
If and when I don't feel I have the courage to fight, you take me on a lifetime journey.
When I feel insecure, you take me on a lifetime journey.
If and when I feel guilt in any way, you take me on a lifetime journey.
When I need you the most, you take me on a lifetime journey.
When I am not myself, you take me on a lifetime journey.
When I feel alone, you take me on a lifetime journey.
When I face challenging days, you take me on a lifetime journey.
If and when I need to vent, you take me on a lifetime journey.

Look Ur Way

When I look back at my fragile past, I know I can look ur way.
When I face my lifelong fears, I know I can look ur way.
When I try and break my lifelong issues that affect me, I know I can look ur way,
When I try and overcome the loneliness I feel, I know I can look ur way.
When I feel down, I know I can look ur way.
If and when I feel broken, I know I can look ur way.
When I feel like I'm in a dark place, I know I can look ur way.

When I feel like I'm struggling, I know I can look ur way.
When my inner cries take its toll on me, I know I can look ur way.
When I don't feel strong enough, I know I can look ur way.
When I don't feel brave enough, I know I can look ur way.
When I feel low, I know I can look ur way.
When I feel lost in any way, I know I can look ur way.
When I need a shoulder to cry on, I know I can look ur way.
If and when I don't feel good enough, I know I can look ur way.

When I feel like an outsider, I know I can look ur way.
If and when I feel rejected, I know I can look ur way.
When I feel like giving up, I know I can look ur way.
If and when I feel unwanted, I know I can look ur way.
If and when I feel worthless, I know I can look ur way.
When I feel like I am entering an unknown trap, I know I can look ur way.
When I feel like I'm in denial, I know I can look ur way.
If and when I have nowhere to turn, I know I can look my way.
If and when I don't feel I have the courage to fight, I know I can look ur way.
When I feel insecure, I know I can look ur way.
If and when I feel guilt in any way, I know I can look ur way.
When I need you the most, I know I can look ur way.
When I am not myself, I know I can look ur way.
When I feel alone, I know I can look ur way.
When I face challenging days, I know I can look ur way.
If and when I need to vent, I know I can look ur way.

You Ease

You ease my fragile past
You ease my lifelong fears
You ease my lifelong issues
You ease my pain
You ease my insecurities
You ease my emotional strain
You ease my loneliness
You ease my guilt
You ease the hateful things that come my way
You ease my worries
You ease my state of mind
You ease my dark days

Bulletproof

Bulletproof my fragile past.
Bulletproof my safe space.
Bulletproof my demons
Bulletproof my carefree existence
Bulletproof my precious experiences
Bulletproof my extraordinary memories.
Bulletproof the real me
Bulletproof the true me
Bulletproof the protection of the people in my life
Bulletproof my pain
Bulletproof my heart
Bulletproof my soul.
Bulletproof my hurt
Bulletproof my rare ways
Bulletproof me from harm.
Bulletproof me from dark moments
Bulletproof me from the wrong direction
Bulletproof me from my inner cries
Bulletproof the words I hear.
Bulletproof my happy moments
Bulletproof the people I care about.

Won't Leave Me Out In The Cold

When I look back at my fragile past, I know you won't leave me out in the cold.
When I face my lifelong fears, I know you won't leave me out in the cold.
When I try and break my lifelong issues that affect me, I know you won't leave me out in the cold.
When I try and overcome the loneliness I feel, I know you won't leave me out in the cold.
When I feel down, I know you won't leave me out in the cold.
If and when I feel broken, I know you won't leave me out in the cold.
When I feel like I'm in a dark place, I know you won't leave me out in the cold.
When I feel like I'm struggling, I know you won't leave me out in the cold.
When my inner cries take its toll on me, I know you won't leave me out in the cold.
When I don't feel strong enough, I know you won't leave me out in the cold.
When I don't feel brave enough, I know you won't leave me out in the cold.
When I feel low, I know you won't leave me out in the cold.

When I feel lost in any way, I know you won't leave me out in the cold.
When I need a shoulder to cry on, I know you won't leave me out in the cold.
If and when I don't feel good enough, I know you won't leave me out in the cold.

When I feel like an outsider, I know you won't leave me out in the cold.
If and when I feel rejected, I know you won't leave me out in the cold..
When I feel like giving up, I know you won't leave me out in the cold.
If and when I feel unwanted, I know you won't leave me out in the cold.
If and when I feel worthless, I know you won't leave me out in the cold.
When I feel like I am entering an unknown trap, I know you won't leave me out in the cold.
When I feel like I'm in denial, I know you won't leave me out in the cold.
If and when I have nowhere to turn, I know you won't leave me out in the cold.
If and when I don't feel I have the courage to fight, I know you won't leave me out in the cold.
When I feel insecure, I know you won't leave me out in the cold.
If and when I feel guilt in any way, I know you won't leave me out in thee cold.
When I need you the most, I know you won't leave me out in the cold.
When I am not myself, I know you won't leave me out in the cold.
When I feel alone, I know you won't leave me out in the cold.
When I face challenging days, I know you won't leave me out in the cold.
If and when I need to vent, I know you won't leave me out in the cold.

Reach Out To You

When I look back at my fragile past, I know I can reach out to you.
When I face my lifelong fears, I know I can reach out to you.
When I try and break my lifelong issues that affect me, I know I can reach out to you.
When I try and overcome the loneliness I feel, I know I can reach out to you.
When I feel down, I know I can reach out to you.
If and when I feel broken, I know I can reach out to you.
When I feel like I'm in a dark place, I know i can reach out to you.
When I feel like I'm struggling, I know I can reach out to you.
When my inner cries take its toll on me, I know I can reach out to you.
When I don't feel strong enough, I know I can reach out to you.
When I don't feel brave enough, I know I can reach out to you.
When I feel low, I know I can reach out to you.
When I feel lost in any way, I know I can reach out to you.
When I need a shoulder to cry on, I know I can reach out to you.

If and when I don't feel good enough, I know I can reach out to you.

When I feel like an outsider, I know I can reach out to you.
If and when I feel rejected, I know I can reach out to you.
When I feel like giving up, I know I can reach out to you.
If and when I feel unwanted, I know I can reach out to you.
If and when I feel worthless, I know I can reach out to you.
When I feel like I am entering an unknown trap, I know I can reach out to you.
When I feel like I'm in denial, I know I can reach out to you.
If and when I have nowhere to turn, I know I can reach out to you.
If and when I don't feel I have the courage to fight, I know I can reach out to you.
When I feel insecure, I know I can reach out to you
If and when I feel guilt in any way, I know I can reach out to you.
When I need you the most, I know I can reach out to you
When I am not myself, I know I can reach out to you.
When I feel alone, I know I can reach out to you.
When I face challenging days, I know I can reach out to you.
If and when I need to vent, I know I can reach out to you.

Rely On You

When I look back at my fragile past, I know I can rely on you.
When I face my lifelong fears, I know I can rely on you.
When I try and break my lifelong issues that affect me, I know I can rely on you.
When I try and overcome the loneliness I feel, I know I can rely on you.
When I feel down, I know I can rely on you.
If and when I feel broken, I know I can rely on you.
When I feel like I'm in a dark place, I know I can rely on you.
When I feel like I'm struggling, I know I can rely on you.
When my inner cries take its toll on me, I know I can rely on you.
When I don't feel strong enough, I know I can rely on you.
When I don't feel brave enough, I know I can rely on you.
When I feel low, I know I can rely on you.
When I feel lost in any way, I know I can rely on you.
When I need a shoulder to cry on, I know I can rely on you.
If and when I don't feel good enough, I know I can rely on you.

When I feel like an outsider, I know I can rely on you.
If and when I feel rejected, I know I can rely on you.
When I feel like giving up, I know I can rely on you.

If and when I feel unwanted, I know I can rely on you.
If and when I feel worthless, I know I can rely on you.
When I feel like I am entering an unknown trap, I know I can rely on you.
When I feel like I'm in denial, I know I can rely on you.
If and when I have nowhere to turn, I know I can rely on you.
If and when I don't feel I have the courage to fight, I know I can rely on you.
When I feel insecure, I know I can rely on you.
If and when I feel guilt in any way, I know I can rely on you.
When I need you the most, I know I can rely on you.
When I am not myself, I know I can rely on you.
When I feel alone, I know I can rely on you.
When I face challenging days, I know I can rely on you.
If and when I need to vent, I know I can rely on you.

Count On You

When I look back at my fragile past, I know I can count on you.
When I face my lifelong fears, I know I can count on you.
When I try and break my lifelong issues that affect me, I know I can count on you.
When I try and overcome the loneliness I feel, I know I can count on you.
When I feel down, I know I can count on you
If and when I feel broken, I know I can count on you.
When I feel like I'm in a dark place, I know I can count on you.
When I feel like I'm struggling, I know I can count on you.
When my inner cries take its toll on me, I know I can count on you.
When I don't feel strong enough, I know I can count on you.
When I don't feel brave enough, I know I can count on you.
When I feel low, I know I can count on you.
When I feel lost in any way, I know I can count on you.
When I need a shoulder to cry on, I know I can count on you.
If and when I don't feel good enough, I know I can count on you.

When I feel like an outsider, I know I can count on you.
If and when I feel rejected, I know I can count on you.
When I feel like giving up, I know I can count on you.
If and when I feel unwanted, I know I can count on you.
If and when I feel worthless, I know I can count on you.
When I feel like I am entering an unknown trap, I know I can count on you.
When I feel like I'm in denial, I know I can count on you.
If and when I have nowhere to turn, I know I can count on you.

If and when I don't feel I have the courage to fight, I know I can count on you.
When I feel insecure, I know I can count on you.
If and when I feel guilt in any way, I know I can count on you.
When I need you the most, I know I can count on you.
When I am not myself, I know I can count on you.
When I feel alone, I know I can count on you.
When I face challenging days, I know I can count on you.
If and when I need to vent, I know I can count on you.

Lean On You

When I look back at my fragile past, I know I can lean on you.
When I face my lifelong fears, I know I can lean on you.
When I try and break my lifelong issues that affect me, I know I can lean on you.
When I try and overcome the loneliness I feel, I know I can lean on you.
When I feel down, I know I can lean on you.
If and when I feel broken, I know I can lean on you.
When I feel like I'm in a dark place, I know I can lean on you.
When I feel like I'm struggling, I know I can lean on you.
When my inner cries take its toll on me, I know I can lean on you.
When I don't feel strong enough, I know I can lean on you.
When I don't feel brave enough, I know I can lean on you.
When I feel low, I know I can lean on you.
When I feel lost in any way, I know I can lean on you.
When I need a shoulder to cry on, I know I can lean on you.
If and when I don't feel good enough, I know I can lean on you.

When I feel like an outsider, I know I can lean on you.
If and when I feel rejected, I know I can lean on you.
When I feel like giving up, I know I can lean on you.
If and when I feel unwanted, I know I can lean on you.
If and when I feel worthless, I know I can lean on you.
When I feel like I am entering an unknown trap, I know I can lean on you.
When I feel like I'm in denial, I know I can lean on you.
If and when I have nowhere to turn, I know I can lean on you
If and when I don't feel I have the courage to fight, I know I can lean on you.
When I feel insecure, I know I can lean on you.
If and when I feel guilt in any way, I know I can lean on you.
When I need you the most, I know I can lean on you.
When I am not myself, I know I can lean on you.
When I feel alone, I know I can lean on you.

When I face challenging days, I know I can lean on you.
If and when I need to vent, I know I can lean on you.

Warrior In Me

When I look back at my fragile past, you bring out the warrior in me.
When I face my lifelong fears, you bring out the warrior in me.
When I try and break my lifelong issues that affect me, you bring out the warrior in me.
When I try and overcome the loneliness I feel, you bring out the warrior in me.
When I feel down, you bring out the warrior in me.
If and when I feel broken, you bring out the warrior in me.
When I feel like I'm in a dark place, you bring out the warrior in me.
When I feel like I'm struggling, you bring out the warrior in me.
When my inner cries take its toll on me, you bring out the warrior in me,
When I don't feel strong enough, you bring out the warrior in me.
When I don't feel brave enough, you bring out the warrior in me.
When I feel low, you bring out the warrior in me.
When I feel lost in any way, you bring out the warrior in me.
When I need a shoulder to cry on, you bring out the warrior in me.
If and when I don't feel good enough, you bring out the warrior in me.

When I feel like an outsider, you bring out the warrior in me.
If and when I feel rejected, you bring out the warrior in me.
When I feel like giving up, you bring out the warrior in me.
If and when I feel unwanted, you bring out the warrior in me.
If and when I feel worthless, you bring out the warrior in me.
When I feel like I am entering an unknown trap, you bring out the warrior in me.
When I feel like I'm in denial, you bring out the warrior in me.
If and when I have nowhere to turn, you bring out the warrior in me.
If and when I don't feel I have the courage to fight, you bring out the warrior in me.
When I feel insecure, you bring out the warrior in me.
If and when I feel guilt in any way, you bring out the warrior in me.
When I need you the most, you bring out the warrior in me.
When I am not myself, you bring out the warrior in me.
When I feel alone, you bring out the warrior in me.
When I face challenging days, you bring out the warrior in me.
If and when I need to vent, you bring out the warrior in me.

Untangle Me

When I look back at my fragile past, you untangle me.
When I face my lifelong fears, you untangle me.
When I try and break my lifelong issues that affect me, you untangle me.
When I try and overcome the loneliness I feel, you untangle me.
When I feel down, you untangle me.
If and when I feel broken, you untangle me.
When I feel like I'm in a dark place, you untangle me.
When I feel like I'm struggling, you untangle me.
When my inner cries take its toll on me, you untangle me.
When I don't feel strong enough, you untangle me.
When I don't feel brave enough, you untangle me.
When I feel low, you untangle me.
When I feel lost in any way, you untangle me.
When I need a shoulder to cry on, you untangle me.
If and when I don't feel good enough, you untangle me.

When I feel like an outsider, you untangle me.
If and when I feel rejected, you untangle me.
When I feel like giving up, you untangle me.
If and when I feel unwanted, you untangle me.
If and when I feel worthless, you untangle me.
When I feel like I am entering an unknown trap, you untangle me.
When I feel like I'm in denial, you untangle me.
If and when I have nowhere to turn, you untangle me.
If and when I don't feel I have the courage to fight, you untangle me.
When I feel insecure, you untangle me.
If and when I feel guilt in any way, you untangle me.
When I need you the most, you untangle me.
When I am not myself, you untangle me.
When I feel alone, you untangle me.
When I face challenging days, you untangle me.
If and when I need to vent, you untangle me.

Bring out the wild side of me

When I look back at my fragile past, you bring out the wild side of me.
When I face my lifelong fears, you bring out the wild side of me.
When I try and break my lifelong issues that affect me, you bring out the wild side of me.

When I try and overcome the loneliness I feel, you bring out the wild side of me.
When I feel down, you bring out the wild side of me.
If and when I feel broken, you bring out the wild side of me.
When I feel like I'm in a dark place, you bring out the wild side of me.
When I feel like I'm struggling, you bring out the wild side of me.
When my inner cries take its toll on me, you bring out the wild side of me.
When I don't feel strong enough, you bring out the wild side of me.
When I don't feel brave enough, you bring out the wild side of me.
When I feel low, you bring out the wild side of me.
When I feel lost in any way, you bring out the wild side of me.
When I need a shoulder to cry on, you bring out the wild side of me.
If and when I don't feel good enough, you bring out the wild side of me.

When I feel like an outsider, you bring out the wild side of me.
If and when I feel rejected, you bring out the wild side of me.
When I feel like giving up, you bring out the wild side of me.
If and when I feel unwanted, you bring out the wild side of me.
If and when I feel worthless, you bring out the wild side of me.
When I feel like I am entering an unknown trap, you bring out the wild side of me.
When I feel like I'm in denial, you bring out the wild side of me.
If and when I have nowhere to turn, you bring out the wild side of me.
If and when I don't feel I have the courage to fight, you bring out the wild side of me.
When I feel insecure, you bring out the wild side of me.
If and when I feel guilt in any way, you bring out the wild side of me.
When I need you the most, you bring out the wild side of me.
When I am not myself, you bring out the wild side of me.
When I feel alone, you bring out the wild side of me.
When I face challenging days, you bring out the wild side of me.
If and when I need to vent, you bring out the wild side of me.

Bring Out The Reckless Side Of Me

When I look back at my fragile past, you bring out the reckless side of me.
When I face my lifelong fears, you bring out the reckless side of me.
When I try and break my lifelong issues that affect me, you bring out the reckless side of me.
When I try and overcome the loneliness I feel, you bring out the reckless side of me.
When I feel down, you bring out the reckless side of me.

If and when I feel broken, you bring out the reckless side of me.
When I feel like I'm in a dark place, you bring out the reckless side of me.
When I feel like I'm struggling, you bring out the reckless side of me.
When my inner cries take its toll on me, you bring out the reckless side of me.
When I don't feel strong enough, you bring out the reckless side of me.
When I don't feel brave enough, you bring out the reckless side of me.
When I feel low, you bring out the reckless side of me.
When I feel lost in any way, you bring out the reckless side of me.
When I need a shoulder to cry on, you bring out the reckless side of me.
If and when I don't feel good enough, you bring out the reckless side of me.

When I feel like an outsider, you bring out the reckless side of me.
If and when I feel rejected, you bring out the reckless side of me.
When I feel like giving up, you bring out the reckless side of me.
If and when I feel unwanted, you bring out the reckless side of me.
If and when I feel worthless, you bring out the reckless side of me.
When I feel like I am entering an unknown trap, you bring out the reckless side of me.
When I feel like I'm in denial, you bring out the reckless side of me.
If and when I have nowhere to turn, you bring out the reckless side of me.
If and when I don't feel I have the courage to fight, you bring out the reckless side of me.
When I feel insecure, you bring out the reckless side of me.
If and when I feel guilt in any way, you bring out the reckless side of me.
When I need you the most, you bring out the reckless side of me.
When I am not myself, you bring out the reckless side of me.
When I feel alone, you bring out the reckless side of me.
When I face challenging days, you bring out the reckless side of me.
If and when I need to vent, you bring out the reckless side of me.

Bring Me Out Of My Shell

When I look back at my fragile past, you bring me out of my shell.
When I face my lifelong fears, you bring me out of my shell.
When I try and break my lifelong issues that affect me, you bring me out of my shell.
When I try and overcome the loneliness I feel, you bring me out of my shell.
When I feel down, you bring me out of my shell.
If and when I feel broken, you bring me out of my shell.
When I feel like I'm in a dark place, you bring me out of my shell.
When I feel like I'm struggling, you bring me out of my shell.

When my inner cries take its toll on me, you bring me out of my shell.
When I don't feel strong enough, you bring me out of my shell.
When I don't feel brave enough, you bring me out of my shell.
When I feel low, you bring me out of my shell.
When I feel lost in any way, you bring me out of my shell.
When I need a shoulder to cry on, you bring me out of my shell.
If and when I don't feel good enough, you bring me out of my shell.

When I feel like an outsider, you bring me out of my shell.
If and when I feel rejected, you bring me out of my shell.
When I feel like giving up, you bring me out of my shell.
If and when I feel unwanted, you bring me out of my shell.
If and when I feel worthless, you bring me out of my shell.
When I feel like I am entering an unknown trap, you bring me out of my shell.
When I feel like I'm in denial, you bring me out of my shell.
If and when I have nowhere to turn, you bring me out of my shell.
If and when I don't feel I have the courage to fight, you bring me out of my shell.
When I feel insecure, you bring me out of my shell.
If and when I feel guilt in any way, you bring me out of my shell.
When I need you the most, you bring me out of my shell.
When I am not myself, you bring me out of my shell.
When I feel alone, you bring me out of my shell.
When I face challenging days, you bring me out of my shell.
If and when I need to vent, you bring me out of my shell.

Vent To You

When I look back at my fragile past, I know I can vent to you.
When I face my lifelong fears, I know I can vent to you.
When I try and break my lifelong issues that affect me, I know I can vent to you.
When I try and overcome the loneliness I feel, I know I can vent to you.
When I feel down, I know I can vent to you.
If and when I feel broken, I know I can vent to you.
When I feel like I'm in a dark place, I know I can vent to you.
When I feel like I'm struggling, I know I can vent to you.
When my inner cries take its toll on me, I know I can vent to you.
When I don't feel strong enough, I know I can vent to you.
When I don't feel brave enough, I know I can vent to you.
When I feel low, I know I can vent to you.
When I feel lost in any way, I know I can vent to you.

When I need a shoulder to cry on, I know I can vent to you.
If and when I don't feel good enough, I know I can vent to you.

When I feel like an outsider, I know I can vent to you.
If and when I feel rejected, I know I can vent to you.
When I feel like giving up, I know I can vent to you.
If and when I feel unwanted, I know I can vent to you.
If and when I feel worthless, I know I can vent to you..
When I feel like I am entering an unknown trap, I know I can vent to you.
When I feel like I'm in denial, I know I can vent to you.
If and when I have nowhere to turn, I know I can vent to you.
If and when I don't feel I have the courage to fight, I know I can vent to you.
When I feel insecure, I know I can vent to you.
If and when I feel guilt in any way, I know I can vent to you.
When I need you the most, I know I can vent to you.
When I am not myself, I know I can vent to you.
When I feel alone, I know I can vent to you.
When I face challenging days, I know I can vent to you.
If and when I need to vent, I know I can vent to you.

Bring Out The Adventurous Side Of Me

When I look back at my fragile past, you bring out the adventurous side of me.
When I face my lifelong fears, you bring out the adventurous side of me.
When I try and break my lifelong issues that affect me, you bring out the adventurous side of me.
When I try and overcome the loneliness I feel, you bring out the adventurous side of me.
When I feel down, you bring out the adventurous side of me.
If and when I feel broken, you bring out the adventurous side of me.
When I feel like I'm in a dark place, you bring out the adventurous side of me.
When I feel like I'm struggling, you bring out the adventurous side of me.
When my inner cries take its toll on me, you bring out the adventurous side of me.
When I don't feel strong enough, you bring out the adventurous side of me.
When I don't feel brave enough, you bring out the adventurous side of me.
When I feel low, you bring out the adventurous side of me.
When I feel lost in any way, you bring out the adventurous side of me.
When I need a shoulder to cry on, you bring out the adventurous side of me.
If and when I don't feel good enough, you bring out the adventurous side of me.

When I feel like an outsider, you bring out the adventurous side of me.
If and when I feel rejected, you bring out the adventurous side of me.
When I feel like giving up, you bring out the adventurous side of me.
If and when I feel unwanted, you bring out the adventurous side of me.
If and when I feel worthless, you bring out the adventurous side of me.
When I feel like I am entering an unknown trap, you bring out the adventurous side of me.
When I feel like I'm in denial, you bring out the adventurous side of me.
If and when I have nowhere to turn, you bring out the adventurous side of me.
If and when I don't feel I have the courage to fight, you bring out the adventurous side of me.
When I feel insecure, you bring out the adventurous side of me.
If and when I feel guilt in any way, you bring out the adventurous side of me.
When I need you the most, you bring out the adventurous side of me.
When I am not myself, you bring out the adventurous side of me.
When I feel alone, you bring out the adventurous side of me.
When I face challenging days, you bring out the adventurous side of me.
If and when I need to vent, you bring out the adventurous side of me.

Bring Out The Rebel In Me

When I look back at my fragile past, you bring out the rebel in me.
When I face my lifelong fears, you bring out the rebel in me.
When I try and break my lifelong issues that affect me, you bring out the rebel in me.
When I try and overcome the loneliness I feel, you bring out the rebel in me.
When I feel down, you bring out the rebel in me.
If and when I feel broken, you bring out the rebel in me.
When I feel like I'm in a dark place, you bring out the rebel in me.
When I feel like I'm struggling, you bring out the rebel in me.
When my inner cries take its toll on me, you bring out the rebel in me.
When I don't feel strong enough, you bring out the rebel in me.
When I don't feel brave enough, you bring out the rebel in me.
When I feel low, you bring out the rebel in me.
When I feel lost in any way, you bring out the rebel in me.
When I need a shoulder to cry on, you bring out the rebel in me.
If and when I don't feel good enough, you bring out the rebel in me.

When I feel like an outsider, you bring out the rebel in me.
If and when I feel rejected, you bring out the rebel in me.
When I feel like giving up, you bring out the rebel in me.

If and when I feel unwanted, you bring out the rebel in me.
If and when I feel worthless, you bring out the rebel in me.
When I feel like I am entering an unknown trap, you bring out the rebel in me.
When I feel like I'm in denial, you bring out the rebel in me.
If and when I have nowhere to turn, you bring out the rebel in me.
If and when I don't feel I have the courage to fight, you bring out the rebel in me.
When I feel insecure, you bring out the rebel in me.
If and when I feel guilt in any way, you bring out the rebel in me..
When I need you the most, you bring out the rebel in me.
When I am not myself, you bring out the rebel in me.
When I feel alone, you bring out the rebel in me.
When I face challenging days, you bring out the rebel in me.
If and when I need to vent, you bring out the rebel in me.

Bring Me Out Of My Comfort Zone

When I look back at my fragile past, you bring me out of my comfort zone
When I face my lifelong fears, you bring me out of my comfort zone
When I try and break my lifelong issues that affect me, you bring me out of my comfort zone
When I try and overcome the loneliness I feel, you bring me out of my comfort zone
When I feel down, you bring me out of my comfort zone
If and when I feel broken, you bring me out of my comfort zone
When I feel like I'm in a dark place, you bring me out of my comfort zone
When I feel like I'm struggling, you bring me out of my comfort zone
When my inner cries take its toll on me, you bring me out of my comfort zone
When I don't feel strong enough, you bring me out of my comfort zone
When I don't feel brave enough, you bring me out of my comfort zone
When I feel low, you bring me out of my comfort zone
When I feel lost in any way, you bring me out of my comfort zone
When I need a shoulder to cry on, you bring me out of my comfort zone
If and when I don't feel good enough, you bring me out of my comfort zone

When I feel like an outsider, you bring me out of my comfort zone.
If and when I feel rejected, you bring me out of my comfort zone
When I feel like giving up, you bring me out of my comfort zone
If and when I feel unwanted, you bring me out of my comfort zone.
If and when I feel worthless, you bring me out of my comfort zone

When I feel like I am entering an unknown trap, you bring me out of my comfort zone
When I feel like I'm in denial, you bring me out of my comfort zone
If and when I have nowhere to turn, you bring me out of my comfort zone
If and when I don't feel I have the courage to fight, you bring me out of my comfort zone
When I feel insecure, you bring me out of my comfort zone
If and when I feel guilt in any way, you bring me out of my comfort zone
When I need you the most, you bring me out of my comfort zone
When I am not myself, you bring me out of my comfort zone
When I feel alone you bring me out of my comfort zone
When I face challenging days you bring me out of my comfort zone.
If and when I need to vent, you bring me out of my comfort zone

Bring Out The Real Me

When I look back at my fragile past, you bring out the real me.
When I face my lifelong fears, you bring out the real me.
When I try and break my lifelong issues that affect me, you bring out the real me.
When I try and overcome the loneliness I feel, you bring out the real me.
When I feel down, you bring out the real me.
If and when I feel broken, you bring out the real me.
When I feel like I'm in a dark place, you bring out the real me.
When I feel like I'm struggling, you bring out the real me.
When my inner cries take its toll on me, you bring out the real me.
When I don't feel strong enough, you bring out the real me.
When I don't feel brave enough, you bring out the real me.
When I feel low, you bring out the real me.
When I feel lost in any way, you bring out the real me.
When I need a shoulder to cry on, you bring out the real me.
If and when I don't feel good enough, you bring out the real me.

When I feel like an outsider, you bring out the real me..
If and when I feel rejected, you bring out the real me.
When I feel like giving up, you bring out the real me.
If and when I feel unwanted, you bring out the real me.
If and when I feel worthless, you bring out the real me.
When I feel like I am entering an unknown trap, you bring out the real me.
When I feel like I'm in denial, you bring out the real me.
If and when I have nowhere to turn, you bring out the real me.

If and when I don't feel I have the courage to fight, you bring out the real me.
When I feel insecure, you bring out the real me.
If and when I feel guilt in any way, you bring out the real me.
When I need you the most, you bring out the real me.
When I am not myself, you bring out the real me.
When I feel alone, you bring out the real me.
When I face challenging days, you bring out the real me.
If and when I need to vent, you bring out the real me.

When I Felt Numb

When I look back at my fragile past, you know when I felt numb.
When I face my lifelong fears, you know when I felt numb.
When I try and break my lifelong issues that affect me, you know when I felt numb.
When I try and overcome the loneliness I feel, you know when I felt numb.
When I feel down, you know when I felt numb.
If and when I feel broken, you know when I felt numb.
When I feel like I'm in a dark place, you know when I felt numb.
When I feel like I'm struggling, you know when I felt numb.
When my inner cries take its toll on me, you know when I felt numb.
When I don't feel strong enough, you know when I felt numb.
When I don't feel brave enough, you know when I felt numb.
When I feel low, you know when I felt numb.
When I feel lost in any way, you know when I felt numb.
When I need a shoulder to cry on, you know when I felt numb.
If and when I don't feel good enough, you know when I felt numb.

When I feel like an outsider, you know when I felt numb.
If and when I feel rejected, you know when I felt numb.
When I feel like giving up, you know when I felt numb.
If and when I feel unwanted, you know when I felt numb.
If and when I feel worthless, you know when I felt numb.
When I feel like I am entering an unknown trap, you know when I felt numb.
When I feel like I'm in denial, you know when I felt numb.
If and when I have nowhere to turn, you know when I felt numb.
If and when I don't feel I have the courage to fight, you know when I felt numb.
When I feel insecure, you know when I felt numb.
If and when I feel guilt in any way, you know when I felt numb.
When I need you the most, you know when I felt numb.
When I am not myself, you know when I felt numb.

When I feel alone, you know when I felt numb.
When I face challenging days, you know when I felt numb.
If and when I need to vent, you know when I felt numb.

When I Am At My Lowest

When I look back at my fragile past, you know when I am at my lowest.
When I face my lifelong fears, you know when I am at my lowest.
When I try and break my lifelong issues that affect me, you know when I am at my lowest.
When I try and overcome the loneliness I feel, you know when I am at my lowest.
When I feel down, you know when I am at my lowest.
If and when I feel broken, you know when I am at my lowest.
When I feel like I'm in a dark place, you know when I am at my lowest.
When I feel like I'm struggling, you know when I am at my lowest.
When my inner cries take its toll on me, you know when I am at my lowest.
When I don't feel strong enough, you know when I am at my lowest.
When I don't feel brave enough, you know when I am at my lowest.
When I feel low, you know when I am at my lowest.
When I feel lost in any way, you know when I am at my lowest.
When I need a shoulder to cry on, you know when I am at my lowest.
If and when I don't feel good enough, you know when I am at my lowest.

When I feel like an outsider, you know when I am at my lowest..
If and when I feel rejected, you know when I am at my lowest.
When I feel like giving up, you know when I am at my lowest.
If and when I feel unwanted, you know when I am at my lowest.
If and when I feel worthless, you know when I am at my lowest.
When I feel like I am entering an unknown trap, you know when I am at my lowest.
When I feel like I'm in denial, you know when I am at my lowest.
If and when I have nowhere to turn, you know when I am at my lowest.
If and when I don't feel I have the courage to fight, you know when I am at my lowest.
When I feel insecure, you know when I am at my lowest.
If and when I feel guilt in any way, you know when I am at my lowest.
When I need you the most, you know when I am at my lowest.
When I am not myself, you know when I am at my lowest.
When I feel alone, you know when I am at my lowest.
When I face challenging days, you know when I am at my lowest.

If and when I need to vent, you know when I am at my lowest.

When I Am At Breaking Point

When I look back at my fragile past, you know when I am at breaking point
When I face my lifelong fears, you know when I am at breaking point
When I try and break my lifelong issues that affect me, you know when I am at breaking point
When I try and overcome the loneliness I feel, you know when I am at breaking point
When I feel down, you know when I am at breaking point
If and when I feel broken, you know when I am at breaking point
When I feel like I'm in a dark place, you know when I am at breaking point
When I feel like I'm struggling, you know when I am at breaking point
When my inner cries take its toll on me, you know when I am at breaking point
When I don't feel strong enough, you know when I am at breaking point
When I don't feel brave enough, you know when I am at breaking point
When I feel low, you know when I am at breaking point
When I feel lost in any way, you know when I am at breaking point
When I need a shoulder to cry on, you know when I am at breaking point
If and when I don't feel good enough, you know when I am at breaking point

When I feel like an outsider, you know when I am at breaking point
If and when I feel rejected, you know when I am at breaking point
When I feel like giving up, you know when I am at breaking point
If and when I feel unwanted, you know when I am at breaking point
If and when I feel worthless, you know when I am at breaking point
When I feel like I am entering an unknown trap, you know when I am at breaking point
When I feel like I'm in denial, you know when I am at breaking point
If and when I have nowhere to turn, you know when I am at breaking point
If and when I don't feel I have the courage to fight, you know when I am at breaking point
When I feel insecure, you know when I am at breaking point
If and when I feel guilt in any way, you know when I am at breaking point
When I need you the most, you know when I am at breaking point
When I am not myself, you know when I am at breaking point
When I feel alone, you know when I am at breaking point
When I face challenging days, you know when I am at breaking point
If and when I need to vent, you know when I am at breaking point

Dark Place

When I look back at my fragile past, I know you won't let me go back to that dark place I was in.
When I face my lifelong fears, I know you won't let me go back to that dark place I was in.
When I try and break my lifelong issues that affect me, I know you won't let me go back to that dark place I was in.
When I try and overcome the loneliness I feel, I know you won't let me go back to that dark place I was in.
When I feel down, I know you won't let me go back to that dark place I was in.
If and when I feel broken, I know you won't let me go back to that dark place I was in.
When I feel like I'm in a dark place, I know you won't let me go back to that dark place I was in.
When I feel like I'm struggling, I know you won't let me go back to that dark place I was in.
When my inner cries take its toll on me, I know you won't let me go back to that dark place I was in.
When I don't feel strong enough, I know you won't let me go back to that dark place I was in.
When I don't feel brave enough, I know you won't let me go back to that dark place I was in.
When I feel low, I know you won't let me go back to that dark place I was in.
When I feel lost in any way, I know you won't let me go back to that dark place I was in.
When I need a shoulder to cry on, I know you won't let me go back to that dark place I was in.
If and when I don't feel good enough, I know you won't let me go back to that dark place I was in.

When I feel like an outsider, I know you won't let me go back to that dark place I was in.
If and when I feel rejected, I know you won't let me go back to that dark place I was in.
When I feel like giving up, I know you won't let me go back to that dark place I was in.
If and when I feel unwanted, I know you won't let me go back to that dark place I was in.
If and when I feel worthless, I know you won't let me go back to that dark place I was in.

When I feel like I am entering an unknown trap, I know you won't let me go back to that dark place I was in.
When I feel like I'm in denial, I know you won't let me go back to that dark place I was in.
If and when I have nowhere to turn, I know you won't let me go back to that dark place I was in.
If and when I don't feel I have the courage to fight, I know you won't let me go back to that dark place I was in.
when I feel insecure, I know you won't let me go back to that dark place I was in.
If and when I feel guilt in any way, I know you won't let me go back to that dark place I was in.
When I need you the most, I know you won't let me go back to that dark place I was in.
When I am not myself, I know you won't let me go back to that dark place I was in.
When I feel alone, I know you won't let me go back to that dark place I was in.
When I face challenging days, I know you won't let me go back to that dark place I was in.
If and when I need to vent, I know you won't let me go back to that dark place I was in.

Mask

I mask the fragile me
I mask the fears within me
I mask the sadness in me
I mask the hurtfulness I feel
I mask the painfulness I carry
I mask the damaged me
I mask the emptiness I hold within
I mask the hatred I feel
I mask the rejection I feel from people I wish didn't reject me
I mask the feeling of being alone
I mask the guilt I feel
I mask the broken me

I Am Never Alone

When I look back at my fragile past, I know I am never alone.
When I face my lifelong fears, I know I am never alone.
When I try and break my lifelong issues that affect me, I know I am never alone.
When I try and overcome the loneliness I feel, I know I am never alone.
When I feel down, I know I am never alone.
If and when I feel broken, I know I am never alone.
When I feel like I'm in a dark place, I know I am never alone.
When I feel like I'm struggling, I know I am never alone.

When my inner cries take its toll on me, I know I am not alone.
When I don't feel strong enough, I know I am not alone.
When I don't feel brave enough, I know I am not alone.
When I feel low, I know I am not alone.
When I feel lost in any way, I know I am not alone.
When I need a shoulder to cry on, I know I am not alone.
If and when I don't feel good enough, I know I am not alone.
When I feel like an outsider, I know I am never alone.
If and when I feel rejected, I know I am never alone.
When I feel like giving up, I know I am never alone.
If and when I feel unwanted, I know I am never alone.
If and when I feel worthless, I know I am never alone.
When I feel like I am entering an unknown trap, I know I am never alone.
When I feel like I'm in denial, I know I am never alone.
If and when I have nowhere to turn, I know I am never alone.
If and when I don't feel I have the courage to fight, I know I am never alone.

When I feel insecure, I know I am never alone.
If and when I feel guilt in any way, I know I am never alone.
When I need you the most, I know I am never alone.
When I am not myself, I know I am never alone.
When I feel alone, I know I am never alone.
When I face challenging days, I know I am never alone.
If and when I need to vent, I know I am never alone.

Kerry

You are so amazing
you are so fearless
you are true to those around you
you are so beautiful
you are so fabulous
you are one in a million
you are so loyal to those close to you
you are so extraordinary
you are so spectacular
you are so outstanding
you are carefree
you are wonderful
you are truly incredible
you are truly out of this world.
You have such a golden heart
You have such a lively sprit about you
You are remarkable
You are so special in so many ways
You know ur mind
You are a go getter
You are marvellous
You are mega
You always make me smile
You always help other when they need you
You are tremendous
You always take troubled lost souls and take them under ur wing
You are a strong

Drain You

When you look back at your fragile past, I won't let anything drain you.
When you face your lifelong fears, I won't let anything drain you.
When you try and break your lifelong issues that affect you, I won't let anything drain you.
When you try and overcome the loneliness you feel, I won't let anything drain you.
When you feel down, I won't let anything drain you.
If and when you feel broken, I won't let anything drain you.
When you feel like you're in a dark place, I won't let anything drain you.

When you feel like you're struggling, I won't let anything drain you.
When your inner cries take its toll on you, I won't let anything drain you.
When you don't feel strong enough, I won't let anything drain you.
When you don't feel brave enough, I won't let anything drain you.
When you feel low, I won't let anything drain you.
When you feel lost in any way, I won't let anything drain you.
When you need a shoulder to cry on, I won't let anything drain you.
If and when you don't feel good enough, I won't let anything drain you.

When you feel like an outsider, I won't let anything drain you.
If and when you feel rejected, I won't let anything drain you.
When you feel like giving up, I won't let anything drain you.
If and when you feel unwanted, I won't let anything drain you.
If and when you feel worthless, I won't let anything drain you.
When you feel like you're entering an unknown trap, I won't let anything drain you.
When you feel like I'm in denial, I won't let anything drain you.
If and when you have nowhere to turn, I won't let anything drain you.
If and when you don't feel you have the courage to fight, I won't let anything drain you.
When you feel insecure, I won't let anything drain you.
If and when you feel guilt in any way, I won't let anything drain you.
When you need me the most, I won't let anything drain you.
When you are not yourself, I won't let anything drain you.
When you feel alone, I won't let anything drain you.
When you face challenging days, I won't let anything drain you.
If and when you need to vent, I won't let anything drain you.

In A Heartbeat

When you look back at your fragile past, I will be there in a heartbeat.
When you face your lifelong fears, I will be there in a heartbeat.
When you try and break your lifelong issues that affect you, I will be there in a heartbeat.
When you try and overcome the loneliness you feel, I will be there in a heartbeat.
When you feel down, I will be there in a heartbeat.
If and when you feel broken, I will be there in a heartbeat.
When you feel like you're in a dark place, I will be there in a heartbeat.
When you feel like you're struggling, I will be there in a heartbeat.
When your inner cries take its toll on you, I will be there in a heartbeat.
When you don't feel strong enough, I will be there in a heartbeat.

When you don't feel brave enough, I will be there in a heartbeat.
When you feel low, I will be there in a heartbeat.
When you feel lost in any way, I will be there in a heartbeat.
When you need a shoulder to cry on, I will be there in a heartbeat.
If and when you don't feel good enough, I will be there in a heartbeat.

When you feel like an outsider, I will be there in a heartbeat.
If and when you feel rejected, I will be there in a heartbeat.
When you feel like giving up, I will be there in a heartbeat.
If and when you feel unwanted, I will be there in a heartbeat.
If and when you feel worthless, I will be there in a heartbeat.
When you feel like you're entering an unknown trap, I will be there in a heartbeat.
When you feel like I'm in denial, I will be there in a heartbeat.
If and when you have nowhere to turn, I will be there in a heartbeat.
If and when you don't feel you have the courage to fight, I will be there in a heartbeat.
When you feel insecure, I will be there in a heartbeat.
If and when you feel guilt in any way, I will be there in a heartbeat.
When you need me the most, I will be there in a heartbeat.
When you are not yourself, I will be there in a heartbeat.
When you feel alone, I will be there in a heartbeat.
When you face challenging days, I will be there in a heartbeat.
If and when you need to vent, I will be there in a heartbeat.

Ups & Downs

When you look back at your fragile past, I won't let you go through ups and downs without me.
When you face your lifelong fears, I won't let you go through ups and downs without me.
When you try and break your lifelong issues that affect you, I won't let you go through ups and downs without me.
When you try and overcome the loneliness you feel, I won't let you go through ups and downs without me.
When you feel down, I won't let you go through ups and downs without me.
If and when you feel broken, I won't let you go through ups and downs without me.
When you feel like you're in a dark place, I won't let you go through ups and downs without me.

When you feel like you're struggling, I won't let you go through ups and downs without me.
When your inner cries take its toll on you, I won't let you go through ups and downs without me.
When you don't feel strong enough, I won't let you go through ups and downs without me.
When you don't feel brave enough, I won't let you go through ups and downs without me.
When you feel low, I won't let you go through ups and downs without me.
When you feel lost in any way, I won't let you go through ups and downs without me.
When you need a shoulder to cry on, I won't let you go through ups and downs without me.
If and when you don't feel good enough, I won't let you go through ups and downs without me.

When you feel like an outsider, I won't let you go through ups and downs without me.
If and when you feel rejected, I won't let you go through ups and downs without me.
When you feel like giving up, I won't let you go through ups and downs without me.
If and when you feel unwanted, I won't let you go through ups and downs without me.
If and when you feel worthless, I won't let you go through ups and downs without me.
When you feel like you're entering an unknown trap, I won't let you go through ups and downs without me.
When you feel like I'm in denial, I won't let you go through ups and downs without me.
If and when you have nowhere to turn, I won't let you go through ups and downs without me.
If and when you don't feel you have the courage to fight, I won't let you go through ups and downs without me.
When you feel insecure, I won't let you go through ups and downs without me.
If and when you feel guilt in any way, I won't let you go through ups and downs without me.
When you need me the most, I won't let you go through ups and downs without me.
When you are not yourself, I won't let you go through ups and downs without me.
When you feel alone, I won't let you go through ups and downs without me.

When you face challenging days, I won't let you go through ups and downs without me.
If and when you need to vent, I won't let you go through ups and downs without me.

Get You Down

When you look back at your fragile past, I won't let anything get you down.
When you face your lifelong fears, I won't let anything get you down.
When you try and break your lifelong issues that affect you, I won't let anything get you down.
When you try and overcome the loneliness you feel, I won't let anything get you down.
When you feel down, I won't let anything get you down.
If and when you feel broken, I won't let anything get you down.
When you feel like you're in a dark place, I won't let anything get you down.
When you feel like you're struggling, I won't let anything get you down.
When your inner cries take its toll on you, I won't let anything get you down.
When you don't feel strong enough, I won't let anything get you down.
When you don't feel brave enough, I won't let anything get you down.
When you feel low, I won't let anything get you down.
When you feel lost in any way, I won't let anything get you down.
When you need a shoulder to cry on, I won't let anything get you down.
If and when you don't feel good enough, I won't let anything get you down.

When you feel like an outsider, I won't let anything get you down.
If and when you feel rejected, I won't let anything get you down.
When you feel like giving up, I won't let anything get you down.
If and when you feel unwanted, I won't let anything get you down.
If and when you feel worthless, I won't let anything get you down.
When you feel like you're entering an unknown trap, I won't let anything get you down.
When you feel like I'm in denial, I won't let anything get you down.
If and when you have nowhere to turn, I won't let anything get you down.
If and when you don't feel you have the courage to fight, I won't let anything get you down.
 when you feel insecure, I won't let anything get you down.
If and when you feel guilt in any way, I won't let anything get you down.
When you need me the most, I won't let anything get you down.
When you are not yourself, I won't let anything get you down.
When you feel alone, I won't let anything get you down.

When you face challenging days, I won't let anything get you down.
If and when you need to vent, I won't let anything get you down.

The Weight Of Everything You Carry On Ur Shoulders

When you look back at your fragile past, I'll carry the weight of everything you hold within you on my shoulders.
When you face your lifelong fears, I'll carry the weight of everything you hold within you on my shoulders.
When you try and break your lifelong issues that affect you, I'll carry the weight of everything you hold within you on my shoulders.
When you try and overcome the loneliness you feel, I'll carry the weight of everything you hold within you on my shoulders.
When you feel down, I'll carry the weight of everything you hold within you on my shoulders.
If and when you feel broken, I'll carry the weight of everything you hold within you on my shoulders.
When you feel like you're in a dark place, I'll carry the weight of everything you hold within you on my shoulders.
When you feel like you're struggling, I'll carry the weight of everything you hold within you on my shoulders.
When your inner cries take its toll on you, I'll carry the weight of everything you hold within you on my shoulders.
When you don't feel strong enough, I'll carry the weight of everything you hold within you on my shoulders.
When you don't feel brave enough, I'll carry the weight of everything you hold within you on my shoulders.
When you feel low, I'll carry the weight of everything you hold within you on my shoulders.
When you feel lost in any way, I'll carry the weight of everything you hold within you on my shoulders.
When you need a shoulder to cry on, I'll carry the weight of everything you hold within you on my shoulders.
If and when you don't feel good enough, I'll carry the weight of everything you hold within you on my shoulders.

When you feel like an outsider, I'll carry the weight of everything you hold within you on my shoulders.
If and when you feel rejected, I'll carry the weight of everything you hold within you on my shoulders.

When you feel like giving up, I'll carry the weight of everything you hold within you on my shoulders.
If and when you feel unwanted, I'll carry the weight of everything you hold within you on my shoulders.
If and when you feel worthless, I'll carry the weight of everything you hold within you on my shoulders.
When you feel like you're entering an unknown trap, I'll carry the weight of everything you hold within you on my shoulders.
When you feel like I'm in denial, I'll carry the weight of everything you hold within you on my shoulders.
If and when you have nowhere to turn, I'll carry the weight of everything you hold within you on my shoulders.
If and when you don't feel you have the courage to fight, I'll carry the weight of everything you hold within you on my shoulders.
When you feel insecure, I'll carry the weight of everything you hold within you on my shoulders.
If and when you feel guilt in any way, I'll carry the weight of everything you hold within you on my shoulders.
When you need me the most, I'll carry the weight of everything you hold within you on my shoulders.
When you are not yourself, I'll carry the weight of everything you hold within you on my shoulders.
When you feel alone, I'll carry the weight of everything you hold within you on my shoulders.
When you face challenging days, I'll carry the weight of everything you hold within you on my shoulders.
If and when you need to vent, I'll carry the weight of everything you hold within you on my shoulders.

Take On Everything You Hold Within

When you look back at your fragile past, I'll always take on everything that you hold within you.
When you face your lifelong fears, I'll always take on everything that you hold within you.
When you try and break your lifelong issues that affect you, I'll always take on everything that you hold within you.
When you try and overcome the loneliness you feel, I'll always take on everything that you hold within you.
When you feel down, I'll always take on everything that you hold within you.

If and when you feel broken, I'll always take on everything that you hold within you.
When you feel like you're in a dark place, I'll always take on everything that you hold within you.
When you feel like you're struggling, I'll always take on everything that you hold within you.
When your inner cries take its toll on you, I'll always take on everything that you hold within you.
When you don't feel strong enough, I'll always take on everything that you hold within you.
When you don't feel brave enough, I'll always take on everything that you hold within you.
When you feel low, I'll always take on everything that you hold within you.
When you feel lost in any way, I'll always take on everything that you hold within you.
When you need a shoulder to cry on, I'll always take on everything that you hold within you.
If and when you don't feel good enough, I'll always take on everything that you hold within you.

When you feel like an outsider, I'll always take on everything that you hold within you.
If and when you feel rejected, I'll always take on everything that you hold within you.
When you feel like giving up, I'll always take on everything that you hold within you.
If and when you feel unwanted, I'll always take on everything that you hold within you.
If and when you feel worthless, I'll always take on everything that you hold within you.
When you feel like you're entering an unknown trap, I'll always take on everything that you hold within you.
When you feel like I'm in denial, I'll always take on everything that you hold within you.
If and when you have nowhere to turn, I'll always take on everything that you hold within you.
If and when you don't feel you have the courage to fight, I'll always take on everything that you hold within you.
When you feel insecure, I'll always take on everything that you hold within you.
If and when you feel guilt in any way, I'll always take on everything that you hold within you.

When you need me the most, I'll always take on everything that you hold within you.
When you are not yourself, I'll always take on everything that you hold within you.
When you feel alone, I'll always take on everything that you hold within you.
When you face challenging days, I'll always take on everything that you hold within you.
If and when you need to vent, I'll always take on everything that you hold within you.

Disguise You

Disguise you from the past that comes in like a ton of bricks.
Disguise you from the trouble that exposes without ur knowledge.
Disguise you from the fears that trap you in a place that you try so hard to escape from.
Disguise the hurt that other people inflict on you.
Disguise you from breaking into a thousand million pieces.
Disguise you from heartache that others but me understands.
Disguise you from the cruelty of this world.
Disguise you from the bad intentions of others that wanna see you fall
Disguise you from messes that you find urself in.
Disguise you from insults that people who are not happy with themselves trying to make themselves feel so big and you miserable.
Disguise you from feeling so down that you feel no one is around but you know in ur heart that you have people who will be there for you
Disguise you from feeling low as you know people will lift you up.
Disguise you from circumstances that leave you so fragile

Fly Alone

When I look back at my fragile past, I know I won't fly alone as you fly beside me.
When I face my lifelong fears, I know I won't fly alone as you fly beside me.
When I try and break my lifelong issues that affect me, I know I won't fly alone as you fly beside me.
When I try and overcome the loneliness I feel, I know I won't fly alone as you fly beside me.
When I feel down, I know I won't fly alone as you fly beside me.
If and when I feel broken, I know I won't fly alone as you fly beside me.

When I feel like I'm in a dark place, I know I won't fly alone as you fly beside me.
When I feel like I'm struggling, I know I won't fly alone as you fly beside me.
When my inner cries take its toll on me, I know I won't fly alone as you fly beside me.
When I don't feel strong enough, I know I won't fly alone as you fly beside me.
When I don't feel brave enough, I know I won't fly alone as you fly beside me.
When I feel low, I know I won't fly alone as you fly beside me.
When I feel lost in any way, I know I won't fly alone as you fly beside me.
When I need a shoulder to cry on, I know I won't fly alone as you fly beside me.
If and when I don't feel good enough, I know I won't fly alone as you fly beside me.
When I feel like an outsider, I know I won't fly alone as you fly beside me.
If and when I feel rejected, I know I won't fly alone as you fly beside me.
When I feel like giving up, I know I won't fly alone as you fly beside me.
If and when I feel unwanted, I know I won't fly alone as you fly beside me.
If and when I feel worthless, I know I won't fly alone as you fly beside me.
When I feel like I am entering an unknown trap, I know I won't fly alone as you fly beside me.
When I feel like I'm in denial, I know I won't fly alone as you fly beside me.
If and when I have nowhere to turn, I know I won't fly alone as you fly beside me.
If and when I don't feel I have the courage to fight, I know I won't fly alone as you fly beside me.
When I feel insecure, I know I won't fly alone as you fly beside me.
If and when I feel guilt in any way, I know I won't fly alone as you fly beside me.
When I need you the most, I know I won't fly alone as you fly beside me.
When I am not myself, I know I won't fly alone as you fly beside me.
When I feel alone, I know I won't fly alone as you fly beside me.
When I face challenging days, I know I won't fly alone as you fly beside me.
If and when I need to vent, I know I won't fly alone as you fly beside me.

You Won't Fly Alone

When you look back at your fragile past, know you won't fly alone as I will fly beside you.
When you face your lifelong fears, know you won't fly alone as I will fly beside you.
When you try and break your lifelong issues that affect you, know you won't fly alone as I will fly beside you.

When you try and overcome the loneliness you feel, know you won't fly alone as I will fly beside you.
When you feel down, know you won't fly alone as I will fly beside you.
If and when you feel broken, know you won't fly alone as I will fly beside you.
When you feel like you're in a dark place, know you won't fly alone as I will fly beside you.
When you feel like you're struggling, know you won't fly alone as I will fly beside you.
When your inner cries take its toll on you, know you won't fly alone as I will fly beside you.
When you don't feel strong enough. know you won't fly alone as I will fly beside you.
When you don't feel brave enough, know you won't fly alone as I will fly beside you.
When you feel low, know you won't fly alone as I will fly beside you.
When you feel lost in any way, know you won't fly alone as I will fly beside you.
When you need a shoulder to cry on, know you won't fly alone as I will fly beside you.
If and when you don't feel good enough, know you won't fly alone as I will fly beside you.

When you feel like an outsider, know you won't fly alone as I will fly beside you.
If and when you feel rejected, know you won't fly alone as I will fly beside you.
When you feel like giving up, know you won't fly alone as I will fly beside you.
If and when you feel unwanted, know you won't fly alone as I will fly beside you.
If and when you feel worthless, know you won't fly alone as I will fly beside you.
When you feel like you're entering an unknown trap, know you won't fly alone as I will fly beside you.
When you feel like I'm in denial, know you won't fly alone as I will fly beside you.
If and when you have nowhere to turn, know you won't fly alone as I will fly beside you.
If and when you don't feel you have the courage to fight, know you won't fly alone as I will fly beside you.
when you feel insecure, know you won't fly alone as I will fly beside you.
If and when you feel guilt in any way, know you won't fly alone as I will fly beside you.
When you need me the most, know you won't fly alone as I will fly beside you.

When you are not yourself, know you won't fly alone as I will fly beside you.
When you feel alone, know you won't fly alone as I will fly beside you.
When you face challenging days, know you won't fly alone as I will fly beside you.
If and when you need to vent, know you won't fly alone as I will fly beside you.

I Find My Voice

When I look back at my fragile past, I find my voice as you showed me, I have a voice and I will be heard.
When I face my lifelong fears, I find my voice as you showed me, I have a voice and I will be heard.
When I try and break my lifelong issues that affect me, I find my voice as you showed me, I have a voice and I will be heard.
When I try and overcome the loneliness I feel, I find my voice as you showed me, I have a voice and I will be heard.
When I feel down, I find my voice as you showed me, I have a voice and I will be heard.
If and when I feel broken, I find my voice as you showed me, I have a voice and I will be heard.
When I feel like I'm in a dark place, I find my voice as you showed me, I have a voice and I will be heard.
When I feel like I'm struggling, I find my voice as you showed me, I have a voice and I will be heard.
When my inner cries take its toll on me, I find my voice as you showed me, I have a voice and I will be heard.
When I don't feel strong enough, I find my voice as you showed me, I have a voice and I will be heard.
When I don't feel brave enough, I find my voice as you showed me, I have a voice and I will be heard.
When I feel low, I find my voice as you showed me, I have a voice and I will be heard.
When I feel lost in any way, I find my voice as you showed me, I have a voice and I will be heard.
When I need a shoulder to cry on, I find my voice as you showed me, I have a voice and I will be heard.
If and when I don't feel good enough, I find my voice as you showed me, I have a voice and I will be heard.

When I feel like an outsider, I find my voice as you showed me, I have a voice and I will be heard.

If and when I feel rejected, I find my voice as you showed me, I have a voice and I will be heard.
When I feel like giving up, I find my voice as you showed me, I have a voice and I will be heard.
If and when I feel unwanted, I find my voice as you showed me, I have a voice and I will be heard.
If and when I feel worthless, I find my voice as you showed me, I have a voice and I will be heard.
When I feel like I am entering an unknown trap, I find my voice as you showed me, I have a voice and I will be heard.
When I feel like I'm in denial, I find my voice as you showed me, I have a voice and I will be heard.
If and when I have nowhere to turn, I find my voice as you showed me, I have a voice and I will be heard.
If and when I don't feel I have the courage to fight, I find my voice as you showed me, I have a voice and I will be heard.
 when I feel insecure, I find my voice as you showed me, I have a voice and I will be heard.
If and when I feel guilt in any way, I find my voice as you showed me, I have a voice and I will be heard.
When I need you the most, I find my voice as you showed me, I have a voice and I will be heard.
When I am not myself, I find my voice as you showed me, I have a voice and I will be heard.
When I feel alone, I find my voice as you showed me, I have a voice and I will be heard.
When I face challenging days, I find my voice as you showed me, I have a voice and I will be heard.
If and when I need to vent, I find my voice as you showed me, I have a voice and I will be heard.

Karma

You know when karma catches up with ur fragile past.
You know when karma catches up with the endless fears that terrorise you to no end.
You know when karma catches up with the troubles that always follow you.
You know when karma catches up with the bad choices you make.
You know when karma catches up with the dilemmas you face through your lifetime.
Karma will sneak up on you when you least expect it to.

Karma will sneak up on you from out of the blue.
Karma will be behind you when you feel people betray you without you realizing the reason behind why to give them a taste of their own actions.

Window Of Opportunity

When I look back at my fragile past, know that you give me a window of opportunity to show you that no matter what I will be able to have every opportunity that comes my way when I really work for it and want it so badly.

When I face my lifelong fears, know that you give me a window of opportunity to show you that no matter what I will be able to have every opportunity that comes my way when I really work for it and want it so badly.

When I try and break my lifelong issues that affect me, know that you give me a window of opportunity to show you that no matter what I will be able to have every opportunity that comes my way when I really work for it and want it so badly.

When I try and overcome the loneliness I feel, know that you give me a window of opportunity to show you that no matter what I will be able to have every opportunity that comes my way when I really work for it and want it so badly.

When I feel down, know that you give me a window of opportunity to show you that no matter what I will be able to have every opportunity that comes my way when I really work for it and want it so badly.

If and when I feel broken, know that you give me a window of opportunity to show you that no matter what I will be able to have every opportunity that comes my way when I really work for it and want it so badly.

When I feel like I'm in a dark place, know that you give me a window of opportunity to show you that no matter what I will be able to have every opportunity that comes my way when I really work for it and want it so badly.

When I feel like I'm struggling, know that you give me a window of opportunity to show you that no matter what I will be able to have every opportunity that comes my way when I really work for it and want it so badly.

When my inner cries take its toll on me, know that you give me a window of opportunity to show you that no matter what I will be able to have every opportunity that comes my way when I really work for it and want it so badly.

When I don't feel strong enough, know that you give me a window of opportunity to show you that no matter what I will be able to have every opportunity that comes my way when I really work for it and want it so badly.

When I don't feel brave enough, know that you give me a window of opportunity to show you that no matter what I will be able to have every opportunity that comes my way when I really work for it and want it so badly.

When I feel low, know that you give me a window of opportunity to show you that no matter what I will be able to have every opportunity that comes my way when I really work for it and want it so badly.

When I feel lost in any way, know that you give me a window of opportunity to show you that no matter what I will be able to have every opportunity that comes my way when I really work for it and want it so badly.

When I need a shoulder to cry on, know that you give me a window of opportunity to show you that no matter what I will be able to have every opportunity that comes my way when I really work for it and want it so badly.

If and when I don't feel good enough, know that you give me a window of opportunity to show you that no matter what I will be able to have every opportunity that comes my way when I really work for it and want it so badly.

When I feel like an outsider, know that you give me a window of opportunity to show you that no matter what I will be able to have every opportunity that comes my way when I really work for it and want it so badly.

If and when I feel rejected, know that you give me a window of opportunity to show you that no matter what I will be able to have every opportunity that comes my way when I really work for it and want it so badly.

When I feel like giving up, know that you give me a window of opportunity to show you that no matter what I will be able to have every opportunity that comes my way when I really work for it and want it so badly.

If and when I feel unwanted, know that you give me a window of opportunity to show you that no matter what I will be able to have every opportunity that comes my way when I really work for it and want it so badly.

If and when I feel worthless, know that you give me a window of opportunity to show you that no matter what I will be able to have every opportunity that comes my way when I really work for it and want it so badly.

When I feel like I am entering an unknown trap, know that you give me a window of opportunity to show you that no matter what I will be able to have every opportunity that comes my way when I really work for it and want it so badly.

When I feel like I'm in denial, know that you give me a window of opportunity to show you that no matter what I will be able to have every opportunity that comes my way when I really work for it and want it so badly.

If and when I have nowhere to turn, know that you give me a window of opportunity to show you that no matter what I will be able to have every opportunity that comes my way when I really work for it and want it so badly.

If and when I don't feel I have the courage to fight, know that you give me a window of opportunity to show you that no matter what I will be able to have every opportunity that comes my way when I really work for it and want it so badly.

when I feel insecure, know that you give me a window of opportunity to show you that no matter what I will be able to have every opportunity that comes my way when I really work for it and want it so badly.

If and when I feel guilt in any way, know that you give me a window of opportunity to show you that no matter what I will be able to have every opportunity that comes my way when I really work for it and want it so badly.

When I need you the most, know that you give me a window of opportunity to show you that no matter what I will be able to have every opportunity that comes my way when I really work for it and want it so badly.

When I am not myself, know that you give me a window of opportunity to show you that no matter what I will be able to have every opportunity that comes my way when I really work for it and want it so badly.

When I feel alone, know that you give me a window of opportunity to show you that no matter what I will be able to have every opportunity that comes my way when I really work for it and want it so badly.

When I face challenging days, know that you give me a window of opportunity to show you that no matter what I will be able to have every opportunity that comes my way when I really work for it and want it so badly.

If and when I need to vent, know that you give me a window of opportunity to show you that no matter what I will be able to have every opportunity that comes my way when I really work for it and want it so badly.

Escape Route

When I look back at my fragile past, know that you showed me that there is an escape route when I need me time to stop everything getting on top of me.

When I face my lifelong fears, know that you showed me that there is an escape route when I need me time to stop everything getting on top of me.

When I try and break my lifelong issues that affect me, know that you showed me that there is an escape route when I need me time to stop everything getting on top of me.

When I try and overcome the loneliness, I feel, know that you showed me that there is an escape route when I need me time to stop everything getting on top of me.

When I feel down, know that you showed me that there is an escape route when I need me time to stop everything getting on top of me.

If and when I feel broken, know that you showed me that there is an escape route when I need me time to stop everything getting on top of me.

When I feel like I'm in a dark place, know that you showed me that there is an escape route when I need me time to stop everything getting on top of me.

When I feel like I'm struggling, know that you showed me that there is an escape route when I need me time to stop everything getting on top of me.
When my inner cries take its toll on me, know that you showed me that there is an escape route when I need me time to stop everything getting on top of me.
When I don't feel strong enough, know that you showed me that there is an escape route when I need me time to stop everything getting on top of me.
When I don't feel brave enough, know that you showed me that there is an escape route when I need me time to stop everything getting on top of me.
When I feel low, know that you showed me that there is an escape route when I need me time to stop everything getting on top of me.
When I feel lost in any way, know that you showed me that there is an escape route when I need me time to stop everything getting on top of me.
When I need a shoulder to cry on, know that you showed me that there is an escape route when I need me time to stop everything getting on top of me.
If and when I don't feel good enough, know that you showed me that there is an escape route when I need me time to stop everything getting on top of me.
When I feel like an outsider, know that you showed me that there is an escape route when I need me time to stop everything getting on top of me.
If and when I feel rejected, know that you showed me that there is an escape route when I need me time to stop everything getting on top of me.
When I feel like giving up, know that you showed me that there is an escape route when I need me time to stop everything getting on top of me.
If and when I feel unwanted, know that you showed me that there is an escape route when I need me time to stop everything getting on top of me.
If and when I feel worthless, know that you showed me that there is an escape route when I need me time to stop everything getting on top of me.
When I feel like I am entering an unknown trap, know that you showed me that there is an escape route when I need me time to stop everything getting on top of me.
When I feel like I'm in denial, know that you showed me that there is an escape route when I need me time to stop everything getting on top of me.
If and when I have nowhere to turn, know that you showed me that there is an escape route when I need me time to stop everything getting on top of me.
If and when I don't feel I have the courage to fight, know that you showed me that there is an escape route when I need me time to stop everything getting on top of me.
 when I feel insecure, know that you showed me that there is an escape route when I need me time to stop everything getting on top of me.
If and when I feel guilt in any way, know that you showed me that there is an escape route when I need me time to stop everything getting on top of me.
When I need you the most, know that you showed me that there is an escape route when I need me time to stop everything getting on top of me.

When I am not myself, know that you showed me that there is an escape route when I need me time to stop everything getting on top of me.
When I feel alone, know that you showed me that there is an escape route when I need me time to stop everything getting on top of me.
When I face challenging days, know that you showed me that there is an escape route when I need me time to stop everything getting on top of me.
If and when I need to vent, know that you showed me that there is an escape route when I need me time to stop everything getting on top of me.

Massive Influence On Me & My Life.

When I look back at my fragile past, know that you have a massive influence on me & my life.
When I face my lifelong fears, know that you have a massive influence on me & my life.
When I try and break my lifelong issues that affect me, know that you have a massive influence on me & my life.
When I try and overcome the loneliness, I feel, know you have a massive influence on me & my life.
When I feel down, know that you have a massive influence on me & my life.
If and when I feel broken, know that you have a massive influence on me & my life.
When I feel like I'm in a dark place, know that you have a massive influence on me & my life.
When I feel like I'm struggling, know that you have a massive influence on me & my life.
When my inner cries take its toll on me, know that you have a massive influence on me & my life.
When I don't feel strong enough, know that you have a massive influence on me & my life.
When I don't feel brave enough, know that you have a massive influence on me & my life.
When I feel low, know that you have a massive influence on me & my life.
When I feel lost in any way, know that you have a massive influence on me & my life.
When I need a shoulder to cry on, know that you have a massive influence on me & my life.
If and when I don't feel good enough, know that you have a massive influence on me & my life.
When I feel like an outsider, know that you have a massive influence on me & my life.

If and when I feel rejected, know that you have a massive influence on me & my life.
When I feel like giving up , know that you have a massive influence on me & my life.
If and when I feel unwanted, know that you have a massive influence on me & my life.
If and when I feel worthless, know that you have a massive influence on me & my life.
When I feel like I am entering an unknown trap, know that you have a massive influence on me & my life.
When I feel like I'm in denial, know that you have a massive influence on me & my life.
If and when I have nowhere to turn, know that you have a massive influence on me & my life.
If and when I don't feel I have the courage to fight, know that you have a massive influence on me & my life.
when I feel insecure, know that you have a massive influence on me & my life.
If and when I feel guilt in any way, know that you have a massive influence on me & my life.
When I need you the most, know that you have a massive influence on me & my life.
When I am not myself, know that you have a massive influence on me & my life.
When I feel alone, know that you make a massive influence on me & my life.
When I face challenging days, know that you have a massive influence on me & my life.
If and when I need to vent, know that you have a massive influence on me & my life.

Catch Every Tear

When I look back at my fragile past, know that you catch every tear that falls down my face when I cry.
When I face my lifelong fears, know that you catch every tear that falls down my face when I cry.
When I try and break my lifelong issues that affect me, know that you catch every tear that falls down my face when I cry.
When I try and overcome the loneliness, I feel, know that you catch every tear that falls down my face when I cry.
When I feel down, know that you catch every tear that falls down my face when I cry.

If and when I feel broken, know that you catch every tear that falls down my face when I cry.
When I feel like I'm in a dark place, know that you catch every tear that falls down my face when I cry.
When I feel like I'm struggling, know that you catch every tear that falls down my face when I cry.
When my inner cries take its toll on me, know that you catch every tear that falls down my face when I cry.
When I don't feel strong enough, know that you catch every tear that falls down my face when I cry.
When I don't feel brave enough, know that you catch every tear that falls down my face when I cry.
When I feel low, know that you catch every tear that falls down my face when I cry.
When I feel lost in any way, know that you catch every tear that falls down my face when I cry.
When I need a shoulder to cry on, know that you catch every tear that falls down my face when I cry.
If and when I don't feel good enough, know that you catch every tear that falls down my face when I cry.
When I feel like an outsider, know that you catch every tear that falls down my face when I cry.
If and when I feel rejected, know that you catch every tear that falls down my face when I cry.
When I feel like giving up, know that you catch every tear that falls down my face when I cry.
If and when I feel unwanted, know that you catch every tear that falls down my face when I cry.
If and when I feel worthless, know that you catch every tear that falls down my face when I cry.
When I feel like I am entering an unknown trap, know that you catch every tear that falls down my face when I cry.
When I feel like I'm in denial, know that you catch every tear that falls down my face when I cry.
If and when I have nowhere to turn, know that you catch every tear that falls down my face when I cry.
If and when I don't feel I have the courage to fight, know that you catch every tear that falls down my face when I cry.
when I feel insecure, know that you catch every tear that falls down my face when I cry.
If and when I feel guilt in any way, know that you catch every tear that falls down my face when I cry.

When I need you the most, know that you catch every tear that falls down my face when I cry.
When I am not myself, know that you catch every tear that falls down my face when I cry.
When I feel alone, know that you catch every tear that falls down my face when I cry.
When I face challenging days, know that you catch every tear that falls down my face when I cry.
If and when I need to vent, know that you catch every tear that falls down my face when I cry.

Drop My Guard

When I look back at my fragile past, know that I drop my guard when I'm around you.
When I face my lifelong fears, know that I drop my guard when I'm around you.
When I try and break my lifelong issues that affect me, know that I drop my guard when I'm around you.
When I try and overcome the loneliness, know that I drop my guard when I'm around you.
When I feel down, know that I drop my guard when I'm around you.
If and when I feel broken, know that I drop my guard when I'm around you.
When I feel like I'm in a dark place, know that I drop my guard when I'm around you.
When I feel like I'm struggling, know that I drop my guard when I'm around you.
When my inner cries take its toll on me, know that I drop my guard when I'm around you.
When I don't feel strong enough, know that I drop my guard when I'm around you.
When I don't feel brave enough, know that I drop my guard when I'm around you.
When I feel low, know that I drop my guard when I'm around you.
When I feel lost in any way, know that I drop my guard when I'm around you.
When I need a shoulder to cry on, know that I drop my guard when I'm around you.
If and when I don't feel good enough, know that I drop my guard when I'm around you.
When I feel like an outsider, know that I drop my guard when I'm around you.
If and when I feel rejected, know that I drop my guard when I'm around you.
When I feel like giving up, know that I drop my guard when I'm around you.

If and when I feel unwanted, know that I drop my guard when I'm around you.
If and when I feel worthless, know that I drop my guard when I'm around you.
When I feel like I am entering an unknown trap, know that I drop my guard when I'm around you.
When I feel like I'm in denial, know that I drop my guard when I'm around you.
If and when I have nowhere to turn, know that I drop my guard when I'm around you.
If and when I don't feel I have the courage to fight, know that I drop my guard when I'm around you.
when I feel insecure, know that I drop my guard when I'm around you.
If and when I feel guilt in any way, know that I drop my guard when I'm around you.
When I need you the most, know that I drop my guard when I'm around you.
When I am not myself, know that I drop my guard when I'm around you.
When I feel alone, know that I drop my guard when I'm around you.
When I face challenging days, know that I drop my guard when I'm around you.
If and when I need to vent, know that I drop my guard when I'm around you.

Cast A Doubt

When I look back at my fragile past, you know when I cast a doubt that shadows me.
When I face my lifelong fears, you know when I cast a doubt that shadows me.
When I try and break my lifelong issues that affect me, you know when I cast a doubt that shadows me.
When I try and overcome the loneliness, I feel, you know when I cast a doubt that shadows me.
When I feel down, you know when I cast a doubt that shadows me.
If and when I feel broken, you know when I cast a doubt that shadows me.
When I feel like I'm in a dark place, you know when I cast a doubt that shadows me.
When I feel like I'm struggling, you know when I cast a doubt that shadows me.
When my inner cries take its toll on me, you know when I cast a doubt that shadows me.
When I don't feel strong enough, you know when I cast a doubt that shadows me.
When I don't feel brave enough, you know when I cast a doubt that shadows me.
When I feel low, you know when I cast a doubt that shadows me.
When I feel lost in any way, you know when I cast a doubt that shadows me.
When I need a shoulder to cry on, you know when I cast a doubt that shadows me.

If and when I don't feel good enough, you know when I cast a doubt that shadows me.
When I feel like an outsider, you know when I cast a doubt that shadows me.
If and when I feel rejected, you know when I cast a doubt that shadows me.
When I feel like giving up , you know when I cast a doubt that shadows me.
If and when I feel unwanted, you know when I cast a doubt that shadows me.
If and when I feel worthless, you know when I cast a doubt that shadows me.
When I feel like I am entering an unknown trap, you know when I cast a doubt that shadows me.
When I feel like I'm in denial, you know when I cast a doubt that shadows me.
If and when I have nowhere to turn, you know when I cast a doubt that shadows me.
If and when I don't feel I have the courage to fight, you know when I cast a doubt that shadows me.
when I feel insecure, you know when I cast a doubt that shadows me.
If and when I feel guilt in any way, you know when I cast a doubt that shadows me.
When I need you the most, you know when I cast a doubt that shadows me.
When I am not myself, you know when I cast a doubt that shadows me.
When I feel alone, you know when I cast a doubt that shadows me.
When I face challenging days, you know when I cast a doubt that shadows me.
If and when I need to vent, you know when I cast a doubt that shadows me.

Troublesome Road Of Defeat

Ur fragile past is never going to be a troublesome road that you can't defeat without those close to and around you & those who are there for you when you need them to be.
Ur lifelong fears is never going to be a troublesome road that you can't defeat without those close to and around you & those who are there for you when you need them to be.
Ur lifelong issues that affect you is never going to be a troublesome road that you can't defeat without those close to and around you & those who are there for you when you need them to be.
When you try and break the loneliness you feel it is never going to be a troublesome road that you can't defeat without those close to and around you & those who are there for you when you need them to be.
When you feel down it is never going to be a troublesome road that you can't defeat without those close to and around you & those who are there for you when you need them to be.

If and when you feel broken it is never going to be a troublesome road that you can't defeat without those close to and around you & those who are there for you when you need them to be.
When you feel like you're in a dark place it is never going to be a troublesome road that you can't defeat without those close to and around you & those who are there for you when you need them to be.
When you feel like you're struggling it is never going to be a troublesome road that you can't defeat without those close to and around you & those who are there for you when you need them to be.
When your inner cries take its toll on you it is never going to be a troublesome road that you can't defeat without those close to and around you & those who are there for you when you need them to be.
When you don't feel strong enough it is never going to be a troublesome road that you can't defeat without those close to and around you & those who are there for you when you need them to be.
When you don't feel brave enough it is never going to be a troublesome road that you can't defeat without those close to and around you & those who are there for you when you need them to be.
When you feel low it is never going to be a troublesome road that you can't defeat without those close to and around you & those who are there for you when you need them to be.
When you feel lost in any way it is never going to be a troublesome road that you can't defeat without those close to and around you & those who are there for you when you need them to be.
When you need a shoulder to cry on it is never going to be a troublesome road that you can't defeat without those close to and around you & those who are there for you when you need them to be.
If and when you don't feel good enough it is never going to be a troublesome road that you can't defeat without those close to and around you & those who are there for you when you need them to be.
When you feel like an outsider it is never going to be a troublesome road that you can't defeat without those close to and around you & those who are there for you when you need them to be.
If and when you feel rejected it is never going to be a troublesome road that you can't defeat without those close to and around you & those who are there for you when you need them to be.
When you feel like giving up it is never going to be a troublesome road that you can't defeat without those close to and around you & those who are there for you when you need them to be.
If and when you feel unwanted it is never going to be a troublesome road that you can't defeat without those close to and around you & those who are there for you when you need them to be.

If and when you feel worthless it is never going to be a troublesome road that you can't defeat without those close to and around you & those who are there for you when you need them to be.

When you feel like you are entering an unknown trap it is never going to be a troublesome road that you can't defeat without those close to and around you & those who are there for you when you need them to be.

When you feel like you're in denial it is never going to be a troublesome road that you can't defeat without those close to and around you & those who are there for you when you need them to be.

If and when you have nowhere to turn it is never going to be a troublesome road that you can't defeat without those close to and around you & those who are there for you when you need them to be.

If and when you don't feel you have the courage to fight it is never going to be a troublesome road that you can't defeat without those close to and around you & those who are there for you when you need them to be.

When you feel insecure it is never going to be a troublesome road that you can't defeat without those close to and around you & those who are there for you when you need them to be.

If and when you feel guilt in any way it is never going to be a troublesome road that you can't defeat without those close to and around you & those who are there for you when you need them to be.

When you need me the most it is never going to be a troublesome road that you can't defeat without those close to and around you & those who are there for you when you need them to be.

When you are not yourself it is never going to be a troublesome road that you can't defeat without those close to and around you & those who are there for you when you need them to be.

When you feel alone it is never going to be a troublesome road that you can't defeat without those close to and around you & those who are there for you when you need them to be.

When you face challenging days, it is never going to be a troublesome road that you can't defeat without those close to and around you & those who are there for you when you need them to be.

If and when you need to vent it is never going to be a troublesome road that you can't defeat without those close to and around you & those who are there for you when you need them to be.

It's Ok To Show The World Who I Truly Am

When I look back at my fragile past , I know that I've come this far because you showed me its ok to show the world who I truly am and everything I can do is coz you showed me that with those close to and around me my confidence grows day by day and I can be who I wanna be with you always by my side & in my life.

When I face my lifelong fears , I know that I've come this far because you showed me its ok to show the world who I truly am and everything I can do is coz you showed me that with those close to and around me my confidence grows day by day and I can be who I wanna be with you always by my side & in my life.

When I try and break my lifelong issues that affect me , I know that I've come this far because you showed me its ok to show the world who I truly am and everything I can do is coz you showed me that with those close to and around me my confidence grows day by day and I can be who I wanna be with you always by my side & in my life.

When I try and overcome the loneliness, I feel , I know that I've come this far because you showed me its ok to show the world who I truly am and everything I can do is coz you showed me that with those close to and around me my confidence grows day by day and I can be who I wanna be with you always by my side & in my life.

When I feel down , I know that I've come this far because you showed me its ok to show the world who I truly am and everything I can do is coz you showed me that with those close to and around me my confidence grows day by day and I can be who I wanna be with you always by my side & in my life.

If and when I feel broken , I know that ive come this far because you showed me its ok to show the world who I truly am and everything I can do is coz you showed me that with those close to and around me my confidence grows day by day and I can be who I wanna be with you always by my side & in my life.

When I feel like I'm in a dark place , I know that ive come this far because you showed me its ok to show the world who I truly am and everything I can do is coz you showed me that with those close to and around me my confidence grows day by day and I can be who I wanna be with you always by my side & in my life.

When I feel like I'm struggling , I know that I've come this far because you showed me its ok to show the world who I truly am and everything I can do is coz you showed me that with those close to and around me my confidence grows day by day and I can be who I wanna be with you always by my side & in my life.

When my inner cries take its toll on me , I know that I've come this far because you showed me its ok to show the world who I truly am and everything I can do

is coz you showed me that with those close to and around me my confidence grows day by day and I can be who I wanna be with you always by my side & in my life.
When I don't feel strong enough , I know that I've come this far because you showed me its ok to show the world who I truly am and everything I can do is coz you showed me that with those close to and around me my confidence grows day by day and I can be who I wanna be with you always by my side & in my life.
When I don't feel brave enough , I know that I've come this far because you showed me its ok to show the world who I truly am and everything I can do is coz you showed me that with those close to and around me my confidence grows day by day and I can be who I wanna be with you always by my side & in my life.
When I feel low, I know that I've come this far because you showed me its ok to show the world who I truly am and everything I can do is coz you showed me that with those close to and around me my confidence grows day by day and I can be who I wanna be with you always by my side & in my life.
When I feel lost in any way , I know that I've come this far because you showed me its ok to show the world who I truly am and everything I can do is coz you showed me that with those close to and around me my confidence grows day by day and I can be who I wanna be with you always by my side & in my life.
When I need a shoulder to cry on, , I know that I've come this far because you showed me its ok to show the world who I truly am and everything I can do is coz you showed me that with those close to and around me my confidence grows day by day and I can be who I wanna be with you always by my side & in my life.
If and when I don't feel good enough , I know that I've come this far because you showed me its ok to show the world who I truly am and everything I can do is coz you showed me that with those close to and around me my confidence grows day by day and I can be who I wanna be with you always by my side & in my life.
When I feel like an outsider , I know that I've come this far because you showed me its ok to show the world who I truly am and everything I can do is coz you showed me that with those close to and around me my confidence grows day by day and I can be who I wanna be with you always by my side & in my life.
If and when I feel rejected , I know that I've come this far because you showed me its ok to show the world who I truly am and everything I can do is coz you showed me that with those close to and around me my confidence grows day by day and I can be who I wanna be with you always by my side & in my life.
When I feel like giving up , , I know that I've come this far because you showed me its ok to show the world who I truly am and everything I can do is coz you

showed me that with those close to and around me my confidence grows day by day and I can be who I wanna be with you always by my side & in my life.
If and when I feel unwanted , I know that I've come this far because you showed me its ok to show the world who I truly am and everything I can do is coz you showed me that with those close to and around me my confidence grows day by day and I can be who I wanna be with you always by my side & in my life.
If and when I feel worthless, , I know that I've come this far because you showed me its ok to show the world who I truly am and everything I can do is coz you showed me that with those close to and around me my confidence grows day by day and I can be who I wanna be with you always by my side & in my life.
When I feel like I am entering an unknown trap , I know that I've come this far because you showed me its ok to show the world who I truly am and everything I can do is coz you showed me that with those close to and around me my confidence grows day by day and I can be who I wanna be with you always by my side & in my life.
When I feel like I'm in denial , I know that I've come this far because you showed me its ok to show the world who I truly am and everything I can do is coz you showed me that with those close to and around me my confidence grows day by day and I can be who I wanna be with you always by my side & in my life.
If and when I have nowhere to turn , I know that I've come this far because you showed me its ok to show the world who I truly am and everything I can do is coz you showed me that with those close to and around me my confidence grows day by day and I can be who I wanna be with you always by my side & in my life.
If and when I don't feel I have the courage to fight , I know that I've come this far because you showed me its ok to show the world who I truly am and everything I can do is coz you showed me that with those close to and around me my confidence grows day by day and I can be who I wanna be with you always by my side & in my life.
when I feel insecure , I know that I've come this far because you showed me its ok to show the world who I truly am and everything I can do is coz you showed me that with those close to and around me my confidence grows day by day and I can be who I wanna be with you always by my side & in my life.
If and when I feel guilt in any way, I know that I've come this far because you showed me its ok to show the world who I truly am and everything I can do is coz you showed me that with those close to and around me my confidence grows day by day and I can be who I wanna be with you always by my side & in my life.

When I need you the most, I know that I've come this far because you showed me its ok to show the world who I truly am and everything I can do is coz you showed me that with those close to and around me my confidence grows day by day and I can be who I wanna be with you always by my side & in my life.
When I am not myself , I know that I've come this far because you showed me its ok to show the world who I truly am and everything I can do is coz you showed me that with those close to and around me my confidence grows day by day and I can be who I wanna be with you always by my side & in my life.
When I feel alone, I know that I've come this far because you showed me its ok to show the world who I truly am and everything I can do is coz you showed me that with those close to and around me my confidence grows day by day and I can be who I wanna be with you always by my side & in my life.
When I face challenging days, I know that I've come this far because you showed me its ok to show the world who I truly am and everything I can do is coz you showed me that with those close to and around me my confidence grows day by day and I can be who I wanna be with you always by my side & in my life.
If and when I need to vent, I know that I've come this far because you showed me its ok to show the world who I truly am and everything I can do is coz you showed me that with those close to and around me my confidence grows day by day and I can be who I wanna be with you always by my side & in my life.

Trick Me

When I look back at my fragile past, I know you won't let anything or anyone trick me into thinking my past defines me as a person
When I face my lifelong fears, I know you won't let anything or anyone trick me into believing that fears will scare me into a corner they won't as I won't let them corner me.
When I try and break my lifelong issues that affect me, I know you won't let anything or anyone trick me into believing that my lifelong issues that affect me will last forever they won't as I won't let them take control over me.
When I try and overcome the loneliness, I feel, I know you won't let anything or anyone trick me into thinking that loneliness is my only option as I know it's not.
When I feel down, I know you won't let anything or anyone trick me into believing I will always feel down as those who are close to me, beside me and around me and those who care about me will lift me up and keep me up.
If and when I feel broken, I know you won't let anything or anyone trick me into believing I am beyond repairable because I know I am and will be mended by those who are close to me, beside me and around me and those who care about me will always pick me up when I least expect it.

When I feel like I'm in a dark place, I know you won't let anything or anyone trick me into believing I will always be in a dark place as I know I won't as I travel into the light as I continue my journey with the people close to me, beside me, and around me.

When I feel like I'm struggling, I know you won't let anything or anyone trick me into believing I will always struggle when I know I won't as I will not let my struggles take control over me, I will take control over them.

When my inner cries take its toll on me, I know you won't let anything or anyone trick me into thinking that my inner cries have control over me as I know they don't.

When I don't feel strong enough, I know you won't let anything or anyone trick me into believing I am not strong as I know I will be again in an unexpected way.

When I don't feel brave enough, I know you won't let anything or anyone trick me into believing I will never be brave again as I know I will be.

When I feel low, I know you won't let anything or anyone trick me into thinking I will always feel low in myself when I know I won't as I have those close to me, beside me and around me to make sure I never feel this way again.

When I feel lost in any way, I know you won't let anything or anyone trick me into thinking I am lost and I won't find my way back because I know I will as I have those close to me, beside me and around me to show me the way back.

When I need a shoulder to cry on, I know you won't let anything or anyone trick me into thinking I don't have a shoulder to cry on when I need to as I know I do as I have those close to me, beside me and around me.

If and when I don't feel good enough, I know you won't let anything or anyone trick me into thinking I am not good enough as I know I am good enough to those close to me, beside me and around me.

When I feel like an outsider, I know you won't let anything or anyone trick me into thinking I am a stranger to those close to me, beside me and around me as I know I'm not.

If and when I feel rejected, I know you won't let anything or anyone trick me into thinking I am rejected because I know as i have people close to me, beside me and around me that won't reject me.

When I feel like giving up , I know you won't let anything or anyone trick me into thinking its ok to give up I won't as it will only show those who wanted me to give up that I did and I know I won't because I have people close to me, beside me and around me that will keep me motivated.

If and when I feel unwanted, I know you won't let anything or anyone trick me into thinking I am not wanted when I know I am wanted by the people in my life, beside me, close to me and around me.

If and when I feel worthless, I know you won't let anything or anything trick me into thinking I am not worthless as I know I am worth everything to the people beside me, close to me and around me.
When I feel like I am entering an unknown trap, I know you won't let anything or anyone trick me into believing there's an unknown trap I would fall into and not come out of as I know I will.
When I feel like I'm in denial, I know you won't let anything or anyone trick me into thinking I am in denial as I know I may have been before but now I'm not as I have nothing to be in denial over.
If and when I have nowhere to turn, I know you won't let anything or anyone trick me into thinking I don't have anywhere to go for a breather when I need to as I know I do.
If and when I don't feel I have the courage to fight, I know you won't let anything or anyone trick me into thinking I will never find the courage to fight.
when I feel insecure, I know you won't let anything or anyone trick me into thinking I have insecurities as I know I've overruled them and they are no longer visible.
If and when I feel guilt in any way, I know you won't let anything or anyone trick me into feeling guilty for something I didn't do.
When I need you the most, I know you won't let anything or anyone trick me into thinking I don't need anyone when I know I do.
When I am not myself, I know you won't let anything or anyone trick me into thinking I am not worth someone coming to find me when I'm feeling like I am not myself
When I feel alone, I know you won't let anything or anyone trick me into believing that no one will be here with me as I turn to those close to and around me so I don't feel alone
When I face challenging days, I know you won't let anything or anyone trick me into not facing these challenges with those close to and around me.
If and when I need to vent, I know you won't let anything or anyone trick me into not venting away to those close to and around me.

Confessions

Confessions are never simple
Confessions are difficult to bring up
Confessions are different to come to terms with
Confessions are really hard to believe something
Confessions can destroy the atmosphere
Confessions can tear apart a relationship
Confessions is honestly

Confessions are brave to admit
Confessions give you a clear way of thinking
Confessions gives whoever committed the wrong doing a chance to start afresh
Confessions is a chance to build trust
Confessions is a way to build a stronger relationship with the someone close to and around you
Confessions allows you to take a step in the right direction

Destructive Way

Destructive way of my fragile past that I feel I know I will turn it around.
Destructive way of my lifelong fears that terrorise me to no end as I know I will turn it around.
Destructive way of my troubles that follow me around everywhere I go, as I know I will turn it around.
Destructive way of my existence that I felt was invisible for those close to me and around me although I know I will turn it around
Destructive way of the pain I went through as I know I will turn it around.
Destructive way of the hurt I felt as I know I will turn it around.
Destructive way of my failure as I know I will turn it around.
Destructive way of my dark nights that haunt me as I know I will turn it around.
Destructive way of my true self that jumps out at me when I least expect it as I know I will turn it around.
Destructive ways of the real me that so badly wants to show the world what it can do within as I know I will turn it around.
Destructive ways to my dark days, hard days, painful days, that creep up on me when I don't expect it to as I know I can turn it around.
Destructive ways of my struggles I face as I know I will turn it around.

Upper Hand

You know I will have the upper hand when it comes to facing my fragile past in the face and defeating it in my own way keeping it from returning.
You know I will have the upper hand when it comes to facing my lifelong fears that terrorise me to no end and defeating it in my own way to keep it from returning.
You know I will have the upper hand when it comes to facing my lifelong issues that affect me and defeating it in my own way keeping it from returning.
You know I will have the upper hand when it comes to facing my loneliness and defeating it in my own way keeping it from returning.

You know I will have the upper hand when it comes to facing the hurt I feel and defeating it in my own way keeping it from returning.
You know I will have the upper hand when it comes to facing the pain ive had to deal with and defeating it in my own way keeping it from returning.
You know I will have the upper hand when it comes to when I don't feel strong enough defeating it in my own way keeping it from returning.
You know I will have the upper hand when it comes to when I don't feel brave enough defeating it in my own way keeping it from returning.
You know I will have the upper hand when it comes to facing demons that scare me into hiding away defeating it in my own way keeping it from returning.
You know I will have the upper hand when it comes to facing battles that I know I will win defeating it in my own way keeping it from returning.
You know I will have the upper hand over the way my life plays out with those close to and around me to help me work out a way to defeating it in my own way and keeping it from returning.
You know I will have the upper hand when it comes to facing the hard times I endure with those close to and around to help me find a way of defeating it and keeping it from returning.
You know I will have the upper hand over the way my dark days come about and how often with those close to and around me to help me find a way of defeating it and keeping it from returning.
You know I will have the upper hand when it comes to facing my struggles and defeating it in my own way keeping it from returning.
You know I will have the upper hand when it comes to confrontations with people who hate me and don't want me to be around doing what I do best defeating them and keeping them from stopping me.
You know I will have the upper hand when it comes to how hard or if I hit the ground and stopping myself from hitting the ground by defeating it and keeping it from returning.

Approval

Approval doesn't define you as a person.
Approval doesn't shape ur past.
Approval doesn't shape the fears that terrorise you to no end.
Approval doesn't change the person you are meant to be.
Approval doesn't shape the loneliness you feel.
Approval doesn't shape the way life plays out for you.
Approval doesn't shape the pain you endured.
Approval doesn't shape the bravery you show the outside world
Approval doesn't shape the hurt you endured.

Approval doesn't shape the way you act.
Approval doesn't shape up the endless damage you endured.
Approval doesn't shape the existence of you.
Approval doesn't shape the future you make for urself.
Approval doesn't shape the determination you have within.
Approval doesn't shape the endless emotion you feel within.
Approval doesn't shape the worthiness within you.
Approval doesn't shape the courage you show the outside world.
Approval doesn't shape the way you look at the world.
Approval doesn't shape the difficulties you faced head on.
Approval doesn't shape the feeling of when you don't feel good enough within urself.
Approval doesn't shape the chances that come ur way.
Approval doesn't shape the options available to you.
Approval doesn't shape the optimism you have within.
Approval doesn't shape the fragile you.
Approval doesn't shape the opportunities that come ur way.
Approval doesn't shape the dreams you have.
Approval doesn't shape the people close to & around you.
Approval doesn't shape the difference you make within urself.
Approval doesn't shape the difference you make to other people's lives.
Approval doesn't shape the difference people make to ur life.
Approval doesn't shape the influence people have on you.
Approval doesn't shape the influence you have on other people's lives.
Approval doesn't shape who is apart of ur life.
Approval doesn't shape who you have in ur circle of closeness.
Approval doesn't shape the lifetime experience you face.
Approval doesn't shape the good memories you make with those close to and around you.
Approval doesn't shape the good & bad times you endured.
Approval doesn't shape the way you empower the way you achieve the goals & dreams you have.
Approval doesn't shape the screams of good & bad days.
Approval doesn't shape what's true & what's fake.
Approval doesn't shape who you are loyal to.
Approval doesn't shape the choices & decisions you make.
Approval doesn't shape the regrets you have.

Uncertainty

When you look back at your fragile past, I'll get you through all the uncertainty.
When you face your lifelong fears, I'll get you through all the uncertainty.
When you try and break your lifelong issues that affect you, I'll get you through all the uncertainty.
When you try and overcome the loneliness you feel I'll get you through all the uncertainty.
When you feel down, I'll get you through all the uncertainty.
If and when you feel broken, I'll get you through all the uncertainty.
When you feel like you're in a dark place I'll get you through all the uncertainty.
When you feel like you're struggling I'll get you through all the uncertainty.
When your inner cries take its toll on you, I'll get you through all the uncertainty.

When you don't feel strong enough, I'll get you through all the uncertainty.
When you don't feel brave enough, I'll get you through all the uncertainty.
When you feel low, I'll get you through all the uncertainty.
When you feel lost in any way, I'll get you through all the uncertainty.
When you need a shoulder to cry on, I'll get you through all the uncertainty.
If and when you don't feel good enough, I'll get you through all the uncertainty.
When you feel like an outsider. I'll get you through all the uncertainty.
If and when you feel rejected, I'll get you through all the uncertainty.
When you feel like giving up, I'll get you through all the uncertainty.
If and when you feel unwanted. I'll get you through all the uncertainty.
If and when you feel worthless. I'll get you through all the uncertainty.
When you feel like you are entering an unknown trap, I'll get you through all the uncertainty.
When you feel like you're in denial I'll get you through all the uncertainty.
If and when you have nowhere to turn, I'll get you through all the uncertainty.
If and when you don't feel you have the courage to fight, I'll get you through all the uncertainty.
When you feel insecure, I'll get you through all the uncertainty.
If and when you feel guilt in any way, I'll get you through all the uncertainty.
When you need me the most, I'll get you through all the uncertainty.
When you are not yourself, I'll get you through all the uncertainty.
When you feel alone, I'll get you through all the uncertainty.
When you face challenging days, I'll get you through all the uncertainty.
If and when you need to vent, I'll get you through all the uncertainty.

Hold You Together

When you look back at your fragile past, know I will hold you together no matter what.
When you face your lifelong fears, know I will hold you together no matter what.
When you try and break your lifelong issues that affect you, know I will hold you together no matter what.
When you   try and overcome the loneliness you feel, know I will hold you together no matter what.
When you feel down, know I will hold you together no matter what.
If and when you feel broken, know I will hold you together no matter what.
When you feel like you're in a dark place, know I will hold you together no matter what.
When you feel like you're struggling, know I will hold you together no matter what.
When your inner cries take its toll on you, know I will hold you together no matter what.

When you don't feel strong enough, know I will hold you together no matter what.
When you don't feel brave enough, know I will hold you together no matter what.
When you feel low, know I will hold you together no matter what.
When you feel lost in any way, know I will hold you together no matter what.
When you need a shoulder to cry on, know I will hold you together no matter what.
If and when you don't feel good enough, know I will hold you together no matter what.
When you feel like an outsider. know I will hold you together no matter what.
If and when you feel rejected, know I will hold you together no matter what.
When you feel like giving up, know I will hold you together no matter what.
When you feel like giving up,

If and when you feel unwanted. know I will hold you together no matter what.
If and when you feel worthless. know I will hold you together no matter what.
When you feel like you are entering an unknown trap, know I will hold you together no matter what.
When you feel like you're in denial know I will hold you together no matter what.
If and when you have nowhere to turn, know I will hold you together no matter what.

If and when you don't feel you have the courage to fight, know I will hold you together no matter what.
When you feel insecure, know I will hold you together no matter what.
If and when you feel guilt in any way, know I will hold you together no matter what.
When you need me the most, know I will hold you together no matter what.
When you are not yourself, know I will hold you together no matter what.
When you feel alone, know I will hold you together no matter what.
When you face challenging days, know I will hold you together no matter what.
If and when you need to vent, know I will hold you together no matter what.

Value You

When you look back at your fragile past, I will always value you no matter what.
When you face your lifelong fears, I will always value you no matter what.
When you try and break your lifelong issues that affect you, I will always value you no matter what.
When you try and overcome the loneliness you feel, I will always value you no matter what.
When you feel down, I will always value you no matter what.
If and when you feel broken, I will always value you no matter what.
When you feel like you're in a dark place, I will always value you no matter what.
When you feel like you're struggling, I will always value you no matter what.
When your inner cries take its toll on you, I will always value you no matter what.

When you don't feel strong enough, I will always value you no matter what.
When you don't feel brave enough, I will always value you no matter what.
When you feel low, I will always value you no matter what.
When you feel lost in any way, I will always value you no matter what.
When you need a shoulder to cry on, I will always value you no matter what.
If and when you don't feel good enough, I will always value you no matter what.
When you feel like an outsider. I will always value you no matter what.
If and when you feel rejected, I will always value you no matter what.
When you feel like giving up, I will always value you no matter what.
If and when you feel unwanted. I will always value you no matter what.
If and when you feel worthless. I will always value you no matter what.
When you feel like you are entering an unknown trap, I will always value you no matter what.
When you feel like you're in denial will always value you no matter what.

If and when you have nowhere to turn, I will always value you no matter what.
If and when you don't feel you have the courage to fight, I will always value you no matter what.
When you feel insecure, know I will always value you no matter what.
If and when you feel guilt in any way, I will always value you no matter what.
When you need me the most, I will always value you no matter what.
When you are not yourself, I will always value you no matter what.
When you feel alone, I will always value you no matter what.
When you face challenging days, I will always value you no matter what.
If and when you need to vent, know I will always value you no matter what.

My Door Will Always Be Open For You.

When you look back at your fragile past, my door will always be open for you day or night I will always be here no matter what.
When you face your lifelong fears, my door will always be open for you day or night I will always be here no matter what.
When you try and break your lifelong issues that affect you, my door will always be open for you day or night I will always be here no matter what.
When you try and overcome the loneliness you feel, my door will always be open for you day or night I will always be here no matter what.
When you feel down, my door will always be open for you day or night I will always be here no matter what.
If and when you feel broken, my door will always be open for you day or night I will always be here no matter what.
When you feel like you're in a dark place, my door will always be open for you day or night I will always be here no matter what.
When you feel like you're struggling, my door will always be open for you day or night I will always be here no matter what.
When your inner cries take its toll on you, my door will always be open for you day or night I will always be here no matter what.

When you don't feel strong enough, my door will always be open for you day or night I will always be here no matter what.
When you don't feel brave enough, my door will always be open for you day or night I will always be here no matter what.
When you feel low, my door will always be open for you day or night I will always be here no matter what.
When you feel lost in any way, my door will always be open for you day or night I will always be here no matter what.

When you need a shoulder to cry on, my door will always be open for you day or night I will always be here no matter what.
If and when you don't feel good enough, my door will always be open for you day or night I will always be here no matter what.
When you feel like an outsider. my door will always be open for you day or night I will always be here no matter what.
If and when you feel rejected, my door will always be open for you day or night I will always be here no matter what.
When you feel like giving up, my door will always be open for you day or night I will always be here no matter what.
If and when you feel unwanted. my door will always be open for you day or night I will always be here no matter what.
If and when you feel worthless. my door will always be open for you day or night I will always be here no matter what.
When you feel like you are entering an unknown trap, my door will always be open for you day or night I will always be here no matter what.
When you feel like you're in denial my door will always be open for you day or night I will always be here no matter what.
If and when you have nowhere to turn, my door will always be open for you day or night I will always be here no matter what.
If and when you don't feel you have the courage to fight, my door will always be open for you day or night I will always be here no matter what.
When you feel insecure, my door will always be open for you day or night I will always be here no matter what.
If and when you feel guilt in any way, my door will always be open for you day or night I will always be here no matter what.
When you need me the most, my door will always be open for you day or night I will always be here no matter what.
When you are not yourself, my door will always be open for you day or night I will always be here no matter what.
When you feel alone, my door will always be open for you day or night I will always be here no matter what.
When you face challenging days, my door will always be open for you day or night I will always be here no matter what.
If and when you need to vent, my door will always be open for you day or night I will always be here no matter what.

Searching For Something Within Me

Searching for something within me with you right beside me is never simple.
Searching for something within me with you right beside me is never easy.
searching for the something within me with you right beside me is always so alarming like you never thought it existed.
searching for something within me with you right beside me shows that it is valid to keep looking.
Searching for something within me with you right beside me and finding the reason behind my fragile past.
Searching for something within me with you right beside me trying to find endless fears from terrorising the daylight out of me.
Searching for something within me with you right beside me trying to solve the issues that affect me.
Searching for something within me with you right beside me trying to figure myself out the only way we know how.
Searching for something within me with you right beside me trying to figure out why I am here.
Searching for something within me with you right beside me trying to find who will stay and who won't.
Searching for something within me with you right beside me trying to work out what's missing.
Searching for something within me with you right beside me trying to figure out why I feel abandoned.
Searching for something within me with you right beside me trying to fight the endless demons that come at me.
Searching for something within me with you right beside me trying to fight the endless pain I feel.
Searching for something within me with you right beside me trying to fight the loneliness I feel.
Searching for something within me with you right beside me trying to fight the endless hurt I feel.

Burning Bridges

Burning bridges is never simple
Burning bridges is never easy
Burning bridges there's no turning back
Burning bridges there is no way forward
Burning bridges can tear you apart
Burning bridges can leave you feel alone
Burning bridges can leave you feeling isolated

Burning bridges can leave you devastated
Burning bridges can leave you feeling like everything is against you.
Burning bridges can leave you feeling like no one wants you around.
Burning bridges can leave you blaming yourself for the way things turned out.
Burning bridges can damage you in a way you don't see coming
Burning bridges can last forever if you allow it
Burning bridges won't put out the fire you alight,

Witness

Witness of my fragile past
Witness of my lifelong fears that terrorise me to no end.
Witness of my lifelong issues that affect me
Witness of the pain I feel
Witness of the hurt I feel
Witness of the battles I face
Witness of the dark days I face
Witness of the struggles I face.
Witness of my downfall.
Witness of when I feel down
Witness of my breaking point
Witness of the fragile me
Witness of when I feel low.
Witness of the rejection I felt
Witness of my downwards spiral
Witness of my sadness
Witness of my tears
Witness of seeing me excel
Witness of seeing the best in me
Witness of my achievements
Witness of my big heart
Witness of my true self
Witness of the fact I know I can turn to you in my hour of need
Witness of my happiness
Witness of the good in me
Witness of me never feeling abandoned
Witness of me never feeling let down.
Witness of me never feeling alone
Witness to what I hide from others but you
Witness to when I am not myself
Witness when I feel broken.

Crisis

When I look back at my fragile past, you help me when I am in a crisis
When I face my lifelong fears, you help me when I am in a crisis
When I try and break my lifelong issues that affect me, you help me when I am in a crisis
When I try and overcome the loneliness I feel, you help me when I am in a crisis
When I feel down, you help me when I am in a crisis
If and when I feel broken, you help me when I am in a crisis
When I feel like I'm in a dark place, you help me when I am in a crisis
When I feel like I'm struggling, you help me when I am in a crisis
When my inner cries take its toll on me, you help me when I am in a crisis
When I don't feel strong enough, you help me when I am in a crisis
When I don't feel brave enough, you help me when I am in a crisis
When I feel low, you help me when I am in a crisis
When I feel lost in any way, you help me when I am in a crisis
When I need a shoulder to cry on, you help me when I am in a crisis
If and when I don't feel good enough, you help me when I am in a crisis

When I feel like an outsider, you help me when I am in a crisis.
If and when I feel rejected, you help me when I am in a crisis
When I feel like giving up, you help me when I am in a crisis
If and when I feel unwanted, you help me when I am in a crisis
If and when I feel worthless, you help me when I am in a crisis
When I feel like I am entering an unknown trap, you help me when I am in a crisis
When I feel like I'm in denial, you help me when I am in a crisis
If and when I have nowhere to turn, you help me when I am in a crisis
If and when I don't feel I have the courage to fight, you help me when I am in a crisis
When I feel insecure, you help me when I am in a crisis
If and when I feel guilt in any way, you help me when I am in a crisis
When I need you the most, you help me when I am in a crisis
When I am not myself, you help me when I am in a crisis
When I feel alone, you help me when I am in a crisis
When I face challenging days, you help me when I am in a crisis
If and when I need to vent, you help me when I am in a crisis

I'll Be Right Here Waiting

When you look back at your fragile past, I'll be right here waiting for you
When you face your lifelong fears, I'll be right here waiting for you
When you try and break your lifelong issues that affect you, I'll be right here waiting for you
When you try and overcome the loneliness you feel, I'll be right here waiting for you
When you feel down, I'll be right here waiting for you
If and when you feel broken, I'll be right here waiting for you
When you feel like you're in a dark place, I'll be right here waiting for you
When you feel like you're struggling, I'll be right here waiting for you
When your inner cries take its toll on you, I'll be right here waiting for you
When you don't feel strong enough, I'll be right here waiting for you
When you don't feel brave enough, I'll be right here waiting for you
When you feel low, I'll be right here waiting for you
When you feel lost in any way, I'll be right here waiting for you
When you need a shoulder to cry on, I'll be right here waiting for you
If and when you don't feel good enough, I'll be right here waiting for you

When you feel like an outsider, I'll be right here waiting for you
If and when you feel rejected, I'll be right here waiting for you
When you feel like giving up, I'll be right here waiting for you
If and when you feel unwanted, I'll be right here waiting for you
If and when you feel worthless, I'll be right here waiting for you
When you feel like you are entering an unknown trap, I'll be right here waiting for you
When you feel like you're in denial, I'll be right here waiting for you
If and when you have nowhere to turn, I'll be right here waiting for you
If and when you don't feel you have the courage to fight, I'll be right here waiting for you
When you feel insecure, I'll be right here waiting for you
If and when you feel guilt in any way, I'll be right here waiting for you
When you need me the most, I'll be right here waiting for you
When you are not yourself, I'll be right here waiting for you
When you feel alone, I'll be right here waiting for you
When you face challenging days, I'll be right here waiting for you
If and when you need to vent, I'll be right here waiting for you

Won't Let You Struggle

When you look back at your fragile past, I won't let you struggle.
When you face your lifelong fears, I won't let you struggle.
When you try and break your lifelong issues that affect you. I won't let you struggle.
When you try and overcome the loneliness you feel, I won't let you struggle.

When you feel down, I won't let you struggle.
If and when you feel broken, I won't let you struggle.
When you feel like you're in a dark place, I won't let you Struggle.
When you feel like you're struggling, I won't let you struggle.

When your inner cries take its toll on you, I won't let you struggle.
When you don't feel strong enough, I won't let you struggle.
When you don't feel brave enough, I won't let you struggle.
When you feel low, I won't let you struggle.

When you feel lost in any way, I won't let you struggle.
When you need a shoulder to cry on, I won't let you struggle.
If and when you don't feel good enough, I won't let you struggle.
When you feel like an outsider, I won't let you struggle.
If and when you feel rejected, I won't let you struggle.
When you feel like giving up, I won't let you struggle.
If and when you feel unwanted, I won't let you struggle.
If and when you feel worthless, I won't let you struggle.

When you feel like you're entering an unknown trap, I won't let you struggle.
When you feel like you're in denial, I won't let you struggle.
If and when you have nowhere to turn, I won't let you struggle.
If and when you don't feel you have the courage to fright, I won't let you struggle.

If and when you feel insecure, I won't let you struggle.
If and when you feel guilt, I won't let you struggle.
When you need me the most, I won't let you struggle.
When you are not yourself, I won't let you struggle.
When you feel alone, I won't let you struggle.
When you face challenging days, I will walk alongside you and I won't let you struggle.
If and when you need to vent, I won't let you struggle.

Won't Let You Feel Insecure

When you look back at your fragile past, know I will not let you feel insecure
When you face your lifelong fears, know I will not let you feel insecure.
When you try and break your lifelong issues that affect you, know I will not let you feel insecure.
When you try and overcome the loneliness you feel, know I will not let you feel insecure.
When you feel down, know I will not let you feel insecure.
If and when you feel broken, know I will not let you feel insecure.
When you feel like you're in a dark place, know I will not let you feel insecure.
When you feel like you're struggling, know I will not let you feel insecure.

When your inner cries take its toll on you, know I will not let you feel insecure.
When you don't feel strong enough, know I will not let you feel insecure.
When you don't feel brave enough, know I will not let you feel insecure.
When you feel low, know I will not let you feel insecure.

When you feel lost in any way, know I will not let you feel insecure.
When you need a shoulder to cry on, know I will not let you feel insecure.
If and when you don't feel good enough, know I will not let you feel insecure.
When you feel like an outsider, know I will not let you feel insecure.

If and when you feel rejected, know I will not let you feel insecure.
When you feel like giving up, know I will not let you feel insecure.
If and when you feel unwanted, know I will not let you feel insecure.
If and when you feel worthless, know I will not let you feel insecure.

When you feel like you are entering an unknown trap, knowI will not let you feel insecure.
When you feel like you're in denial, know I will not let you feel insecure.
If and when you have nowhere to turn, know I will not let you feel insecure.
If and when you don't feel you have the courage to fight, know I will not let you feel insecure.
If and when you feel insecure, know I will not let you feel insecure.
If and when you feel guilt in any way, know I will not let you feel insecure.
When you need me the most, know I will not let you feel insecure.
When you are not yourself, know I will not let you feel insecure.
When you feel alone, know I will not let you feel insecure.
When you face challenging days, I will walk alongside you and know I will not let you feel insecure.
If and when you need to vent, know I will not let you feel insecure.

Daylight Or Not

When you look back at your fragile past, know I will be there daylight or not.
When you face you your lifelong fears, know I will be there daylight or not.
When you try and break your lifelong issues that affect you, know I will be daylight or not.
When you try and overcome the loneliness you feel, know I will be there daylight or not.
When you feel down, know I will be there daylight or not.
If and when you feel broken, know I will be there daylight or not.
When you feel like you're in a dark place, know I will be there daylight or not.
When you feel like you're struggling, know I will be there daylight or not.

When your inner cries take its toll on you, know I will be there daylight or not.
When you don't feel strong enough, know I will be there daylight or not.
When you don't feel brave enough, know I will be there daylight or not.
When you feel low, know I will be there daylight or not.

When you feel lost in any way, know I will be there daylight or not.
When you need a shoulder to cry on, know I will be there daylight or not.
If and when you don't feel good enough, know I will be there daylight or not.
When you feel like an outsider, know I will be there daylight or not.

If and when you feel rejected, know I will be there daylight or not.
When you feel like giving up, know I will be there daylight or not.
If and when you feel unwanted, know I will be there daylight or not.
If and when you feel worthless, know I will be there daylight or not.

When you feel like you are entering an unknown trap, know I will be there daylight or not.
When you feel like you're in denial, know I will be there daylight or not.
If and when you have nowhere to turn, know I will be there daylight or not.
If and when you don't feel you have the courage to fight, know I will be there daylight or not.
If and when you feel insecure, know I will be there daylight or not.
If and when you feel guilt in any way, know I will be there daylight or not.
When you need me the most, know I will be there daylight or not.
When you are not yourself, know I will be there daylight or not.
When you feel alone, know I will be there daylight or not.
When you face challenging days, I will walk alongside you and know I will be there daylight or not.
If and when you need to vent, know I will be there daylight or not.

Never Let You Face A Mess Alone

When you look back at your fragile past, know I will never let you face a mess alone we are in this mess together I will always help you any way I can.

When you face you your lifelong fears, know I will never let you face a mess alone we are in this mess together I will always help you any way I can.

When you try and break your lifelong issues that affect you, know I will never let you face a mess alone we are in this mess together I will always help you any way I can.

When you try and overcome the loneliness you feel, know I will never let you face a mess alone we are in this mess together I will always help you any way I can.

When you feel down, know I will never let you face a mess alone we are in this mess together I will always help you any way I can.

If and when you feel broken, know I will never let you face a mess alone we are in this mess together I will always help you any way I can.

When you feel like you're in a dark place, know I will never let you face a mess alone we are in this mess together I will always help you any way I can.

When you feel like you're struggling, know I will never let you face a mess alone we are in this mess together I will always help you any way I can.

When your inner cries take its toll on you, know I will never let you face a mess alone we are in this mess together I will always help you any way I can.

When you don't feel strong enough, know I will never let you face a mess alone we are in this mess together I will always help you any way I can.

When you don't feel brave enough, know I will never let you face a mess alone we are in this mess together I will always help you any way I can.

When you feel low, know I will never let you face a mess alone we are in this mess together I will always help you any way I can.

When you feel lost in any way, know I will never let you face a mess alone we are in this mess together I will always help you any way I can.

When you need a shoulder to cry on, know I will never let you face a mess alone we are in this mess together I will always help you any way I can.

If and when you don't feel good enough, know I will never let you face a mess alone we are in this mess together I will always help you any way I can.

When you feel like an outsider, know I will never let you face a mess alone we are in this mess together I will always help you any way I can.

If and when you feel rejected, know I will never let you face a mess alone we are in this mess together I will always help you any way I can.

When you feel like giving up, know I will never let you face a mess alone we are in this mess together I will always help you any way I can.

If and when you feel unwanted, know I will never let you face a mess alone we are in this mess together I will always help you any way I can.
If and when you feel worthless, know I will never let you face a mess alone we are in this mess together I will always help you any way I can.
When you feel like you are entering an unknown trap, know I will never let you face a mess alone we are in this mess together I will always help you any way I can.
When you feel like you're in denial, know I will never let you face a mess alone we are in this mess together I will always help you any way I can.
If and when you have nowhere to turn, know I will never let you face a mess alone we are in this mess together I will always help you any way I can.
If and when you don't feel you have the courage to fight, know I will never let you face a mess alone we are in this mess together I will always help you any way I can.
If and when you feel insecure, know I will never let you face a mess alone we are in this mess together I will always help you any way I can.
If and when you feel guilt in any way, know I will never let you face a mess alone we are in this mess together I will always help you any way I can.
When you need me the most, know I will never let you face a mess alone we are in this mess together I will always help you any way I can.
When you are not yourself, know I will never let you face a mess alone we are in this mess together I will always help you any way I can.
When you feel alone, know I will never let you face a mess alone we are in this mess together I will always help you any way I can.
When you face challenging days, I will never let you face a mess alone we are in this mess together I will always help you any way I can.
If and when you need to vent, know I will never let you face a mess alone we are in this mess together I will always help you any way I can.

Never Abandon You

When you look back at your fragile past, know I will never abandon you.
When you face your lifelong fears, know I will never abandon you.
When you try and break your lifelong issues that affect you, know I will never abandon you.
When you try and overcome the loneliness you feel, know I will never abandon you.
When you feel down, know I will never abandon you.
If and when you feel broken, know I will never abandon you.
When you feel like you're in a dark place, know I will never abandon you.
When you feel like you're struggling, know I will never abandon you.

When your inner cries take its toll on you, know I will never abandon you.
When you don't feel strong enough, know I will never abandon you.
When you don't feel brave enough, know I will never abandon you.
When you feel low, know I will never abandon you.
When you feel lost in any way, know I will never abandon you.
When you need a shoulder to cry on, know I will never abandon you.
If and when you don't feel good enough, know I will never abandon you.

When you feel like an outsider, know I will never abandon you.
If and when you feel rejected, know I will never abandon you.
When you feel like giving up, know I will never abandon you.
If and when you feel unwanted, know I will never abandon you.
If and when you feel worthless, know I will never abandon you.
When you feel like you are entering an unknown trap, know I will never abandon you.
When you feel like you're in denial, know I will never abandon you.
If and when you have nowhere to turn, know I will never abandon you.
If and when you don't feel you have the courage to fight, know I will never abandon you.
If and when you feel insecure, know I will never abandon you.
If and when you feel guilt in any way, know I will never abandon you.
When you need me the most, know I will never abandon you.
When you are not yourself, know I will never abandon you.
When you feel alone, know I will never abandon you.
When you face challenging days, I will never abandon you.
If and when you need to vent, know I will never abandon you.

Always Make Time For You

When you look back at your fragile past, know I will always make time for you.
When you face your lifelong fears, know I will always make time for you.
When you try and break your lifelong issues that affect you, know I will always make time for you.
When you try and overcome the loneliness you feel, know I will always make time for you.
When you feel down, know I will always make time for you.
If and when you feel broken, know I will always make time for you.
When you feel like you're in a dark place, know I will always make time for you.
When you feel like you're struggling, know I will always make time for you.

When your inner cries take its toll on you, know I will always make time for you.
When you don't feel strong enough, know I will always make time for you.
When you don't feel brave enough, know I will always make time for you.
When you feel low, know I will always make time for you.
When you feel lost in any way, know I will always make time for you.
When you need a shoulder to cry on, know I will always make time for you.
If and when you don't feel good enough, know I will always make time for you.

When you feel like an outsider, know I will always make time for you.
If and when you feel rejected, know I will always make time for you.
When you feel like giving up, know I will always make time for you.
If and when you feel unwanted, know I will always make time for you.
If and when you feel worthless, know I will always make time for you.
When you feel like you are entering an unknown trap, know I will always make time for you.
When you feel like you're in denial, know I will always make time for you.
If and when you have nowhere to turn, know I will always make time for you.
If and when you don't feel you have the courage to fight, know I will always make time for you
If and when you feel insecure, know I will always make time for you.
If and when you feel guilt in any way, know I will always make time for you.
When you need me the most, know I will always make time for you.
When you are not yourself, know I will always make time for you.
When you feel alone, know I will always make time for you.
When you face challenging days, I will always make time for you.
If and when you need to vent, know I will always make time for you.

Always Watch Over You

When you look back at your fragile past, know I will always watch over you.
When you face your lifelong fears, know I will always watch over you.
When you try and break your lifelong issues that affect you, know I will always watch over you.
When you try and overcome the loneliness you feel, know I will always watch over you.
When you feel down, know I will always watch over you.
If and when you feel broken, know I will always watch over you.
When you feel like you're in a dark place, know I will always watch over you.
When you feel like you're struggling, know I will always watch over you.
When your inner cries take its toll on you, know I will always watch over you.

When you don't feel strong enough, know I will always watch over you.
When you don't feel brave enough, know I will always watch over you.
When you feel low, know I will always watch over you.
When you feel lost in any way, know I will always watch over you.
When you need a shoulder to cry on, know I will always watch over you.
If and when you don't feel good enough, know I will always watch over you.

When you feel like an outsider, know I will always watch over you.
If and when you feel rejected, know I will always watch over you.
When you feel like giving up, know I will always watch over you.
If and when you feel unwanted, know I will always watch over you.
If and when you feel worthless, know I will always watch over you.
When you feel like you are entering an unknown trap, know I will always watch over you.
When you feel like you're in denial, know I will always watch over you.
If and when you have nowhere to turn, know I will always watch over you.
If and when you don't feel you have the courage to fight, know I will always watch over you.
If and when you feel insecure, know I will always watch over you.
If and when you feel guilt in any way, know I will always watch over you.
When you need me the most, know I will always watch over you.
When you are not yourself, know I will always watch over you.
When you feel alone, know I will always watch over you.
When you face challenging days, I will always watch over you.
If and when you need to vent, know I will always watch over you.

Make Me Feel Good Enough

When I look back at my fragile past, know you always make me feel good enough.
When I face my lifelong fears, know you always make me feel good enough.
When I try and break your lifelong issues that affect me, know you always make me feel good enough.
When I try and overcome the loneliness I feel, know you always make me feel good enough.
When I feel down, know you always make me feel good enough.
If and when I feel broken, know you always make me feel good enough.
When I feel like I'm in a dark place, know you always make me feel good enough.
When I feel like I'm struggling, know you always make me feel good enough.

When my inner cries take its toll on me, know you always make me feel good enough.
When I don't feel strong enough, know you always make me feel good enough.
When I don't feel brave enough, know you always make me feel good enough.
When I feel low, know you always make me feel good enough.
When I feel lost in any way, know you always make me feel good enough.
When I need a shoulder to cry on, know you always make me feel good enough.
If and when I don't feel good enough, know you always make me feel good enough.

When I feel like an outsider, know you always make me feel good enough.
If and when I feel rejected, know you always make me feel good enough.
When I feel like giving up, know you always make me feel good enough.
If and when I feel unwanted, know you always make me feel good enough.
If and when I feel worthless, know you always make me feel good enough.
When I feel like I am entering an unknown trap, know you always make me feel good enough.
When I feel like I'm in denial, know you always make me feel good enough.
If and when I have nowhere to turn, know you always make me feel good enough.
If and when I don't feel I have the courage to fight, know you always make me feel good enough.
If and when I feel insecure, know you always make me feel good enough.
If and when I feel guilt in any way, know you always make me feel good enough.
When I need you the most, know you always make me feel good enough.
When I am not myself, know you always make me feel good enough.
When I feel alone, know you always make me feel good enough.
When I face challenging days, you always make me feel good enough.
If and when I need to vent, know you always make me feel good enough

Burn Out

When you look back at your fragile past, know I will not let you burn out.
When you face your lifelong fears, know I will not let you burn out.
When you try and break your lifelong issues that affect you, know I will not let you burn out.
When you try and overcome the loneliness you feel, know I will not let you burn out
When you feel down, know I will not let you burn out.
If and when you feel broken, know I will not let you burn out.

When you feel like you're in a dark place, know I will not let you burn out
When you feel like you're struggling, know I will not let you burn.

When your inner cries take its toll on you, know I will not let you burn out
When you don't feel strong enough, know I will not let you burn out.
When you don't feel brave enough, know I will not let you burn out
When you feel low, know I will not let you burn out.

When you feel lost in any way, know I will not let you burn out.
When you need a shoulder to cry on, know I will not let you burn out
If and when you don't feel good enough, know I will not let you burn out.
When you feel like an outsider, know I will not let you burn out.

If and when you feel rejected, know I will not let you burn out.
When you feel like giving up, know I will not let you burn out.
If and when you feel unwanted, know I will not let you burn out
If and when you feel worthless, know I will not let you burn out.

When you feel like you are entering an unknown trap, know I will not let you burn out
When you feel like you're in denial, know I will not let you burn out.
If and when you have nowhere to turn, know I will not let you burn out.
If and when you don't feel you have the courage to fight, know I will not let you burn out.
If and when you feel insecure, know I will not let you burn out.
If and when you feel guilt in any way, know I will not let you burn out.
When you need me the most, know I will not let you burn out.
When you are not yourself, know I will not let you burn out.
When you feel alone, know I will not let you burn out.
When you face challenging days, I will walk alongside you and know I will not let you burn out.
If and when you need to vent, know I will not let you burnout

Go To The End Of The Earth For You

When you look back at your fragile past, know I will go to the end of the earth for you.
When you face your lifelong fears, know I will go to the end of the earth for you.
When you try and break your lifelong issues that affect you, know I will go to the end of the earth for you.

When you try and overcome the loneliness you feel, know I will go to the end of the earth for you.
When you feel down, know I will go to the end of the earth for you.
If and when you feel broken, know I will go to the end of the earth for you.
When you feel like you're in a dark place, know I will go to the end of the earth for you.
When you feel like you're struggling, know I will go to the end of the earth for you.

When your inner cries take its toll on you, know I will go to the end of the earth for you.
When you don't feel strong enough, know I will go to the end of the earth for you.
When you don't feel brave enough, know I will go to the end of the earth for you.
When you feel low, know I will go to the end of the earth for you.

When you feel lost in any way, know I will go to the end of the earth for you.
When you need a shoulder to cry on, know I will go to the end of the earth for you.
If and when you don't feel good enough, know I will go to the end of the earth for you.
When you feel like an outsider, know I will go to the end of the earth for you.

If and when you feel rejected, know I will go to the end of the earth for you.
When you feel like giving up, know I will go to the end of the earth for you.
If and when you feel unwanted, know I will go to the end of the earth for you.
If and when you feel worthless, know I will go to the end of the earth for you.
When you feel like you are entering an unknown trap, know I will go to the end of the earth for you.
When you feel like you're in denial, know I will go to the end of the earth for you.
If and when you have nowhere to turn, know I will go to the end of the earth for you.
If and when you don't feel you have the courage to fight, know I will go to the end of the earth for you.
If and when you feel insecure, know I will go to the end of the earth for you.
If and when you feel guilt in any way, know I will go to the end of the earth for you.
When you need me the most, know I will go to the end of the earth for you.
When you are not yourself, know I will go to the end of the earth for you.
When you feel alone, know I will go to the end of the earth for you.

When you face challenging days, I will walk alongside you and know I will go to the end of the earth for you.
If and when you need to vent, know I will go to the end of the earth for you.

Won't Let You Carry A Black Cloud Around With You

When you look back at your fragile past, know I will not let you carry a black cloud around with you, know you can tell me anything.
When you face your lifelong fears, know I will not let you carry a black cloud around with you, know you can tell me anything.
When you try and break your lifelong issues that affect you, know I will not let you carry a black cloud around with you, know you can tell me anything.
When you try and overcome the loneliness you feel, know I will not let you carry a black cloud around with you, know you can tell me anything.
When you feel down, know I will not let you carry a black cloud around with you, know you can tell me anything.
If and when you feel broken, know I will not let you carry a black cloud around with you, know you can tell me anything.
When you feel like you're in a dark place, know I will not let you carry a black cloud around with you, know you can tell me anything.
When you feel like you're struggling, know I will not let you carry a black cloud around with you, know you can tell me anything.
When your inner cries take its toll on you, know I will not let you carry a black cloud around with you, know you can tell me anything.
When you don't feel strong enough, know I will not let you carry a black cloud around with you, know you can tell me anything.
When you don't feel brave enough, know I will not let you carry a black cloud around with you, know you can tell me anything.
When you feel low, know I will not let you carry a black cloud around with you, know you can tell me anything.
When you feel lost in any way, know I will not let you carry a black cloud around with you, know you can tell me anything.
When you need a shoulder to cry on, know I will not let you carry a black cloud around with you, know you can tell me anything.
If and when you don't feel good enough, know I will not let you carry a black cloud around with you, know you can tell me anything.
When you feel like an outsider, know I will not let you carry a black cloud around with you, know you can tell me anything.
If and when you feel rejected, know I will not let you carry a black cloud around with you, know you can tell me anything.

When you feel like giving up, know I will not let you carry a black cloud around with you, know you can tell me anything.
If and when you feel unwanted, know I will not let you carry a black cloud around with you, know you can tell me anything.
If and when you feel worthless, know I will not let you carry a black cloud around with you, know you can tell me anything.
When you feel like you are entering an unknown trap, know I will not let you carry a black cloud around with you, know you can tell me anything.
When you feel like you're in denial, know I will not let you carry a black cloud around with you, know you can tell me anything.
If and when you have nowhere to turn, know I will not let you carry a black cloud around with you, know you can tell me anything.
If and when you don't feel you have the courage to fight, know I will not let you carry a black cloud around with you, know you can tell me anything.
If and when you feel insecure, know I will not let you carry a black cloud around with you, know you can tell me anything.
If and when you feel guilt in any way, know I will not let you carry a black cloud around with you, know you can tell me anything.
When you need me the most, know I will not let you carry a black cloud around with you, know you can tell me anything.
When you are not yourself, know I will not let you carry a black cloud around with you, know you can tell me anything.
When you feel alone, know I will not let you carry ta black cloud around with you, know you can tell me anything.
When you face challenging days, I will walk alongside you and know I will not let you carry a black cloud around with you, know you can tell me anything.
If and when you need to vent, know I will not let you carry a black cloud around with you, know you can tell me anything.

Don't Have To Keep Me In The Dark

When you look back at your fragile past know you don't have to keep me in the dark.
When you face your lifelong fears, know you don't have to keep me in the dark.
When you try and break your lifelong issues that affect you, know you don't have to keep me in the dark.
When you try and overcome the loneliness you feel know you don't have to keep me in the dark.
When you feel down know you don't have to keep me in the dark.
If and when you feel broken know you don't have to keep me in the dark.

When you feel like you're in a dark place know you don't have to keep me in the dark.
When you feel like you're struggling know you don't have to keep me in the dark.

When your inner cries take its toll on you, know you don't have to keep me in the dark.
When you don't feel strong enough know you don't have to keep me in the dark.
When you don't feel brave enough know I won't keep you in the dark.
When you feel low know you don't have to keep me in the dark.

When you feel lost in any way know you don't have to keep me in the dark
When you need a shoulder to cry on know you don't have to keep me in the dark.
If and when you don't feel good enough know you don't have to keep me in the dark.
When you feel like an outsider know you don't have to keep me in the dark.

If and when you feel rejected know you don't have to keep me in the dark.
When you feel like giving up know you don't have to keep me in the dark.
If and when you feel unwanted know you don't have to keep me in the dark.
If and when you feel worthless know you don't have to keep me in the dark.

When you feel like you're entering an unknown trap know you don't have to keep me in the dark.
When you feel like you're in denial know you don't have to keep me in the dark.
If and when you have nowhere to turn know you don't have to keep me in the dark.
If and when you don't feel you have the courage to fight know you don't have to keep me in the dark.
If and when you feel insecure know you don't have to keep me in the dark.
If and when you feel guilt know you don't have to keep me in the dark.
When you need me the most know you don't have to keep me in the dark.
When you are not yourself know you don't have to keep me in the dark.
When you feel alone know you don't have to keep me in the dark.
When you face challenging days, I will walk alongside you and know you don't have to keep me in the dark
If and when you need to vent know you don't have to keep me in the dark.

When I Am A Mess

When I look back at my fragile past, you know when I am a mess.
When I face my lifelong fears, you know when I am a mess.
When I try and break my lifelong issues that affect me, you know when I am a mess.
When I try and overcome the loneliness I feel, you know when I am a mess.
When I feel down, you know when I am a mess.
If and when I feel broken, you know when I am a mess.
When I feel like I'm in a dark place, you know when I am a mess,
When I feel like I'm struggling, you know when I am a mess.
When my inner cries take its toll on me, you know when I am a mess.
When I don't feel strong enough, you know when I am a mess.
When I don't feel brave enough, you know when I am a mess.
When I feel low, you know when I am a mess.
When I feel lost in any way, you know when I am a mess.
When I need a shoulder to cry on, you know when I am a mess.
If and when I don't feel good enough, you know when I am a mess.

When I feel like an outsider, you know when I am a mess.
If and when I feel rejected, you know when I am a mess.
When I feel like giving up, you know when I am a mess,
If and when I feel unwanted, you know when I am a mess,
If and when I feel worthless, you know when I am a mess,
When I feel like I am entering an unknown trap, you know when I am a mess.
When I feel like I'm in denial, you know when I am a mess.
If and when I have nowhere to turn, you know when I am a mess.
If and when I don't feel I have the courage to fight, you know when I am a mess.
When I feel insecure, you know when I am a mess.
If and when I feel guilt in any way, you know when I am a mess
When I need you the most, you know when I am a mess.
When I am not myself, you know when I am a mess.
When I feel alone, you know when I am a mess.
When I face challenging days, you know when I am a mess.
If and when I need to vent, you know when I am a mess.

Stick By Ur Word

When I look back at my fragile past, you stick by ur word.
When I face my lifelong fears, you stick by ur word.
When I try and break my lifelong issues that affect me, you tick by ur word.
When I try and overcome the loneliness I feel, you stick by ur word.
When I feel down, you stick by ur word.
If and when I feel broken, you stick by ur word.
When I feel like I'm in a dark place, you stick by ur word.
When I feel like I'm struggling, you stick by ur word.
When my inner cries take its toll on me, you stick by ur word.
When I don't feel strong enough, you stick by ur word.
When I don't feel brave enough, you stick by ur word.
When I feel low, you stick by ur word.
When I feel lost in any way, you stick by ur word.
When I need a shoulder to cry on, you stick by ur word.
If and when I don't feel good enough, you stick by ur word.
When I feel like an outsider, you stick by ur word.
If and when I feel rejected, you stick by ur word.
When I feel like giving up, you stick by ur word.
If and when I feel unwanted, you stick by ur word.
If and when I feel worthless, you stick by ur word.
When I feel like I am entering an unknown trap, you stick by ur word.
When I feel like I'm in denial, you stick by ur word.
If and when I have nowhere to turn, you stick by ur word.
If and when I don't feel I have the courage to fight, you stick by ur word.
 when I feel insecure, you stick by ur word.
If and when I feel guilt in any way, you stick by ur word.
When I need you the most, you stick by ur word.
When I am not myself, you stick by ur word.
When I feel alone, you stick by ur word.
When I face challenging days, you stick ur word.
If and when I need to vent, you stick by ur word.

Face It With Me

When I look back at my fragile past, when I face anything you face it with me.
When I face my lifelong fears, when I face anything you face it with me.
When I try and break my lifelong issues that affect me, when I face anything you face it with me.
When I try and overcome the loneliness I feel, when I face anything you face it with me.
When I feel down, when I face anything you face it with me.
If and when I feel broken, when I face anything you face it with me.
When I feel like I'm in a dark place, when I face anything you face it with me.
When I feel like I'm struggling, when I face anything you face it with me.
When my inner cries take its toll on me, when I face anything you face it with me.
When I don't feel strong enough, when I face anything you face it with me.
When I don't feel brave enough, when I face anything you face it with me.
When I feel low, when I face anything you face it with me.
When I feel lost in any way, when I face anything you face it with me.
When I need a shoulder to cry on, when I face anything you face it with me.
If and when I don't feel good enough, when I face anything you face it with me,

When I feel like an outsider, when I face anything you face it with me.
If and when I feel rejected, when I face anything you face it with me.
When I feel like giving up, when I face anything you face it with me.
If and when I feel unwanted, when I face anything you face it with me.
If and when I feel worthless, when I face anything you face it with me.
When I feel like I am entering an unknown trap, when I face anything you face it with me.
When I feel like I'm in denial, when I face anything you face it with me.
If and when I have nowhere to turn, when I face anything you face it with me.
If and when I don't feel I have the courage to fight, when I face anything you face it with me.
When I feel insecure, when I face anything you face it with me.
If and when I feel guilt in any way, when I face anything you face it with me.
When I need you the most, when I face anything you face it with me.
When I am not myself, when I face anything you face it with me.
When I feel alone, when I face anything you face it with me.
When I face challenging days, when I face anything you face it with me.
If and when I need to vent, when I face anything you face it with me.

Ur World Of Possibilities

When I look back at my fragile past, you take me into ur world of possibilities.
When I face my lifelong fears, you take me into ur world of possibilities.
When I try and break my lifelong issues that affect me, you take me into ur world of possibilities.
When I try and overcome the loneliness I feel, you take me into ur world of possibilities.
When I feel down, you take me into ur world of possibilities.
If and when I feel broken, you take me into ur world of possibilities.
When I feel like I'm in a dark place, you take me into ur world of possibilities.
When I feel like I'm struggling, you take me into ur world of possibilities.
When my inner cries take its toll on me, you take me into ur world of possibilities.
When I don't feel strong enough, you take me into ur world of possibilities.
When I don't feel brave enough, you take me into ur world of possibilities.
When I feel low, you take me into ur world of possibilities.
When I feel lost in any way, you take me into ur world of possibilities.
When I need a shoulder to cry on, you take me into ur world of possibilities.
If and when I don't feel good enough, you take me into ur world of possibilities.

When I feel like an outsider, you take me into ur world of possibilities.
If and when I feel rejected, you take me into ur world of possibilities.
When I feel like giving up, you take me into ur world of possibilities.
If and when I feel unwanted, you take me into ur world of possibilities.
If and when I feel worthless, you take me into ur world of possibilities.
When I feel like I am entering an unknown trap, you take me into ur world of possibilities.
When I feel like I'm in denial, you take me into ur world of possibilities.
If and when I have nowhere to turn, you take me into ur world of possibilities.
If and when I don't feel I have the courage to fight, you take me into ur world of possibilities.
when I feel insecure, you take me into ur world of possibilities.
If and when I feel guilt in any way, you take me into ur world of possibilities.
When I need you the most, you take me into ur world of possibilities.
When I am not myself, you take me into ur world of possibilities.
When I feel alone, you take me into ur world of possibilities.
When I face challenging days, you take me into ur world of possibilities.
If and when I need to vent, you take me into ur world of possibilities.

Know When I Start To Stumble

When I look back at my fragile past, you know when I start to stumble
When I face my lifelong fears, you know when I start to stumble
When I try and break my lifelong issues that affect me, you know when I start to stumble
When I try and overcome the loneliness I feel, you know when I start to stumble
When I feel down, you know when I start to stumble
If and when I feel broken, you know when I start to stumble
When I feel like I'm in a dark place, you know when I start to stumble
When I feel like I'm struggling, you know when I start to stumble
When my inner cries take its toll on me, you know when I start to stumble
When I don't feel strong enough, you know when I start to stumble
When I don't feel brave enough, you know when I start to stumble
When I feel low, you know when I start to stumble
When I feel lost in any way, you know when I start to stumble.
When I need a shoulder to cry on, you know when I start to stumble
If and when I don't feel good enough, you know when I start to stumble

When I feel like an outsider, you know when I start to stumble
If and when I feel rejected, you know when I start to stumble
When I feel like giving up, you know when I start to stumble
If and when I feel unwanted, you know when I start to stumble.
If and when I feel worthless, you know when I start to stumble.
When I feel like I am entering an unknown trap, you know when I start to stumble.
When I feel like I'm in denial, you know when I start to stumble.
If and when I have nowhere to turn, you know when I start to stumble.
If and when I don't feel I have the courage to fight, you know when I start to stumble.
When I feel insecure, you know when I start to stumble.
If and when I feel guilt in any way, you know when I start to stumble.
When I need you the most, you know when I start to stumble.
When I am not myself, you know when I start to stumble.
When I feel alone, you know when I start to stumble.
When I face challenging days, you know when I start to stumble.
If and when I need to vent, you know when I start to stumble.

Always Matter To Me

When you look back at your fragile past, you know you will always matter to me.
When you face your lifelong fears, you know you will always matter to me.
When you try and break your lifelong issues that affect you, you know you will always matter to me.
When you try and overcome the loneliness you feel, you know you will always matter to me.
When you feel down, you know you will always matter to me.
If and when you feel broken, you know you will always matter to me.
When you feel like you're in a dark place, you know you will always matter to me.
When you feel like you're struggling, you know you will always matter to me.
When your inner cries take its toll on you, you know you will always matter to me.
When you don't feel strong enough, you know you will always matter to me.
When you don't feel brave enough, you know you will always matter to me.
When you feel low, you know you will always matter to me.
When you feel lost in any way, you know you will always matter to me.
When you need a shoulder to cry on, you know you will always matter to me.
If and when you don't feel good enough, you know you will always matter to me.

When you feel like an outsider, you know you will always matter to me.
If and when you feel rejected, you know you will always matter to me.
When you feel like giving up, you know you will always matter to me.
If and when you feel unwanted, you know you will always matter to me.
If and when you feel worthless, you know you will always matter to me.
When you feel like you're entering an unknown trap, you know you will always matter to me.
When you feel like I'm in denial, you know you will always matter to me.
If and when you have nowhere to turn, you know you will always matter to me.
If and when you don't feel you have the courage to fight, you know you will always matter to me.
When you feel insecure, you know you will always matter to me.
If and when you feel guilt in any way, you know you will always matter to me.
When you need me the most, you know you will always matter to me.
When you are not yourself, you know you will always matter to me.
When you feel alone, you know you will always matter to me.
When you face challenging days, you know you will always matter to me.
If and when you need to vent, you know you will always matter to me.

Always Matter To You

When I look back at my fragile past, I know I will always matter to you.
When I face my lifelong fears, I know I will always matter to you.
When I try and break my lifelong issues that affect me, I know I will always matter to you.
When I try and overcome the loneliness I feel, I know I will always matter to you.
When I feel down, I know I will always matter to you.
If and when I feel broken, I know I will always matter to you.
When I feel like I'm in a dark place, I know I will always matter to you.
When I feel like I'm struggling, I know I will always matter to you.
When my inner cries take its toll on me, I know I will always matter to you.
When I don't feel strong enough, I know I will always matter to you.
When I don't feel brave enough, I know I will always matter to you.
When I feel low, I know I will always matter to you.
When I feel lost in any way, I know I will always matter to you.
When I need a shoulder to cry on, I know I will always matter to you.
If and when I don't feel good enough, I know I will always matter to you.

When I feel like an outsider, I know I will always matter to you.
If and when I feel rejected, I know I will always matter to you.
When I feel like giving up, I know I will always matter to you.
If and when I feel unwanted, I know I will always matter to you.
If and when I feel worthless, I know I will always matter to you.
When I feel like I am entering an unknown trap, I know I will always matter to you.
When I feel like I'm in denial, I know I will always matter to you.
If and when I have nowhere to turn, I know I will always matter to you.
If and when I don't feel I have the courage to fight, I know I will always matter to you.
When I feel insecure, I know I will always matter to you.
If and when I feel guilt in any way, I know I will always matter to you.
When I need you the most, I know I will always matter to you.
When I am not myself, I know I will always matter to you.
When I feel alone, I know I will always matter to you.
When I face challenging days, I know I will always matter to you.
If and when I need to vent, I know I will always matter to you.

Comfort Me

When I look back at my fragile past, you comfort me when I need it.
When I face my lifelong fears, you comfort me when I need it.
When I try and break my lifelong issues that affect me, you comfort me when I need it.
When I try and overcome the loneliness I feel, you comfort me when I need it.
When I feel down, you comfort me when I need it.
If and when I feel broken, you comfort me when I need it.
When I feel like I'm in a dark place, you comfort me when I need it.
When I feel like I'm struggling, you comfort me when I need it.
When my inner cries take its toll on me, you comfort me when I need it.
When I don't feel strong enough, you comfort me when I need it.
When I don't feel brave enough, you comfort me when I need it.
When I feel low, you comfort me when I need it.
When I feel lost in any way, you comfort me when I need it.
When I need a shoulder to cry on, you comfort me when I need it.
If and when I don't feel good enough, you comfort me when I need it.

When I feel like an outsider, you comfort me when I need it.
If and when I feel rejected, you comfort me when I need it.
When I feel like giving up, you comfort me when I need it.
If and when I feel unwanted, you comfort me when I need it.
If and when I feel worthless, you comfort me when I need it.
When I feel like I am entering an unknown trap, you comfort me when I need it.
When I feel like I'm in denial, you comfort me when I need it.
If and when I have nowhere to turn, you comfort me when I need it.
If and when I don't feel I have the courage to fight, you comfort me when I need it.
When I feel insecure, you comfort me when I need it.
If and when I feel guilt in any way, you comfort me when I need it.
When I need you the most, you comfort me when I need it.
When I am not myself, you comfort me when I need it.
When I feel alone, you comfort me when I need it.
When I face challenging days, you comfort me when I need it.
If and when I need to vent, you comfort me when I need it.

Nothing Will Stop Me Achieving My Goals.

When I look back at my fragile past, you show me nothing will stop me achieving my goals.
When I face my lifelong fears, you show me nothing will stop me achieving my goals.
When I try and break my lifelong issues that affect me, you show me nothing will stop me achieving my goals.
When I try and overcome the loneliness I feel, you show me nothing will stop me achieving my goals.
When I feel down, you show me nothing will stop me achieving my goals.
If and when I feel broken, you show me nothing will stop me achieving my goals.
When I feel like I'm in a dark place, you show me nothing will stop me achieving my goals.
When I feel like I'm struggling, you show me nothing will stop me achieving my goals.
When my inner cries take its toll on me, you show me nothing will stop me achieving my goals.
When I don't feel strong enough, you show me nothing will stop me achieving my goals.
When I don't feel brave enough, you show me nothing will stop me achieving my goals..
When I feel low, you show me nothing will stop me achieving my goals.
When I feel lost in any way, you show me nothing will stop me achieving my goals.
When I need a shoulder to cry on, you show me nothing will stop me achieving my goals.
If and when I don't feel good enough, you show me nothing will stop me achieving my goals.

When I feel like an outsider, you show me nothing will stop me achieving my goals.
If and when I feel rejected, you show me nothing will stop me achieving my goals.
When I feel like giving up, you show me nothing will stop me achieving my goals.
If and when I feel unwanted, you show me nothing will stop me achieving my goals.
If and when I feel worthless, you show me nothing will stop me achieving my goals.

When I feel like I am entering an unknown trap, you show me nothing will stop me achieving my goals.
When I feel like I'm in denial, you show me nothing will stop me achieving my goals.
If and when I have nowhere to turn, you show me nothing will stop me achieving my goals.
If and when I don't feel I have the courage to fight, you show me nothing will stop me achieving my goals.
When I feel insecure, you show me nothing will stop me achieving my goals.
If and when I feel guilt in any way, you show me nothing will stop me achieving my goals.
When I need you the most, you show me nothing will stop me achieving my goals.
When I am not myself, you show me nothing will stop me achieving my goals.
When I feel alone, you show me nothing will stop me achieving my goals.
When I face challenging days, you show me nothing will stop me achieving my goals.
If and when I need to vent, you show me nothing will stop me achieving my goals.

A Force To Be Reckoned With

When I look back at my fragile past, I know I am a force to be reckoned with.
When I face my lifelong fears, I know I am a force to be reckoned with.
When I try and break my lifelong issues that affect me, I know I am a force to be reckoned with.
When I try and overcome the loneliness I feel, I know I am a force to be reckoned with.
When I feel down, I know I am a force to be reckoned with.
If and when I feel broken, I know I am a force to be reckoned with.
When I feel like I'm in a dark place, I know I am a force to be reckoned with.
When I feel like I'm struggling, I know I am a force to be reckoned with.
When my inner cries take its toll on me, I know I am a force to be reckoned with.
When I don't feel strong enough, I know I am a force to be reckoned with.
When I don't feel brave enough, I know I am a force to be reckoned with.
When I feel low, I know I am a force to be reckoned with.
When I feel lost in any way, I know I am a force to be reckoned with.
When I need a shoulder to cry on, I know I am a force to be reckoned with.
If and when I don't feel good enough, I know I am a force to be reckoned with.

When I feel like an outsider, I know I am a force to be reckoned with.

If and when I feel rejected, I know I am a force to be reckoned with.
When I feel like giving up, I know I am a force to be reckoned with.
If and when I feel unwanted, I know I am a force to be reckoned with.
If and when I feel worthless, I know I am a force to be reckoned with.
When I feel like I am entering an unknown trap, I know I am a force to be reckoned with.
When I feel like I'm in denial, I know I am a force to be reckoned with.
If and when I have nowhere to turn, I know I am a force to be reckoned with.
If and when I don't feel I have the courage to fight, I know I am a force to be reckoned with.
When I feel insecure, I know I am a force to be reckoned with.
If and when I feel guilt in any way, I know I am a force to be reckoned with.
When I need you the most, I know I am a force to be reckoned with.
When I am not myself, I know I am a force to be reckoned with.
When I feel alone, I know I am a force to be reckoned with.
When I face challenging days, I know I am a force to be reckoned with.
If and when I need to vent, I know I am a force to be reckoned with.

Won't Let Me Slip Under The Cracks.

When I look back at my fragile past, I know you won't let me slip under the cracks.
When I face my lifelong fears, I know you won't let me slip under the cracks.
When I try and break my lifelong issues that affect me, I know you won't let me slip under the cracks.
When I try and overcome the loneliness I feel, I know you won't let me slip under the cracks.
When I feel down, I know you won't let me slip under the cracks.
If and when I feel broken, I know you won't let me slip under the cracks.
When I feel like I'm in a dark place, I know you won't let me slip under the cracks.
When I feel like I'm struggling, I know you won't let me slip under the cracks.
When my inner cries take its toll on me, I know you won't let me slip under the cracks.
When I don't feel strong enough, I know you won't let me slip under the cracks.
When I don't feel brave enough, I know you won't let me slip under the cracks.
When I feel low, I know you won't let me slip under the cracks.
When I feel lost in any way, I know you won't let me slip under the cracks.
When I need a shoulder to cry on, I know you won't let me slip under the cracks.
If and when I don't feel good enough, I know you won't let me slip under the cracks.

When I feel like an outsider, I know you won't let me slip under the cracks..
If and when I feel rejected, I know you won't let me slip under the cracks.
When I feel like giving up, I know you won't let me slip under the cracks.
If and when I feel unwanted, I know you won't let me slip under the cracks.
If and when I feel worthless, I know you won't let me slip under the cracks.
When I feel like I am entering an unknown trap, I know you won't let me slip under the cracks.
When I feel like I'm in denial, I know you won't let me slip under the cracks.
If and when I have nowhere to turn, I know you won't let me slip under the cracks.
If and when I don't feel I have the courage to fight, I know you won't let me slip under the cracks.
When I feel insecure, I know you won't let me slip under the cracks
If and when I feel guilt in any way, know you won't let me slip under the cracks.
When I need you the most, know you won't let me slip under the cracks.
When I am not myself, I know you won't let me slip under the cracks.
When I feel alone, I know you won't let me slip under the cracks.
When I face challenging days, know you won't let me slip under the cracks.
If and when I need to vent, I know you won't let me slip under the cracks

Loyal To Me For Life

When I look back at my fragile past, I know you will always be loyal to me for life
When I face my lifelong fears, I know you will always be loyal to me for life
When I try and break my lifelong issues that affect me, I know you will always be loyal to me for life
When I try and overcome the loneliness I feel, I know you will always be loyal to me for life
When I feel down, I know you will always be loyal to me for life
If and when I feel broken, I know you will always be loyal to me for life
When I feel like I'm in a dark place, I know you will always be loyal to me for life
When I feel like I'm struggling, I know you will always be loyal to me for life
When my inner cries take its toll on me, I know you will always be loyal to me for life
When I don't feel strong enough, I know you will always be loyal to me for life
When I don't feel brave enough, I know you will always be loyal to me for life
When I feel low, I know you will always be loyal to me for life
When I feel lost in any way, I know you will always be loyal to me for life
When I need a shoulder to cry on, I know you will always be loyal to me for life

If and when I don't feel good enough, I know you will always be loyal to me for life

When I feel like an outsider, I know you will always be loyal to me for life
If and when I feel rejected, I know you will always be loyal to me for life
When I feel like giving up, I know you will always be loyal to me for life
If and when I feel unwanted, I know you will always be loyal to me for life
If and when I feel worthless, I know you will always be loyal to me for life
When I feel like I am entering an unknown trap, I know you will always be loyal to me for life
When I feel like I'm in denial, I know you will always be loyal to me for life
If and when I have nowhere to turn, I know you will always be loyal to me for life
If and when I don't feel I have the courage to fight, I know you will always be loyal to me for life
When I feel insecure, I know you will always be loyal to me for life
If and when I feel guilt in any way, I know you will always be loyal to me for life
When I need you the most, I know you will always be loyal to me for life
When I am not myself, I know you will always be loyal to me for life.
When I feel alone, I know you will always be loyal to me for life
When I face challenging days, I know you will always be loyal to me for life
If and when I need to vent, I know you will always be loyal to me for life

You Give Me A Helping Hand

When I look back at my fragile past, you know when I need a helping hand.
When I face my lifelong fears, you know when I need a helping hand.
When I try and break my lifelong issues that affect me, you know when I need a helping hand.
When I try and overcome the loneliness I feel, you know when I need a helping hand.
When I feel down, you know when I need a helping hand.
If and when I feel broken, you know when I need a helping hand.
When I feel like I'm in a dark place, you know when I need a helping hand.
When I feel like I'm struggling, you know when I need a helping hand.
When my inner cries take its toll on me, you know when I need a helping hand.
When I don't feel strong enough, you know when I need a helping hand.
When I don't feel brave enough, you know when I need a helping hand.
When I feel low, you know when I need a helping hand.
When I feel lost in any way, you know when I need a helping hand.

When I need a shoulder to cry on, you know when I need a helping hand.
If and when I don't feel good enough, you know when I need a helping hand.

When I feel like an outsider, you know when I need a helping hand.
If and when I feel rejected, you know when I need a helping hand.
When I feel like giving up, you know when I need a helping hand.
If and when I feel unwanted, you know when I need a helping hand.
If and when I feel worthless. you know when I need a helping hand.
When I feel like I am entering an unknown trap, you know when I need a helping hand.
When I feel like I'm in denial, you know when I need a helping hand.
If and when I have nowhere to turn, you know when I need a helping hand.
If and when I don't feel I have the courage to fight, you know when I need a helping hand.
When I feel insecure, you know when I need a helping hand.
If and when I feel guilt in any way, you know when I need a helping hand.
When I need you the most, you know when I need a helping hand.
When I am not myself, you know when I need a helping hand.
When I feel alone, you know when I need a helping hand.
When I face challenging days, you know when I need a helping hand.
If and when I need to vent, you know when I need a helping hand.

Believe In Myself

When I look back at my fragile past, you have shown me that I can believe in myself.
When I face my lifelong fears, you have shown me that I can believe in myself.
When I try and break my lifelong issues that affect me, you have shown me that I can believe in myself.
When I try and overcome the loneliness I feel, you have shown me that I can believe in myself.
When I feel down, you have shown me that I can believe in myself.
If and when I feel broken, you have shown me that I can believe in myself.
When I feel like I'm in a dark place, you have shown me that I can believe in myself.
When I feel like I'm struggling, you have shown me that I can believe in myself.
When my inner cries take its toll on me, you have shown me that I can believe in myself.
When I don't feel strong enough, you have shown me that I can believe in myself.
When I don't feel brave enough, you have shown me that I can believe in myself.

When I feel low, you have shown me that I can believe in myself.
When I feel lost in any way, you have shown me that I can believe in myself.
When I need a shoulder to cry on, you have shown me that I can believe in myself.
If and when I don't feel good enough, you have shown me that I can believe in myself.

When I feel like an outsider, you have shown me that I can believe in myself.
If and when I feel rejected, you have shown me that I can believe in myself.
When I feel like giving up, you have shown me that I can believe in myself.
If and when I feel unwanted, you have shown me that I can believe in myself.
If and when I feel worthless, you have shown me that I can believe in myself.
When I feel like I am entering an unknown trap, you know I will always stand up for what I believe.
When I feel like I'm in denial, you have shown me that I can believe in myself.
If and when I have nowhere to turn, you have shown me that I can believe in myself.
If and when I don't feel I have the courage to fight, you have shown me that I can believe in myself.
When I feel insecure, you have shown me that I can believe in myself.
If and when I feel guilt in any way, you have shown me that I can believe in myself.
When I need you the most, you have shown me that I can believe in myself.
When I am not myself, you have shown me that I can believe in myself.
When I feel alone, you have shown me that I can believe in myself.
When I face challenging days, you have shown me that I can believe in myself.
If and when I need to vent, you have shown me that I can believe in myself.

Surface From Below

When I look back at my fragile past, you know when it will surface from below.
When I face my lifelong fears, you know when it will surface from below.
When I try and break my lifelong issues that affect me, you know when it will surface from below.
When I try and overcome the loneliness I feel, you know when it surfaces from below.
When I feel down, you know when it will surface from below.
If and when I feel broken, you know when it will surface from below.
When I feel like I'm in a dark place, you know when it will surface from below.
When I feel like I'm struggling, you know when it will surface from below.

When my inner cries take its toll on me, you know when it will surface from below.
When I don't feel strong enough, you know when it surfaces from below.
When I don't feel brave enough, you know when it surfaces from below.
When I feel low, you know when it will surface from below.
When I feel lost in any way, you know when it surfaces from below.
When I need a shoulder to cry on, you know when it surfaces from below.
If and when I don't feel good enough, you know when it surfaces from below.

When I feel like an outsider, you know when it surfaces from below.
If and when I feel rejected, you know when it surfaces from below.
When I feel like giving up, you know when it surfaces from below.
If and when I feel unwanted, you know when it surfaces from below.
If and when I feel worthless, you know when it will surface from below.
When I feel like I am entering an unknown trap, you know when it will surface from below.
When I feel like I'm in denial, you know when it will surface from below.
If and when I have nowhere to turn, you know when it will surface from below.
If and when I don't feel I have the courage to fight, you know when it will surface from below.
When I feel insecure, you know when it will surface from below.
If and when I feel guilt in any way, you know when it will surface from below.
When I need you the most, you know when It will surface from below.
When I am not myself, you know when it will surface from below.
When I feel alone, you know when it will surface from below.
When I face challenging days, you know when it will surface from below.
If and when I need to vent, you know when it will surface from below.

Jump To My Defence

When I look back at my fragile past, you jump to my defence
When I face my lifelong fears, you jump to my defence
When I try and break my lifelong issues that affect me, you jump to my defence
When I try and overcome the loneliness I feel, you jump to my defence
When I feel down, you jump to my defence
If and when I feel broken, you jump to my defence
When I feel like I'm in a dark place, you jump to my defence
When I feel like I'm struggling, you jump to my defence
When my inner cries take its toll on me, you jump to my defence
When I don't feel strong enough, you jump to my defence
When I don't feel brave enough, you jump to my defence

When I feel low, you jump to my defence
When I feel lost in any way, you jump to my defence
When I need a shoulder to cry on, you jump to my defence
If and when I don't feel good enough, you jump to my defence

When I feel like an outsider, you jump to my defence
If and when I feel rejected, you jump to my defence
When I feel like giving up, you jump to my defence
If and when I feel unwanted, you jump to my defence
If and when I feel worthless, you jump to my defence.
When I feel like I am entering an unknown trap, you jump to my defence
When I feel like I'm in denial, you jump to my defence
If and when I have nowhere to turn, you jump to my defence
If and when I don't feel I have the courage to fight, you jump to my defence
When I feel insecure, you jump to my defence
If and when I feel guilt in any way, you jump to my defence
When I need you the most, you jump to my defence
When I am not myself, you jump to my defence
When I feel alone, you jump to my defence
When I face challenging days, you jump to my defence
If and when I need to vent, you jump to my defence

Patch Me Up

When I look back at my fragile past, you patch me up.
When I face my lifelong fears, you patch me up.
When I try and break my lifelong issues that affect me, you patch me up.
When I try and overcome the loneliness I feel, you patch me up.
When I feel down, you patch me up.
If and when I feel broken, you patch me up.
When I feel like I'm in a dark place, you patch me up.
When I feel like I'm struggling, you patch me up.
When my inner cries take its toll on me, you patch me up.
When I don't feel strong enough, you patch me up.
When I don't feel brave enough, you patch me up.
When I feel low, you patch me up.
When I feel lost in any way, you patch me up.
When I need a shoulder to cry on, you patch me up.
If and when I don't feel good enough, you patch me up.

When I feel like an outsider, you patch me up.

If and when I feel rejected, you patch me up.
When I feel like giving up, you patch me up.
If and when I feel unwanted, you patch me up.
If and when I feel worthless, you patch me up.
When I feel like I am entering an unknown trap, you patch me up.
When I feel like I'm in denial, you patch me up.
If and when I have nowhere to turn, you patch me up.
If and when I don't feel I have the courage to fight, you patch me up.
When I feel insecure, you patch me up.
If and when I feel guilt in any way, you patch me up.
When I need you the most, you patch me up.
When I am not myself, you patch me up.
When I feel alone, you patch me up.
When I face challenging days, you patch me up.
If and when I need to vent, you patch me up.

Never Let Anything Go Wrong When I'm Around You.

When I look back at my fragile past, you never let anything go wrong when I'm around you.
When I face my lifelong fears, you never let anything go wrong when I'm around you.
When I try and break my lifelong issues that affect me, you never let anything go wrong when I'm around you.
When I try and overcome the loneliness I feel, you never let anything go wrong when I'm around you.
When I feel down, you never let anything go wrong when I'm around you.
If and when I feel broken, you never let anything go wrong when I'm around you.
When I feel like I'm in a dark place, you never let anything go wrong when I'm around you.
When I feel like I'm struggling, you never let anything go wrong when I'm around you.
When my inner cries take its toll on me, you never let anything go wrong when I'm around you.
When I don't feel strong enough, you never let anything go wrong when I'm around you.
When I don't feel brave enough, you never let anything go wrong when I'm around you.
When I feel low, you never let anything go wrong when I'm around you.

When I feel lost in any way, you never let anything go wrong when I'm around you.
When I need a shoulder to cry on, you never let anything go wrong when I'm around you.
If and when I don't feel good enough, you never let anything go wrong when I'm around you.

When I feel like an outsider, you never let anything go wrong when I'm around you.
If and when I feel rejected, you never let anything go wrong when I'm around you.
When I feel like giving up, you never let anything go wrong when I'm around you.
If and when I feel unwanted, you never let anything go wrong when I'm around you.
If and when I feel worthless, you never let anything go wrong when I'm around you.
When I feel like I am entering an unknown trap, you never let anything go wrong when I'm around you.
When I feel like I'm in denial, you never let anything go wrong when I'm around you.
If and when I have nowhere to turn, you never let anything go wrong when I'm around you.
If and when I don't feel I have the courage to fight, you never let anything go wrong when I'm around you.
when I feel insecure, you never let anything go wrong when I'm around you.
If and when I feel guilt in any way, you never let anything go wrong when I'm around you.
When I need you the most, you never let anything go wrong when I'm around you.
When I am not myself, you never let anything go wrong when I'm around you.
When I feel alone, you never let anything go wrong when I'm around you.
When I face challenging days, you never let anything go wrong when I'm around you.
If and when I need to vent, you never let anything go wrong when I'm around you.

Always Watch Over Me

When I look back at my fragile past, you always watch over me
When I face my lifelong fears, you always watch over me
When I try and break my lifelong issues that affect me, you always watch over me
When I try and overcome the loneliness I feel, you always watch over me
When I feel down, you always watch over me
If and when I feel broken, you always watch over me
When I feel like I'm in a dark place, you always watch over me
When I feel like I'm struggling, you always watch over me
When my inner cries take its toll on me, you always watch over me
When I don't feel strong enough, you always watch over me
When I don't feel brave enough, you always watch over me
When I feel low, you always watch over me
When I feel lost in any way, you always watch over me.
When I need a shoulder to cry on, you always watch over me
If and when I don't feel good enough, you always watch over me

When I feel like an outsider, you always watch over me
If and when I feel rejected, you always watch over me
When I feel like giving up, you always watch over me
If and when I feel unwanted, you always watch over me
If and when I feel worthless, you always watch over me
When I feel like I am entering an unknown trap, you always watch over me
When I feel like I'm in denial, you always watch over me
If and when I have nowhere to turn, you always watch over me
If and when I don't feel I have the courage to fight, you always watch over me
When I feel insecure, you always watch over me
If and when I feel guilt in any way, you always watch over me
When I need you the most, you always watch over me
When I am not myself, you always watch over me
When I feel alone, you always watch over me
When I face challenging days, you always watch over me
If and when I need to vent, you always watch over me

Always Make Sure I'm Ok

When I look back at my fragile past, you always make sure I'm ok.
When I face my lifelong fears, you always make sure I'm ok.
When I try and break my lifelong issues that affect me, you always make sure I'm ok.
When I try and overcome the loneliness I feel, you always make sure I'm ok.
When I feel down, you always make sure I'm ok.
If and when I feel broken, you always make sure I'm ok.
When I feel like I'm in a dark place, you always make sure I'm ok.
When I feel like I'm struggling, you always make sure I'm ok.
When my inner cries take its toll on me, you always make sure I'm ok.
When I don't feel strong enough, you always make sure I'm ok.
When I don't feel brave enough, you always make sure I'm ok.
When I feel low, you always make sure I'm ok.
When I feel lost in any way, you always make sure I'm ok.
When I need a shoulder to cry on, you always make sure I'm ok.
If and when I don't feel good enough, you always make sure I'm ok.

When I feel like an outsider, you always make sure I'm ok.
If and when I feel rejected, you always make sure I'm ok.
When I feel like giving up, you always make sure I'm ok.
If and when I feel unwanted, you always make sure I'm ok.
If and when I feel worthless, you always make sure I'm ok.
When I feel like I am entering an unknown trap, you always make sure I'm ok.
When I feel like I'm in denial, you always make sure I'm ok.
If and when I have nowhere to turn, you always make sure I'm ok.
If and when I don't feel I have the courage to fight, you always make sure I'm ok.
When I feel insecure, you always make sure I'm ok.
If and when I feel guilt in any way, you always make sure I'm ok.
When I need you the most, you always make sure I'm ok.
When I am not myself, you always make sure I'm ok.
When I feel alone, you always make sure I'm ok.
When I face challenging days, you always make sure I'm ok.
If and when I need to vent, you always make sure I'm ok.

Confide In Me

You can confide in me about ur fragile past.
You can confide in me about your lifelong fears that terrorize me to no end.
You can confide in me about your lifelong issues that affect you.
You can confide in me about the hateful things you have to deal with.
You can confide in me when you don't feel strong enough.
You can confide in me when you don't feel brave enough.
You can confide in me because you can trust me totally.
You can confide in me when you feel low.
You can confide in me when you feel broken.
You can confide in me when you don't feel like yourself.
You can confide in me about things you can't tell anyone else.
You can confide in me when you feel unwanted.
You can confide in me when you feel scared.
You can confide in me when you feel let down by others.
You can confide in me when you feel you can't keep your tears from rolling down your face.
You can confide in me when you don't feel good enough.
You can confide in me because you feel I'm the only one you feel able to talk to.
You can confide in me when you feel damaged.
You can confide in me because you know you are never alone.
I confide in you because I know I can be me when I'm around you
You can confide in me when you need me the most.
You can confide in me during your dark times
You can confide in me during your hour of need.
You can confide in me during your darkest points in life.
You can confide in me when there is no other way.
You can confide in me because you see what others don't
You can confide in me because we are lifelong friends and inseparable for life.

Knock Me Down

When I look back at my fragile past, I know you won't let anyone knock me down.
When I face my lifelong fears, I know you won't let anyone knock me down.
When I try and break my lifelong issues that affect me, I know you won't let anyone knock me down.
When I try and overcome the loneliness I feel, I know you won't let anyone knock me down.
When I feel down, I know you won't let anyone knock me down.

If and when I feel broken, I know you won't let anyone knock me down.
When I feel like I'm in a dark place, I know you won't let anyone knock me down.
When I feel like I'm struggling, I know you won't let anyone knock me down.
When my inner cries take its toll on me, I know you won't let anyone knock me down.
When I don't feel strong enough, I know you won't let anyone knock me down.
When I don't feel brave enough, I know you won't let anyone knock me down.
When I feel low, I know you won't let anyone knock me down.
When I feel lost in any way, I know you won't let anyone knock me down.
When I need a shoulder to cry on, I know you won't let anyone knock me down.
If and when I don't feel good enough, I know you won't let anyone knock me down.
When I feel like an outsider, I know you won't let anyone knock me down.
If and when I feel rejected, I know you won't let anyone knock me down.
When I feel like giving up, I know you won't let anyone knock me down.
If and when I feel unwanted, I know you won't let anyone knock me down.
If and when I feel worthless, I know you won't let anyone knock me down.
When I feel like I am entering an unknown trap, I know you won't let anyone knock me down.
When I feel like I'm in denial, I know you won't let anyone knock me down.
If and when I have nowhere to turn, I know you won't let anyone knock me down.
If and when I don't feel I have the courage to fight, I know you won't let anyone knock me down.
When I feel insecure, I know you won't let anyone knock me down.
If and when I feel guilt in any way, I know you won't let anyone knock me down.
When I need you the most, I know you won't let anyone knock me down.
When I am not myself, I know you won't let anyone knock me down.
When I feel alone, I know you won't let anyone knock me down.
When I face challenging days, I know you won't let anyone knock me down.
If and when I need to vent, I know you won't let anyone knock me down.

Put Me Down

When I look back at my fragile past, I know you won't let anyone put me down.
When I face my lifelong fears, I know you won't let anyone put me down.
When I try and break my lifelong issues that affect me, I know you won't let anyone put me down.
When I try and overcome the loneliness I feel, I know you won't let anyone put me down.
When I feel down, I know you won't let anyone put me down.
If and when I feel broken, I know you won't let anyone put me down.
When I feel like I'm in a dark place, I know you won't let anyone put me down.
When I feel like I'm struggling, I know you won't let anyone put me down.
When my inner cries take its toll on me, I know you won't let anyone put me down.
When I don't feel strong enough, I know you won't let anyone put me down.
When I don't feel brave enough, I know you won't let anyone put me down.
When I feel low, I know you won't let anyone put me down.
When I feel lost in any way, I know you won't let anyone put me down..
When I need a shoulder to cry on, I know you won't let anyone put me down.
If and when I don't feel good enough, I know you won't let anyone put me down.

When I feel like an outsider, I know you won't let anyone put me down.
If and when I feel rejected, I know you won't let anyone put me down.
When I feel like giving up, I know you won't let anyone put me down.
If and when I feel unwanted, I know you won't let anyone put me down.
If and when I feel worthless, I know you won't let anyone put me down.
When I feel like I am entering an unknown trap, I know you won't let anyone put me down.
When I feel like I'm in denial, I know you won't let anyone put me down.
If and when I have nowhere to turn, I know you won't let anyone put me down.
If and when I don't feel I have the courage to fight, I know you won't let anyone put me down.
When I feel insecure, I know you won't let anyone put me down.
If and when I feel guilt in any way, I know you won't let anyone put me down.
When I need you the most, I know you won't let anyone put me down.
When I am not myself, I know you won't let anyone put me down.
When I feel alone, I know you won't let anyone put me down.
When I face challenging days, I know you won't let anyone put me down.
If and when I need to vent, I know you won't let anyone put me down.

Rashma Mehta

Make Me Stronger Than Ever Before

When I look back at my fragile past, you make me stronger than ever before.
When I face my lifelong fears, you make me stronger than ever before.
When I try and break my lifelong issues that affect me, you make me stronger than ever before.
When I try and overcome the loneliness I feel, you make me stronger than ever before.
When I feel down, you make me stronger than ever before.
If and when I feel broken, you make me stronger than ever before.
When I feel like I'm in a dark place, you make me stronger than ever before.
When I feel like I'm struggling, you make me stronger than ever before.
When my inner cries take its toll on me, you make me stronger than ever before.
When I don't feel strong enough, you make me stronger than ever before.
When I don't feel brave enough, you make me stronger than ever before.
When I feel low, you make me stronger than ever before.
When I feel lost in any way, you make me stronger than ever before.
When I need a shoulder to cry on, you make me stronger than ever before.
If and when I don't feel good enough, you make me stronger than ever before.

When I feel like an outsider, you make me stronger than ever before..
If and when I feel rejected, you make me stronger than ever before.
When I feel like giving up, you make me stronger than ever before.
If and when I feel unwanted, you make me stronger than ever before.
If and when I feel worthless, you make me stronger than ever before.
When I feel like I am entering an unknown trap, you make me stronger than ever before.
When I feel like I'm in denial, you make me stronger than ever before.
If and when I have nowhere to turn, you make me stronger than ever before.
If and when I don't feel I have the courage to fight, you make me stronger than ever before.
When I feel insecure, you make me stronger than ever before.
If and when I feel guilt in any way, you make me stronger than ever before.
When I need you the most, you make me stronger than ever before.
When I am not myself, you make me stronger than ever before.
When I feel alone, you make me stronger than ever before.
When I face challenging days, you make me stronger than ever before.
If and when I need to vent, you make me stronger than ever before.

Won't Shatter Into A Million Tiny Pieces

When I look back at my fragile past, I know I won't shatter into a million tiny pieces
When I face my lifelong fears, I know I won't shatter into a million tiny pieces
When I try and break my lifelong issues that affect me, I know I won't shatter into a million tiny pieces
When I try and overcome the loneliness I feel, I know I won't shatter into a million tiny pieces
When I feel down, I know I won't shatter into a million tiny pieces
If and when I feel broken, I know I won't shatter into a million tiny pieces

When I feel like I'm in a dark place, I know I won't shatter into a million tiny pieces
When I feel like I'm struggling, I know I won't shatter into a million tiny pieces
When my inner cries take its toll on me, I know I won't shatter into a million tiny pieces
When I don't feel strong enough, I know I won't shatter into a million tiny pieces
When I don't feel brave enough, I know I won't shatter into a million tiny pieces
When I feel low, I know I won't shatter into a million tiny pieces
When I feel lost in any way, I know I won't shatter into a million tiny pieces
When I need a shoulder to cry on, I know I won't shatter into a million tiny pieces
If and when I don't feel good enough, I know I won't shatter into a million tiny pieces

When I feel like an outsider, I know I won't shatter into a million tiny pieces
If and when I feel rejected, I know I won't shatter into a million tiny pieces
When I feel like giving up, I know I won't shatter into a million tiny pieces
If and when I feel unwanted, I know I won't shatter into a million tiny pieces
If and when I feel worthless, I know I won't shatter into a million tiny pieces

When I feel like I am entering an unknown trap, I know I won't shatter into a million tiny pieces
When I feel like I'm in denial, I know I won't shatter into a million tiny pieces
If and when I have nowhere to turn, I know I won't shatter into a million tiny pieces
If and when I don't feel I have the courage to fight, I know I won't shatter into a million tiny pieces
When I feel insecure, I know I won't shatter into a million tiny pieces

If and when I feel guilt in any way, I know I won't shatter into a million tiny pieces
When I need you the most, you know when I start to question myself.
When I am not myself, I know I won't shatter into a million tiny pieces
When I feel alone, I know I won't shatter into a million tiny pieces
When I face challenging days, I know I won't shatter into a million tiny pieces
If and when I need to vent, I know I won't shatter into a million tiny pieces

Drag Me Down

When I look back at my fragile past, I know you won't let anyone drag me down.
When I face my lifelong fears, I know you won't let anyone drag me down.
When I try and break my lifelong issues that affect me, I know you won't let anyone drag me down.
When I try and overcome the loneliness I feel, I know you won't let anyone drag me down.
When I feel down, I know you won't let anyone drag me down.
If and when I feel broken, I know you won't let anyone drag me down.
When I feel like I'm in a dark place, I know you won't let anyone drag me down.
When I feel like I'm struggling, I know you won't let anyone drag me down.
When my inner cries take its toll on me, I know you won't let anyone drag me down.
When I don't feel strong enough, I know you won't let anyone drag me down.
When I don't feel brave enough, I know you won't let anyone drag me down.
When I feel low, I know you won't let anyone drag me down.
When I feel lost in any way, I know you won't let anyone drag me down.
When I need a shoulder to cry on, I know you won't let anyone drag me down.
If and when I don't feel good enough, I know you won't let anyone drag me down.

When I feel like an outsider, I know you won't let anyone drag me down.
If and when I feel rejected, I know you won't let anyone drag me down.
When I feel like giving up, I know you won't let anyone drag me down.
If and when I feel unwanted, I know you won't let anyone drag me down.
If and when I feel worthless, I know you won't let anyone drag me down.
When I feel like I am entering an unknown trap, I know you won't let anyone drag me down.
When I feel like I'm in denial, I know you won't let anyone drag me down.
If and when I have nowhere to turn, I know you won't let anyone drag me down.

If and when I don't feel I have the courage to fight, I know you won't let anyone drag me down.
When I feel insecure, I know you won't let anyone drag me down.
If and when I feel guilt in any way, I know you won't let anyone drag me down.
When I need you the most, I know you won't let anyone drag me down.
When I am not myself, I know you won't let anyone drag me down.
When I feel alone, I know you won't let anyone drag me down.
When I face challenging days, I know you won't let anyone drag me down.
If and when I need to vent, I know you won't let anyone drag me down.

Walk All Over Me

When I look back at my fragile past, I know you won't let anyone walk all over me.
When I face my lifelong fears, I know you won't let anyone walk all over me.
When I try and break my lifelong issues that affect me, I know you won't let anyone walk all over me
When I try and overcome the loneliness I feel, I know you won't let anyone walk all over me.
When I feel down, I know you won't let anyone walk all over me.
If and when I feel broken, I know you won't let anyone walk all over me.
When I feel like I'm in a dark place, I know you won't let anyone walk all over me.
When I feel like I'm struggling, I know you won't let anyone walk all over me.
When my inner cries take its toll on me, I know you won't let anyone walk all over me.
When I don't feel strong enough, I know you won't let anyone walk all over me.
When I don't feel brave enough, I know you won't let anyone walk all over me.
When I feel low, I know you won't let anyone walk all over me.
When I feel lost in any way, I know you won't let anyone walk all over me.
When I need a shoulder to cry on, I know you won't let anyone walk all over me.
If and when I don't feel good enough, I know you won't let anyone walk all over me.

When I feel like an outsider, I know you won't let anyone walk all over me.
If and when I feel rejected, I know you won't let anyone walk all over me.
When I feel like giving up, I know you won't let anyone walk all over me..
If and when I feel unwanted, I know you won't let anyone walk all over me.
If and when I feel worthless, I know you won't let anyone walk all over me.
When I feel like I am entering an unknown trap, I know you won't let anyone walk all over me.

When I feel like I'm in denial, I know you won't let anyone walk all over me.
If and when I have nowhere to turn, I know you won't let anyone walk all over me.
If and when I don't feel I have the courage to fight, I know you won't let anyone walk all over me.
when I feel insecure, I know you won't let anyone walk all over me.
If and when I feel guilt in any way, I know you won't let anyone drag me down.
When I need you the most, I know you won't let anyone walk all over me.
When I am not myself, I know you won't let anyone walk all over me.
When I feel alone, I know you won't let anyone walk all over me.
When I face challenging days, I know you won't let anyone walk all over me.
If and when I need to vent, I know you won't let anyone walk all over me.

Shed A Tear On You When I Cry

When I look back at my fragile past, I know I can shed a tear on you when I cry.
When I face my lifelong fears, I know I can shed a tear on you when I cry.
When I try and break my lifelong issues that affect me, I know I can shed a tear on you when I cry.
When I try and overcome the loneliness I feel, I know I can shed a tear on you when I cry.
When I feel down, I know I can shed a tear on you when I cry.
If and when I feel broken, I know I can shed a tear on you when I cry.
When I feel like I'm in a dark place, I know you won't let anyone walk all over me.
When I feel like I'm struggling, I know I can shed a tear on you when I cry.
When my inner cries take its toll on me, I know I can shed a tear on you when I cry.
When I don't feel strong enough, I know I can shed a tear on you when I cry.
When I don't feel brave enough, I know I can shed a tear on you when I cry.
When I feel low, I know I can shed a tear on you when I cry.
When I feel lost in any way, I know I can shed a tear on you when I cry.
When I need a shoulder to cry on, I know I can shed a tear on you when I cry.
If and when I don't feel good enough, I know I can shed a tear on you when I cry.

When I feel like an outsider, I know I can shed a tear on you when I cry.
If and when I feel rejected, I know I can shed a tear on you when I cry.
When I feel like giving up, I know I can shed a tear on you when I cry.
If and when I feel unwanted, I know I can shed a tear on you when I cry.
If and when I feel worthless, I know I can shed a tear on you when I cry.

When I feel like I am entering an unknown trap, I know I can shed a tear on you when I cry.
When I feel like I'm in denial, I know I can shed a tear on you when I cry.
If and when I have nowhere to turn, I know I can shed a tear on you when I cry.
If and when I don't feel I have the courage to fight, I know I can shed a tear on you when I cry.
When I feel insecure, I know I can shed a tear on you when I cry.
If and when I feel guilt in any way, I know I can shed a tear on you when I cry.
When I need you the most, I know I can shed a tear on you when I cry.
When I am not myself, I know I can shed a tear on you when I cry.
When I feel alone, I know I can shed a tear on you when I cry.
When I face challenging days, I know I can shed a tear on you when I cry.
If and when I need to vent, I know I can shed a tear on you when I cry.

Escape My Reality

When I look back at my fragile past, you know when I need to escape my reality.
When I face my lifelong fears, you know when I need to escape my reality.
When I try and break my lifelong issues that affect me, you know when I need to escape my reality.
When I try and overcome the loneliness I feel, you know when I need to escape my reality.
When I feel down, you know when I need to escape my reality.
If and when I feel broken, you know when I need to escape my reality.
When I feel like I'm in a dark place, you know when I need to escape my reality.
When I feel like I'm struggling, you know when I need to escape my reality.
When my inner cries take its toll on me, you know when I need to escape my reality.
When I don't feel strong enough, you know when I need to escape my reality.
When I don't feel brave enough, you know when I need to escape my reality.
When I feel low, you know when I need to escape my reality.
When I feel lost in any way, you know when I need to escape my reality.
When I need a shoulder to cry on, you know when I need to escape my reality.
If and when I don't feel good enough, you know when I need to escape my reality.

When I feel like an outsider, you know when I need to escape my reality.
If and when I feel rejected, you know when I need to escape my reality..
When I feel like giving up, you know when I need to escape my reality.
If and when I feel unwanted, you know when I need to escape my reality.
If and when I feel worthless, you know when I need to escape my reality.

When I feel like I am entering an unknown trap, you know when I need to escape my reality.
When I feel like I'm in denial, you know when I need to escape my reality.
If and when I have nowhere to turn, you know when I need to escape my reality.
If and when I don't feel I have the courage to fight, you know when I need to escape my reality.
When I feel insecure, you know when I need to escape my reality.
If and when I feel guilt in any way, you know when I need to escape my reality.
When I need you the most, you know when I need to escape my reality.
When I am not myself, you know when I need to escape my reality.
When I feel alone, you know when I need to escape my reality.
When I face challenging days, you know when I need to escape my reality.
If and when I need to vent, you know when I need to escape my reality.

Find A Way To Make Me Smile

When I look back at my fragile past, you always find a way to make me smile.
When I face my lifelong fears, you always find a way to make me smile.
When I try and break my lifelong issues that affect me, you always find a way to make me smile.
When I try and overcome the loneliness I feel, you always find a way to make me smile.
When I feel down, you always find a way to make me smile.
If and when I feel broken, you always find a way to make me smile.
When I feel like I'm in a dark place, you always find a way to make me smile.
When I feel like I'm struggling, you always find a way to make me smile.
When my inner cries take its toll on me, you always find a way to make me smile.
When I don't feel strong enough, you always find a way to make me smile.
When I don't feel brave enough, you always find a way to make me smile.
When I feel low, you always find a way to make me smile.
When I feel lost in any way, you always find a way to make me smile.
When I need a shoulder to cry on, you always find a way to make me smile.
If and when I don't feel good enough, you always find a way to make me smile.

When I feel like an outsider, you always find a way to make me smile.
If and when I feel rejected, you always find a way to make me smile..
When I feel like giving up, you always find a way to make me smile.
If and when I feel unwanted, you always find a way to make me smile.
If and when I feel worthless, you always find a way to make me smile.

When I feel like I am entering an unknown trap, you always find a way to make me smile.
When I feel like I'm in denial, you always find a way to make me smile.
If and when I have nowhere to turn, you always find a way to make me smile.
If and when I don't feel I have the courage to fight, you always find a way to make me smile.
When I feel insecure, you always find a way to make me smile.
If and when I feel guilt in any way, you always find a way to make me smile.
When I need you the most, you always find a way to make me smile.
When I am not myself, you always find a way to make me smile.
When I feel alone, you always find a way to make me smile.
When I face challenging days, you always find a way to make me smile.
If and when I need to vent, you always find a way to make me smile.

Keep You Down

When you look back at your fragile past, you know I won't let anything keep you down.
When you face your lifelong fears, you know I won't let anything keep you down.
When you try and break your lifelong issues that affect you, you know I won't let anything keep you down.
When you try and overcome the loneliness you feel, you know I won't let anything keep you down.
When you feel down, you know I won't let anything keep you down.
If and when you feel broken, you know I won't let anything keep you down.
When you feel like you're in a dark place, you know I won't let anything keep you down.
When you feel like you're struggling, you know I won't let anything keep you down.
When your inner cries take its toll on you, you know I won't let anything keep you down.
When you don't feel strong enough, you know I won't let anything keep you down.
When you don't feel brave enough, you know I won't let anything keep you down.
When you feel low, you know I won't let anything keep you down.
When you feel lost in any way, you know I won't let anything keep you down.
When you need a shoulder to cry on, you know I won't let anything keep you down.

If and when you don't feel good enough, you know I won't let anything keep you down.

When you feel like an outsider, you know I won't let anything keep you down.
If and when you feel rejected, you know I won't let anything keep you down.
When you feel like giving up, you know I won't let anything keep you down.
If and when you feel unwanted, you know I won't let anything keep you down.
If and when you feel worthless, you know I won't let anything keep you down.
When you feel like you're entering an unknown trap, you know I won't let anything keep you down.
When you feel like I'm in denial, you know I won't let anything keep you down.
If and when you have nowhere to turn, you know I won't let anything keep you down.
If and when you don't feel you have the courage to fight, you know I won't let anything keep you down.
When you feel insecure, you know I won't let anything keep you down.
If and when you feel guilt in any way, you know I won't let anything keep you down.
When you need me the most, you know I won't let anything keep you down.
When you are not yourself, you know I won't let anything keep you down.
When you feel alone, you know I won't let anything keep you down.
When you face challenging days, you know I won't let anything keep you down.
If and when you need to vent. you know I won't let anything keep you down.

Precious To Me

When you look back at your fragile past, you will always be very precious to me.
When you face your lifelong fears, you will always be very precious to me.
When you try and break your lifelong issues that affect you, you will always be very precious to me.
When you try and overcome the loneliness you feel, you will always be very precious to me.
When you feel down, you will always be very precious to me.
If and when you feel broken, you will always be very precious to me.
When you feel like you're in a dark place, you will always be very precious to me.
When you feel like you're struggling, you will always be very precious to me.
When your inner cries take its toll on you, you will always be very precious to me.
When you don't feel strong enough, you will always be very precious to me.
When you don't feel brave enough, you will always be very precious to me.

When you feel low, you will always be very precious to me.
When you feel lost in any way, you will always be very precious to me.
When you need a shoulder to cry on, you will always be very precious to me.
If and when you don't feel good enough, you will always be very precious to me.

When you feel like an outsider, you will always be very precious to me.
If and when you feel rejected, you will always be very precious to me..
When you feel like giving up, you will always be very precious to me.
If and when you feel unwanted, you will always be very precious to me.
If and when you feel worthless, you will always be very precious to me.
When you feel like you're entering an unknown trap, you will always be very precious to me.
When you feel like I'm in denial, you will always be very precious to me.
If and when you have nowhere to turn, you will always be very precious to me.
If and when you don't feel you have the courage to fight, you will always be very precious to me.
When you feel insecure, you will always be very precious to me.
If and when you feel guilt in any way, you will always be very precious to me.
When you need me the most, you will always be very precious to me.
When you are not yourself, you will always be very precious to me.
When you feel alone, you will always be very precious to me.
When you face challenging days, you will always be very precious to me.
If and when you need to vent, you will always be very precious to me.

Precious To You.

When I look back at my fragile past, I know I will always be very precious to you.
When I face my lifelong fears, I know I will always be very precious to you.
When I try and break my lifelong issues that affect me, I know I will always be very precious to you.
When I try and overcome the loneliness I feel, I know I will always be very precious to you.
When I feel down, I know I will always be very precious to you.
If and when I feel broken, I know I will always be very precious to you.
When I feel like I'm in a dark place, I know I will always be very precious to you.
When I feel like I'm struggling, I know I will always be very precious to you.
When my inner cries take its toll on me, I know I will always be very precious to you.
When I don't feel strong enough, I know I will always be very precious to you.

When I don't feel brave enough, I know I will always be very precious to you.
When I feel low, I know I will always be very precious to you.
When I feel lost in any way, I know I will always be very precious to you.
When I need a shoulder to cry on, I know I will always be very precious to you.
If and when I don't feel good enough, I know I will always be very precious to you.

When I feel like an outsider, I know I will always be very precious to you.
If and when I feel rejected, I know I will always be very precious to you.
When I feel like giving up, I know I will always be very precious to you.
If and when I feel unwanted, I know I will always be very precious to you.
If and when I feel worthless, I know I will always be very precious to you.
When I feel like I am entering an unknown trap, I know I will always be very precious to you.
When I feel like I'm in denial, I know I will always be very precious to you.
If and when I have nowhere to turn, I know I will always be very precious to you.
If and when I don't feel I have the courage to fight, I know I will always be very precious to you.
When I feel insecure, I know I will always be very precious to you.
If and when I feel guilt in any way, I know I will always be very precious to you.
When I need you the most, I know I will always be very precious to you.
When I am not myself, I know I will always be very precious to you.
When I feel alone, I know I will always be very precious to you.
When I face challenging days, I know I will always be very precious to you.
If and when I need to vent, I know I will always be very precious to you.

Won't Let You Go Without A Fight

When you look back at your fragile past, I know I won't let you go without a fight.
When you face your lifelong fears, I know I won't let you go without a fight.
When you try and break your lifelong issues that affect you, I know I won't let you go without a fight.
When you try and overcome the loneliness you feel, I know I won't let you go without a fight.
When you feel down, I know I won't let you go without a fight.
If and when you feel broken, I know I won't let you go without a fight.
When you feel like you're in a dark place, I know I won't let you go without a fight.
When you feel like you're struggling, I know I won't let you go without a fight.

When your inner cries take its toll on you, I know I won't let you go without a fight.
When you don't feel strong enough, I know I won't let you go without a fight.
When you don't feel brave enough, I know I won't let you go without a fight.
When you feel low, I know I won't let you go without a fight.
When you feel lost in any way, I know I won't let you go without a fight.
When you need a shoulder to cry on, I know I won't let you go without a fight.
If and when you don't feel good enough, I know I won't let you go without a fight.

When you feel like an outsider, I know I won't let you go without a fight.
If and when you feel rejected, I know I won't let you go without a fight.
When you feel like giving up, I know I won't let you go without a fight.
If and when you feel unwanted, I know I won't let you go without a fight.
If and when you feel worthless, I know I won't let you go without a fight.
When you feel like you're entering an unknown trap, I know I won't let you go without a fight.
When you feel like I'm in denial, I know I won't let you go without a fight.
If and when you have nowhere to turn, I know I won't let you go without a fight.
If and when you don't feel you have the courage to fight, I know I won't let you go without a fight.
When you feel insecure, I know I won't let you go without a fight.
If and when you feel guilt in any way, I know I won't let you go without a fight.
When you need me the most, I know I won't let you go without a fight.
When you are not yourself, I know I won't let you go without a fight.
When you feel alone, I know I won't let you go without a fight.
When you face challenging days, I know I won't let you go without a fight.
If and when you need to vent, I know I won't let you go without a fight.

Whatever Life Throws My Way

When I look back at my fragile past, whatever life throws my way I know we will get through it together.
When I face my lifelong fears, whatever life throws my way I know we will get through it together.
When I try and break my lifelong issues that affect me, whatever life throws my way I know we will get through it together.
When I try and overcome the loneliness I feel, whatever life throws my way I know we will get through it together.
When I feel down, whatever life throws my way I know we will get through it together.

If and when I feel broken, whatever life throws my way I know we will get through it together.
When I feel like I'm in a dark place, whatever life throws my way I know we will get through it together.
When I feel like I'm struggling, whatever life throws my way I know we will get through it together.
When my inner cries take its toll on me, whatever life throws my way I know we will get through it together.
When I don't feel strong enough, whatever life throws my way I know we will get through it together.
When I don't feel brave enough, whatever life throws my way I know we will get through it together.
When I feel low, whatever life throws my way I know we will get through it together.
When I feel lost in any way, whatever life throws my way I know we will get through it together.
When I need a shoulder to cry on, whatever life throws my way I know we will get through it together.
If and when I don't feel good enough, whatever life throws my way I know we will get through it together.

When I feel like an outsider, whatever life throws my way I know we will get through it together.
If and when I feel rejected, whatever life throws my way I know we will get through it together.
When I feel like giving up, whatever life throws my way I know we will get through it together.
If and when I feel unwanted, whatever life throws my way I know we will get through it together.
If and when I feel worthless, whatever life throws my way I know we will get through it together.
When I feel like I am entering an unknown trap, whatever life throws my way I know we will get through it together.
When I feel like I'm in denial, whatever life throws my way I know we will get through it together.
If and when I have nowhere to turn, whatever life throws my way I know we will get through it together.
If and when I don't feel I have the courage to fight, whatever life throws my way I know we will get through it together.
When I feel insecure, whatever life throws my way I know we will get through it together.

If and when I feel guilt in any way, whatever life throws my way I know we will get through it together.
When I need you the most, whatever life throws my way I know we will get through it together.
When I am not myself, whatever life throws my way I know we will get through it together.
When I feel alone, whatever life throws my way I know we will get through it together.
When I face challenging days, whatever life throws my way I know we will get through it together.
If and when I need to vent, whatever life throws my way I know we will get through it together.

Whatever Life Throws Ur Way

When you look back at your fragile past, whatever life throws ur way I know we will get through it together.
When you face your lifelong fears, whatever life throws ur way I know we will get through it together.
When you try and break your lifelong issues that affect you, whatever life throws ur way I know we will get through it together.
When you try and overcome the loneliness you feel, whatever life throws ur way I know we will get through it together.
When you feel down, whatever life throws ur way I know we will get through it together.
If and when you feel broken, whatever life throws ur way I know we will get through it together.
When you feel like you're in a dark place, whatever life throws ur way I know we will get through it together.
When you feel like you're struggling, whatever life throws ur way I know we will get through it together.
When your inner cries take its toll on you, whatever life throws ur way I know we will get through it together.
When you don't feel strong enough, whatever life throws ur way I know we will get through it together.
When you don't feel brave enough, whatever life throws ur way I know we will get through it together.
When you feel low, whatever life throws ur way I know we will get through it together.
When you feel lost in any way, whatever life throws ur way I know we will get through it together.

When you need a shoulder to cry on, whatever life throws ur way I know we will get through it together.
If and when you don't feel good enough, whatever life throws ur way I know we will get through it together.

When you feel like an outsider, whatever life throws ur way I know we will get through it together.
If and when you feel rejected, whatever life throws ur way I know we will get through it together.
When you feel like giving up, whatever life throws ur way I know we will get through it together.
If and when you feel unwanted, whatever life throws ur way I know we will get through it together.
If and when you feel worthless, whatever life throws ur way I know we will get through it together.
When you feel like you're entering an unknown trap, whatever life throws ur way I know we will get through it together.
When you feel like I'm in denial, whatever life throws ur way I know we will get through it together.
If and when you have nowhere to turn, whatever life throws ur way I know we will get through it together.
If and when you don't feel you have the courage to fight, whatever life throws ur way I know we will get through it together.
 when you feel insecure, whatever life throws ur way I know we will get through it together.
If and when you feel guilt in any way, whatever life throws ur way I know we will get through it together.
When you need me the most, whatever life throws ur way I know we will get through it together.
When you are not yourself, whatever life throws ur way I know we will get through it together.
When you feel alone, whatever life throws ur way I know we will get through it together.
When you face challenging days, whatever life throws ur way I know we will get through it together.
If and when you need to vent, whatever life throws ur way I know we will get through it together.

Won't Let Us Get Ripped Apart

When I look back at my fragile past, I know you won't let us be ripped apart again.
When I face my lifelong fears, I know you won't let us be ripped apart again.
When I try and break my lifelong issues that affect me, I know you won't let us be ripped apart again.
When I try and overcome the loneliness I feel, I know you won't let us be ripped apart again.
When I feel down, I know you won't let us be ripped apart again.
If and when I feel broken, I know you won't let us be ripped apart again.
When I feel like I'm in a dark place, I know you won't let us be ripped apart again.
When I feel like I'm struggling, I know you won't let us be ripped apart again.
When my inner cries take its toll on me, I know you won't let us be ripped apart again.
When I don't feel strong enough, I know you won't let us be ripped apart again.
When I don't feel brave enough, I know you won't let us be ripped apart again.
When I feel low, I know you won't let us be ripped apart again.
When I feel lost in any way, I know you won't let us be ripped apart again.
When I need a shoulder to cry on, I know you won't let us be ripped apart again.
If and when I don't feel good enough, I know you won't let us be ripped apart again.

When I feel like an outsider, I know you won't let us be ripped apart again.
If and when I feel rejected, I know you won't let us be ripped apart again.
When I feel like giving up, I know you won't let us be ripped apart again.
If and when I feel unwanted, I know you won't let us be ripped apart again.
If and when I feel worthless, I know you won't let us be ripped apart again.
When I feel like I am entering an unknown trap, I know you won't let us be ripped apart again.
When I feel like I'm in denial, I know you won't let us be ripped apart again.
If and when I have nowhere to turn, I know you won't let us be ripped apart again.
If and when I don't feel I have the courage to fight, I know you won't let us be ripped apart again.
When I feel insecure, I know you won't let us be ripped apart again.
If and when I feel guilt in any way, I know you won't let us be ripped apart again.
When I need you the most, I know you won't let us be ripped apart again.
When I am not myself, I know you won't let us be ripped apart again.
When I feel alone, I know you won't let us be ripped apart again.

When I face challenging days, I know you won't let us be ripped apart again.
If and when I need to vent, I know you won't let us be ripped apart again.

Treasure Me

When I look back at my fragile past, I know you will always treasure me.
When I face my lifelong fears, I know you will always treasure me.
When I try and break my lifelong issues that affect me, I know you will always treasure me.
When I try and overcome the loneliness I feel, I know you will always treasure me.
When I feel down, I know you will always treasure me.
If and when I feel broken, I know you will always treasure me
When I feel like I'm in a dark place, I know you will always treasure me.
When I feel like I'm struggling, I know you will always treasure me.
When my inner cries take its toll on me, I know you will always treasure me.
When I don't feel strong enough, I know you will always treasure me
When I don't feel brave enough, I know you will always treasure me always.
When I feel low, I know you will treasure me.
When I feel lost in any way, I know you will treasure me always.
When I need a shoulder to cry on, I know you will treasure me always.
If and when I don't feel good enough, I know you will treasure me always.

When I feel like an outsider, I know you will always treasure me
If and when I feel rejected, I know you will always treasure me.
When I feel like giving up, I know you will always treasure me.
If and when I feel unwanted, I know you will always treasure me.
If and when I feel worthless, I know you will always treasure me.
When I feel like I am entering an unknown trap, I know you will always treasure me.
When I feel like I'm in denial, I know you will always treasure me.
If and when I have nowhere to turn, I know you will always treasure me
If and when I don't feel I have the courage to fight, I know you will always treasure me.
When I feel insecure, I know you will always treasure me.
If and when I feel guilt in any way, I know you will always treasure me.
When I need you the most, I know you will always treasure me.
When I am not myself, I know you will always treasure me.
When I feel alone, I know you will always treasure me.
When I face challenging days, I know you will always treasure me.
If and when I need to vent, I know you will always treasure me.

Treasure You.

When you look back at your fragile past, I will always treasure you.
When you face your lifelong fears, I will always treasure you.
When you try and break your lifelong issues that affect you, I will always treasure you.
When you try and overcome the loneliness you feel, I will always treasure you.
When you feel down, I will always treasure you.
If and when you feel broken, I will always treasure you.
When you feel like you're in a dark place, I will always treasure you.
When you feel like you're struggling, I will always treasure you.
When your inner cries take its toll on you, I will always treasure you.
When you don't feel strong enough, I will always treasure you.
When you don't feel brave enough, I will always treasure you.
When you feel low, I will always treasure you.
When you feel lost in any way, I will always treasure you.
When you need a shoulder to cry on, I will always treasure you.
If and when you don't feel good enough, I will always treasure you.

When you feel like an outsider, I will always treasure you.
If and when you feel rejected, I will always treasure you.
When you feel like giving up, I will always treasure you.
If and when you feel unwanted, I will always treasure you.
If and when you feel worthless, I will always treasure you.
When you feel like you're entering an unknown trap, I will always treasure you.
When you feel like I'm in denial, I will always treasure you.
If and when you have nowhere to turn, I will always treasure you.
If and when you don't feel you have the courage to fight, I will always treasure you.
When you feel insecure, I will always treasure you.
If and when you feel guilt in any way, I will always treasure you.
When you need me the most, I will always treasure you.
When you are not yourself, I will always treasure you.
When you feel alone, I will always treasure you.
When you face challenging days, I will always treasure you.
If and when you need to vent, I will always treasure you.

Trapped No Longer

When I look back at my fragile past, I no longer feel trapped.
When I face my lifelong fears, I no longer feel trapped.
When I try and break my lifelong issues that affect me, I no longer feel trapped.
When I try and overcome the loneliness I feel, I no longer feel trapped.
When I feel down, I no longer feel trapped.
If and when I feel broken, I no longer feel trapped.
When I feel like I'm in a dark place, I no longer feel trapped.
When I feel like I'm struggling, I no longer feel trapped.
When my inner cries take its toll on me, I no longer feel trapped.
When I don't feel strong enough, I no longer feel trapped.
When I don't feel brave enough, I no longer feel trapped.
When I feel low, I no longer feel trapped.
When I feel lost in any way, I no longer feel trapped.
When I need a shoulder to cry on, I no longer feel trapped.
If and when I don't feel good enough, I no longer feel trapped.

When I feel like an outsider, I no longer feel trapped.
If and when I feel rejected, I no longer feel trapped.
When I feel like giving up, I no longer feel trapped.
If and when I feel unwanted, I no longer feel trapped.
If and when I feel worthless, I no longer feel trapped.
When I feel like I am entering an unknown trap, I no longer feel trapped.
When I feel like I'm in denial, I no longer feel trapped.
If and when I have nowhere to turn, I no longer feel trapped.
If and when I don't feel I have the courage to fight, I no longer feel trapped.
When I feel insecure, I no longer feel trapped.
If and when I feel guilt in any way, I no longer feel trapped.
When I need you the most, I no longer feel trapped.
When I am not myself, I no longer feel trapped.
When I feel alone, I no longer feel trapped.
When I face challenging days, I no longer feel trapped.
If and when I need to vent, I no longer feel trapped.

Nothing To Fear When Ur In My Life & Around Me.

When you look back at your fragile past, you know you have nothing to fear when ur in my life & around me.
When you face your lifelong fears, you know you have nothing to fear when ur in my life & around me.
When you try and break your lifelong issues that affect you, you know you have nothing to fear when ur in my life & around me.
When you try and overcome the loneliness you feel, you know you have nothing to fear when ur in my life & around me.
When you feel down, you know you have nothing to fear when ur in my life & around me.
If and when you feel broken, you know you have nothing to fear when ur in my life & around me.
When you feel like you're in a dark place, you know you have nothing to fear when ur in my life & around me.
When you feel like you're struggling, you know you have nothing to fear when ur in my life & around me.
When your inner cries take its toll on you, you know you have nothing to fear when ur in my life & around me.
When you don't feel strong enough, you know you have nothing to fear when ur in my life & around me.
When you don't feel brave enough, you know you have nothing to fear when ur in my life & around me.
When you feel low, you know you have nothing to fear when ur in my life & around me.
When you feel lost in any way, you know you have nothing to fear when ur in my life & around me.
When you need a shoulder to cry on, you know you have nothing to fear when ur in my life & around me.
If and when you don't feel good enough, you know you have nothing to fear when ur in my life & around me.

When you feel like an outsider, you know you have nothing to fear when ur in my life & around me.
If and when you feel rejected, you know you have nothing to fear when ur in my life & around me.
When you feel like giving up, you know you have nothing to fear when ur in my life & around me.
If and when you feel unwanted, you know you have nothing to fear when ur in my life & around me.

If and when you feel worthless, you know you have nothing to fear when ur in my life & around me.
When you feel like you're entering an unknown trap, you know you have nothing to fear when ur in my life & around me.
When you feel like I'm in denial, you know you have nothing to fear when ur in my life & around me.
If and when you have nowhere to turn, you know you have nothing to fear when ur in my life & around me.
If and when you don't feel you have the courage to fight, you know you have nothing to fear when ur in my life & around me.
 when you feel insecure, you know you have nothing to fear when ur in my life & around me.
If and when you feel guilt in any way, you know you have nothing to fear when ur in my life & around me.
When you need me the most, you know you have nothing to fear when ur in my life & around me.
When you are not yourself, you know you have nothing to fear when ur in my life & around me.
When you feel alone, you know you have nothing to fear when ur in my life & around me.
When you face challenging days, you know you have nothing to fear when ur in my life & around me.
If and when you need to vent, you know you have nothing to fear when ur in my life & around me.

Have Nothing To Fear When I'm In Ur Life & Around You

When I look back at my fragile past, I have nothing to fear when I'm in ur life & around you
When I face my lifelong fears, I have nothing to fear when I'm in ur life & around you
When I try and break my lifelong issues that affect me, I have nothing to fear when I'm in ur life & around you
When I try and overcome the loneliness I feel, I have nothing to fear when I'm in ur life & around you

When I feel down, I have nothing to fear when I'm in ur life & around you
If and when I feel broken, I have nothing to fear when I'm in ur life & around you

When I feel like I'm in a dark place, I have nothing to fear when ur in my life & around you.
When I feel like I'm struggling, I have nothing to fear when I'm in ur life & around you
When my inner cries take its toll on me, I have nothing to fear when I'm in ur life & around you
When I don't feel strong enough, I have nothing to fear when I'm in ur life & around you
When I don't feel brave enough, I have nothing to fear when I'm in ur life & around you
When I feel low, I have nothing to fear when I'm in ur life & around you

When I feel lost in any way, I have nothing to fear when I'm in ur life & around you
When I need a shoulder to cry on, I have nothing to fear when I'm in ur life & around you
If and when I don't feel good enough, I have nothing to fear when I'm in ur life & around you

When I feel like an outsider, I have nothing to fear when I'm in ur life & around you.
If and when I feel rejected, I have nothing to fear when I'm in ur life & around you
When I feel like giving up, I have nothing to fear when I'm in ur life & around you
If and when I feel unwanted, I have nothing to fear when I'm in ur life & around you
If and when I feel worthless, I have nothing to fear when I'm in ur life & around you
When I feel like I am entering an unknown trap, I have nothing to fear when I'm in ur life & around you
When I feel like I'm in denial, I have nothing to fear when I'm in ur life & around you
If and when I have nowhere to turn, I have nothing to fear when I'm in ur life & around you
If and when I don't feel I have the courage to fight, I have nothing to fear when I'm in ur life & around you
When I feel insecure, I have nothing to fear when I'm in ur life & around you
If and when I feel guilt in any way, I have nothing to fear when I'm in ur life & around you
When I need you the most, I have nothing to fear when I'm in ur life & around you

When I am not myself, I have nothing to fear when I'm in ur life & around you
When I feel alone, I have nothing to fear when I'm in ur life & around you
When I face challenging days, I have nothing to fear when I'm in ur life & around you
If and when I need to vent, I know I have nothing to fear when I'm in ur life & around you

Won't Let Anything Come Between Us

When I look back at my fragile past, I know you won't let anything come between us.
When I face my lifelong fears, I know you won't let anything come between us.
When I try and break my lifelong issues that affect me, I know you won't let anything come between us.
When I try and overcome the loneliness I feel, I know you won't let anything come between us.
When I feel down, I know you won't let anything come between us.
If and when I feel broken, I know you won't let anything come between us.
When I feel like I'm in a dark place, I know you won't let anything come between us.
When I feel like I'm struggling, I know you won't let anything come between us.
When my inner cries take its toll on me, I know you won't let anything come between us.
When I don't feel strong enough, I know you won't let anything come between us.
When I don't feel brave enough, I know you won't let anything come between us.
When I feel low, I know you won't let anything come between us.
When I feel lost in any way, I know you won't let anything come between us.
When I need a shoulder to cry on, I know you won't let anything come between us.
If and when I don't feel good enough, I know you won't let anything come between us.

When I feel like an outsider, I know you won't let anything come between us.
If and when I feel rejected, I know you won't let anything come between us.
When I feel like giving up, I know you won't let anything come between us.
If and when I feel unwanted, I know you won't let anything come between us.
If and when I feel worthless, I know you won't let anything come between us.

When I feel like I am entering an unknown trap, I know you won't let anything come between us.
When I feel like I'm in denial, I know you won't let anything come between us.
If and when I have nowhere to turn, I know you won't let anything come between us. If and when I don't feel I have the courage to fight, I know you won't let anything come between us.
when I feel insecure, I know you won't let anything come between us.
If and when I feel guilt in any way, I know you won't let anything come between us.
When I need you the most, I know you won't let anything come between us.
When I am not myself, I know you won't let anything come between us.
When I feel alone, I know you won't let anything come between us.
When I face challenging days, I know you won't let anything come between us.
If and when I need to vent, I know you won't let anything come between us.

When I Am A Lost Soul

When I look back at my fragile past, you know when I am a lost soul.
When I face my lifelong fears, you know when I am a lost soul.
When I try and break my lifelong issues that affect me, you know when I am a lost soul.
When I try and overcome the loneliness I feel, you know when I am a lost soul.
When I feel down, you know when I am a lost soul.
If and when I feel broken, you know when I am a lost soul.
When I feel like I'm in a dark place, you know when I am a lost soul.
When I feel like I'm struggling, you know when I am a lost soul.
When my inner cries take its toll on me, you know when I am a lost soul.
When I don't feel strong enough, you know when I am a lost soul.
When I don't feel brave enough, you know when I am a lost soul.
When I feel low, you know when I am a lost soul.
When I feel lost in any way, you know when I am a lost soul.
When I need a shoulder to cry on, you know when I am a lost soul.
If and when I don't feel good enough, you know when I am a lost soul.

When I feel like an outsider, you know when I am a lost soul.
If and when I feel rejected, you know when I am a lost soul.
When I feel like giving up, you know when I am a lost soul.
If and when I feel unwanted, you know when I am a lost soul.
If and when I feel worthless, you know when I am a lost soul.
When I feel like I am entering an unknown trap, you know when I am a lost soul.
When I feel like I'm in denial, you know when I am a lost soul.

If and when I have nowhere to turn, you know when I am a lost soul.
If and when I don't feel I have the courage to fight, you know when I am a lost soul.
When I feel insecure, you know when I am a lost soul.
If and when I feel guilt in any way, you know when I am a lost soul.
When I need you the most, you know when I am a lost soul.
When I am not myself, you know when I am a lost soul.
When I feel alone, you know when I am a lost soul.
When I face challenging days, you know when I am a lost soul.
If and when I need to vent, you know when I am a lost soul.

Keep Me Afloat

When I look back at my fragile past, you keep me afloat.
When I face my lifelong fears, you keep me afloat.
When I try and break my lifelong issues that affect me, you keep me afloat.
When I try and overcome the loneliness I feel, you keep me afloat.
When I feel down, you keep me afloat.
If and when I feel broken, you keep me afloat.
When I feel like I'm in a dark place, you keep me afloat.
When I feel like I'm struggling, you keep me afloat.
When my inner cries take its toll on me, you keep me afloat.
When I don't feel strong enough, you keep me afloat.
When I don't feel brave enough, you keep me afloat.
When I feel low, you keep me afloat.
When I feel lost in any way, you keep me afloat.
When I need a shoulder to cry on, you keep me afloat.
If and when I don't feel good enough, you keep me afloat.

When I feel like an outsider, you keep me afloat.
If and when I feel rejected, you keep me afloat.
When I feel like giving up , you keep me afloat.
If and when I feel unwanted, you keep me afloat.
If and when I feel worthless, you keep me afloat.
When I feel like I am entering an unknown trap, you keep me afloat.
When I feel like I'm in denial, you keep me afloat.
If and when I have nowhere to turn, you keep me afloat.
If and when I don't feel I have the courage to fight, you keep me afloat.
When I feel insecure, you keep me afloat.
If and when I feel guilt in any way, you keep me afloat.
When I need you the most, you keep me afloat.

When I am not myself, you keep me afloat.
When I feel alone, you keep me afloat.
When I face challenging days, you keep me afloat.
If and when I need to vent, you keep me afloat.

Get Me Down

I won't let my past get me down.
I won't let my fears get me down.
I won't let my issues that affect me get me down.
I won't let the loneliness get me down.
I won't let rejection get me down.
I won't let feeling alone get me down.
I won't let my circumstances get me down.
I won't let my way of life get me down.
I won't let the emptiness I felt get me down.
I won't let the feeling of being fragile get me down
I won't let hateful words get me down.
I won't let people who are not interested in me get me down
I won't let my unspoken words get me down.
I won't let my surroundings get me down.
I won't let the fact that I felt like a black sheep get me down.
I won't let the fact that I live my life differently to others around me get me down.
I won't let the fact that I didn't exist in those of my loved one's eyes get me down.
I won't let the fact I haven't got what I want in the same way as those around me as I know I will get it in my own way.
I won't let the fact that I have a different ability within myself to others around me get me down.
I won't let the dark place I was in get me down.
I won't let the fact I felt broken at one stage get me down.
I won't let the fact I felt down at one stage get me down.
I won't let the fact that I felt unwanted get me down as I know I am wanted.
I won't let the fact that I wasn't strong enough get me down.
I won't let the fact that I wasn't brave enough get me down.
I won't let the fact that I struggled to get where I wanna be get me down.
I won't let the fact I felt abandoned get me down as I know I am not abandoned anymore.

Come Out Stronger, Braver And Best You Can Be.

When you look back at your fragile past, I know ur fragile but that won't last forever as I know you will always come out stronger, braver and best you can be.
When you face your lifelong fears, I know ur fragile but that won't last forever as I know you will always come out stronger, braver and best you can be.
When you try and break your lifelong issues that affect you, I know ur fragile but that won't last forever as I know you will always come out stronger, braver and best you can be.
When you try and overcome the loneliness you feel, I know ur fragile but that won't last forever as I know you will always come out stronger, braver and best you can be.
When you feel down, I know ur fragile but that won't last forever as I know you will always come out stronger, braver and best you can be.
If and when you feel broken, I know ur fragile but that won't last forever as I know you will always come out stronger, braver and best you can be.
When you feel like you're in a dark place, I know ur fragile but that won't last forever as I know you will always come out stronger, braver and best you can be.
When you feel like you're struggling, I know ur fragile but that won't last forever as I know you will always come out stronger, braver and best you can be.
When your inner cries take its toll on you, I know ur fragile but that won't last forever as I know you will always come out stronger, braver and best you can be.
When you don't feel strong enough, I know ur fragile but that won't last forever as I know you will always come out stronger, braver and best you can be.
When you don't feel brave enough, I know ur fragile but that won't last forever as I know you will always come out stronger, braver and best you can be.
When you feel low, I know ur fragile but that won't last forever as I know you will always come out stronger, braver and best you can be.
When you feel lost in any way, I know ur fragile but that won't last forever as I know you will always come out stronger, braver and best you can be.
When you need a shoulder to cry on, I know ur fragile but that won't last forever as I know you will always come out stronger, braver and best you can be.
If and when you don't feel good enough, I know ur fragile but that won't last forever as I know you will always come out stronger, braver and best you can be.

When you feel like an outsider, I know ur fragile but that won't last forever as I know you will always come out stronger, braver and best you can be.
If and when you feel rejected, I know ur fragile but that won't last forever as I know you will always come out stronger, braver and best you can be.
When you feel like giving up, I know ur fragile but that won't last forever as I know you will always come out stronger, braver and best you can be.

If and when you feel unwanted, I know ur fragile but that won't last forever as I know you will always come out stronger, braver and best you can be.
If and when you feel worthless, I know ur fragile but that won't last forever as I know you will always come out stronger, braver and best you can be.
When you feel like you're entering an unknown trap, I know ur fragile but that won't last forever as I know you will always come out stronger, braver and best you can be.
When you feel like you're in denial, I know ur fragile but that won't last forever as I know you will always come out stronger, braver and best you can be.
If and when you have nowhere to turn, I know ur fragile but that won't last forever as I know you will always come out stronger, braver and best you can be.
If and when you don't feel you have the courage to fight, I know ur fragile but that won't last forever as I know you will always come out stronger, braver and best you can be.
When you feel insecure, I know ur fragile but that won't last forever as I know you will always come out stronger, braver and best you can be.
If and when you feel guilt in any way, I know ur fragile but that won't last forever as I know you will always come out stronger, braver and best you can be.
When you need me the most, I know ur fragile but that won't last forever as I know you will always come out stronger, braver and best you can be.
When you are not yourself, I know ur fragile but that won't last forever as I know you will always come out stronger, braver and best you can be.
When you feel alone, I know ur fragile but that won't last forever as I know you will always come out stronger, braver and best you can be.
When you face challenging days, I know ur fragile but that won't last forever as I know you will always come out stronger, braver and best you can be.
If and when you need to vent, I know ur fragile but that won't last forever as I know you will always come out stronger, braver and best you can be.

Backstab Me

When I look back at my fragile past, you make sure no one backstabs me.
When I face my lifelong fears, you make sure no one backstabs me.
When I try and break my lifelong issues that affect me, you make sure no one backstabs me.
When I try and overcome the loneliness I feel, you make sure no one backstabs me.
When I feel down, you make sure no one backstabs me.
If and when I feel broken, you make sure no one backstabs me.
When I feel like I'm in a dark place, you make sure no one backstabs me.
When I feel like I'm struggling, you make sure no one backstabs me.

When my inner cries take its toll on me, you make sure no one backstabs me.
When I don't feel strong enough, you make sure no one backstabs me.
When I don't feel brave enough, you make sure no one backstabs me.
When I feel low, you make sure no one backstabs me.
When I feel lost in any way, you make sure no one backstabs me.
When I need a shoulder to cry on, you make sure no one backstabs me.
If and when I don't feel good enough, you make sure no one backstabs me.

When I feel like an outsider, you make sure no one backstabs me..
If and when I feel rejected, you make sure no one backstabs me.
When I feel like giving up, you make sure no one backstabs me.
If and when I feel unwanted, you make sure no one backstabs me.
If and when I feel worthless, you make sure no one backstabs me.
When I feel like I am entering an unknown trap, you make sure no one backstabs me.
When I feel like I'm in denial, you make sure no one backstabs me.
If and when I have nowhere to turn, you make sure no one backstabs me.
If and when I don't feel I have the courage to fight, you make sure no one backstabs me.
When I feel insecure, you make sure no one backstabs me.
If and when I feel guilt in any way, you make sure no one backstabs me.
When I need you the most, you make sure no one backstabs me.
When I am not myself, you make sure no one backstabs me.
When I feel alone, you make sure no one backstabs me.
When I face challenging days, you make sure no one backstabs me.
If and when I need to vent, you make sure no one backstabs me.

Doubt Myself

When I look back at my fragile past, you know when I doubt myself.
When I face my lifelong fears, you know when I doubt myself.
When I try and break my lifelong issues that affect me, you know when I doubt myself.
When I try and overcome the loneliness I feel, you know when I doubt myself.
When I feel down, you know when I doubt myself.
If and when I feel broken, you know when I doubt myself.
When I feel like I'm in a dark place, you know when I doubt myself.
When I feel like I'm struggling, you know when I doubt myself.
When my inner cries take its toll on me, you know when I doubt myself.
When I don't feel strong enough, you know when I doubt myself.
When I don't feel brave enough, you know when I doubt myself.

When I feel low, you know when I doubt myself.
When I feel lost in any way, you know when I doubt myself.
When I need a shoulder to cry on, you know when I doubt myself.
If and when I don't feel good enough, you know when I doubt myself.

When I feel like an outsider, you know when I doubt myself.
If and when I feel rejected, you know when I doubt myself.
When I feel like giving up, you know when I doubt myself.
If and when I feel unwanted, you know when I doubt myself.
If and when I feel worthless, you know when I doubt myself.
When I feel like I am entering an unknown trap, you know when I doubt myself.
When I feel like I'm in denial, you know when I doubt myself.
If and when I have nowhere to turn, you know when I doubt myself.
If and when I don't feel I have the courage to fight, you know when I doubt myself.
When I feel insecure, you know when I doubt myself.
If and when I feel guilt in any way, you know when I doubt myself.
When I need you the most, you know when I doubt myself.
When I am not myself, you know when I doubt myself.
When I feel alone, you know when I doubt myself.
When I face challenging days, you know when I doubt myself.
If and when I need to vent, you know when I doubt myself.

Know How Fragile I Can Be

When I look back at my fragile past, you know how fragile I can be.
When I face my lifelong fears, you know how fragile I can be.
When I try and break my lifelong issues that affect me, you know how fragile I can be.
When I try and overcome the loneliness I feel, you know how fragile I can be.
When I feel down, you know how fragile I can be.
If and when I feel broken, you know how fragile I can be.
When I feel like I'm in a dark place, you know how fragile I can be.
When I feel like I'm struggling, you know how fragile I can be.
When my inner cries take its toll on me, you know how fragile I can be.
When I don't feel strong enough, you know how fragile I can be.
When I don't feel brave enough, you know how fragile I can be.
When I feel low, you know how fragile I can be.
When I feel lost in any way, you know how fragile I can be.
When I need a shoulder to cry on, you know how fragile I can be.
If and when I don't feel good enough, you know how fragile I can be.

When I feel like an outsider, you know how fragile I can be.
If and when I feel rejected, you know how fragile I can be.
When I feel like giving up, you know how fragile I can be.
If and when I feel unwanted, you know how fragile I can be.
If and when I feel worthless, you know how fragile I can be.
When I feel like I am entering an unknown trap, you know how fragile I can be.
When I feel like I'm in denial, you know how fragile I can be.
If and when I have nowhere to turn, you know how fragile I can be.
If and when I don't feel I have the courage to fight, you know how fragile I can be.
When I feel insecure, you know how fragile I can be.
If and when I feel guilt in any way, you know how fragile I can be.
When I need you the most, you know how fragile I can be.
When I am not myself, you know how fragile I can be.
When I feel alone, you know how fragile I can be.
When I face challenging days, you know how fragile I can be.
If and when I need to vent, you know how fragile I can be.

Lead Me Astray

When I look back at my fragile past, I know you won't lead me astray
When I face my lifelong fears, I know you won't lead me astray
When I try and break my lifelong issues that affect me, I know you won't lead me astray
When I try and overcome the loneliness, I know you won't lead me astray
When I feel down, I know you won't lead me astray
If and when I feel broken, I know you won't lead me astray
When I feel like I'm in a dark place, I know you won't lead me astray
When I feel like I'm struggling, I know you won't lead me astray
When my inner cries take its toll on me, I know you won't lead me astray
When I don't feel strong enough, I know you won't lead me astray
When I don't feel brave enough, I know you won't lead me astray
When I feel low, I know you won't lead me astray
When I feel lost in any way, I know you won't lead me astray
When I need a shoulder to cry on, I know you won't lead me astray
If and when I don't feel good enough, I know you won't lead me astray

When I feel like an outsider, I know you won't lead me astray
If and when I feel rejected, I know you won't lead me astray
When I feel like giving up, I know you won't lead me astray

If and when I feel unwanted, I know you won't lead me astray
If and when I feel worthless, I know you won't lead me astray
When I feel like I am entering an unknown trap, I know you won't lead me astray
When I feel like I'm in denial, I know you won't lead me astray
If and when I have nowhere to turn, I know you won't lead me astray
If and when I don't feel I have the courage to fight, I know you won't lead me astray
When I feel insecure, I know you won't lead me astray
If and when I feel guilt in any way, I know you won't lead me astray
When I need you the most, I know you won't lead me astray
When I am not myself, I know you won't lead me astray
When I feel alone, I know you won't lead me astray
When I face challenging days, I know you won't lead me astray
If and when I need to vent, I know you won't lead me astray

Won't Let Me Feel Isolated

When I look back at my fragile past, I know you won't let me feel isolated.
When I face my lifelong fears, I know you won't let me feel isolated.
When I try and break my lifelong issues that affect me, I know you won't let me feel isolated.
When I try and overcome the loneliness, I know you won't let me feel isolated.
When I feel down, I know you won't let me feel isolated.
If and when I feel broken, I know you won't let me feel isolated.
When I feel like I'm in a dark place, I know you won't let me feel isolated.
When I feel like I'm struggling, I know you won't let me feel isolated.
When my inner cries take its toll on me, I know you won't let me feel isolated.
When I don't feel strong enough, I know you won't let me feel isolated.
When I don't feel brave enough, I know you won't let me feel isolated.
When I feel low, I know you won't let me feel isolated.
When I feel lost in any way, I know you won't let me feel isolated.
When I need a shoulder to cry on, I know you won't let me feel isolated.
If and when I don't feel good enough, I know you won't let me feel isolated.

When I feel like an outsider, I know you won't let me feel isolated.
If and when I feel rejected, I know you won't let me feel isolated.
When I feel like giving up, I know you won't let me feel isolated.
If and when I feel unwanted, I know you won't let me feel isolated.
If and when I feel worthless, I know you won't let me feel isolated.

When I feel like I am entering an unknown trap, I know you won't let me feel isolated.
When I feel like I'm in denial, I know you won't let me feel isolated.
If and when I have nowhere to turn, I know you won't let me feel isolated.
If and when I don't feel I have the courage to fight, I know you won't let me feel isolated.
When I feel insecure, I know you won't let me feel isolated.
If and when I feel guilt in any way, I know you won't let me feel isolated.
When I need you the most, I know you won't let me feel isolated.
When I am not myself, I know you won't let me feel isolated.
When I feel alone, I know you won't let me feel isolated.
When I face challenging days, I know you won't let me feel isolated.
If and when I need to vent, I know you won't let me feel isolated.

Not Invisible To You.

When I look back at my fragile past, I know I'm not invisible to you.
When I face my lifelong fears, I know I'm not invisible to you.
When I try and break my lifelong issues that affect me, I know I'm not invisible to you.
When I try and overcome the loneliness, I know I'm not invisible to you.
When I feel down, I know I'm not invisible to you.
If and when I feel broken, I know I'm not invisible to you.
When I feel like I'm in a dark place, I know I'm not invisible to you.
When I feel like I'm struggling, I know I'm not invisible to you.
When my inner cries take its toll on me, I know I'm not invisible to you.
When I don't feel strong enough, I know I'm not invisible to you.
When I don't feel brave enough, I know I'm not invisible to you..
When I feel low, I know I'm not invisible to you.
When I feel lost in any way, I know I'm not invisible to you.
When I need a shoulder to cry on, I know I'm not invisible to you.
If and when I don't feel good enough, I know I'm not invisible to you.

When I feel like an outsider, I know I'm not invisible to you.
If and when I feel rejected, I know I'm not invisible to you.
When I feel like giving up, I know I'm not invisible to you.
If and when I feel unwanted, I know I'm not invisible to you.
If and when I feel worthless, I know I'm not invisible to you.
When I feel like I am entering an unknown trap, I know I'm not invisible to you.
When I feel like I'm in denial, I know I'm not invisible to you.
If and when I have nowhere to turn, I know I'm not invisible to you.

If and when I don't feel I have the courage to fight, I know I'm not invisible to you.
When I feel insecure, I know I'm not invisible to you.
If and when I feel guilt in any way, I know I'm not invisible to you.
When I need you the most, I know I'm not invisible to you.
When I am not myself, I know I'm not invisible to you.
When I feel alone, I know I'm not invisible to you.
When I face challenging days, I know I'm not invisible to you.
If and when I need to vent, I know I'm not invisible to you.

Find Closure

When you look back at your fragile past, I know you will find closure.
When you face your lifelong fears, I know you will find closure.
When you try and break your lifelong issues that affect you, I know you will find closure.
When you try and overcome the loneliness you feel, I know you will find closure.
When you feel down, I know you will find closure.
If and when you feel broken, I know you will find closure.
When you feel like you're in a dark place, I know you will find closure.
When you feel like you're struggling, I know you will find closure.
When your inner cries take its toll on you, I know you will find closure.
When you don't feel strong enough. I know you will find closure.
When you don't feel brave enough, I know you will find closure.
When you feel low, I know you will find closure.
When you feel lost in any way, I know you will find closure.
When you need a shoulder to cry on, I know you will find closure.
If and when you don't feel good enough, I know you will find closure.

When you feel like an outsider, I know you will find closure.
If and when you feel rejected, I know you will find closure.
When you feel like giving up, I know you will find closure.
If and when you feel unwanted, I know you will find closure.
If and when you feel worthless, I know you will find closure.
When you feel like you're entering an unknown trap, I know you will find closure.
When you feel like I'm in denial, I know you will find closure.
If and when you have nowhere to turn, I know you will find closure.
If and when you don't feel you have the courage to fight, I know you will find closure.

When you feel insecure, I know you will find closure.
If and when you feel guilt in any way, I know you will find closure.
When you need me the most, I know you will find closure.
When you are not yourself, I know you will find closure.
When you feel alone, I know you will find closure.
When you face challenging days, I know you will find closure.
If and when you need to vent, I know you will find closure.

You Changed My Life

When I look back at my fragile past, you changed my life just by being apart of it.
When I face my lifelong fears, you changed my life just by being apart of it.
When I try and break my lifelong issues that affect me, you changed my life just by being apart of it.
When I try and overcome the loneliness I feel, you changed my life just by being apart of it.
When I feel down, you changed my life just by being apart of it.
If and when I feel broken, you changed my life just by being apart of it.
When I feel like I'm in a dark place, you changed my life just by being apart of it.
When I feel like I'm struggling, you changed my life just by being apart of it.
When my inner cries take its toll on me, you changed my life just by being apart of it.
When I don't feel strong enough, you changed my life just by being apart of it.
When I don't feel brave enough, you changed my life just by being apart of it.
When I feel low, you changed my life just by being apart of it.
When I feel lost in any way, you changed my life just by being apart of it.
When I need a shoulder to cry on, you changed my life just by being apart of it.
If and when I don't feel good enough, you changed my life just by being apart of it.

When I feel like an outsider, you changed my life just by being apart of it.
If and when I feel rejected, you changed my life just by being apart of it.
When I feel like giving up, you changed my life just by being apart of it.
If and when I feel unwanted, you changed my life just by being apart of it.
If and when I feel worthless, you changed my life just by being apart of it.
When I feel like I am entering an unknown trap, you changed my life just by being apart of it.
When I feel like I'm in denial, you changed my life just by being apart of it.
If and when I have nowhere to turn, you changed my life just by being apart of it.

If and when I don't feel I have the courage to fight, you changed my life just by being apart of it.
When I feel insecure, you changed my life just by being apart of it.
If and when I feel guilt in any way, you changed my life just by being apart of it.
When I need you the most, you changed my life just by being apart of it.
When I am not myself, you changed my life just by being apart of it.
When I feel alone, you changed my life just by being apart of it.
When I face challenging days, you changed my life just by being apart of it.
If and when I need to vent, you changed my life just by being apart of it.

I Turned My Life Around

When I look back at my fragile past, I turned my life around as you showed me it was possible for me to be who I wanna be.
When I face my lifelong fears, I turned my life around as you showed me it was possible for me to be who I wanna be.
When I try and break my lifelong issues that affect me, I turned my life around as you showed me it was possible for me to be who I wanna be.
When I try and overcome the loneliness I feel, I turned my life around as you showed me it was possible for me to be who I wanna be.
When I feel down, I turned my life around as you showed me it was possible for me to be who I wanna be.
If and when I feel broken, I turned my life around as you showed me it was possible for me to be who I wanna be.
When I feel like I'm in a dark place, I turned my life around as you showed me it was possible for me to be who I wanna be.
When I feel like I'm struggling, I turned my life around as you showed me it was possible for me to be who I wanna be.
When my inner cries take its toll on me, I turned my life around as you showed me it was possible for me to be who I wanna be.
When I don't feel strong enough, I turned my life around as you showed me it was possible for me to be who I wanna be.
When I don't feel brave enough, I turned my life around as you showed me it was possible for me to be who I wanna be.
When I feel low, I turned my life around as you showed me it was possible for me to be who I wanna be.
When I feel lost in any way, I turned my life around as you showed me it was possible for me to be who I wanna be.
When I need a shoulder to cry on, I turned my life around as you showed me it was possible for me to be who I wanna be.

If and when I don't feel good enough, I turned my life around as you showed me it was possible for me to be who I wanna be.

When I feel like an outsider, I turned my life around as you showed me it was possible for me to be who I wanna be.
If and when I feel rejected, I turned my life around as you showed me it was possible for me to be who I wanna be.
When I feel like giving up, I turned my life around as you showed me it was possible for me to be who I wanna be.
If and when I feel unwanted, I turned my life around as you showed me it was possible for me to be who I wanna be.
If and when I feel worthless, I turned my life around as you showed me it was possible for me to be who I wanna be.
When I feel like I am entering an unknown trap, I turned my life around as you showed me it was possible for me to be who I wanna be.
When I feel like I'm in denial, I turned my life around as you showed me it was possible for me to be who I wanna be.
If and when I have nowhere to turn, I turned my life around as you showed me it was possible for me to be who I wanna be.
If and when I don't feel I have the courage to fight, I turned my life around as you showed me it was possible for me to be who I wanna be.
when I feel insecure, I turned my life around as you showed me it was possible for me to be who I wanna be.
If and when I feel guilt in any way, I turned my life around as you showed me it was possible for me to be who I wanna be.
When I need you the most, I turned my life around as you showed me it was possible for me to be who I wanna be.
When I am not myself, I turned my life around as you showed me it was possible for me to be who I wanna be.
When I feel alone, I turned my life around as you showed me it was possible for me to be who I wanna be.
When I face challenging days, I turned my life around as you showed me it was possible for me to be who I wanna be.
If and when I need to vent, I turned my life around as you showed me it was possible for me to be who I wanna be.

Index

A Force To Be Reckoned With	347
Admire You	113
Against Me	52
Always Be My Lookout	215
Always Have Me	65
Always Make Sure I'm Ok	358
Always Make Time For You	329
Always Matter To Me	343
Always Matter To You	344
Always Take Me As Me	229
Always Watch Over Me	357
Always Watch Over You	330
Angel Eyez	16
Appreciate You	256
Approach	48
Approval	313
As I Go Under	175
At A Standstill	158
Backstab Me	389
Backstab You	135
Be Ur Sidekick	179
Be Your Rock	61
Because Of You	163
Believe In Myself	351
Believe In You	90
Best Friend	29
Best In Me	251
Best Intentions	125
Best Interest	127
Betray You In Any Way	138
Bite	164
Blame Game	42
Blinded	146
Blink Of A Light	78
Blink Of An Eye	74
Block Out	166
Brave Face	95
Bring Me Back From The Edge	184
Bring Me Out Of My Comfort Zone	273
Bring Me Out Of My Shell	269

Bring Out The Adventurous Side Of Me	271
Bring Out The Best In You	116
Bring Out The Real Me	274
Bring Out The Rebel In Me	272
Bring Out The Reckless Side Of Me	268
Bring Out The Warrior In You	114
Bring Out The Wild Side Of Me	267
Bring Out The Worst In You	120
Bring You Down	131
Bring You Out Of Your Shell	111
Build A Wall Around You	171
Bulletproof	261
Burn Out	332
Burning Bridges	320
Care For You	85
Cast A Doubt	302
Catch Every Tear	299
Cave In	84
Close By	104
Close Chapter	160
Come & Find Me	172
Come Out Stronger, Braver And Best You Can Be.	388
Comfort Me	345
Confessions	311
Confide In Me	359
Confide In You	166
Confidence	152
Connection	17
Count On Me	59
Count On You	264
Crisis	322
Crossroads	24
Crumble	22
Dark Place	278
Daylight Or Not	326
Defeat You	129
Destructive Way	312
Dictate	161
Didn't Know	162
Different Side Of Me	152
Disguise You	289
Don't Have To Be Ashamed Of My Disability	247

Don't Have To Be Ashamed Of My Scars & Burns	245
Don't Have To Cry On The Inside	208
Don't Have To Keep Me In The Dark	336
Don't Have To Say A Word I'll Know	185
Don't Hold It In	167
Doubt Myself	390
Doubt Yourself	141
Drag Me Down	364
Drag You Down	94
Drain You	281
Dreams	131
Drop My Guard	301
Echoes	149
Eliminate	46
Errors	27
Escape My Reality	367
Escape Route	296
Every Inch	24
Face It With Me	340
Fake Smile	97
Fall Out	30
Family Loyalty	21
Find A Way To Make Me Smile	368
Find Closure	395
Fly Alone	289
Found My Way	156
Free Me	204
Free You	81
Get Me Down	387
Get You Down	285
Give In	187
Give Me Courage	250
Give Me Hope	223
Give Me Stability	237
Give Me Strength	224
Give Up	191
Glue You Back Together	72
Go That Extra Mile For You	124
Go To The End Of The Earth For You	333
Good In Me Only You Can See	198
Had My Back	44
Have Nothing To Fear When I'm In Ur Life & Around You	382

Have Your Back	60
Heal Me	53
Hear Me	242
Hear You Call	66
Held My Hand	38
Help Me Find My True Calling	213
Help Me Find Purpose	212
Hit A Brick Wall	139
Hold Back My Honesty	249
Hold Back My Hurt	244
Hold Back My Pain	241
Hold Back My Tears	239
Hold You Together	316
Hold You	31
Host	28
Human Being	35
Hurt You	73
I Am Never Alone	280
I Can	157
I Don't Have To Put On A Brave Face	252
I Don't Wanna Be Awake	159
I Don't Wanna Be Overlooked	154
I Find My Voice	292
I Give You	95
I Know	197
I Pick Myself Back Up	22
I Turned My Life Around	397
I Unlock	51
I'd Jump To Ur Defence	180
I'd Take A Bullet For You	178
I'd Take A Risk On You	176
I'll Be Right Here Waiting	323
I'll Be Ur Lifeline	190
I'll Be Ur Safe Place	189
I'll Be Ur U Turn	192
I'll Be With You Every Step Of The Way	194
I'll Find The Truth	162
I'm So Caught Up	24
Illusion	17
Imperfections	19
Important To Me	174
Imprint	150

In A Flash	88
In A Heartbeat	282
In The Flesh	77
In Your Corner	75
Individuality	18
Inseparable For Life	103
Inspiration	33
Intoxicated	26
It's Hard To Admit	183
Its Ok To Admit	150
It's Ok To Show The World Who I Truly Am	306
Jump To My Defence	353
Karma	293
Keep Close	22
Keep Me Afloat	386
Keep Me On The Straight & Narrow	202
Keep You Down	369
Keep You On The Straight & Narrow	201
Kerry	281
Knock Me Down	359
Knock You Down	82
Know How Fragile I Can Be	391
Know Me Inside Out	218
Know When I Start To Stumble	342
Lead Me Astray	392
Lead You Astray	107
Lean On Me	57
Lean On You	265
Let Me Drown	20
Let My Voice	20
Light Me Up	53
Living Proof	49
Look For Me	83
Look My Way	67
Look Out For You	86
Look Up To Me	110
Look Up To You	109
Look Ur Way	259
Looking In The Mirror	146
Loyal To Me For Life	349
Loyal To You For Life	87
Loyalty	19

Make A Massive Difference To Me & My Life.	234
Make Me Feel Good Enough	331
Make Me Feel Like I Belong	231
Make Me Feel Like Somebody	227
Make Me Feel Valued	228
Make Me Stronger Than Ever Before	362
Make My Day	236
Mask	279
Massive Influence On Me & My Life.	298
My Door Will Always Be Open For You.	318
My Emotional Strain	209
My Hour Of Need	233
My Only Wish	26
My World In Tatters	230
Never Abandon You	328
Never Be Ashamed	147
Never Change You	143
Never Cling	32
Never Judge Me	258
Never Leave Your Side	70
Never Let Anything Go Wrong When I'm Around You.	355
Never Let You Down	71
Never Let You Face A Mess Alone	327
Never Let You Face Anything Alone	91
Never Question	133
Never Run A Mile	123
Not Invisible To You.	394
Nothing To Fear When Ur In My Life & Around Me.	381
Nothing Will Stop Me Achieving My Goals.	346
Only You Can	182
Open With Me	200
Open With You	199
Own Worst Enemy	23
Patch Me Up	354
Perfect To Me	118
Personality	36
Pick Up The Pieces	177
Positive Impression On Me	145
Power	25
Precious To Me	370
Precious To You.	371
Protector	16

Proud Of Me No Matter What	214
Proud Of You No Matter What	216
Push In The Right Direction	148
Put Me Down	361
Put On An Act	99
Reach Out To Me	56
Reach Out To You	262
Reality	119
Reasons	155
Regrets	147
Release	157
Rely On Me	62
Rely On You	263
Reservations	27
Revenge	144
Rise Above It	52
Screw You Over	115
Searching For Something Within Me	320
Shed A Tear On You When I Cry	366
Shed A Teardrop On Me	102
Someone Understands Me	156
Spiral	21
Stand By You Through Thick & Thin	225
Stand Tall	22
Stick By Me Through Thick & Thin	222
Stick By My Word	105
Stick By Ur Word	339
Storm	37
Stuck By Me	255
Surface From Below	352
Take Advantage Of You	136
Take Me On A Lifetime Journey	258
Take Me Under Your Wing	47
Take On Everything You Hold Within	287
Take You Aside And Make You Smile	92
Take You Under My Wing	238
Take You Underground	133
Tear Me Apart	55
Thank You	40
The Weight Of Everything You Carry On Ur Shoulders	286
The Weight On Ur Shoulders	169
There For Me	39

To The Back Of My Mind	164
Trapped No Longer	380
Treasure Me	378
Treasure You.	379
Trick Me	309
Troublesome Road Of Defeat	303
True Friends Like You Are Hard To Find	232
Trust In Me	68
Turn To Me	69
Twist The Truth	168
Uncertainty	315
Untangle Me	267
Untangle You	106
Until You Came Into My Life	153
Upper Hand	312
Ups & Downs	283
Ur Faith In Me	206
Ur World Of Possibilities	341
Value You	317
Vbbs	196
Vent To Me	58
Vent To You	270
Vision Impairment	134
Vision	25
Walk All Over Me	365
Walk All Over You	119
Walk On Fire For You	122
Warrior In Me	266
What If	37
Whatever Life Throws My Way	373
Whatever Life Throws Ur Way	375
When I Am A Lost Soul	385
When I Am A Mess	338
When I Am A Wreck	257
When I Am At Breaking Point	277
When I Am At My Lowest	276
When I Felt Numb	275
When I Question Myself	254
When I	23
When I'm Around You	128
When You Need Me	76
Window Of Opportunity	294

Witness	321
Won't Abandon Me	221
Won't Be Far	193
Won't Leave Me Out In The Cold	261
Won't Leave My Side	211
Won't Leave You Out In The Cold	188
Won't Let Anything Come Between Us	384
Won't Let Me Down	237
Won't Let Me Feel Isolated	393
Won't Let Me Slip Under The Cracks.	348
Won't Let Me Struggle	220
Won't Let Us Get Ripped Apart	377
Won't Let You Carry A Black Cloud Around With You	335
Won't Let You Fall	63
Won't Let You Feel Insecure	325
Won't Let You Feel Rejected	181
Won't Let You Go Without A Fight	372
Won't Let You Quit	195
Won't Let You Struggle	324
Won't Shatter Into A Million Tiny Pieces	363
Won't Turn You Away	64
Won't Walk Away	80
Words	151
You Are A Star	28
You Are Good Enough	173
You Are My Hero	31
You Are My Rock	205
You Are My Role Model	43
You Are Not Invisible To Me	186
You Break Through	18
You Can Be Yourself	100
You Changed My Life	396
You Ease	260
You Give Me A Helping Hand	350
You Have	20
You Helped Me	46
You Make Me Feel	34
You Mean The Absolute World To Me	142
You Reassure Me	160
You Shield Me	130
You Won't Fly Alone	290

MAPublisher Catalogue

ISBN/Titles/Image/Author	Description	ISBN/Titles/Image/Author	Description
978-1-910499-00-9 Father to child By Mayar Akash	This book about poetry of transition to adulthood. Ebook version 978-1-910499-02-3	978-1-910499-14-6 The Halloweeen Poem by Zainab Khan	This is poetry book written by an 8 year old about their Halloween experience.
978-1-910499-15-3 Anthology One By Penny Authors	This is the first Anthology - of poetry from different writers.	978-1-910499-17-7 Anthology Two By Penny Authors	This is the second Anthology - of poetry from different writers.
978-1-910499-29-0 Book of Lived v3 By Penny Authors	This is the third Anthology - of poetry from different writers.	978-1-910499-V4 Book of Lived By Penny Authors	This is the fourth Anthology - of poetry from different writers.
978-1-910499-37-5 When You Look Back By Rashma Mehta	When you look back", who hasn't been there? No matter how strong you are, she manages to take you back to memory lane.	978-1-910499-36-8 Delirious By Liam Newton	This is the first of the Writer's Champion book getting Liam Newton's book of lyrics and poem.
978-1-910499-39-9 Eyewithin By Mayar Akash	This is the 3rd book of Mayar Akash. The book catalogues the lost paintings by himself.	978-1-910499-37-5 My Dream World By Rashma Mehta	This book will keep readers spellbound as they read the stories, poems and lyrics wanting to know more looking into Rashma's dream world.

ISBN/Titles /Image/Author	Description	ISBN/Titles /Image/Author	Description
978-1-910499-43-6 By Mayar Akash	Mayer's poetry in a series of "My Life Book" which catalogues his work so far in life, 2019.	978-1-910499-44-3 By Mayar Akash	Mayar's poetry in a series of "My Life Book" which catalogues his work so far in life, 2019.
978-1-910499-49-8 By B. M. Gandhi	This is B. M. Gandhi's collection of poetry depicting his life, Tanzanian life.	978-1-910499-50-4 Penny Authors	This is the fifth Anthology - of poetry from different writers.

All books are available on-line, Google the titles and they will take you to the sites where you can acquire copies.